Frank B. Goodrich

The Court of Napoleon

Or Society under the First Empire

Frank B. Goodrich

The Court of Napoleon
Or Society under the First Empire

ISBN/EAN: 9783743432895

Manufactured in Europe, USA, Canada, Australia, Japa

Cover: Foto ©ninafisch / pixelio.de

Manufactured and distributed by brebook publishing software (www.brebook.com)

THE COURT OF NAPOLEON.

THE COURT OF NAPOLEON

MARIE LOUISE

BY F. B. GOODRICH

PHILADELPHIA
J. B. LIPPINCOTT & CO.

THE
COURT OF NAPOLEON;

OR,

SOCIETY UNDER THE FIRST EMPIRE.

WITH

Portraits of its Beauties, Wits, and Heroines.

DESIGNED FROM AUTHENTIC ORIGINALS
BY JULES CHAMPAGNE,
AND ENGRAVED UPON STEEL BY
HALPIN, ROGERS, BUTTRE, G. B. HALL, H. B. HALL, AND HOLLYER.

BY FRANK B. GOODRICH.

THIRD EDITION.

PHILADELPHIA:
J. B. LIPPINCOTT & CO.
1864.

ENTERED according to Act of Congress, in the year 1856, by
FRANK B. GOODRICH,
In the Clerk's Office of the District Court of the United States, for the Southern District of New York.

PREFACE.

ALTHOUGH numerous volumes have been written upon Napoleon in this country, there is none whose purpose is to give a general view of his influence upon society. His career has been regarded as exclusively military and political, and to these topics historians and essayists have principally directed their labors. Nor has there been, even in France, a methodical treatise, presenting a delineation of manners and morals under the Empire, at the same time tracing their connection with the court, and noting the effect produced by the Emperor and his system upon the society he had created. It is the object, therefore, of this volume to fill an obvious void, and thus to supply a practical test of the character and influence of Napoleon I.

The name and fame of Napoleon have long since ceased in America to be connected with party interests or associations. Even the romance with which an inherent hero-worship has led us to invest his career, is visibly yielding to a scrutinizing curiosity which demands unadorned reality in place of sentimental fiction. This tendency is aided and accelerated by the contemplation of events now passing in France, where we see a new empire founded upon the souvenirs of the preceding one, and professing to be conceived in its image. To appreciate the present, it is essential to understand the past.

In giving to the public, therefore, the present volume, though it forms a part of the design of the publishers to offer a tasteful example of art, in the various departments coöperating in the production of books, it is still the purpose, or at least the hope, of the author, to contribute something to the philosophy of history, in that portion of it which he has treated. It does not enter into his plan to record the battles and the conquests of the Emperor, nor to describe his foreign policy or his domestic administration. It has been his simple purpose to represent him at home, in his court, and amongst his people; to chronicle his influence upon morals, manners, religion, art, science, literature—the fountains of public life and the basis of national character.

Impartiality is the first requisite in a work of this description, and the author has acted throughout under this conviction. That he has always fulfilled his design can hardly be assumed, though it is believed that every assertion of sufficient importance to require it, has been substantiated by adequate reference. The critical reader will thus be able to test the accuracy of the representations made. This has been deemed the more necessary, as many topics are presented in a light somewhat different from that thrown upon them by popular opinion in this country.

The author may be permitted to add, that while he has thus carefully based his work upon authority, he has still further verified the views therein expressed, by personal observations made during a residence of eight years in France, and that under circumstances which permitted him to become acquainted with the opinions entertained by the French people themselves upon the subjects referred to. This experience has been in many cases of more value than a library of biographies.

With these remarks, the author and publishers submit "THE COURT OF NAPOLEON" to the candid judgment of the American public.

NEW YORK, OCTOBER, 1857.

ADVERTISEMENT

TO THE THIRD EDITION.

IN announcing a third edition of "THE COURT OF NAPOLEON," the Publishers beg leave to state that, in accordance with various suggestions from the Press and the Public, they have caused the Sixteen Portraits which embellish the Work, to be engraved upon steel, in the highest style of the art.

Circumstances over which they had no control, prevented them from giving, in the earlier editions, the portrait of Miss Patterson—afterwards Madame Jerome Bonaparte. This omission is here repaired, and the gallery now contains the faces of three ladies of American birth—Josephine, Miss Patterson, and Grace Ingersoll.

The Work has been submitted to a thorough revision, and the Publishers trust that, in its present shape, it may enjoy a continuance of the favor which was extended to it upon its first appearance.

NEW YORK, OCTOBER, 1857.

LIST OF ILLUSTRATIONS.

JOSEPHINE,	FRONTISPIECE.
MARIE LOUISE,	TITLE.
CHARLOTTE CORDAY,	TO FACE PAGE 30
MADAME ROLAND,	47
MADAME TALLIEN,	79
MADAME JUNOT,	114
MADAME RÉCAMIER,	145
PAULINE BONAPARTE,	190
MADAME DE STAËL,	233
CAROLINE BONAPARTE,	266
HORTENSE,	283
M'LLE LENORMAND,	320
MADAME JEROME BONAPARTE (Miss Patterson),	343
GRACE INGERSOLL,	367
MADAME RÉGNAULT,	381
M'LLE GEORGES,	402

CONTENTS.

CHAPTER I.

The Women of the Revolution—The Girondines and the Scaffold—Théroigne de Méricourt and the Mountain—Madame Tallien and Josephine—Napoleon as the Reformer of Society, . 17

CHAPTER II.

Lucile Duplessis and Camille Desmoulins—Jesus Christ the Sans-culotte—Lucile's Prayer—Her Death and Character—Charlotte Corday—Her Journey to Paris—Her Arrest, Trial, and Execution—Her fifteen Portraits—Her Character as judged by History, ... 21

CHAPTER III.

The Furies of the Guillotine—The first Sans-culottes—Théroigne de Méricourt—An Amazon at the Invalides—Her Address to the Club des Cordeliers—A Royalist Caricature—Olympe de Gouges—Madame Roland—Her Precocity—Her Marriage and Removal to Paris—Her Association with the Girondins—Her Arrest and Condemnation, ... 34

CHAPTER IV.

Society under the Directory—Divorce—Burial of the Dead—Dancing Gardens—Frascati and Tivoli—Supremacy of Matter—National Bankruptcy—Famine—Two Million Francs for a Waistcoat—The Cascade of Discredit—Voltaire's God-daughter in Danger of Starving—Pamphlets, Caricatures and Fans, ... 50

CHAPTER V.

Fashions of the Terror and Directory—Classic Nudities—Iphigenia and the Vestal Virgins in Paris—Fatal Consequences—Cravats, Smallclothes, and a new Pronunciation—Magazines of Fashion, ... 62

CONTENTS.

CHAPTER VI.

Thérésia Cabarrus—Her Marriage with M. de Fontenay—Tallien at Bordeaux—The Pro-Consul exercises Clemency—Thérésia and Josephine in Prison together—Their Signatures still visible upon the Walls—The Fall of Robespierre—Josephine's Letter to Madame Tallien—Barras and Josephine—The Anecdote of Sempronia—The Green Dominos—Rose Thermidor—Public Disapprobation, ... 68

CHAPTER VII.

France prepared for a social Change—Bonaparte lands at Fréjus—Is hailed as a Deliverer from Anarchy—A Deputy dies of sudden Joy—Bonaparte arrives at Paris—The Purpose of this Volume, ... 81

CHAPTER VIII.

The Revival of Manners—Bonaparte urges his Officers to Marry—An Invasion of new Faces—The first Ladies of Honor—The Households of Josephine, of Bonaparte, his Mother and Sisters—The First Reception at the Tuileries—The consular Court established—The Fashions of the Period, ... 85

CHAPTER IX.

Religion during the Revolution—Napoleon a Mahometan in Egypt, a Catholic in France—The Concordat and the Te Deum—Eighty Ladies present at the Ceremony—A disrespectful Audience—Epigrams—The Curate of St. Roch and the Danseuse—The Clergy are refractory—Mass at St. Cloud—The Restoration of the Saints to the Calendar, ... 95

CHAPTER X.

A Courtship and Marriage under Bonaparte—General Junot and M'lle de Permon—The Offer—Consultation with Bonaparte—A singular Obstacle—The Trousseau and Corbeille—The Bride's Toilet—The Ceremony—Bonaparte wagers with Josephine upon the sex of the First-Born—The Baptism of M'lle Junot, ... 106

CHAPTER XI.

An Evening at Madame Récamier's—The Company—The Programme—Talma as Othello—A Gavotte rehearsed—The Wild Boy of the Aveyron—A rustic Wedding—An amateur Performance by Madame de Staël—A Midnight Supper—A Sentiment by the Prussian Ambassador, ... 117

CHAPTER XII.

Bonaparte projects the Legion of Honor—The first Conversation concerning it—The Argument and the Vote—Epigrams and counterfeit Decorations—The Artists, Scientific and Literary Men admitted—Lafayette—The Grand Eagle—Goethe—Young Lafayette—Picard, Talma and Crescentini—Madame de Genlis—Hubert Goffin—Caricatures—The Effect of the Order upon Society, ... 123

CONTENTS.

CHAPTER XIII.

The Empire proclaimed—Attitude of the People—Jests upon the rapid Fortunes of the Bonapartes—The Clamor for Office—Bonapartists, Bourbons and Jacobins—Mock Receptions—Napoleon's Irritation—Brunet and Napoleon's Bust—The Court Journal—Extravagance, 138

CHAPTER XIV.

Madame Récamier—Description of her Personal Appearance—Her Character—Fouché's Proposal—Caroline Bonaparte an Accomplice—Madame Récamier's Banishment—Her Wanderings in England, Italy and Switzerland—The Prince of Prussia and the Duke of Wellington in love with her—Canova's Bust of Dante's Beatrice—The Inconsistencies in her Character—Napoleon's Rejection of the Cooperation of Women, ... 144

CHAPTER XV.

The Code of Etiquette—The Grand Marshal—Governors of the Palaces—Prefects—Chamberlains—Grand Master of the Horse—The Pages—The Aids-de-Camp—Grand Master of Ceremonies—The Palace of the Tuileries—Its Divisions and Apartments—Meals—Punctilio at Table—Napoleon's Opinion on Eating in Public, ... 157

CHAPTER XVI.

The Members of Napoleon's Imperial Household—The Almoners; Chamberlains; Marshals; Masters of the Horse and Hounds; Intendants; Physicians; Surgeons—The Subordinate Service—Napoleon's Fondness for Etiquette—Its Consequences, . . . 168

CHAPTER XVII.

The Household of the Empress Josephine—Prince Ferdinand de Rohan—General Nansouty—The Duchess d'Aiguillon—Madame de Larochefoucauld—Madame de Lavalette—Madame Gazani—M'lle Avrillon—Georgette Ducrest—The Pages, Ushers, Valets, Footmen—Josephine's Extravagance and consequent Quarrels with Napoleon—Talleyrand and Bourrienne the Mediators between them—The Beauties of the Court—The Household of Madame Mère, ... 175

CHAPTER XVIII.

Pauline Bonaparte—Her early Loves—Her Marriage with General Leclerc—The Expedition to St. Domingo—The Widow's Weeds—Don Camillo Borghèse—Extraordinary Scene at St. Cloud—The Statue of Venus Victorious—Pauline's Household at Neuilly—Her Receptions—Her Sedan Chair—Her Taste in Dress—M. Jules de Canonville—Pauline's Impertinence to Marie Louise—Her Banishment—Her Visit to Napoleon at Elba—Her Appeal to Lord Liverpool—Her Death at Florence, ... 187

CHAPTER XIX.

Literature under Napoleon—Oriani and Corneille—Bernardin de St. Pierre—Chénier—Delille—Chateaubriand—Madame de Staël—The Institute—Napoleon's favorite Authors—His Treatment of Literary Men—The Censorship—Ducis—Lemercier—Encouragement extended to Literature and the Sciences—Non-bestowal of the Awards—Liberty of the Press—An Apology for the Penury of Letters under Napoleon—Literature under Napoleon III., . . 208

CHAPTER XX.

Madame de Staël—Her Infancy and Education—Her Marriage—Her Personal Appearance—The Revolution—Her First Meeting and Conversation with Bonaparte—Interview with Josephine—Her Portrait and Character—Her Repartees—Exile—Delphine—Auguste de Staël and Napoleon—Private Theatricals—Corinne—Police Interference—Travels in Foreign Countries—Her Illness and Death—Effect of Napoleon's Persecution upon the Literary Position of Madame de Staël, ... 224

CHAPTER XXI.

Liberty of the Press—The Moniteur—Official Bulletins—Registry of Marriages—Suppression of Newspapers—The British Press—Control of Public Opinion—Mutilated Editions of the Classics—Dramatic Censorship—Edward in Scotland—Lax Criticism—Josephine and Cadet-Roussel—Violation of the Mails—The Dark Closet—Napoleon's Correspondents—Napoleon and Public Opinion, ... 243

CHAPTER XXII.

Elisa Bonaparte—Her Marriage and Residence at Paris—Her Government of Lucca—Baron Capelle—Paganini—Elisa in Tuscany—Her Exile and Death—Caroline Bonaparte—Her Marriage with Murat—Her Portrait—Intrigue with General Junot—Murat's Military Dress—The Throne of Naples—Caroline's Exile and Death, ... 259

CHAPTER XXIII.

Science under Napoleon—The Institute—Speculation and Theory—Progress of Physical Science—Mathematics—Chemistry applied to the Arts—Chaptal, Cuvier, Jussieu, Geoffroy St. Hilaire, Volta, Fulton—The Gregorian Calendar restored—The Republican Year—The Decimal System—Dr. Gall—Maelzel's Automaton—The Comet of 1811—Napoleon's Influence upon Science, ... 272

CHAPTER XXIV.

Hortense de Beauharnais—Her Education—Talent for Amateur Theatricals—Calumny—A Maniac Lover—Duroc—Louis Bonaparte—Official Poetry—The Throne of Holland—Death of Napoleon-Charles—Birth of Louis Napoleon and de Morny—Hortense at Aix; at Malmaison; at the Court of Louis XVIII.—The Return of Napoleon—The Necklace—Chateau of Arenenberg—Death and Will of Queen Hortense—Education and Life of de Morny—Modern French Biography, ... 282

CHAPTER XXV.

The Art of Painting under Louis XIV.—Watteau—Painting under Louis XV.—Boucher—Napoleon and David—The Picture of the Coronation—Cardinal Caprara and his Wig—The Portrait of Napoleon and the Marquis of Douglas—David's Coat of Arms—Gérard—Girodet—Guérin—Isabey—Gros—The Plague of Jaffa—Napoleon and Desgenettes—Géricault—The Spoliation of Italy—Foreign Works of Art at the Louvre—Their Restoration by the Allies—Sculpture under Napoleon—Canova at Paris—His Interview with Napoleon—Houdon—Chaudet—Music during the Empire—Méhul—Lesueur—Boieldieu—Spontini—Cherubini—Napoleon's Influence upon Art, ...   297

CHAPTER XXVI.

Astrology during the Empire—M'lle Lenormand—Her first Prophecy—Her Education and Choice of Studies—Predictions made to Mirabeau, M'lle Montansier, Bernadotte, Murat, Robespierre, St. Just—The Horoscope of Josephine—Napoleon—M'lle Lenormand's Cabinet of Consultation—Her Prediction to Madame de Staël—Her Arrest, Interrogatory and Release—Predictions to Horace Vernet, Potier, Alexander and Von Malchus—Her Adventures in Brussels—Her Works—Her Death and Character—Her Faith in her own Powers—The Processes to which she had Recourse—Hermann the Soothsayer—An Intrigue at the Tuileries,   .   .   .   318

CHAPTER XXVII.

Napoleon's Early Loves—M'lle du Colombier—M'lle Eugénie Clary—Madame de Permon—Josephine—Her Education and First Marriage—Separation from her Husband—Josephine and Barras—Josephine's Marriage with Napoleon—The Honeymoon at Milan—M. Charles—Bonaparte's return from Egypt—His quarrel and reconciliation with Josephine—The conduct of the latter during the Consulate—Her Jealousies—Her proposal to resort to a Political Fraud—The Divorce—Josephine at Malmaison and Navarre—Her Death—Misapprehensions in regard to her Character—Reasons for this Misapprehension—French views of Private Character—Marie Louise—Her Youth and Education—The Overtures of Napoleon—A Marriage by proxy—Journey to Paris—Proceedings upon the Bavarian Frontier—The first interview of Napoleon and Marie Louise—The Marriage—Organization of the Household—Adventures of M. Biennais, M. Paër, and M. Leroy—Birth of the King of Rome—The Russian Campaign—The Treaty of Fontainebleau—Marie Louise at Blois—Her life at Parma—The Count de Neipperg—Death of Marie Louise—Napoleon's Ignorance of her Conduct,   .   .   .   334

CHAPTER XXVIII.

Napoleon's Manners towards Women—Grace Ingersoll, the Belle of New Haven—Her Marriage and Transfer to the Court of the Tuileries—Her Presentation to Napoleon—His Amiable Speech—Death of Grace Ingersoll—Her Two Daughters—Madame de Chevreuse—Her Epigrams and Smart Speeches—Her Persecution by Napoleon—Her Exile and Death—The Journey to Cythera—Napoleon appointed Doorkeeper—Madame Charpentier—A Scene in the Gallery of Diana—Madame Fourès—Her Connection with Napoleon—Her Divorce and Second Marriage—Napoleon's Estimate of Women—His Opinions upon Love—" How many Children have you?"—Perpetual Vows—Madame Regnault de St. Jean d'Angely—Napoleon's Speech to her—Her Reply—Napoleon expresses Regret at St. Helena,   .   .   .   366

CONTENTS.

CHAPTER XXIX.

The Drama under Napoleon—Imperial Patronage of Actors—The Decree of Moscow—Epigrams upon this Decree—Talma—His Education and early Tastes—His First Appearance—Charles IX.—Talma a Girondin—Talma and Napoleon—Character of Talma's Genius—Criticisms of the Emperor—Talma at Erfurth—His Letter to John Kemble—His two Marriages—His Death—Lafon—Fleury—St. Prix—M'lle Mars—Character of her Talent—The Mysterious Ring—Political Constancy of M'lle Mars—M'lle Duchesnois—M'lle Georges—Circumstances attending her Birth—Her Infant Performances—Her First Appearance—Stage Riots—M'lle Georges and Lucien Bonaparte—M'lle Georges and Napoleon—She Visits St. Petersburg, Stockholm and Dresden—The Romantic School of Modern Dramatic Literature, . . 383

CHAPTER XXX.

Features of Society under Napoleon—Mystification: the Princess Dolgoroucky and the Institute—Cafés under the Empire—Gastronomy—Conversation—Effect of Official Eulogy upon the French Language—Affectation and Exaggeration—The Soldier in Society—Epigrams, Jests and Libels—Moreau and the Legion of Honor—Napoleon's Mother and the Pope nicknamed—Napoleon and the Beet-root—Puns at the expense of Marie Louise—Desertion of Napoleon—The Race of Apostasy—Adhesion and Renunciation—The allied Sovereigns at the Theatre—Defection in the Army—Napoleon's Fall hailed as a Deliverance—Conclusion, ... 405

THE

COURT OF NAPOLEON;

OR,

SOCIETY UNDER THE FIRST EMPIRE.

CHAPTER I.

The Women of the Revolution—The Girondines and the Scaffold—Théroigne de Méricourt and the Mountain—Madame Tallien and Josephine—Napoleon as the Reformer of Society.

THE women of the episodic period in French history, which reaches from the destruction of the Bastille, in 1789, to the landing of Bonaparte at Fréjus, in 1799, were, beyond all controversy, the most extraordinary race since Cornelia and the Spartan mother, on the one hand, or since the Amazons and the Eumenides on the other. The annals of no nation, certainly not those of any other period of anarchy and dismemberment, present such a picture of female influence, heroism, and virtue, and at the same time, of female excess, violence, and infamy, as those of the Revolution, Terror, and Directory.

Marie Antoinette and the Duchess de Polignac had introduced and commenced the era of feminine ascendency: they controlled the court, the camp, and the city. Lafayette, on his return from the War of American Independence, received a more enthusiastic welcome from the ladies of Paris than from the soldiers of the Champ de Mars. The milliners composed caps à la Lafayette, and tunics à la d'Estaing, to occupy and satisfy this feminine revolutionary effervescence. Madame Helvetius, who was "so happy with three acres of land," and at whose house Franklin had been so intimate, Madame de Genlis and the Marquise de Condorcet made their parlors the rendezvous of the disaffected and the enthusiasts of the epoch, guiding their speech, moulding their opinions, directing their acts. The Fête of the Federation, the preparations for which 12,000 workmen could not accomplish in time, was successful only through the eager coöperation of the women of Paris: danseuse and dairymaid, bayadère and benedictine, labored together with wheelbarrow and spade. Necker, the Minister of Finance, was so openly assisted by his wife that he was popularly called Necker the Hermaphrodite.

Then, a year or two later, what lustre was lent to martyrdom, what grace was shed upon the pillory and the scaffold, what glory was derived even from ignominy by the modest heroism of the sublime, yet unconscious Girondines! Charlotte Corday—illumined, if not inspired—the protest and the vengeance of outraged humanity; Madame Roland, the sententious philosopher and discreet lawgiver of the Revolution; Lucile Desmoulins, amiable, lovely, and yet undaunted: three women, rare, even had they been isolated and consecutive, and trebly admirable in their joint and contemporaneous glories! From the upas and cypress which encompassed their death and shadowed their graves, history has woven them a crown of laurel and a wreath of amaranth.

Théroigne de Méricourt, acting under a poignant sense of personal wrong, did as much to exasperate and embitter the hostility of the plebeians to the aristocracy, as did Danton: her eloquence was as persuasive as that of Mirabeau. Olympe de Gouges had no rival in either sex for club oratory or pamphlet satire. Then, altogether at the other extreme, were the Women of the Mountain, who, with grotesque and hideous energy, with squalid and ruthless turbulence, spread menace and consternation from Vincennes to Versailles. They made the Mountain a French Sinai, which issued its decrees of eternal justice amid the thunders of their applause, and the reverberations of their riotous vivats.[1]

Later still: To whom does France owe the fall of Robespierre and the cessation of the Terror? To a woman, Madame Tallien, the voluptuous and enchanting Andalusian. To whom does history owe the first link in the chain of events that led to Napoleon Bonaparte? To a woman, Josephine de Beauharnais, the gentle and seductive Creole. Upon another field, and in another sphere, other women were at the same moment acquiring humbler fame, by courage in battle or devotion in the ambulance. Local chronicle still cherishes, however national history may have forgotten it, the intrepidity of Liberté Barreau, the charity of Rose Bouillon, and the patriotism of Félicité and Théophile Fernig.

A late writer thus speaks of this singular inversion of society, referring in the passage quoted to the state of things under the Directory, just previous to Napoleon: "No age can show a more conspicuous example of the fall and annihilation of man, and of the triumph, the publicity, and influence of woman. Never did woman so occupy the public gaze; never did she so openly mix in the conduct of the nation's affairs. Women controlled the choice of generals; they bespoke for them success or reverse, and had their reputation made to order. Not only was public opinion submissive to their behests—not only was their written recommendation virtually a patent of impunity—but they pilfered the keys of the treasury from the girdle of the sleeping guardians, and they guided the pens of those who awarded plethoric contracts, and who fingered sealed proposals."[2]

It is essential to study and understand this period, before it is possible to present an intelligible view of Napoleon as the reformer of society, and, if not the regenerator of morals, at least the restorer of appearances and the reviver of opinion. It was Napoleon's mission—for we are not to consider him here as a soldier or a legislator—to repress the abuses which crept or strode into society during the interregnum between '89 and '99. It is indispensable to expose, in some detail, the situation of the mind and heart of France throughout the three episodes which separate Louis XVI. from Bonaparte—the Revolution, Terror, and Directory. This can be attained in no better manner, within the limits and according to the purpose of this volume, than by concisely narrating the experience of the most conspicuous women of the epoch, though some may have been heroines and some harlots. The Women of the Revolution will thus naturally provoke a comparison with the Women of the Empire: the latter being as remarkable for their deprivation of influence as were the former for its enjoyment and exercise.

The Women of the Empire who attained to fame were few: without exception, they suffered persecution. Madame de Staël was exiled for her opinions; Madame Récamier was banished for her unrelenting beauty and her sturdy virtue; Madame de Chevreuse, the embodiment of the Legitimist protestation against Napoleon, was exiled for an epigram; Madame Tallien underwent exclusion from the Tuileries, because she had been divorced; Josephine suffered repudiation, because, being a wife without a child, the throne was without an heir. Historically and socially, these five women were the first of their time. Properly to appreciate a period in which women were so subjected to oppression, and so denuded of influence, it is well to understand the previous period, in which example was of their setting, and when laws were of their making.

CHAPTER II.

Lucile Duplessis and Camille Desmoulins—Jesus Christ the Sans-culotte—Lucile's Prayer—Her Death and Character—Charlotte Corday—Her Journey to Paris—Her Arrest, Trial, and Execution—Her fifteen Portraits—Her Character as judged by History.

THE sketches which follow, and which precede the advent of Napoleon, will prepare the reader, by the insight they give him into the state of France during the Republic, for a proper comparison of the two periods. Considering Napoleon as the reconstructor of society, it is important to know what elements he drew from the ruins and dismemberment of the edifice which the Revolution had overthrown, for that which, in its turn, the Restoration was to destroy.

Lucile Duplessis, young, lovely, and thoughtless, was the type of that class of women who, without reproach or complaint, marched to the scaffold from the nursery of their children. Being the daughter of rich parents, she seemed unlikely to wed her penniless lover, Camille Desmoulins. But she waited from the age of twelve till the age of twenty: she waited till Camille, overcoming a hesitation in his speech, became a vehement and impassioned orator. She waited till the 12th of July, 1789, when, mounted upon a table in the Palais Royal, he pronounced the brief and celebrated harangue which gave the first impulse to the Revolution. "Citizens," he cried, "let us wear rosettes, by which to know friends from foes. What color do you choose? Green, the color of hope, or the blue of Cincinnatus, the color of American liberty? Green, is it? Let the rallying signal, then, be a green leaf plucked from the garden and worn upon the hat as a cockade." The trees were denuded of their foliage, and dense masses of men—Macbeth's Birnam wood animated and in march—strode at the heels of the impetuous Camille. Two days afterwards, the Bastille was in the hands of the insurgents, and the people danced among its smoking ruins.

Lucile Duplessis now became Lucile Desmoulins. She soon shared the revolutionary zeal of her husband. As he wrote the successive numbers of his pamphlet, "Les Révolutions de France et de Brabant," she listened to them in manuscript, expressing her disapprobation of passages by dancing her cat upon the keys of a piano. She received from a society of patriots the bust of Lafayette, then as much beloved in France as in America. She gave to her first son the Roman name of Horace: his father offered him to the country, upon an altar erected for the purpose. Danton, who now became Minister of Justice, made his friend Camille secretary-general of his department. This rapid promotion overcame his better reason, and for a brief period he indulged the instincts of a reflected, not native, ferocity. Repentance and remorse followed. "Would that I were as obscure as I am infamously famous!" he wrote at this period to his father. "Where is the asylum or the cavern which may conceal me from every eye, with my infant and my books?"

He now established the since famous journal, entitled "Le Vieux Cordelier." Disguisedly at first, openly in the sequel, he pleaded the cause of humanity, and begged a suspension of the Reign of Terror. His friends besought him not to compromise himself out of season and without possible fruit. But his resolution was taken: he could only redeem the errors he had committed and the excesses he had shared, by a bold disavowal of the past. "Let Camille fulfill his mission," said Lucile, on one of these occasions, as she was preparing the morning's meal; "he is destined to save his country. No one who opposes him shall taste my chocolate for breakfast." Camille Desmoulins was speedily denounced, arrested, and brought before the bar of the Convention.

Danton and Camille were tried on the same day. The replies of both to the first questions asked them, are brilliant examples of French epigrammatic repartee. Danton was told to give his home and his name. "My home will soon be in chaos," he replied, "my name will forever live in history." Camille was summoned to tell his age. "Thirty-three years," he returned, "exactly the age of Jesus Christ, the sans-culotte." French sentiment as well as the French language permits such an allusion without intended profanity. On their way to the scaffold, Danton contemplated the howling multitude with tranquillity and disdain, while Camille gave vent to his feelings in detached fragments of vehement imprecation. On passing the residence of Robespierre, he uttered the famous philippic: "Thou shalt follow us, Robespierre: thy house shall be razed, and salt shall be sown upon the soil which it cumbers." He perished holding a lock of Lucile's hair in his clenched and trembling hand.

Such was the train of circumstances which was to transform Lucile Desmoulins from the gay and thoughtless woman, unknown to history, into the heroine destined to grace the portrait gallery of France. She had written a touching appeal to Robespierre— but lately her suitor—in behalf of Camille: she had sent letters, her portrait and her hair, to her husband in prison. She had watched days and nights at the dungeon windows: and the chronicles of the time accuse her of having plotted an attack upon the prison and the deliverance of the captives. It was upon this charge that she was arrested and brought to trial. She arrayed herself in her most elegant toilet; her black hair was tressed in a gauze handkerchief of snowy whiteness. Her complicity in the alleged plot was not proved, but her guilt was pronounced. She arose and thus addressed her judges: "So, in a few moments, I shall have the delight of meeting my dear Camille

In leaving the earth, where I no longer possess that which attached me to life, I am much happier than you, for you shall live tormented by that remorse which is the fruit of crime. Do you not know that the blood of a woman is always fatal to tyrants? Do you not remember that the blood of a woman drove the Tarquins and the decemvirs from Rome? Rejoice, O my country! and receive with transport this augury of thy salvation!"

A prayer, fragmentary and half illegible, was found among her papers, and is doubtless to be connected with this period of her life. It ran thus: "O thou, whom the earth adores, *if indeed thou art*, receive the offering of a heart that worships thee. Oh, enlighten my soul and illumine my reason! When, O God, may I fly into thy bosom, and raise my humid eyelids upon thy glory? Art thou a spirit, art thou a flame? I adore without comprehending thee: I implore without knowing thee: I feel, yet I cannot divine thee. Thou art the source of life, and the secret of nature. There is no happiness but in thee: all else is vain illusion." Having made her peace with Heaven, having provided for her two children upon earth, content to lose her hold upon the past, and confident of redemption in the future, she ascended the fatal chariot, smiling and serene. She conversed gaily with a young man, on the road to the scaffold. She mounted the steps without aid, and died composedly and unaffectedly braving the horrors of a public, violent, and ignominious death.

History has not told, and philosophy has hardly inquired, what it was in the influence of the times or the contagion of the atmosphere, which gave to the women of this period the grandeur, now child-like and now solemn, with which they supported calamity and endured defeat. Up to the age of twenty-three, Lucile Desmoulins had displayed no higher qualities than a persevering constancy, a tried devotion, and the natural, earnest affections of a wife and a mother. Suddenly suspicion entered her house, and death desolated her home. The scaffold soon menaced her life, and orphanage lowered about her children. It was now that she received, as by inspiration, gifts that she did not seem to possess either by nature or education. She found a new faith in her heart, unbidden tears upon her eyelids, and an unknown eloquence upon her lips. She showed the abnegation of a Christian, the fortitude of a stoic, the hope of a martyr. After twenty-three years of a life which, though not frivolous, was certainly not austere, she met the catastrophe which terminated it, in a spirit at once Spartan in its simplicity, and Roman in its sacrifice. Her death furnishes instruction to mankind, and to history a relieving light to mingle with its accumulated shadows.

Marie-Anne-Charlotte de Corday was born on the 27th of July, 1768, at Argentan, in Normandy. Her father was a direct descendant, in the fourth generation, of one of the sisters of Corneille, the dramatist, another of whose sisters gave birth to Fontenelle. His family consisted of two sons and three daughters; they lived in a condition bordering upon indigence, though sustained with dignity; their annual income not exceeding fifteen hundred francs. On the death of Madame de Corday, which occurred shortly after Charlotte's birth, the latter was placed with her sisters at a convent in the town of Caen, where they remained till the revolution of 1789. At the latter date, Charlotte found an asylum at the house of an aunt, with whom she remained till July, 1793, the period of her journey to Paris, on the mission which has made her immortal.

Though she lived in retirement, and avoided systematically all political assemblages, she was seen at this epoch by numerous persons, who have left us their impressions of her appearance, character, and manners. She was of a contemplative, almost melancholy mood, and passed much of her time in study and reflection. Her favorite authors were Corneille, Racine, and Rousseau, and it does not appear that she gave any considerable portion of her time to political reading, though her subsequent acts show how profoundly she was interested in the affairs of the state. M. Dubois, Secretary-general of the Prefecture, who met her often during the three months preceding her departure from home, gives the following description of her appearance:

"I at once noticed M'lle de Corday for her noble yet simple beauty. She was five feet one inch in height, and appeared tall; her form was classic and harmonious. Young, fresh, interesting and elegant, modest in her attitudes, she seemed to veil, as with a tinge of melancholy, the vivacity of her expression; her lips and cheeks were faultlessly colored; the waving curls of her brown hair, and the fine arch of her black eyebrows, gave to her face, which was regularly oval, the most charming character; her blue eyes, at once intelligent, tender and modest, gave an infinite charm to the modulations of her voice; her conversation was precise, elegant and reserved; and her ideas, as she gave them expression, were remarkable for their justice, clearness and measure. Her intonation was delicate, melodious and seductive."

It was during the months of June and July of 1793, that the exasperation and disgust of the provinces, at the fierce and wanton excesses of the revolutionary tribunal at Paris, attained their highest point. Normandy and Brittany collected their best citizens, formed them into columns, and prepared to send them against the capital, now completely in the power of Robespierre and Marat. Caen was the focus of this organized resistance, and Charlotte Corday lived in an atmosphere of discontent and rebellion. Marat was considered the worst of the three demagogues, and appeared then, as history has painted him since, the most odious and the most dangerous, because the most influential with the populace.

Charlotte, we learn from her own declaration at her trial, believed that in destroying Marat, she should deprive anarchy of its chief, and civil war of its motive: she hoped to arrest the shedding of innocent blood and to preserve the thousands of lives and liberties that were threatened by the continuance of his power. So, animated by this noble purpose, without any apparent effort to nerve herself to the act, though sure to lose her life in the attempt, concealing from all the object of her journey, and giving her father and sisters, at Argentan, to understand that she was going to England, she bade adieu to her friends at Caen, and on Tuesday, the 9th of July, took the diligence for Paris. Her passport was three months old, and was signed Marie Corday. Being a republican, she omitted the nobiliary particle *de* before her family name.

On Thursday, the 11th, she arrived in Paris, after two days' travel, and alighted at the Hôtel de la Providence. She went to bed at five in the afternoon, and slept without interruption till eight the next morning. On Saturday, the 13th, she bought at the Palais Royal an ebony-handled knife, for which she paid forty sous: she then called at Marat's house, but was not admitted. She returned home and wrote to Marat the following letter, which she sent through the post:

"CITIZEN.—I have just arrived from Caen. Your love for your country leads me to presume that you would be glad to learn the unhappy occurrences in that part of the republic. I will call upon you at one o'clock. Have the kindness to receive me, and to grant me a moment's interview: I will enable you to render France a signal service.—CHARLOTTE CORDAY."

To this she received no answer. She then wrote another letter, and, taking it with her, again called at Marat's residence, at seven in the evening. For this second letter, however, she had no use, as she was admitted. It was found upon her person, when she was searched.

Marat was at this moment in his bath, writing; his countenance was much disfigured by leprosy. He heard the servants refusing admittance to the applicant, and learning that it was the person who had written to him in the morning, he ordered her to be introduced. He questioned her upon the events which had transpired at Caen, and asked her the names of the deputies who had taken refuge in that city. These he wrote upon his lists of proscription, and then said, "I will soon have these people guillotined at Paris." Charlotte Corday immediately advanced towards him, and drawing from her bosom and unsheathing her knife, she plunged it into his side. Marat could only exclaim, "Help, my love, help," speaking to the woman whom he called his "governess:" he expired immediately, and almost without a groan.

The people of the house at once rushed into the room; Laurent Basse, the carrier of Marat's newspaper, seized a chair and felled Charlotte to the ground. Albertine, the governess, trampled on her with her feet. A tumultuous crowd assembled under the windows and demanded the assassin's head. It was with difficulty that the populace could be induced to allow the carriage to pass in which she was conveyed to the prison of the Abbaye.

The next morning, the 14th, a member of the Convention made to that body a report upon the occurrence, in which he said: "This woman bears the audacity of crime stamped upon her very countenance; she is capable of the worst designs; she is one of those monsters that Nature vomits forth occasionally, to be the scourge of humanity." Marat was buried on the 15th, and on the 16th Charlotte Corday was transferred from the Abbaye to the Conciergerie, to undergo her trial on the morrow. At eight in the evening, she sat down to write to the deputy Barbaroux, a refugee at Caen. One passage runs thus: "I do not know how the last moments of my life will pass: it is the end which crowns the work. I have no need of affecting insensibility to my fate; for thus far I have no fear of death. I have never put any value upon life, except as an opportunity for usefulness."

She then wrote a short letter to her father, in which were the following passages: "Pardon me, my dear father, if I have disposed of my life without your consent. I have avenged many innocent victims; I have prevented many disasters. . . . Adieu, my dear father! I pray you to forget me, or rather to rejoice at my fate. You know I could not have been actuated by an unworthy motive. Kiss my sister, whom I love with all my heart, as I do all my relatives. . . . I am to be tried to-morrow, at eight o'clock."

At the appointed hour the tribunal was opened. Montané presided, the infamous Fouquier Tinville officiating as public accuser. Charlotte Corday was at once introduced, and placed upon the prisoners' bench. She advanced with a composure and dignity of carriage, and a serenity of countenance, which she preserved through the trial and the delivery of the sentence. The president, perceiving in the chamber M. Chauveau de Lagarde—afterwards the advocate of Marie Antoinette—empowered him to assume the prisoner's defense. He at once took a seat beside her, and, as he himself says in his notes of the trial, read in her countenance, as she gazed at him, the silent declaration that any defense unworthy of her would be instantly disavowed. He adds that the appearance of this imposing heroine, calmly and confidently braving this fierce and fanatic tribunal, produced a powerful effect upon president, jury and spectators; they seemed to take her for a judge about to summon them to their last account.

The trial lasted but half an hour. Some of her answers to the questions put to her bespeak the sincerity of her convictions and the purity of her motives. The judge inquired what had led her to the assassination of Marat. "His crimes," she replied. "What do you mean by his crimes?" "The disasters he has caused since the Revolution." "Who induced you to kill him?" "No one: the idea was my own." "Still, the idea must have been suggested by some one?" "No: one executes ill what he has not himself planned. I knew that he was perverting France. I have slain one man to save a hundred thousand. I was a republican long before the Revolution, and have never been deficient in energy." "What do you mean by energy?" "The quality which leads one to lay aside personal interests, and sacrifice himself for his country." "Did you not practise on other persons before striking Marat?" "No: I am not an assassin!"

At about this period of the trial, Charlotte noticed a young man in the audience engaged in sketching her portrait. She at once turned towards him, that he might the more readily reproduce her features. This incident is noticed in the official report of the trial, in the Moniteur of the 27th of July. This portrait, and another, taken as she was on her way to the scaffold, are the originals of all the likenesses now in existence. These number over fifteen; the best is preserved with care at Caen.*

One of the witnesses stated that at the moment of her arrest, Charlotte said she would have preferred killing Marat in his seat at the Convention; for she would then have been at once murdered by the people, and as her family believed her at London, her name would never have been known. She cut the depositions of several witnesses short, by saying, "Yes, it was I that killed him."

Fouquier Tinville here summed up the evidence, and called upon the jury for a sentence to death. While he was speaking, Chauveau de Lagarde received from the jury instructions to decline the defense, and from the judge, advice to consider the prisoner demented. "Their desire was," he adds, "that I should humiliate her." He rose: confused sounds at first met his ear, but they soon subsided into a death-like silence. He looked for the last time at his client, and reading in her glance a positive injunction to attempt no justification, he delivered the following appeal:

"The prisoner acknowledges with coolness the horrible crime she has committed: she acknowledges with coolness a long premeditation: she acknowledges it in all its details: in one word, her acknowledgment is complete, and she seeks no justification.

---

* The portrait of Charlotte Corday, upon the opposite page, is from the original picture by Ary Scheffer, in the gallery of the Luxembourg. Though believed to be somewhat idealized, the public has accepted it as an authentic likeness; no other portrait of the Norman heroine would now be received in France.

This, citizen jurymen, is her whole defense. This imperturbable tranquillity, this entire self-forgetfulness, this calmness and this devotion, in one respect sublime, are not natural. They can only be explained by the ardor of the political fanaticism which has placed the poignard in her hand. It is your duty, citizen jurymen, to determine what weight must be given to this consideration in the balance of justice. I leave it to your prudence."

The question was now put to the jury. The vote was unanimous, and the president at once pronounced her sentence to death, and the confiscation of her property. Being asked if she had anything to say, she caused herself to be led to Lagarde, whom she addressed as follows: "Sir, I thank you for the courage and delicacy with which you have defended me: it was worthy of you and of me. But I desire to give you a greater proof of my gratitude. These gentlemen," turning towards the jury, "confiscate my property: I beg you, therefore, to pay for me what I owe at the prison, and I shall count upon your generosity." Her debts amounted to thirty-six francs, which Lagarde paid to the porter of the Abbaye the next morning.

Charlotte Corday was at once conveyed back to the Conciergerie, where she soon received the visit of a priest. She declined listening to him, saying, "Give my thanks to the persons who sent you, but I have no need of your services." She had already said before the tribunal that she had never confessed to a priest. Soon afterwards the executioner entered her cell. She was to die that evening.

At seven o'clock, dressed in the red chemise that, by law, convicted assassins were compelled to wear, she was placed upon the chariot and conveyed to the Place de la Révolution. The streets were filled by an excited populace, who assailed her with maledictions and gibes. Some few expressed their admiration, and encouraged her by word and look. Her attitude, during this trying scene, was calm and dignified, though she was somewhat agitated by the near approach of her martyrdom. Her color was high, and she seemed to enjoy a foretaste of immortality. At the sight of the scaffold, she manifested a momentary alarm, but ascended its steps with resolution. As the executioner removed the handkerchief which covered her bosom, her countenance showed that the fear of death was a sentiment secondary to that of offended modesty. She placed her head upon the block, and perished an eager and willing martyr to the cause she had espoused, but which she failed to serve.

The titled executioner of Paris, Sanson, had delegated his office, for this occasion, to one of his aids, named Legros. This person presented the severed head to the people, and as he did so, dealt it a sturdy blow upon either cheek. The spectators murmured their disapprobation, and Legros was imprisoned for the outrage. At the moment of committing it, the bystanders noticed that the cheeks of the victim became suffused with a deep flush. This incident gave rise to an animated scientific discussion, in 1795, in the Magazin Encyclopédique. The fact was explained by some, by supposing that the brain momentarily survives decollation, and that in Charlotte Corday's case, the blush was occasioned by indignation. Others accounted for it anatomically, while others still, denied the circumstance altogether. It would seem, however, to be as well authenticated as anything can be, dependent upon popular evidence and public belief.

Charlotte Corday ranks as the first French heroine, not even excepting Jeanne d'Arc. Her ancestry was illustrious and her birth noble. Her morals were pure and her life was spotless. Her tastes and associations were refined. Her motive for the act which has given her immortality was purely patriotic. She offered her own life upon the altar of humanity. In the pursuance of her design she displayed judgment and resolution, and she met her fate with composure and fortitude. That nothing might be wanting to complete a portrait and a character already so perfect, she was the possessor of unusual beauty of face and form, and enjoyed enduring health. She failed only in her choice of a victim. Marat was sinking under the effects of his disease, and the leading Girondins regarded him as merely the puppet of Robespierre and Danton.

Posterity has done her full justice. Historians, poets and dramatists have chronicled her praise ; painters and sculptors have perpetuated her features. Had success crowned her efforts, her country would have judged her worthy of the Girondin deputy's epitaph — a daring composition, for which he suffered death :

"CHARLOTTE CORDAY:

GREATER THAN BRUTUS."

CHAPTER III.

The Furies of the Guillotine—The first Sans-culottes—Théroigne de Méricourt—An Amazon at the Invalides—Her Address to the Club des Cordeliers—A Royalist Caricature—Olympe de Gouges—Madame Roland—Her Precocity—Her Marriage and Removal to Paris—Her Association with the Girondins—Her Arrest and Condemnation.

MIRABEAU had one day remarked at Versailles, during the scenes which preluded the Revolution, that an insurrection would be impossible, unless women took an active part in it, and made themselves its sponsors and its leaders. This observation was doubtless uttered with a meaning; for the eloquent tribune had learned from history, what pitiless ferocity and sanguinary intensity may be communicated to a social or political revolt, by the coöperation of those whom license and depravity have disinherited of the gentler privileges of their sex. At periods of social disorganization—at least in France—no hate is more venomous, no emancipation from restraint more turbulent, than that of the woman whose transgressions deny her the name of wife or of mother. The allusion of Mirabeau was eagerly seized upon and colported at Paris. It was not long before a band of women, possessing something of the discipline and concentration of a military organization, burst upon the astonished city. These women, the opprobrium of their sex, the shame of the Revolution, soon deserved and acquired the title of "Les Furies de Guillotine."

They began their political existence in the halls of the National Assembly and of the Jacobin Club. They drowned the conciliatory proposals of the Girondins in a deluge of murmurs and imprecations, receiving the violent appeals of the Mountain, and the denunciations of the Committee of Public Safety, with formidable salvos of applause. Their riotous behavior gave to French revolutionary language its most celebrated epithet: the Abbé Maury, annoyed by their interruptions, said to the president: "Pray, sir, call to order this pack of sans-culottes!" The name of sans-culotte, or trowserless politician, has since been applied to any person professing extreme opinions, or urging violent measures.

They soon appeared upon the place of public execution, where they rendered the Terror good service. The people had been but lately struck with horror and moved to pity, by the fearful struggles of la Dubarry with the executioner upon the scaffold. Several isolated cries of "Grace! grace!" were heard in reply to her frantic appeals for mercy. The people were tiring of these bloody saturnalia: another such desperate resistance might incline them to interference and rescue. The decapitation of Chatel, Mayor of St. Denis, first revealed the presence of these implacable Eumenides; they stifled the first whisper of compassion under a storm of menace and invective. They now made it their mission and their pleasure to attend upon and haunt the instrument of death. They augmented the horror of the victim by their demoniacal clamor; they clung to the frame-work of the guillotine, vociferating atrocious taunts upon the pallor of the criminal, counterfeiting his last shudder and caricaturing his expiring agony; they besought the executioner to allow one of their number to officiate in his place; and when, in their hideous dialect, the victim "had sneezed in the bag," they danced the carmagnole about his mutilated body—that frantic rigadoon, half dance, half ditty—with which the king had been insulted, and with which death was now blasphemed and eternity profaned![1]

They arrogated to themselves the right of inflicting personal

1 Les Femmes Célèbres, II. 200.

chastisement upon persons of their own sex suspected of aristocracy, or convicted of contumacy, by declining to wear the tricolored rosette. They seized women in the open street, and, heedless of their supplications, flagellated them publicly—subjecting them to the ignominy of the treatment undergone at Rome by the Vestals who neglected the sacred fire. They broke into a convent of Sisters of Charity, under pretense of searching for a refractory priest; they dragged the recluses forth into the street, and there, making jest of their mission of consolation and mercy, and tearing a portion of their garments from their persons, they whipped them till the indignant mob interfered.

These Tisiphones of the Revolution disappeared upon the promulgation of the Constitution of 1795: their last act was to hoot at Barras and his colleagues, as they proceeded to the Institute to inaugurate the government of the Directory.

Théroigne de Méricourt, at one period the leader of the Furies de Guillotine, was, in her youth, a peasant of the environs of Liége. A victim, at the age of seventeen, of a cruel deception and abandonment on the part of a man of high position, she fled from her native village, carrying with her an ardent hatred of the social institutions to which she owed her disgrace. The artificial distinctions of rank had caused her portion to be seduction and desertion instead of marriage: her fall was due to a system which, she said, destroyed love by destroying equality. She nourished this germ of retributive vengeance till it became a towering and controlling passion: she lived to make her name famous as that of a vindictive, insatiable, and remorseless leveller.

She fled at once to England, where her beauty won her the homage of the Prince of Wales; on returning to France, she became the Aspasia of the day, choosing Mirabeau for her Pericles. The vengeance which she was, at a later period, to direct against a class and against masses, she now waged against individuals. Many were the nobles whom she stripped of their fortune, or disgraced in position. Already, and with only such influence as a courtesan could command, she dealt vigorous blows at privilege and caste. But nature had not intended her to exercise her varied talents upon a field so limited, and by processes so degrading: the Revolution, the effervescence of the streets, and the tumult of the camp, taught her the true sphere of her influence. Aspasia became Bellona.

She now assumed the costume of an Amazon: her tight-fitting bodice and short skirt were of blue cloth; her hat, à la Henri IV., was worn martially upon one ear; a heavy sabre hung at her side, and two pistols garnished her belt. The whip which she carried in her hand, ostensibly an instrument of masculine intent, in reality bore witness to still lingering feminine apprehensions. The ball of the handle was filled with aromatic salts, to be used in case of fainting, and to "neutralize the emanations of the crowd:" a dainty and fastidious sentiment for a lady holding popular and democratic views! She adopted an energetic and descriptive motto, with which to spur and sustain her own courage: A crime to punish—a people to avenge—a king to dethrone!

She led the attack upon the Invalides, in quest of weapons with which to arm the insurrection. The governor opened the gates to the infuriated rabble, whom it were madness to resist. In ten minutes, the huge castle swarmed from cellar to dome; the armory was ransacked, and the park of artillery seized. Théroigne assumed and maintained a grade equal to that of the acknowledged leaders, Hulin and Ethis de Corny. She posted piquets, enrolled and drilled undisciplined recruits, intercepted the king's despatches from Versailles, gave orders and enforced obedience. She was one of the first to scale the ramparts of the Bastille; for this she received an honorary sabre, and was placed upon the national list of the conquerors of the dungeon.

She now adopted an austere and mystic severity of manner; she abandoned her debaucheries, and frequented only the society of journalists and of literary men. She stored her memory with poetic passages most calculated to impress and agitate a miscellaneous and excitable audience. Her oratory, seasoned by a strong Flemish accent, and adorned by images almost exclusively drawn from Pindar and the Bible, was in the highest degree picturesque and seductive. Her address to the Club des Cordeliers, upon the shame of lodging the king in a palace, and the deputies in a riding-school, is a masterpiece of revolutionary eloquence. Having been introduced to the club as the Queen of Sheba visiting Solomon, she seized upon the allusion with ready wit, and made it the occasion of her exordium: "Yes," she said, "it was Solomon's mission to build one temple, and if you possess his wisdom, hasten to construct another for the National Assembly. The executive inhabits the finest palace of the universe, while the legislature, like the dove loosed from Noah's ark, and which found no resting-place for the sole of its foot, wanders from the Storehouse to the Circus, and from the Circus to the Tennis-court. The last stone of the lowest cell of the Bastille has been laid at the feet of the Senate. The site of the fortress is vacant; one hundred thousand laborers call for work. Why do you delay, illustrious patriots, republicans, and Romans? Open a subscription to erect the national palace upon the foundations of the Bastille. Let us cut the cedars of Lebanon, and the savins of Mount Ida. Oh! if ever stones moved from impulse of their own, it was not to build the walls of Thebes, but to construct the Temple of Liberty! The French, like the Jews, are given to idolatry; they yield their worship to the external emblems which captivate their senses. Divert, then, their eyes from the pavilion of Flora and the colonnades of the Louvre, to a temple more beautiful than St. Paul's at London, or St. Peter's at Rome!"

Théroigne was the soul of the fearful disorders that followed the announcement that the king sought to reduce Paris by famine. She was the chief of a horde of women armed with clubs, muskets, and cutlasses. Dressed in red, and with a red plume floating from her cap, bearing a lance in her hand and a carbine upon her shoulder, with dishevelled hair and impassioned gesture, she stood aloft upon a cannon, brandishing the tricolor and tossing imprecations at the royal body-guard and the regiment of Flanders. At massacre and bivouac, at plot, council, orgie, and carnage, Théroigne was the master-spirit and the prime agitator—an ardent and remorseless Pythoness, breathing upon the masses that were subject to her will the invisible spirit which inspired her own breast.[1]

Théroigne now became the butt of the royalist pamphleteers. A drama in verse was written to chronicle and celebrate her marriage with Populus. One of the scenes represented the birth of their first boy at the Assembly. By some mischance, the infant rolls upon the president's table, overturns two hundred and sixteen motions and one hundred and thirty-eight amendments, and slightly rings the bell; he finally stops at a bundle of the writings of the Abbé Sieyès, and goes to sleep upon them, which is considered a proof of good taste. The president announces an examination of the child in order to discover and verify his paternity; every demagogue asserts his claim to that distinguished honor. Several stains, as it were of blood, seem to indicate that the sanguinary Barnave is the author of his days. A marked difference in the size of his feet would appear to connect his birth with Talleyrand. His formidable voice allies him, by general consent, with Mirabeau; but then a sort of alert restlessness equally assimilates him to Mathieu de Montmorency; while an inconstant eye, half martial, half pacific, inclines Charles Lameth to recognize him as his son. His sex not being distinctly proved, however, the Duc d'Aiguillon claims him, having puzzled the town about his own sex, by his famous disguise as a fishwoman.[2] Such was a political caricature in 1793.

Théroigne was present at, and took an active part in, the

[1] Les 12 Journées de la Révolution.—A Poem [2] Actes des Apôtres, chap. 38

September massacres at the prisons. In her infuriate thirst for blood, she was not altogether indiscriminate, choosing her victims, by preference, among aristocrats, either suspected or denounced. At the Abbaye she met the young nobleman who had betrayed her. Hesitating for a moment at this dramatic rencontre, apparently vacillating between vengeance and mercy, massacre and reprieve, she plunged her sabre into his breast. The purpose of her life was fulfilled at the age of thirty-two. Her reason was not destined long to survive this early accomplishment of what she had made the object and end of existence.

Upon the capture of the Bastille, Théroigne had been deputed to deliver the keys of the fortress to a member of the municipality, named Brissot. An earnest friendship sprang up between the two, which continued even when the latter became leader of the moderate party. He was one day assailed in the garden of the Tuileries by a band of the "Furies de Guillotine." Théroigne threw herself between them, and zealously took his defense. "Ah, you are a Brissotine, are you?" they cried. "Then you shall pay for yourself and him!" They seized, bound and flagellated her, in the midst of a hooting populace. She lost consciousness, and finally reason. She disappeared from public life, and, when again heard of, was an inmate of a mad-house. She lived, a hopeless and revolting maniac, through the Directory, the Consulate and Empire, and died under Louis XVIII., after having suffered twenty-four years of durance.

Olympe de Gouges, a courtesan in her youth, an author in her maturer years, possessing an ardent imagination, an impetuous temper, a rapid and burning eloquence, and an intrepid spirit, embraced with enthusiasm the principles of the Revolution. She became the most conspicuous and brilliant political adventurer of her sex. It was she who proposed the establishment of female clubs, that women might take part in public debate and influence the action of government; and she herself was the first woman to harangue an auditory of citoyennes. In these discourses she displayed a profundity of thought and a vigor of logic which a statesman might have envied : a warmth and fervor of expression equalled by few orators of greater fame. She was not a demagogue nor a fanatic, for she deprecated and deplored intestine commotion or bloodshed. The excesses of the Revolution shocked her, and induced in her the most contradictory fluctuations and reactions of opinion. She regretted the throne while she preached the Republic : she shed tears over the captive king while her lips still dallied with the advancing Revolution.

When it became apparent that Louis Capet, the last of the Bourbons, suffering for errors of which he was not the author, and held responsible for calamities he could not avert, must appear like a criminal at the bar of the Convention, her democracy abandoned her, and she wept over the degradation of her legitimate king. She wrote to the President of the Convention, proposing to associate herself with Malesherbes in the defense of the monarch. "What matters my sex?" she asked. "The soul is the point. Louis deserves exile, but not death. Rome won immortality by the exile of its king: England has earned infamy by the murder of Charles I."

This open espousal of the principles of the moderate party exposed her to the suspicions of her late associates, the Jacobins. She replied to their taunts by pamphlets unequalled by anything in the language for their energetic, yet crude eloquence. She thus apostrophized Robespierre : "Thou thinkest thyself a Cato, Robespierre ; but thou art nought but Cato's caricature. Thou livest in the hope of making thyself a place among memorable usurpers. Thy reason, caressed by the example of Cromwell, is subjugated by that of Mahomet. Oh, Maximilien! Maximilien! Thou proclaimest peace to the world, and wagest war against the human race. Thou callest thyself the sole author of the Revolution, but thou art nothing but its eternal opprobrium and its lasting execration. Thy breath taints the air, and the hairs of thy head can hardly number the crimes of thy hand. When thou speakest of thy virtues, why is it that high heaven does not launch forth its thunders, to drown the sacrilege of thy impious lips!"

Olympe de Gouges was condemned in November, 1793. When the executioner cut off her hair, she asked for a looking-glass. "Heaven be praised," she exclaimed, "my face does not play me false: I am not pale." At the foot of the scaffold, she said, "They ought to be content: they have destroyed the tree and the branch." Thus perished a woman, whose talents, had they been guided by principle, and exercised in their proper sphere, might have made her the equal of Madame Roland, her illustrious contemporary. But the faculties that Heaven bestowed to be employed with earnest purpose and for enduring benefit, she frittered away in the consuming excitements of a dissolute life, in a futile pursuit of literature, and in a brilliant but unsteady political career. With the eloquence of Mirabeau, the wit of Talleyrand, and the courage of Bayard, she has left posterity little to admire, and nothing to imitate.

Manon Philipon, afterwards Madame Roland—the greatest of the Women of the Revolution—was born at Paris in the year 1756. Her memoirs, written in prison at the close of her life and at the age of thirty-seven, supply the best existing account of her career. These are dated at Ste. Pelagie, 1793, and commence as follows: "Daughter of an artist, wife of a philosopher, who when a minister of state remained a man of virtue; now a prisoner, destined perhaps to a violent and unexpected death—I have known happiness and adversity: I have learned what glory is, and have suffered injustice. Born in an humble condition, but of respectable parents, I passed my youth in the bosom of the arts and amidst the delights of study, knowing no superiority but that of merit, and no grandeur but that of virtue."

Pencils and paper, graving tools, books and a guitar were placed early in Manon's hands. She read at the age of four, and eagerly perused everything which chance threw in her way—

Locke, Pascal, Montesquieu, Voltaire, Don Quixote. She understood astronomy and algebra, and was the best dancer among the young society she was accustomed to meet; and again, quitting her austere studies and her social gaieties, could skim the pot and prepare the meals of the family. At the age of eight, a book was placed in her hands, which formed her character and decided her fate. This was Plutarch's Lives of illustrious Greeks and Romans. It became her bosom companion; she carried it to church with her and slept with it under her pillow. At fourteen she wept that her birth had not made her a Spartan. Greece and Italy filled her mind and absorbed her thoughts: she lived in an ideal republic, enjoying wise laws, pure morals, secure institutions: her watchwords were glory, liberty and country. She contrasted the weak and dissolute men of her epoch with the philosophers, sages and heroes, with whom she loved, in imagination, to associate.

From the age of seventeen to twenty, she received numerous offers of marriage, from persons in her own rank in life, but she felt that none but a man of education could satisfy the ideas she had formed. At this period her father entered into speculation and neglected his profession: he lost his property, and at the same time his wife. Manon was overwhelmed with grief, and as she herself says, "was for a long time a burden to myself and to others. At the age of twenty-one, I read the Nouvelle Héloise, and Rousseau made the same impression upon me that Plutarch had done at eight. Plutarch disposed me to republicanism: he inspired me with a true enthusiasm for public virtue and freedom. Rousseau showed me domestic happiness and the ineffable felicity I was capable of enjoying." She now resumed her studies and committed many of her reflections to paper. Though advised to publish her writings, she declined, and thus explains her refusal: "My chief object was my own happiness, and I never knew the public interfere with this for any one without spoiling it. There is nothing more delightful than being appreciated by those with whom we live, and nothing so empty as the admiration of those whom we are never to meet."

At this time, M. Roland, a laborious writer and philosopher, a man of known probity and simplicity of character, sought her acquaintance. He was not calculated to make a favorable impression upon a young woman. He was formal in his manners, careless in his dress, and advanced in life. He waited five years before declaring to Manon the attachment he felt for her. His avowal did not displease her, though she rejected the offer. She felt that the family of Roland, which, though not noble, had acquired official dignity, would oppose an alliance with a person of humble birth. Roland persisted, and being referred by Manon to her father, was definitively refused.

Philipon's affairs now became extremely embarrassed, and Manon, wishing to secure her own independence, purchased an annuity of six hundred francs, with which she obtained a room at a convent, where she lived, by dint of extreme economy. In six months Roland again presented himself as a suitor, and, after some deliberation on Manon's part, was accepted. She says, in her memoirs, "if marriage was, as I thought, an austere union, in which the woman usually burdens herself with the happiness of two individuals, it seemed better that I should exert my abilities and my courage in so honorable a task, than in the solitude in which I lived." She was married at the age of twenty-six, and soon became her husband's constant friend and companion. They travelled together in England and Switzerland, and finally settled in Lyons, where Roland became inspector of the manufactories. Madame Roland devoted herself to the education of her infant daughter, and to the genial task of rendering her home a happy one. The revolution of 1789 disturbed this peaceful existence.

Madame Roland welcomed this event with joy. Her husband was sent by the manufacturers of Lyons, to represent to the National Assembly at Paris the distress suffered by their interest, and she and their daughter accompanied him. Her house soon became the rendezvous of the Girondins, and she obtained great influence in their councils, through her talents, beauty and enthusiasm. Her husband yielded insensibly to her superior ascendency. She wrote much for him, and inspired him with ardor and energy, though she sedulously avoided all appearance of exerting the influence she possessed.

In December, 1792, Louis XVI., seeking succor amid his adversaries, resolved to choose a minister from among the Girondins. This choice fell upon Roland, and was at once justified by his assiduity, his knowledge, zeal and probity. But the simplicity of his costume and the severity of his manners shocked the court, and the unvarnished truth of his advice annoyed the king and his council. Being alone in opinion in the cabinet, upon a certain measure, he presented an individual remonstrance to the king. This was written, at a single sitting, by his wife: it was couched in daring, even menacing language. It exists as a remarkable monument of the times, and of the genius of her who wrote it. Roland was dismissed from office the next day.

The appearance of Madame Roland at this period is thus described: "Her eyes, hair and face were of remarkable beauty; her delicate complexion had a freshness and color which, joined to her reserved yet ingenuous appearance, imparted to her a singular air of youth. She spoke well and without affectation: wit, good sense, propriety of expression, keen reasoning, natural grace, all flowing without effort from her rosy lips. Her husband resembled a Quaker, and she looked like his daughter. Her child flitted about her with ringlets down to her waist. Her mind was excited, but her heart remained gentle. Although the monarchy was not yet overturned, she did not conceal the fact that symptoms of anarchy began to appear, and she declared herself ready to resist them unto death. I remember the resolute tone in which she announced herself as prepared, if need be, to place her head upon the block. I confess that the image of that charming head delivered over to the axe of the executioner made an indelible impression upon me : for party excesses had not yet accustomed us to such frightful ideas."

Roland was soon after recalled to the ministry, upon the suspension of the royal authority. He maintained a long struggle with the anarchists who were daily gaining strength in the Convention, and who had become all-powerful with the mob. Madame Roland thus wrote to a friend upon the state of affairs at Paris: "Danton is the chief: Robespierre is his puppet: Marat holds his torch and dagger. This ferocious tribune is supreme, and we are its slaves till we shall become its victims. You are aware of my enthusiasm for the Revolution : well, I am ashamed of it; it is deformed by monsters, and has become hideous. It is degrading to remain, but we are not allowed to leave the city; they shut us up to murder us when occasion serves."

Discouraged and sick at heart, Roland retired from office, and he and his wife prepared to return to the country. On the overthrow of the Girondins, on the 31st of May, Madame Roland was arrested, by order of the Convention; her husband had already left the city, and was in a place of safety. She was taken to the prison of the Abbaye, through streets crowded with rioters, to whom her moderation rendered her odious.

She at once determined to occupy her hours of captivity in writing the history of her times, and in sketching the portraits of the distinguished men with whom she had been thrown in contact. She obtained a few books, her admired Plutarch being among the number. She had hardly bent herself to her task, however, before she was transferred to another prison; the jailers practising upon her the odious deception of announcing to her that she was at liberty, and under pretext of escorting her home, conveying her to Ste. Pelagie. She was here placed in the same building with the most hardened criminals, having no other associates in the apartment she occupied, than women of dissolute and abandoned life. Their situation excited her pity, and she

resolved to restrict herself to the most abstemious diet, and at a later period, she even sold her silver, in order to alleviate their misery. She had always practised benevolence according to her means, and during the ministry of her husband, had set apart one thousand francs a month for that purpose.*

It was during this imprisonment of five months, the rigors of which were somewhat softened by the humanity of the jailer's wife, that she wrote her "Private Memoirs," in which she narrates the events of the earlier portions of her life: the "Anecdotes" of the crimes and atrocities of the epoch, and the "Portraits" of some twenty Girondins with whom she had been intimate. She entrusted her writings to two friends, one of whom was arrested; during his captivity the package was discovered and burned. The other concealed his portion of the deposit for eight months, in the hollow of a rock in the forest of Montmorency; these papers still exist. The loss of the others was communicated to Madame Roland in time for her, by a new effort of application, to make it good.

In one of her letters written about this period, she says, "All is over: you know the affection which the English call heart-break: I am hopelessly attacked, and I care not to stay its effects." She now formed a plan for committing suicide, and considered it maturely for many days. She gives her motives for the project in a paper entitled "Last Thoughts." She felt a gloomy satisfaction in thus baffling her tyrants, and dying by her own hand, the mistress of herself and of her actions. Moreover, by perishing before her trial and condemnation, her property would descend to her daughter, whereas a sentence by the Revolutionary Tribunal involved of necessity the confiscation of all her possessions. Her first resolve was to allow herself to starve, but it was evident the jailer would discover and oppose the attempt. She next decided

---

* The portrait of Madame Roland, upon the opposite page, is taken from the only original profile of her in existence, and which has served as a model for the very numerous copies now in circulation. The name of the artist is not known.

upon taking opium, and communicated her plan to a friend in whom she had confidence. This friend dissuaded her from the step; considering it best that she should fasten the crime of her death upon the Tribunal, and feeling that she owed a sacrifice to her cause and an example to her friends. Madame Roland reflected, and decided to accept the scaffold, "not with the transport of an enthusiast who seeks for martyrdom, but with the stern resolution of a stoic who accomplishes a duty."

She was summoned to appear on the 10th of November, before the Revolutionary Tribunal. M. Chauveau de Lagarde, but lately the advocate of Charlotte Corday, requested permission to defend her. He saw her several times at the Conciergerie, and on the 9th, in the evening, was admitted to communicate to her his plan of defense. This she discussed with him, and at eleven o'clock, as he rose to take his leave, she drew a ring from her finger, and gave it to him, saying, "To assume my cause, would be endangering yourself without benefiting me. Let me not have to deplore the death of an upright man! Do not come to the tribunal; I shall disavow you, should you do so. Accept this ring, the only expression of my gratitude that I can offer. To-morrow I shall be no more!"

During the night which followed, Madame Roland composed an address for her own defense. This plea, eloquent and logical, is still in existence, though it was not delivered. She was not allowed to speak at her trial, and was condemned to death, for complicity with the Girondins. She was dressed in white, this attire symbolizing, as she said, the purity of her soul.

Associated with Madame Roland, in the last terrible scene, was a man whose resignation was not equal to hers. She devoted herself, on the way to the scaffold, to an effort to revive his courage. It was her privilege to die first, but, unwilling to expose him to the horror of witnessing her execution, she renounced it in his favor. As he hesitated to accept, she said, "What, do you refuse a woman her last request?" He yielded to her entreaties, and Madame Roland witnessed his death without a shudder. Then turning to the statue of Liberty, she pronounced these memorable words: "O Liberty, how many crimes are committed in thy name!" Another version of this scene, however, gives her apostrophe thus: "O Liberty! how thou art betrayed!" She then yielded herself into the hands of the executioner.

"Without being regularly beautiful," says a late author, "Madame Roland possessed her own style of beauty. Her form was elegant, her movements were graceful and natural; her expression was sweet, her smile was winning: her attitude was that of candor and serenity: her large black eyes, sparkling with vivacity, arched with brows of the same dark chestnut as her hair, reflected by their constant changes the passing emotions of her heart. Endowed with a man's character, tempered by a woman's graces: with a brilliant and flexible wit: with a sonorous and pliant voice: possessing infinite power of pleasing in conversation, and an eloquence whose source was in her soul: a pupil of Rousseau and Plutarch, and enthusiastically devoted to liberty, she subjugated her husband, at the same time sustaining him by her inspirations: and she controlled her friends of the Gironde by her irresistible ascendency. She was, as it were, a chaste Aspasia, but without a Pericles."[1]

Such were the Women of the Revolution. Their lives, as they have been thus briefly sketched, shed sufficient light, for our purpose, upon the mental and moral condition of the country. The succeeding epoch demands a more intimate and detailed analysis, for it was the disorder and the social anarchy of this period which rendered Bonaparte's usurpation possible, not to say desirable and beneficial.

[1] Tissot's Hist. de la Rév. Française, iii. '5.

CHAPTER IV.

Society under the Directory—Divorce—Burial of the Dead—Dancing Gardens—Frascati and Tivoli—Supremacy of Matter—National Bankruptcy—Famine—Two Million Francs for a Waistcoat—The Cascade of Discredit—Voltaire's God-daughter in Danger of Starving—Pamphlets, Caricatures and Fans.

IN October, 1795, the National Convention terminated its disgraceful career. It was succeeded by a form of government imitated from that of the United States, the "Council of Ancients" representing the Senate, and the "Council of Five Hundred" constituting the popular branch. The Executive power was lodged in the hands of five Directors, composing what was called the Directory. The principal member of this joint executive was Paul Jean François Barras, legislator and voluptuary.

Society, under the Directory, and during the four years of its tenure of power, was little better than a masquerade. It was an inversion, yet a reminiscence, of the society which existed previous to the late episode of anarchy. The Terror had made a new distribution of wealth, and had taken power from those in whose hands education and tradition had placed it, to entrust it to those whom hazard had enriched, and whom the current had swept on to fortune. It had perverted morals and denounced religion: it had confounded ranks and destroyed caste; it had ceased to pay homage to worth or respect to age; it had transferred the scene of family gatherings and of social festivity, from the private house to the public garden: society and fashion danced in the open air.

and bought their invitations at the ticket-office. Punning had superseded conversation; the sexes were reversed, and women pursued and captured men. No fruit was forbidden, and little was stolen, for there was no sin and no secrecy. Decency was so far banished, propriety so far violated, during this foul interregnum, families were so dispersed, relations of friendship and acquaintance so relaxed, that marriage ceased to be a social institution: in this pell-mell of disorder and havoc of anarchy, neither men nor women had the time or the opportunity to seek for those conditions of similar taste and spirit which are essential to a congenial union. Citizen Liardot opened a "husband and wife office," where he kept a register of names and fortunes, and published a semi-weekly "Indicator." Marriage soon became illicit, and wedlock relapsed into intercourse.

The Law of Divorce had fastened upon the country this deep social stain. What was before solemn and indissoluble, was now precarious and transitory. It became easier to put asunder than to join. Libertinism was the pet child of the law, and wantonness the privileged daughter of the code. The marriage ceremony was styled by Sophie Arnould, and in one of the satirical publications of the time, the Sacrament of Adultery.[1] Women were transferable like season-tickets, and negotiable like state stocks: their value fluctuated like real estate; those that became old during the continuance of the law, and before the revival of reason, found themselves bereft of all which, at that period of existence, renders life desirable—the respect of friends, the companionship of children, and the approval of conscience. People divorced after a week's connection, so that marriage became a lease, and separation a clause in the contract, as pithy as a postscript. "People divorce for dissimilarity of inclination; they divorce for a vacation of six months; they divorce for nothing. They marry in order to divorce; and they unmarry to get married again. At the promenade, those who were married yesterday meet, already

[1] Paris, Feb. 1797.

bound by another hymen. They have had time to forget, for they bow as to indifferent acquaintances. A countess divorces, and marries her footman. Soldiers, on going into winter quarters, marry for the dead season. Delville exclaims at the tribune, 'This is a traffic in human flesh that you have introduced into France!' The foundlings of the Year V. number 48,000. The Council of Five Hundred receives the petition of a bereaved husband, who has lost two wives, who were sisters, and now desires to marry their mother."[1]

In this race and battle of inconstancy, women bore the palm. Out of 5,994 divorces in fifteen months, 3,870 were applied for by the gentler sex; and out of 1,145 repudiations for bad temper, 887 were the cases of husbands who had ceased to be acceptable to their wives.

After the profanation of marriage came the blasphemy of death: the society that had ceased to reverence woman now forgot to bury the dead. Death was no longer a warning, for life was no longer a probation: death was the end, because life was the whole. The reign of Terror had made life sweet, inasmuch as it made it short: no institution can compare with the guillotine, in rendering existence material, and making the present paramount. So that only those called upon to die heard the summons with dismay: those they left behind had no time to waste in regret, no affections to perpetuate by remembrance. "Death was but an importunate meddler who called the guests from table; those not bidden hardly rose when he entered, and neglected to count the empty places when he withdrew."[2]

Coffins were borne to the cemetery upon the shoulders of hired carriers. Bodies thus delivered over to impious desecration were often warm, and, in more instances than one, were not inanimate. The carriers laid their burden down at the doors of the taverns, and resuming it after repose, tottered, unsteady with liquor, to the mouth of the common grave. Ragged boys played

[1] Soc. Franç. sous le Directoire, 180.   [2] Ibid. 186.

leapfrog over the coffins, waiting on the tavern steps. No one was there to protest against the sacrilege, for even a father's corpse went unattended by his children, and a sister's hardly lifeless form was thrust away to the gentle charities of a ticket-porter. The municipality were forced to publish a notification to the effect that "it was distressed to see with what barbarous indifference were treated by the survivors the remains of persons who should have been dear to them," and to decree that "an officer of police, with crape about his hat, should follow each coffin to the grave."

Those that lived, lived to outrage propriety and defy constraint. The young, whom five years of fasting and deprivation had made clamorous and impatient, the middle-aged, who turned with horror from the barbarities of the present, and recalled with delight the amiable sociabilities of the past, were impelled, the former by nascent passions claiming the gratification due to their age, the latter by the revival of habit and the promptings of memory, into a whirl of turbulent and fantastic excitements. Unable to reconstitute society, with its system of checks, of control and of compensations, they restored only its pleasures, its frivolities and its vices. The Republic had begun to create disgust, with its hard, anti-social requisitions, its Spartan pretences and its repulsive practices. The reaction was profound and lasting. Pleasure was unsatisfactory, unless it was public and ostentatious: love undesirable, unless gross and scandalous; debauch and riot were unattractive, unless spiced with personal encounters and brutal sensuality. The smouldering energies, the smothered and suppressed vitality of la Jeune France, broke into a violent and consuming flame, and the beauty, and strength, and emotion, and sentiment, that had been gathered during the Revolution and the Terror, were now spent with lavish and prodigal hands. "Girls were beset by a sudden impatience: their hearts had arrived at the age of dreams, and their persons at the age of coquetry, during the sombre years of anarchy; and they threw themselves headlong into the vortex of pleasure, that they might regain the time which they had lost, though not employed."[1]

Paris now possessed six hundred and forty-four public ball-rooms and dancing gardens. The society that aspired to elegance secured admissions by subscription; visitors without pretension paid as they went. Orphans danced to forget the guillotine; lovers, bereaved, pirouetted to drown the memory of the scaffold. Tears were quickly dried during this season of oblivion, and oaths that should have been eternal, vows registered in heaven, were as carelessly recalled or disregarded. The bacchanal became epidemic, and soon all France fell into the measure, and danced an immense and frantic rigadoon.

The most famous and most fashionably attended of the dancing gardens were Tivoli and Frascati, both bearing Italian names, and in their embellishments and scenery, being souvenirs of the environs of Rome. The dances, composed with mathematical precision, were executed on the part of the gentlemen with studied vehemence of body and limb, and on the part of the ladies, with the blandishments of languor, attitude and coquetry. Each figure ended with a tableau—in which the spectacle of arms entwined, of gauze conveniently indiscreet, of eyes that asked and other eyes that answered, of lips that trembled with invitation or whispered encouragement or smiled consent, in an atmosphere of music and moonlight, was one that, more than any other illustration of national manners, has shocked history and offended posterity.

Matter being now supreme, bodily strength, the perfection of form and the cultivation of the limbs, became objects of deep consideration. The dangers of the streets and the necessities of defense had rendered a vigorous fist and a pliant staff essential. So, from the perversion and excess that marked the epoch, force soon came to take precedence of intellect, and muscle became a substitute for brains. Men educated their bodies with earnest

[1] Soc. Franç. sous le Directoire, 185.

solicitude, and strove to be at once plastic and ponderous. They practised the arts of the Gymnasium and revived the Olympic Games. They aimed at the glory of Hercules, and their emulation was the emulation of Centaurs. Their ambition was to be athletic, massive, pagan; and they spent their lives in the discipline of their limbs and the development of their persons.

So far was partisanship carried, that the streets were unsafe and life was insecure. Opinion was manifested in the style of the hair, in the form of the garments, in the color of the fabric; and all were ready, in the maintenance of their opinion, to resort to the argument of blows, at the promenade, the ball-room, or the theatre. Combats on the highway, duels in the public thoroughfares, hand to hand struggles on the brink of the fish-ponds, were of daily, nay hourly, occurrence. The theatres were the rendezvous of party spirit, and the scenes of party violence: the Vaudeville was in the interest of the Royalists; the Comédie Française in that of the Jacobins: allusions which could be applied or tortured into an application, were the signal for bravos or for hisses. Even music was political, and every popular air, from the Marseillaise to the Ça ira, was made to breathe menace or to whisper sympathy. The police was powerless against disorder so universal, and no longer sought to repress such violence as sprang from party and political rancor.

Women became Amazons, then viragos, then men.[1] Their emancipation from restraint made them boisterous and masculine. They lived in the open air, racing like Atalanta, or playing truant from home like Hero. They no longer gave suck to their infants; herds of goats waited idly at the street corners to furnish the nourishment which mothers refused. "Adieu, sweet fireside companion! Adieu, gentle wife and modest hearth-stone! Adieu, dear providence of home! Adieu, the careful housekeeper whose heart was domestic and whose children sat upon her knees! Women now require the street. They carry leather-handled whips,

---

[1] Soc. Franç. sous le Directoire, 185.

and with gloved and gauntleted hands, they saw the rebellious mouths of horses."[1] Thus they lived, imitators of Jehu and rivals of Automedon, till the municipality, shocked and outraged, forbade, by public edict, the indecent exhibition, and prohibited female equestrianism.

This was the period of the depreciation of money, with the fearful miseries and calamities it entailed. Assignats were printed by millions of reams, and on certain days the amount manufactured reached the sum of one hundred millions of francs. The government was on the verge of bankruptcy, if the paper-mills gave out. The depreciation was called the Cascade of Discredit. Prices became absurd, incredible: ninety-eight francs for a pound of candles : one hundred and fifty francs for a handkerchief : four hundred francs for a straw hat : eight hundred for a cravat : three thousand francs for five quill pens : four thousand francs for a cord of wood : and five thousand francs for two dozen crash towels. A woman that cried radishes earned a thousand francs, in assignats, in one day : and the journeyman who had worked an hour, was paid by a bunch of assignats bigger than his two fists. "When a man of our time reads these prices, he may easily imagine himself to be perusing a romance of figures, a fairy tale of addition, or a journey in the kingdom of extravagance, by some Swift in a state of hallucination : for the actual and positive rise in the value of the necessaries of life seems to defy credence and to mock possibility."[2]

The state of things, financially, was such that many who had been rich, were now forced to dispense with the use of salt: that landlords, who had signed leases before the Revolution, and were consequently paid in assignats, at their apparent value, could not purchase a dozen needles with the rent of a house for one year : that persons receiving annuities and pensions, got but one-twelfth of their due, and must wait thirty-seven years for their arrears ; and that men, women and children died of hunger and

---

[1] Soc. Franç. sous le Directoire, 185.   [2] Ibid. 148.

cold. Women were seen struggling with dogs in the mud at night for the possession of a half-gnawed bone ; a man died in a public square, and in his mouth were found blades of grass and stems of plants, at which, in the agonies of starvation, he had snatched. Water was as dear as wine : horseflesh took the place of beef.[1] Sugar gave out in the hospitals, and in the ambulances of the armies there were no more wooden legs![2]

A national bankruptcy, amounting to twenty-three thousand millions of francs, was one of the first fruits of this fearful system of credit—a system "which might, perhaps," says Lacretelle, "have been maintained for six months longer, by guillotining four or five millions of inhabitants,"[3] and thus adapting the population to the finances.

While France was languishing under the régime of paper money, foreign speculators—their governments possessing a metallic currency—swooped down upon the merchantable riches of the country, with that precision of poise and certainty of capture which characterizes specie as distinguished from paper, and cash as compared with credit. The Germans and Dutch bought and exported the yield of the finer wines ; the Russians, not yet embarrassed by the drain of war, purchased the family diamonds which had escaped the spoliations of the Terror. The English obtained, and transported across the channel, choice collections of medals, engravings, paintings and books.

Enormous and dazzling fortunes were made, in the midst of this penury of the nation and exhaustion of the exchequer, by stockjobbers and money brokers. The Bourse controlled the Directory. It fixed the daily value of the specie currency of France ; it appointed daily, for the morrow, the rate of exchange between the louis d'or and the assignat. On the 6th of June, 1796,[4] it ran the louis to the value of twenty-three thousand francs in paper. "The brokers were the tyrants of credit, the arbiters of price ; they controlled the pulse of the expiring public fortune, depressing,

[1] Paris, 1796.   [2] Ibid. 1797.   [3] Lac. Dir. Ex. i. 81.   [4] Censeur des Journaux, 1796.

reviving, checking and resuscitating it at will. The value of the louis was ticketed on the veal pies in the windows of the pastry cooks; and the passer-by who had read the figure 1,000 at noon, might read 1,500 an hour later."[1]

The accumulations of wealth were monstrous, and the uses made of it as impiously luxurious as the excesses of Belshazzar. Clerks, who but lately arrived in rags from some distant province, now possessed palates so pampered and tastes so fastidious, that their tables must be spread with golden pheasants, with lake trout, and with pineapples from the tropics; they were drawn through the streets by twelve horses; and they paid two million francs for a waistcoat. They held lotteries in which every ticket won; they gave balls in which the company was so choice and parvenu, that a lady of the late royal household, who asked for an invitation, could only be gratified with a " billet d'escalier "—a ticket to stand upon the staircase! They were so lavish of pin-money to their wives, that the latter would risk a million upon the turn of an ace. They had literary taste, too, and would extend their patronage to poets that were an-hungered: "their opulence was won to smiles by the verses of some Virgil who had fasted, or of some Horace at half price."[2]

Napoleon, writing from Paris, during this period, to his brother Joseph, at Genoa, says: " Luxury, pleasure, and the arts are reviving here, in a wonderful degree: Phèdre was performed yesterday at the Opera, for the benefit of a retired actress; the crowd was immense as early as two o'clock, although the prices were trebled. Equipages and elegantly dressed gentlemen are reappearing: they only recollect as a long dream, that they have ever ceased to shine. Libraries, historical lectures, courses of botany, chemistry, astronomy, succeed each other in rapid variety. Every thing is accumulated in this country to distract and embellish life; the public tears itself violently from its reflexions: how can one look upon the dark side of things during such an application

[1] Soc. Franç. 154.   [2] Ibid. 156.

of the mind, and during an agitation so restless? Women are everywhere: at the theatres, at the promenades, at the libraries. In the studies of the savans, even, you will find very elegant ladies. Here, the only spot upon the globe, do they deserve to hold the helm : the men are, therefore, madly in love with them ; they think of nothing but them, and only live by, through and for them. A woman needs to remain six months at Paris to learn what is her due, and what empire she may wield."[1]

The success of speculators on a large scale tempted speculators in little ; and a passion for trade and barter seized upon the entire population. Men and women, whether qualified by education and practice or not, bought, sold and exchanged ; their pockets were stuffed with samples, now of cambric or sewing-silk, anon of soap, rice or gunpowder. Ground floors became bazaars ; parlors became store-rooms, bed-chambers granaries, dining-tables counters, and the fairest of hands were begrimed with charcoal, pepper, suet, coffee and oil. Persons brought up to trade sold everything except what they advertised : "the confectioner sold soap, the hatter sold butter, the grocer sold books, and the apothecary sold shoes." A citizen whose antecedents had poorly qualified him for his new calling, invited purchasers to examine his stock, consisting of "two bronze horses, six hundred thousand pounds of good prunes, at thirty-three sous a pound, and a superb electrical machine with a glass wheel three inches thick." Another called attention to a collection comprising a guitar, a cooking-stove, a mechanical bed for the sick, a tambourine, a reindeer skin capable of furnishing an excellent pair of tights, and an Ecce Homo. "From the rich man to the poor, from the master to the valet, runs a chain of purchase and sale, of re-purchase and re-sale, of again buying in and again selling out : from pocket to pocket, from hand to hand, the article passes, passes, passes, gaining, gaining, gaining, or perchance losing, losing, losing."

[1] Mémoires du Roi Joseph, i. 183.

The municipality were unable to suppress or to interfere with this disgraceful and unproductive practice. A castigation now came from the stage; at the close of the famous farce of "The Fashionable Tea-Party, or A Thousand Pounds of Sugar," the actor St. Maurice, addressing the audience and not the characters in the play, said in tones half of indignation and half of persuasion: "Abandon, ladies, let me implore you, abandon this scandalous traffic, which devours the public substance and degrades the human name. Nature has bestowed upon you the talent of amiability and the graces of feature. Use them, I beseech you, to embellish life and dignify society, and seek no longer to adorn commerce or to add lustre to bargain and sale."[1]

The success of this unskilled speculation and of these chance per centages, was of short duration. The small gains were speedily lapped up and passed into the remorseless maw of the heavier operators. The rich became richer and the poor poorer. General de Montalembert, at the age of eighty-three, and after sixty-five years of active service, sold his furniture for food in the year V. Bomare, the author of the Dictionary of Natural History, was reduced to two ounces of black bread a day. Préville, the actor, lately in the annual receipt of forty thousand francs, begged and was refused admission to the Incurables: as did Balbâtre the organist, to whom the Duchess of Choiseul had given one hundred louis for tuning her piano. The dramatic works of Corneille, having outlived the period during which copyright upon them was due to his heirs, had fallen into the public domain: but in view of the fact that Voltaire's god-daughter, Dupuis Corneille Dangely, was in danger of starvation, the theatre Feydeau restored the author's ten per cent, in her favor, upon Don Juan and the Liar.[2]

The fugitive literature of this period—pamphlets, satires, caricatures—forcibly illustrates these singular features of society. Their titles indicate their themes—themes of poverty, national

---

[1] Soc. Franç. sous le Directoire, 168. [2] Ibid 166.

degradation, stock-jobbing, debauchery and violence: The Vultures of the Eighteenth Century: The Grumbler: Intriguers and Plunderers: Discourse upon Tombstones: Women shall no longer lead us, or the Triumph of Beasts of Burden: The Gymnast's Programme: Our Follies, or the Memoirs of a Mussulman: The Rusty Turnspit of Gentlemen once in easy Circumstances: Everybody has a Finger in the Pie, or the Mania for Trade: Curious and Veritable History of the Parvenus of the Revolution: Tournament of Don Quixote against a Windmill: The Ventriloquist, or the Hungry Stomach: The Last Cry of Humanity and Reason: We are dying of Hunger, the People are weary, and this must come to an End. Caricatures represented fish-women bestowing alms upon gentlemen of property: and fans intended for "pensioners, persons in the receipt of annuities, and who but lately enjoyed so much a year," bore an inscription composed of the inflection of a very suggestive preterit: I was, thou wast, he was: you were, they were, we all were.[1]

[1] Soc. Franç. sous le Directoire, 167.

CHAPTER V.

Fashions of the Terror and Directory—Classic Nudities—Iphigenia and the Vestal Virgins in Paris—Fatal Consequences—Cravats, Smallclothes, and a new Pronunciation—Magazines of Fashion.

MARIE ANTOINETTE and her retinue set the fashions up to the period of the first revolutionary outbreak : M'lle Bertin was the court mantuamaker. During the Terror, fashion became democratic, and a style of costume prevailed which gave rise to the descriptive expression, the "anarchy of taste." Ideas were borrowed from foreign nations, and scraps of attire were adapted from distant people, or revived from remote ages. The momentary rage for English fabrics and English styles speedily gave way to the belief that antiquity—Greek and Roman antiquity—with some modifications to suit the climate and the epoch, would best furnish the Republic's wearing apparel. David, the painter, strengthened this conviction by his choice of antique subjects, and his preference either for flowing drapery or the nude flesh. Two assemblies, La Société Républicaine, and Le Club Révolutionnaire, made the subject of a national costume the theme of debate. "A mother of a family" appealing to the former of these for the means of "dressing herself in the antique style," was sent with two members to the costumer of the Théâtre Français, "that he might show the lady how properly to cut her cloth." A deputy exhibited at the Annual Gallery of Art the design of a republican sans-culotte attire, which he proposed that every Frenchman should assume at the age of twenty-one.

From the experiment of the "mother of a family," speedily proceeded a multitude of mythological and classic fashions: robes à la Flore, à la Diane, à la Vestale, tunics à la Cérès, à la Minerve, jackets à la Galatée, à la Sunrise. A peculiar style, the Omphale, required a train sufficiently long to allow the end to be brought back and tucked into the girdle. M'lle Nancy was the mantuamaker for those who affected the Greek revival; Madame Raimbaut for those who preferred the Roman. Coppe was the ton shoemaker, though shoes were now called buskins. His price was sixty francs a pair, but purchasers could forget the cost in the consciousness that the article was "singularly fresh, eloquent and poetic." Coppe was one day summoned to the house of a lady who complained that her buskin burst the first time she tried it. Coppe examined it, and then pronounced the following opinion, with all the solemnity of a verdict: "Madame, I'll lay my life you walked in it!"

Thus far, at least, the styles of dress for women were decent, indeed modest. The throat and arms were covered, and the stuffs employed, principally silk and woollen, were too heavy and opaque for indiscreet revelations. The convenience, the relief, of loose garments, was such that it was soon thought that garments still looser and lighter would be still more convenient. So robes that concealed the bosom and the arms were called robes "à l'hypocrite," and all who could abandon them did so. This was the age of muslin, gossamer, tissue, filigree and gauze. Starch was laid under interdict, and the only permissible color was pure white. The newspapers were filled with allusions, now serious and now jocose, to the prevailing taste. One published an assertion made by Dr. Desessarts, that "he had seen die more young ladies, since the introduction of these 'begauzed nudities,' than in the previous forty years." Another described a lady of its acquaintance as attired "in a transparent robe of muslin, through which was to be seen her form closely fitted by a justaucorps of pink silk, her thighs encircled by rings studded with diamonds." The same paper celebrated the existing mode in verse, of which the following lines are a fair specimen:

> "Grâce à la mode,
> Une chemise suffit,
> Une chemise suffit,
> Ah! que c'est commode!
> Une chemise suffit,
> C'est tout profit!"[1]

As the Greek and Roman costume did not admit of the introduction of pockets, a lady of fashion was obliged to dispense with such anti-classic receptacles; she therefore sheathed her fan in her girdle, dropped her purse into her bosom, and gave her handkerchief to her lover or aspirant to carry at her side.

Those were the most successful votaries of fashion who could best drape themselves after a bas relief from Athens, or could the most nearly approach the simplicity of sculpture. It was not only in the evening, by moonlight, or under the dim revelations of Chinese transparencies, that they assumed the attire of Vestal virgins: it was in this costume that they breakfasted in the morning and shopped at noon. The ladies in the streets were white as phantoms, and they flitted like ghosts awaiting cock-crow. The maiden and the matron were alike undistinguishable in their dress from women of bad life, except perhaps that the latter were the most chaste in their selection of a model, for they adopted the costume of Iphigenia in Aulis.[2]

An elegante of this period was expected to dress, if aspiring to the consideration of a merveilleuse, somewhat after the following fashion: Her hair was short, and fell in crisp curls about her ears and over her eyes; her gown, usually of muslin or cambric, was so short-waisted that it cut the bosom in halves; the sleeves

---

[1] Paris, Oct. 1798.   [2] L'Europe sous Napoléon, de Capefigue, i. 187.

were so tight that the arms became red from suspended circulation; the skirt of the gown was short in front, and displayed the feet and ankles; behind, it was long enough to drag upon the floor, though not sufficiently so to assume the importance of a train

"How," wrote Dr. Desessarts, the Nestor of medicine, "how can I refrain from speaking of the evils multiplying every day, under the influence of these incomprehensible fashions? Can I ever efface from my memory the image of that young lady who, in the full enjoyment of health at six o'clock in the evening, and resplendent with all the charms and graces of youth, attended, at nine, in a costume bordering upon the nude, one of those assemblies that so resemble the saturnalia of Rome, and returned home at midnight benumbed with cold, her chest oppressed, her throat parched and hacked by a violent cough, her reason wavering and her blood wild with fever? Can I ever forget how our art was powerless to relieve her, and how she expiated, in the long agonies of consumption and in a premature death, the imprudence of having revealed what modesty should have taught her to conceal?"

Parisian fashions have from time immemorial been contagious, and it is not singular that we should read in the Russian annals of this epoch, that the Princess Tufaikin fell a victim, at the age of seventeen, to the French epidemic and to the imprudence of having unduly exposed herself to the inclemency of the St. Petersburg season.

The styles of dress for gentlemen presented a singular contrast. They are thus described by a late author: "By the side of ladies thus seeking for all the coquetry and allurements of costume, and who recommend themselves by their very indelicacy, one would say that the men, in a spirit of sacrifice and self-immolation, desire to play the part of foils. They offer their arms to ladies decked with ribbons, spangles, flowers, plumes, feathers and tufts; but they themselves appear habited as English rustics. Not that their garments are those of common life, or are not made to measure: their attire has been a matter of deep and serious consideration; but they apply themselves to appearing untidy, they aim at being soiled, tumbled and uncared for, as if they sought to prepare the costume of Robert Macaire for the masked balls of the future. They require the scissors of the tailor to spoil a garment after a particular manner; and they have haberdashers of great renown to equip them in the guise of caricatures. That bottle-green coat, with pearl buttons—a coat which purposely calumniates its wearer's form, and which seems fashioned to avenge hunchbacks upon the person of an upright man—was cut by the famous Saul Heyl. Heyl gives his customers the air of busts shrouded in bags and mounted on stilts.

"The cravat is an affair of profound importance. No one wears a proper cravat who has not about his neck an enormous muslin goître. Professors will inform you that a cravat must caress the under lip with its upper edge, so that the head, supported upon this pedestal, as it were, may produce at a distance, the effect of a Bologna sausage. The button of the breeches must be skillfully looped at the knee, to give to the leg a deliciously tortuous and bandy aspect.

"They adopt in their conversation a voice like that of invalid women, an infantine lisp, an extinct and inaudible utterance. They have muscles able to kill an ox; and they appear to have a throat so delicate that a consonant would rasp it raw. They put the alphabet upon the bed of Procrustes. The French language—so majestic with its resounding and rolling R, allying the noble rhythm of the Latin with the musical pomp of modern Italian—is nothing more than a warble. Lisping has succeeded pronunciation. The R was banished first, and fashion now insists upon proscription after proscription. The D is next cut out from ma-âme, for the better euphony of the word. Ch is forced to yield its place to S, in order not to startle the "sarmes" of a belle, and G is altogether too guttural to figure in a mention of her "anzelic visase." So, from suppression to suppression, from substitution to substitution, a few thousand people in France have come to speak the most marvellous nightingale dialect that ever trifled with the twenty-one consonants!"[1]

Fashion was thus an absorbing avocation, and a jealous and exacting mistress. Her votaries were well aware of their own follies and extravagance, as the descriptive names that they assumed, or were made to bear, plainly show. The gentlemen of this fantastic period were styled "Incroyables," "Inimaginables;" the ladies were "Impossibles" and "Merveilleuses." Mesdames Raguet, Tallien and Hamelin, the three beauties of the epoch, were the despots that gave the law, in all matters of color and cut. Their decrees were so stern that statesmen and diplomates were forced, from policy, to submit to them. Talleyrand, in order to maintain relations with the society, which, for want of a better, must be considered the elegant society of the period, assumed the dress and manners of an Incroyable: his cravat he preserved and continued to wear, through all changes, for half a century, as a pledge of constancy and immovable opinions.[2]

Scores of magazines, pamphlets and periodicals were published upon this attractive theme: such as the Tableau of Taste; the Correspondence of Ladies; the War of Black Collars; Heads of Hair Shorn, Hooted at, criticised and treated as they Deserve; Journal des Incroyables; Eulogy of Wigs; Parisians, see what you were in 1788, and what you are to-day; Petite Poste; Paris; Journal of Fashion, Amusements of the Toilet, Secret History of all the white Wigs in Paris, The Elegant Manual, How shall I Dress, with philosophical Reflexions, and the Portfolio of Love.

[1] Soc. Franç. 428.   [2] Capefigue i. 188.

CHAPTER VI.

Thérésia Cabarrus—Her Marriage with M. de Fontenay—Tallien at Bordeaux—The Pro-Consul exercises Clemency—Thérésia and Josephine in Prison together—Their Signatures still visible upon the Walls—The Fall of Robespierre—Josephine's Letter to Madame Tallien—Barras and Josephine—The Anecdote of Sempronia—The Green Dominos—Rose Thermidor—Public Disapprobation.

THE name of Madame Tallien has been mentioned as one closely connected with the politics, fashion and gaieties of this epoch. Her influence upon the period entitles her to a detailed biography.

Thérésia Cabarrus, only daughter of the Comte de Cabarrus, a French banker settled in Spain, and of M'lle Galabert, to whom he was secretly married, visited Paris, at the age of sixteen, with her father, who was charged with a mission from Charles III., King of Spain, to the government of Louis XVI. M. Devin, Marquis de Fontenay, counsellor to the Parliament of Paris, was the most fortunate of the numerous aspirants attracted by her extraordinary Andalusian beauty, and married her. This alliance, which made the fair Saragossan a Frenchwoman, was one of the most important events of the epoch: for Thérésia Cabarrus was the proximate cause of the fall of Robespierre, as the sequel will show: she was the occasion of the acquaintance formed between Bonaparte and Josephine—an event which made the former general of the Italian army and leader of the Egyptian expedition. That she diverted the course and changed the character of the French Revolution, all historians allow: that she was at least a link in the chain of circumstances which made Napoleon emperor, no biographer has denied.

Upon her marriage she became the ornament of the society with which she was thrown in contact: Lafayette, then general-in-chief of the National Guard, was a constant visitor at her house. Upon the arrest of the Comte de Cabarrus at Madrid, in 1790, for malversation, she said to Lafayette, "Give me your guard, general, that I may fly to the deliverance of my father." The restoration of the count to favor, however, rendered unnecessary the execution of this fantastic design. Madame de Fontenay was unhappy with her husband: he squandered her dowry, and upon the breaking out of the Revolution, was compelled, in order to save his life, to join the emigration of the nobles: before leaving France, however, he restored his wife to liberty, by obtaining a divorce in due form. A son had been the fruit of the union.

Madame de Fontenay now became an ardent and active republican. She dreamed of little but the practice of civic virtues, and of brows bound with civic laurels. She wrote of fraternity and emancipation, and joined associations whose object was the sacrifice of personal interest to the general welfare. She addressed a communication to the Convention, in behalf of an extension of the influence of women, and in favor of the establishment of an asylum for orphans ; this is a model of fervid style and of close argumentation. In no sense, however, did she quit the legitimate sphere of her duties as a woman: she neither became an Amazon nor a citoyenne. She joined the party of the Girondins, and employed her eloquence and her beauty to assuage the horrors of the Reign of Terror. Upon the dispersion of her friends, she fled hastily towards Spain, where her father was in the enjoyment of fortune and office. An irregularity in her passport drew upon her the suspicions of the police of Bordeaux. She was arrested and thrown into prison. It is at this point that properly commences her national and historical career.

Bordeaux, at the period of which we are speaking, was in the power of a man who for a time at least, was a worthy rival of Robespierre and Danton, in the ferocity of his instincts and the unscrupulousness of their gratification—Jean Lambert Tallien. This man, the son of a cook, possessed the entire confidence of the Jacobins, having prepared and contributed to the execution of the terrible massacres of September. They made him pro-consul at Bordeaux, within whose hospitable walls the scattered remnants of the Girondins had asked and found a refuge. He took lodgings upon the square where he had established the guillotine. He directed the proceedings of the scaffold from his window: and applauded the most skillful decapitations. After thinning the political ranks, he attacked the merchants and the industrial classes. He burthened them with taxes and confiscations, and guillotined those whose engagements were unfulfilled. Famine followed in this train of calamity, and the fierce pro-consul composed new lists of proscription from the names of persons designated as monopolists and forestallers of the grain market. In all these measures he was supported by the Convention, to which he sent regular reports of his proceedings, and from which he received congratulations upon the salutary severity of his pro-consulate.

An event now happened which, in giving a new turn to his thoughts, suspended these saturnalia of blood. Madame de Fontenay, whom he had seen at Paris at the house of Madame Lameth, was now confined in a dungeon at Bordeaux: she wrote to him, imploring his protection or his interference. The terrible inquisitor, who did not bear his character written on his person—for he was of noble aspect, but twenty-four years old, impassioned and eloquent—visited the fair petitioner in her cell. One glance of the enchantress sufficed to open her prison doors: she, on her part, expressed, and probably felt, no reluctance in accepting the implied conditions of her enlargement. She took up her residence in Tallien's house, and speedily obtained over him a controlling and salutary ascendency.

A reign of clemency now succeeded this disastrous period of

persecution. Under the benign control of Madame de Fontenay, Tallien became a humane and beneficent citizen. He ceased to compose lists of proscription, and appended his signature instead, to columns of pardon and reprieve. The lovely suppliant saved many hundreds of lives, and endeared herself to thousands who, while condemning the irregularity of her life, could but admire the excellence of her heart. On one occasion, the ferocity of Tallien's instincts breaking out anew, she arrested the fatal consequences by asking him for his portrait. A painter was summoned, and being instructed by Madame de Fontenay to protract the work, Tallien was absorbed, to the exclusion of his bloody avocations, in the peaceful duty of sitting for his likeness. The Marquis de Paroy, who obtained an audience of Madame de Fontenay, in the hope of enlisting her compassion in behalf of his father confined in prison, was admitted to Tallien's library, now transformed into an artist's studio. He has described it as resembling the boudoir of the Muses: a piano, a harp, a guitar, an easel and loose music, a pallet and color-box, brushes and miniatures, a writing desk upon which lay an unsigned petition for pardon, encumbered the room in picturesque confusion. Tallien was seated in a luxurious arm-chair, dividing his attentions between the painter and his mistress. The latter was diligently embroidering upon satin. She permitted the marquis to hope that her intercession for his father would be effectual. "Lady," he said, on taking his leave, "your talents are universal, but your goodness surpasses them, and nothing can equal your beauty." The daughter of Madame de Genlis, afterwards Madame de Valence, who owed her life to Madame de Fontenay, said of her, "I witnessed the good she did, and I saw her tormented by that which she was obliged to leave undone."

The Convention was soon informed of the apostasy of its emissary. Tallien was denounced and recalled to Paris, accused of having arrested the Revolution. Madame de Fontenay was included in the indictment, as accessory to the "paralysis of the

Republic." Robespierre advised that she be immediately tried at Bordeaux by a military commission. She escaped, but was arrested at Versailles. She was taken to the prison of the Carmes, where she was plunged into an underground cell; she received insufficient food, and her bed was a pallet of straw, unchanged from day to day. In the same prison was confined Josephine de Beauharnais; they often met, and there formed the intimacy which was destined, some months later, to bring about the acquaintance and the marriage of Josephine and Napoleon.

"A tender friendship," says Lamartine, "united these two women, though they had often divided the public admiration and that of the leaders of the army and of the Convention. One was predestined to the throne to which the love of young Bonaparte was to raise her: the other was predestined to overthrow the Republic, by inspiring Tallien with the courage to attack the Committees in the person of Robespierre. The captives were consumed with souvenirs, with impatience and thirst for life. With the points of their scissors, with the teeth of their combs, they scratched upon the plaster of the walls, initials, dates, and bitter invocations to fallen liberty. These inscriptions are still legible: 'Liberty, when wilt thou cease to be a vain word?' 'This is the forty-seventh day of our confinement.' 'They say we shall be set at liberty to-morrow.' 'Delusive hope!' Underneath are the three signatures: 'Citoyenne Tallien,[1] citoyenne Beauharnais, citoyenne d'Aiguillon.'"[2]

Madame de Fontenay had been arrested on the 30th of May, 1794. One of her friends, named Tascherau-Fargeau, exerted his influence with Coffinal and Lavalette to obtain the postponement of her trial: in this he succeeded, and meeting Tallien walking disconsolately upon the Champs Elysées, he said to him, "Do not fear for the citoyenne Cabarrus: she will not be brought at present before the revolutionary tribunal." All the efforts of

---

[1] This signature is singular, for though Madame de Fontenay had lived with Tallien as his wife, the marriage ceremony had not been performed, and she therefore did not bear his name.

[2] Les Girondins, viii. 185.

Tallien in her behalf only served to tighten her chains: it was in vain that he claimed her liberty, urging that she was his wife, and that he would answer for her good behavior. On the 23d of July, Alexandre de Beauharnais, the husband of Josephine, perished upon the scaffold: on the 26th, Josephine and Madame de Fontenay were to be judged and executed. On the 25th the latter wrote as follows to Tallien: "The police administrator has just left me: he came to inform me that I am to be tried, and consequently guillotined, to-morrow. This is very unlike a dream I had last night: I thought that Robespierre was dead and that the prisons were open: but thanks to your signal cowardice, there will very soon be no one left in France capable of realizing my dream." This letter was written in blood. Tallien replied: "Calm yourself, Madame, and be as prudent as I shall be courageous." The morrow was the 27th of July, the NINTH OF THERMIDOR. Tallien, in company with Fréron and Billaud, had plotted the destruction of Robespierre: ascending the tribune, and brandishing a poignard aloft, he accused the tyrant of aspiring to dictatorship and usurpation. The Convention, whose members were in personal fear of the growing ascendency of Robespierre, eagerly profited by the opportunity, and in the midst of tumult and agitation passed sentence of death upon him. Robespierre was executed the next day. His fall terminated the period to which history has given the name of "Terror." Josephine and Madame de Fontenay were soon afterwards placed at liberty. Madame de Fontenay became Madame Tallien on the 26th of December of the same year.

The newly married couple took up their residence at Chaillot, just without the walls of Paris. Madame Tallien's existence was soon absorbed in balls and concerts; and she became the foremost in the whirl of gaiety to which Paris abandoned itself upon the fall of Robespierre. She invited Josephine constantly to her house, and befriended her during the destitution which she suffered until a portion of the confiscated estates of her husband were restored to her. Josephine and Thérésia were now inseparable: a letter from the former to the latter shows to what extent they were absorbed in the frivolous excitements of the period: "There is to be a magnificent ball at Thelusson's, I hear: I do not ask you if you are going, for the fête would languish without you. As it appears to me important that our dresses should be absolutely alike, I write to inform you that I shall wear a red handkerchief in my hair, after the Creole fashion, and with three knots at the temples: we will each of us wear our peach-blossom under-skirt. This, which is rather daring for me, is very natural for you, who are younger, handsomer perhaps, and incomparably fresher. I wish especially to enrage 'les trois Bichons' and 'les bretelles Anglaises.'" These elegant epithets designated rival beauties.

Tallien was now compelled, by the force of a reaction which soon set in, to resume his position as an advanced republican, and he again professed sanguinary opinions. His wife, occupied in reviving the pleasures and the social amenities which the Terror had banished, was somewhat alienated from him, in consequence. This antagonism produced a singular effect: the newspapers in the interest of Tallien did not hesitate to publish the most impertinent attacks upon his wife. Thus, the "Tableau de Paris" would fill its columns with such gibes and innuendoes as the following: "Thérésia Cabarrus pretends to be but twenty-three years old; her enemies give her twenty-eight and twenty-nine. . . . . She is a handsome woman, with the exception of her nose, which certainly is not attractive. Otherwise, her face deserves nothing but praise; and we must admire the splendor of her form and the beauty of her arms. Our description must stop here: those who desire further information may apply, in Germany, to M. de Fontenay; in Switzerland, to M. de Lameth; in England, to M. d'Aiguillon. . . . . As to the character of Thérésia, it is not what many people suppose: her coëxistence with Tallien reminds one of the friendship of the lion and the dog, in the Menagerie. . . . . If you ask her, she will talk English, Italian or Spanish; but we defy you, even though you be of London, Naples or Madrid, to understand one word of the jargon which she offers as specimens of these languages."

In 1795, the Council of Five Hundred succeeded the Convention, and Mesdames Tallien and Beauharnais attached themselves to the person and interests of Barras. The friendship of the two ladies was so sincere that it suffered no interruption from their rivalry in love. Both were too well pleased with possessing so powerful a protector, and enjoying a credit so unlimited, to endanger their position by an inconsiderate quarrel. Josephine, whose extravagance was at this early period ungovernable, drew heavily upon the purse of Barras and of other intimate friends. It was through Madame Tallien that she became acquainted with Barras, and it was Barras himself who presented Napoleon Bonaparte to her: it was also with Barras that originated the idea of an alliance between the two. Such is the intimate connection of Madame Tallien with the fall of Robespierre and the elevation of Napoleon.

The alienation of Tallien and his wife ended in a virtual separation. Her scandalous conduct left him no peace at home, and the bitter reproaches of the journals and the tribune rendered his public life intolerable. He joined Bonaparte's expedition to Egypt, and sailed in May, 1798. He occupied a subordinate position in the department of Political Economy, together with Bourrienne and Regnault de St. Jean d'Angely. Josephine and Madame Tallien continued their intimacy, which gave uneasiness to Bonaparte, who one evening said to Lefebvre at Cairo, "Lefebvre, what is Madame Bonaparte doing at this moment in Paris?" "General, she is weeping." "You are an idiot, Lefebvre; she rides every day to the Bois de Boulogne, upon a white horse, in bad company." The official journal spoke of Madame Tallien at about this period: at a race at la Révolte, a person was knocked over and severely injured by Othello, the winning horse; Madame

Visconti, the Cisalpine ambassadress, sent the unfortunate man to the hospital in her carriage, and Madame Tallien took up a collection in his behalf. An appeal urged by so fair a petitioner was not likely to pass unheeded, and a very considerable sum was realized.[1]

On Bonaparte's return from Egypt—a slight anticipation is unavoidable here—Madame Tallien applied herself to dissipate his suspicions of the infidelity of his wife ; and his reconciliation with Josephine was, in some measure, due to the warmth and the address of her representations. After the revolution which made Bonaparte First Consul, he ordered her exclusion from the Tuileries. Not being warned of this, she visited the palace, and was subjected to the mortification of a repulse. The newspapers not venturing to narrate the anecdote in its original form, disguised it under the dress of a reminiscence of Rome, as follows : "The lovely Sempronia, wife of one of the lieutenants that the great Cæsar left behind him in Egypt to reap the fruit of his victories, desired to present herself before the hero of the Nile. The amiable Sempronia possessed infinite grace and countless attractions. With so many resources with which to please, how was it possible for her to remain constant to a husband now eighteen months absent? Evidence not to be refuted attested the weakness of Sempronia. She nevertheless supposed she might appear before her husband's friend. Cæsar not only refused to see her, but directed his wife to deny her admittance. It is well known that this great man maintained as a principle that the wife of Cæsar should not even be suspected."[2]

Madame Tallien was hurt and annoyed at this repulse, and after numerous unsuccessful attempts, obtained from Bonaparte a rendezvous at a masked ball. Each was to recognize the other by the green ribbon with which both dominos were to be trimmed. The two dominos met : the one uttered complaints and the other offered excuses : the one denounced a system of exclusion which

---

[1] Moniteur, An VI. 240.   [2] Salgues' Memo'rs, iii. 254.

the other hastened to palliate : the one demanded admission to the Tuileries, which the other deliberately refused. Madame Tallien soon justified this harshness by the scandal of a second divorce. There is little doubt that she saw Josephine secretly at Malmaison, and that Napoleon was aware of it : he did not object, however, the publicity of their intercourse being the only feature that displeased him.

Tallien returned from Egypt in 1801, after an absence of three years. Before his departure, his wife had given birth to a daughter, who received the name of Thérésia Rose Thermidor ; she was educated at the expense of Josephine, and subsequently married the Comte de Narbonne Pelet. During his absence, she had three children, all of whom were entered upon the civil register under the maiden name of their mother, Cabarrus. Tallien obtained a divorce on the 8th of April, 1802. These three children, two of whom were daughters, applied to the government, in 1835, for the rectification of the registry of their birth. The tribunal decided that as Tallien, now dead, had not formally disavowed them, and as it had been officially stated in the Moniteur that he had made several voyages to France from Egypt, a fact which rendered the legitimacy of their birth possible in the eyes of the law, such a rectification was necessary and proper. The names of the three applicants were therefore changed upon the register from Cabarrus to Tallien.[1]

The disorders of Madame Tallien's life now drew upon her public disapprobation. The populace in the streets took offence at the transparency of her costume, and on one occasion compelled her by insulting language and menace even of brutality, to escape from the promenade in the carriage of a deputy which fortunately was at hand. A portrait of her was exhibited at the Louvre, in which she was represented in the prison of the Duchess of Lamballe, holding in her hand the shorn hair of the unfortunate victim.[2] This was in allusion to a current witticism, to the effect that instead of receiving the appellation of "Notre-Dame-de bon Secours," in acknowledgment of her humanity at Bordeaux, she rather deserved that of "Notre-Dame-de-Septembre." This, which was due to the royalists, was manifestly unjust and cruel: for the September massacres in the prisons, of which Tallien was in part the author, occurred long before his acquaintance with Madame de Fontenay, and the jest which made her responsible for them was as misplaced as it was harsh.

Madame Tallien soon contracted a third alliance. Though her two previous husbands were still living, she married the Comte Joseph de Caraman, and by the death of one of the relatives of her husband, became soon afterwards La Princesse de Chimay. She gave birth to three sons, during her long and undisturbed union of thirty years. She resided successively at Rome, Florence, Naples and Brussels, being received at court in the three former cities. She died in 1835, preserving her remarkable beauty to the last. The irregularities of her life, which occurred at a period when society seemed to offer no inducements to virtue and no recompense for rectitude, have been condescendingly pardoned by her country, in view of her unrivalled beauty and her beneficent triumphs. She has left an indelible popularity, and occupies a warm corner in the heart of the nation. She is known neither as the Marquise de Fontenay, nor the Comtesse de Caraman, nor the Princesse de Chimay; her national and historical name is Madame Tallien; one which, as she bore it before she possessed it, she continued to wear after she lost it. Tallien himself, when he heard of her third marriage, said, "It is all in vain: her name is Madame Tallien: the country will remember her under that title, long after it has forgotten the Princesse de 'Chimère.'"

"She was the ornament," says Thibaudeau, "of every fête, and the soul of every pleasure: she reigned without the embarrassment of a throne: her empire dried many tears, and I never heard that it caused one. I can speak impartially, for I never

saw her except in society, and never once spoke to her. Her husband I did not esteem, for I feared his ambition."[1]

"In her person," says Lamartine, "were united the fire of the south and the languor of the north. She was the living embodiment of the beauty of every climate. She was one of those women whose charms Nature employs, as a Cleopatra or a Theodora, to conquer those who conquer the world, and to subject tyrants to tyranny. The Republic seemed to her the Nemesis of kings and the Providence of nations. She became the divinity of the pardoning power. The love of a woman transformed the Terror. Bordeaux forgot its seven hundred victims, and smiled at Tallien's oriental pro-consulate."[2]

"In this troop of women," says de Goncourt, "thus amiable beyond propriety and influential beyond reason, among these gay and thoughtless usurpers, there were one or two of the family of Cleopatra—enchantresses who charm posterity—who have but to smile at History to obtain History's smile in return. Of these is Madame Tallien.[3]

"What a beautiful ambassadress is she, commissioned to reconcile women with the Revolution, men with Fashion, commerce with the Republic and France with a court! She is a Pompadour after Lycurgus. With magic voice, she recalls mirth and festivity from exile: she stretches carpets over the stains of blood, and pours out bumpers of Lethe and Nepenthe to a country only too glad to forget and too happy to renounce. She reconstructs about her a Versailles of splendor, luxury and debauch: she preaches extravagance, love, music and dancing; she awakens to life a society but now given over to death. Aiming at every agreeable protectorate, and claiming patronage of all that is elegant and attractive, she summons Art home from emigration, and honors the Picture Gallery with her last new head-dress. She takes the theatres under her tutelage. When she appears at the

[1] Mémoires sur la Convention, I. 181. [2] Les Girondins, vii. 380.
[3] The portrait of Madame Tallien, on the opposite page, is from an original belonging to the Historical Gallery at Versailles. The name of the artist is not known.

promenade in her blood-colored coach, clothed in a white cloud of muslin, Paris bends before her as to the soul and fortune and genius of the Directory.

"Madame Tallien is the fairy of the Luxembourg. She organizes its galas and parties of pleasure, and illumines them with her presence and her smile. She claims the pianos of the civil list, whose melodies had been suffered to slumber, and gives them to hands worthy of re-awakening them. She fills the palace of the Directory with the choice music of Marie Antoinette: and she saves from ruin the declining art of Sèvres, by an uncontrollable caprice for porcelain."[1]

What a flood of light do these passages throw, not only upon the age to which they refer, but upon the genius of the French people! How impossible, out of France, would be such a character and such commentators!

[1] Soc. Franç. 300.

CHAPTER VII.

France prepared for a social Change—Bonaparte lands at Fréjus—Is hailed as a Deliverer from Anarchy—A Deputy dies of sudden Joy—Bonaparte arrives at Paris—The Purpose of this Volume.

EVENTS, as we have shown, were ripe for a change, in 1799. France awaited, almost with impatience, the accident or the man which should be the instrument of her deliverance. The indications of the existence of a deep desire for relief, in the hearts of the people, were visible and legible to those who could read the signs of the times. The Terror had become infamous in conversation and in print; the Convention was remembered only with contempt, and mentioned only with ridicule. The caricatures, pasquinades and libels of the day were deadly satires upon the manners, the pretenses and the failures of the Republic. The tricolored cockade was no longer a fit ornament for the person of a woman; engravings represented it as the appropriate badge of the Furies of the Guillotine. So oppressive was the memory of the Republic, that the virtues it had affected, patriotism, sobriety, self-sacrifice, were now offensive and odious. Ostentation of simplicity and of devotion to the commonwealth, had disgusted society even with honest conviction and with sincere practice. The very frivolity of the manners and dress of the incroyables and merveilleuses argued a monarchical tendency, or was a monarchical reminiscence: for the excess of their absurdity showed the depth of the reaction. The Revolution, which commenced in violence, lay now exhausted in folly; the people that had shed blood in torrents now could not pronounce their R's; the nation was sated with license and debauch, fatigued with anarchy and riot, decrepit from early vice and undue and precocious gratification. Emancipation from the proper prescriptions of nature and the regulating instincts of conscience; emancipation from the law, from the traditional requirements of society, from the obedience due to religion and the deference due to good taste—in one word, emancipation from all humanizing influences and all controlling restraints, had been the one marked feature of the period—a period of perversity and disruption—without parallel in the history of Europe.

Napoleon Bonaparte was at this epoch in Egypt, where he had apostrophized the pyramids and exterminated the Mamelukes. Of the true situation of his army but little was known, and Paris was agitated by contradictory reports, which alternately made him victorious before Constantinople or humiliated at St. Jean d'Acre; he was now the victim of a revolt, and anon the terror of the Sultan. Suddenly the telegraph conveyed to the wonder-stricken city the tidings of his disembarkment at Fréjus. The general had suddenly quitted the army of Egypt, where disaster was accumulating against him, and, favored by auspicious winds and served by a concurrence of circumstances, baffling and outsailing the English squadron, he touched the French coast on the 9th of October, 1799. The harbor of Fréjus was speedily covered with boats filled with men and women, anxious to see the hero whose name had become immortal, and for whose rumored death the British government had but lately ordered a salute of twenty guns. The sanitary regulations of the port were violated, for Bonaparte was in no humor to serve a tedious quarantine: at noon he set foot upon the soil of his adopted country. He set out at once for Paris; his journey was an ovation, varied by occasional incidents of attack and delay, but which seemed attributable rather to highwaymen than to political opponents. The enthusiasm of the people of Lyons, who had suffered severely from anarchy, knew no bounds: a poetaster of the city composed an impromptu entitled "Le Retour du Héros," the performance of which the impatient conqueror was compelled to stay to witness. The cities on the route were illuminated and dressed in flags: honors due only to sovereigns were spontaneously bestowed upon him, from Fréjus to Paris. His name was the watchword of those who hoped for a return of tranquillity—even though it were the tranquillity of despotism: the rallying cry of all who despaired of any liberation from the reign of confusion, but such as a soldier could effect—of any escape from the Scylla of civil convulsion, but into the Charybdis of a military dictatorship. On the 13th of the month, the news of his arrival and of his march towards the capital, reached Paris. It was announced to the audiences gathered at the various theatres, and produced a whirlwind of excitement and long continued vivats. A member of the Council of Five Hundred, Baudin des Ardennes, died of joy on hearing the intelligence. Joseph and Lucien Bonaparte, together with Josephine, at once set out for Lyons, where they hoped to meet the returning hero; but a change of route, on his part, resulted in their missing each other, and in his finding his house at Paris deserted and forlorn.

Bonaparte entered Paris on the 16th. Those who had seen him upon his departure, recognized him with difficulty upon his return. On leaving France, he wore his hair long and powdered: his cheeks were hollow; his complexion was pale and sickly. He came back with short hair, with full cheeks and a skin bronzed by an African sun. A detachment of Mamelukes which attended him, added to the excitement of the occasion and the novelty of the spectacle. He adroitly augmented the curiosity and interest of which he was the object, by affecting a desire for retirement and solitude. He went out but little, and declined receiving the members of the two councils. He withdrew from the Opéra Comique, when embarrassed by the persistent shouts of "Vive

Bonaparte!" He remained in seclusion, studying the state of parties, calculating the chances of revolution, planning usurpation and plotting his coup d'état. He was already preparing the 18TH BRUMAIRE—one short month distant—which should place the destinies of the country in his hands, and present him as the emulator of Cæsar and the successor of Charlemagne.

The revolution of this date, the 9th of November, the only French revolution which cost no lives and which shed no blood, is nevertheless the most important in the modern history of France. It is the design of these pages to show its effect upon society, morals and manners; to note the influence of Napoleon upon the literature, science and art of his time; to chronicle the processes by which he sought to revive religion, to restore the sway of public opinion, to resuscitate the amenities of life, to redeem the country from excess and premature decay, and to lift from the heart of the nation its weight of lassitude and disgust. It will be their purpose to reflect the lights and shadows of this interesting period: making, as far as possible, the actors of the drama pass before the eye of the reader, and thus show alike the successes and the failures, of the master spirit of the age.

Although it is our design to write in the spirit of history, which disdains aught but truth, and of philosophy, which aims chiefly at instruction, still the plan of the work permits us to depart from the formality of a strict arrangement according to dates, on the one hand, and invites, on the other, the admission of incident and anecdote, of personal portraits and sketches, and of the lesser and lighter chronicles of the time, never without their significance in interpreting the heart of society. The collection of these, from a variety of sources, has been deemed a labor essential not only to impart interest and vitality to the narrative, but to render the presentation of the subject sincere, complete and impartial.

CHAPTER VIII.

The Revival of Manners—Bonaparte urges his Officers to Marry—An Invasion of new Faces—The first Ladies of Honor—The Households of Josephine, of Bonaparte, his Mother and Sisters—The First Reception at the Tuileries—The consular Court established—The Fashions of the Period.

WITH the dispersion of the Council of Five Hundred, the fall of the Directory, and the establishment of the Consulate, a brighter day dawned upon French society. With the return of the emigrants and the resuscitation of the Faubourg St. Germain, came the revival of manners and the renewal of intercourse. Bonaparte felt the necessity of reorganizing the fabric of life, and aimed at re-establishing a "social" system by first encouraging a "sociable" system. His efforts tended with constancy and zeal in this direction, and his plan of effecting a fusion between the two camps—between his own, which was to furnish the action, the control and the influence, and that of the Legitimists, which should contribute the tone, the mould and the form—soon promised to be an efficient and a successful one.

Bonaparte had himself had little or no acquaintance with the elegant society of Paris. He had somewhat frequented it, it is true, during his vacations at Brienne, but he was too young then to form permanent associations or to obtain lasting impressions. During the Terror there had been no society, and under the Directory there had been no law and no opinion. Josephine was not noble—for colonial nobility was unrecognized—and her position, before her marriage with Bonaparte, was not such as to give her influence with the royalists after it. Bonaparte, in wedding her, supposed himself to be contracting an alliance with a family equal to that of the Montmorencies; and afterwards, at St. Helena, confessed to a certain degree of disappointment.[1] Nevertheless, legitimacy hardly waited for the installation of the First Consul at the Tuileries to besiege its doors and throng its ante-rooms. Better to judge of, and the nearer to contemplate, the applicants for place and favor, Bonaparte ordered a series of dinners for 300 guests in the gallery of Diana. These took place regularly on Quintidis —the fifth day of the republican decade; invitations were distributed, with little discrimination, among all who had held a position or exercised an influence. There was no etiquette, and as little satisfaction; for in such a motley group, and at such an epoch of transition, there would naturally be no harmony, and as little unity. Bonaparte, however, was observing, reflecting, and deciding: he was choosing the courtiers of his court; and, in this view, scanned faces, asked names, took notes upon station, and made studies of capacity. The wits of the time styled these dinners "reviews."

Bonaparte now urged his officers to marriage, and evinced marked eagerness for the revival of the courtesies and amenities of a well-organized society. "Marry, and open a parlor," he said to his generals; "receive company, and make your house attractive." He could not fail to appreciate the influence of woman in her domestic relations, though he was never forward to acknowledge it; but he plainly acted upon the belief, that to revive social order and to compose the agitations that still rendered home unalluring and the family tie uncertain, the only plan was to invite the aid of wives, mothers, daughters and sisters, in the work of restoration.

The eager obedience of Napoleon's general officers soon extended the circle of Josephine's incipient court. It commenced on the 30th Pluviose, 1800, with the following ladies,[2] as yet hold-

[1] d'Abr. Hist. des Salons de Paris, v. 7.   [2] Ibid. v. 32.

ing no distinct official position: Madame de Larochefoucauld, "short, witty and hunchbacked;" Madame de Lavalette, "kind, engaging and beautiful, in spite of the faint traces of small-pox;" Madame de Lameth, "rotund and bearded, but good and intelligent in compensation;" Madame de Laplace, "who had learned to make even her courtesy geometrically, to please her mathematical husband;" Madame de Lauriston, winning and courteous to all; Madame de Remusat, a lady of superior intellect and high cultivation; Madame de Thalouet, "too mindful of her past beauty, and not sufficiently conscious of her present loss of it;" and Madame d'Harville, "impolite by system, and polite by chance." Then followed an invasion of young and pretty faces, consequent upon the prompt compliance of the staff with the First Consul's desires: Madame Bessières, of lively and elegant manners and equable temper; Madame Mortier, an angel of gentleness and amiability; Madame Junot, whose courtship and wedding we shall have occasion to describe; Madame Savary, a brunette who insisted on wearing the colors suitable to a blonde; and Madame Lannes, a beauty of acknowledged European repute. Somewhat later, came Madame Duroc and Madame Ney, the former as hard and repellant as the latter was winning and prepossessing.

It was not long before the Consulate began to assume the air and etiquette of royalty. Josephine, who had always been familiar and accessible, ceased to visit, on intimate terms, the ladies of her acquaintance, and the wives of the generals. She hardly left the Tuileries, except in state; her friends no longer saw her, unless bidden to an audience, or invited to a levee. Suddenly, Bonaparte appointed to accompany and attend her, four ladies of rank, who formed the original nucleus of what afterwards became the Consular, and, still later, the Imperial Household.

The first of these ladies was Madame de Remusat, a pattern of stately dignity and of kindly influence. She soon acquired a great ascendency over Josephine, whose too cordial and condescending familiarity she stiffened with the starch of reserve and punctilio. Josephine, by nature, would only seek to please, to win, and to make herself beloved: under Madame de Remusat's tuition and example, she learned to inspire respect and to claim the homage due to rank. Madame de Thalouet, Madame de Luçay, haughty and domineering, and Madame Law de Lauriston, gay in the midst of reserve, and at once charming and imposing, were the other three members of the bodyguard. Calumny seems to have spared them, and—a noticeable feature in any court—there was nothing equivocal in their lives, or contagious in their example. Other ladies, in situations less prominent, were successively added to the household, and these were still further classified, and for the most part titled, on the proclamation of the Empire.

At the same time, Bonaparte formed a small household for himself, and upon a similar pattern and scale. M. de Remusat became half Chamberlain and half Master of the Horse; M. de Cramayel introduced the ambassadors, and a rigid system of ceremonial. Of M. de Luçay it was said that he affected to speak low, that his voice might not reverberate through Europe: though he must have been convinced, after the fall of Napoleon, that if Echo sometimes repeats and prolongs the shock of the thunder, it is never Echo which launches it athwart the sky. M. Salmatoris, a Piedmontese, was Prefect of the Palace, and Duroc was governor of the Tuileries.

The aids-de-camp at this period were: Auguste de Caffarelli, whose numerous brothers were so selfish, and worked together so exclusively for their private advancement, that a relative said of them, "Under whatever aspect you regard the ten Caffarellis, I defy you to see more than one;" Law de Lauriston, grand nephew of Law the financier, and one of the first gallants of his time; Lemarrois, loyal, brave and devoted; Generals Rapp and Savary, the former of whom said of the latter: "When I speak to Bonaparte, I speak loud: Savary talks to him as if he had lost his voice. I speak to him to his face: Savary talks in his ear.

Every one knows what I say, but who the devil can tell what Savary says when he whispers?" Estève, who had been a hatter's apprentice at Montpellier, was the treasurer-general, and afterwards intendant of the crown. He died of disappointment and chagrin at not being made Duke of Montpellier, under the empire.

Madame Lætitia, Bonaparte's mother, laid the foundation of an establishment, at this same period, by appointing to her own person an inseparable attendant, Madame de Fontanges: Madame Murat—Caroline Bonaparte—was never seen in public unescorted by Madame Lagrange, and Pauline, at this time Madame Widow Leclerc, rarely ventured into society without her constant chaperone, Madame de Champagny.

The various households being thus installed and organized, it became necessary to open the season and inaugurate the court by an official reception at the Tuileries. The invitations were verbal, and were delivered by the aids-de-camp and orderly officers. Paris was in a ferment of delight at this imminent restoration of the elegant distractions and amenities of peace—the resurrection of commerce, good manners, and manufactures. A government ball at Paris directly or indirectly benefits the whole population—one eminently dependent upon the maintenance of luxury: especially in this case was the promised festivity grateful to the citizens, after so many years passed in anarchy and stagnation.

The palace was profusely decorated and illuminated. Superb battle pieces, recalling the fields of the Republic and the early Consulate; standards from Holland, Prussia, Austria: trophies from Egypt, statues, groups and vases from Italy; flowers from the green-houses, orange trees in full blossom from the conservatories, adorned the novel scene. The diplomatic corps was complete, even to the legation of Lord Whitworth, the English ambassador. Old and revived courtiers of a banished and well-nigh forgotten dynasty displayed their recovered graces and their Bourbon urbanity, by the side of the parvenu retinue and its parvenu master. The costumes were of all ages—a very prism of anachronisms—for as yet Bonaparte had not applied his genius to the shaping of garments, the selection of colors, and the regulation of the fashions.

The company did not wait long for the hostess and heroine. A door was thrown open, and an usher, dressed in black velvet, and preceded by six lackeys in green and gold, advanced two steps into the room, saying in measured and sonorous accents, "MADAME! Femme du Premier Consul." The form of this announcement, which was unusual, took every one by surprise, for the word Madame is, in this sense, at once royal and legitimist. The audience rose, and formed itself into lines and passage ways. Josephine entered, giving her hand to Talleyrand, Minister of Foreign Affairs. She was dressed with elegance and simplicity. Her robe was of white muslin, trimmed with festoons of lace : a girdle of massive gold encircled her waist, attached in front by a pearl clasp. Her bracelets, ear-rings and necklace were of pearls, and completed her attire, with the exception of a flame-colored Cashmere shawl, negligently thrown over her left shoulder.

Talleyrand was dressed, not as an ecclesiastic, but as a cabinet minister. His coat was of black velvet, highly embroidered at the collar, wrists and pockets : and he wore that very unchurchly accoutrement—a sword. Behind Josephine was Madame Lætitia, in a white velvet bonnet trimmed with nacarat feathers, a robe of cherry-colored satin, bordered by deep black blonde. Her ornaments were antique cameos and engraved shells. M'lle Hortense Beauharnais was dressed in pink, with a wreath of roses upon her brow, and emeralds upon her neck and arms.

Madame Bacciochi, the elder of Bonaparte's sisters, appeared in yellow satin flounced with yellow crape, and trimmed with red zephyrs : her person was loaded with a magnificent and profuse display of corals. Madame Murat, whose wonderfully pure complexion was always an object of remark and admiration wherever she appeared, and whose dress of black velvet showed it to great advantage, was the acknowledged belle of the occasion ; for Pauline, the unrivalled beauty, was not present. The hem of her skirt was trimmed with vine leaves and clusters of pearl grapes. Her ear-rings also represented grapes, and were formed of groups of rubies. The consular family were followed by four ladies of honor, the rear being brought up by citizen Bacciochi, in military uniform, and M. Fesch, the half-brother of Madame Lætitia, in his ecclesiastic cassock, girdle and calotte.

Josephine, gallantly led by Talleyrand, made her way through the throng to the seats prepared for her and Bonaparte. Two arm-chairs, entirely new, made of wood heavily gilt, trimmed with green velvet spangled with golden stars, and surmounted by eagles in the place of the Gallic cock, had been placed in front of the fire-place. She was hardly seated before the drums of the consular guard beat to arms, the door of the interior apartments was opened, and twelve green and gold valets and five ushers in black, marched into the room. One of the latter, taking up the announcement which was already heard in the distance, said, "Le Premier Consul, Messieurs!" Duroc, the governor of the Tuileries, with the newly appointed officers of the palace, entered first: then came Bonaparte, then Cambacérès and Lebrun, the second and third consuls, and finally the aids-de-camp, the ministers and a number of orderly officers.

The two subordinate consuls had donned their official apparel, and shone forth in all the effulgence of white and flame-colored satin, thickly embroidered, and of hats à la Henri IV., dancing with white plumes. Bonaparte, who had ordered this luxury of costume in order to strike by contrast, wore a simple military frock, with a white waistcoat, and white cassimere pantaloons. Top boots, conspicuously spurred, a battle hat under his arm, the consular scarf and a sword, completed his attire. A profound silence greeted his approach ; he did not wait for the usual presentation of the diplomatic corps, but commenced at once his round of salutations and his running fire of inquiries.

At this initial festivity of the new régime, Bonaparte at first so markedly avoided, and afterwards so menacingly interrogated, Lord Whitworth, the English ambassador, that the company construed his attitude and his speech into a semi-declaration of war. Meeting one of the late commissaries of the army of Italy, whose depredations had been notorious, and whose ill-gotten wealth was impudently displayed in the diamonds upon his fingers and in the jewels of his hat, Bonaparte said aloud : " Citizen, if a just fairy were to touch you with her wand, in the place of these precious stones, we should see bread, wine and medicine, stolen from my soldiers. Your splendor is odious, and should bring you before the auditor of accounts. Until then, leave my presence : go and make merry elsewhere with the spoils of the army." The commissary cowered and slunk away from the palace, overwhelmed with confusion and shame.

The evening advanced ; there was little music, as little conversation, and no dancing. The occasion was rather political than social, and the evident imminence of trouble with England was a new element of anxiety. The ambassadors were pre-occupied, and the guests generally uneasy, while the ladies were visibly neglected. But the fête, which set the example for others, had fulfilled one of the objects for which it was ordered : it had drawn many hundreds of thousands of francs into the gaping tills of the distressed, but now chuckling shop-keepers.

As time wore on, and as it became apparent that the nation would not resist the re-establishment of a court, Bonaparte gave for a time his almost undivided attention to the subject. Old codes of etiquette, that could furnish precedents ; old courtiers, who could recall forgotten fashions ; old lackeys, who could instruct and drill the young, were consulted and pressed into the consular service. Many of the incongruities of the first period of the revival now rapidly disappeared, and the circle that gathered about the chief of the state and his wife, might already be compared, in point of brilliancy and elegance, to that of the brightest periods of the monarchy. The number of those who rebelled against the regal and imperial tendencies of Bonaparte, and who grieved at the account made of matters so frivolous as fashion, costume, and livery, constantly and steadily diminished.

Under the Consulate, a marked improvement in the fashions took place both in fabric and form. The following was one of the costumes worn by ladies at dinners and similar festivities. Upon the head was a toque, or skull-cap, of black velvet, with two white feathers. The bodice was detached from the skirt, and made in the form of a spencer; it bore the name of "canezou," and was usually richly embroidered and trimmed with Malines or Valenciennes lace. The skirt, of fine India muslin, and long enough behind to form a demi-train, was embroidered along the hem with garlands representing oak-leaves, ivy, or jessamine. Mademoiselle l'Olive was the embroideress of this epoch. A veil of English point lace was often attached to the toque, and allowed to fall in a single fold at the side; a Cashmere shawl of some deep color, and usually red, was thrown over the shoulders. Around the neck was a long Mexican chain, to which was attached a watch from the counter of Leroy. The cost of an equipment of this description was not far from 7,000 francs, and might be thus divided: the shawl, 2,000 francs; the bodice, or canezou, 500 francs; the skirt, 1,200 francs; the veil, 1,000 francs; the watch, 2,000 francs; and the toque, 200 francs.

Bonaparte, who in 1800 had declined "accepting from the nation the Château of St. Cloud during the period of his magistracy, or for a year after its close," took possession of it in 1802, of his own authority, and without further invitation. Mass was said in the palace every Sunday, and audience was given to an indiscriminate attendance immediately afterwards. Josephine received in the afternoon, though some selection was exercised in admissions and exclusions. On Sundays, Wednesdays and Fridays, Napoleon gave dinners to twelve or fifteen guests. By degrees access to his presence became more difficult, and the approach to his person was purposely surrounded with discouraging formalities. Power imposed its charlatanry upon him, and everything about him became a copy of Versailles.[1] He became very strict in the choice of society for Josephine; he would never admit to the court either Madame Gaudin, wife of the Minister of Finance, nor, as has been narrated, Madame Tallien, the beauty of the Directory. The morals of society were improving, though perhaps the improvement was yet but superficial, and consisted rather in a greater respect for public opinion and regard for appearance, than in a radical change of life and conduct. The political prospects of the country were brightening; confidence succeeded to distrust, activity to stagnation, responsibility to corruption. There are few examples on record of a more speedy resurrection of society; and if this instance shows the capacity of the country for regeneration, it also shows how deeply France had taken the lesson taught by calamity, to heart, and how ardently it yearned to recover the social blessings it had lost.

It was at this period that Bonaparte took a step which exerted an important influence upon the manners and morals of the city and the court; he revived the legal connection between Church and State. This measure calls for detailed description, as its bearing upon the condition of society for many subsequent years was close and intimate.

[1] Thib. Hist. de la France, iii. 372.

CHAPTER IX.

Religion during the Revolution—Napoleon a Mahometan in Egypt, a Catholic in France—The Concordat and the Te Deum—Eighty Ladies present at the Ceremony—A disrespectful Audience—Epigrams—The Curate of St. Roch and the Danseuse—The Clergy are refractory—Mass at St. Cloud—The Restoration of the Saints to the Calendar.

THAT the Revolution uprooted the institution of religion, and that the Constituent Assembly abolished the clergy, is not surprising. The priests were possessors of a large part of the soil of France, and yet paid no taxes; they contributed to the support of the state as much or as little as they pleased; their tithes were purely voluntary. They constituted a political body, and were one of the three orders represented at the States-General in 1789. The Constituent Assembly, undoubtedly wise in deciding that the clergy should renounce their landed estates, and should abandon political authority, erred in suppressing the canonical installation of bishops—their confirmation by the Pope—and in exacting of his Holiness the papal approbation and ratification of these changes. It erred still more grievously in demanding of the clergy an oath of fidelity to the civil constitution. This oath was forbidden by the Pope, and an immediate schism was the consequence in France. The priests who took the oath formed the recognized or constitutional clergy; those who refused it suffered interdict, but nevertheless clandestinely administered the sacrament to immense numbers of the faithful. The civil war of La Vendée followed; and then came the persecution, transportation, and during the Terror, the execution upon the scaffold, of the insubordinate clergy; and, finally, the deistical Proclamation of the Supreme Being and the Worship of Reason. This rendered the rupture between the Republic and the Vatican complete; and such was the state of things in religious affairs upon the usurpation of power by Bonaparte.[1]

Napoleon has left ample records of his own opinions upon the subject of a state religion: "Man," he said, many years subsequent to this period, "man, once launched into life, asks himself the question, Whence do I come? What am I? Whither am I going? These are all mysterious questions which precipitate him toward religion. We hasten to meet it, a natural inclination leads us toward it; but education arrests us: education and history are the two great enemies of true religion, thus disfigured by the imperfections of men. Why is the religion of Paris different from that of London or of Berlin? Why is the religion of St. Petersburg distinct from that of Constantinople? Why is the latter different from that of China, Persia or of the Ganges? Why is the religion of antiquity different from that of to-day? Reason, staggered by these questions, returns back upon itself, exclaiming that religions are the children of men. We believe willingly in God, because everything around us proclaims him, and because the greatest minds have acknowledged him—not only Bossuet, whose business it was to preach him, but Newton and Leibnitz, whose investigations led them elsewhere. But we know not what to think of the doctrines we are taught, and we still find ourselves to be watches which tick, though we cannot discover the watchmaker."[2]

That he believed religion to be necessary to society, we know. "In the midst of contradictions," he said, "man feels an imperious and irresistible impulse to form for himself a definite belief; and he does form one, either true or false, ridiculous or sublime. Everywhere, in every age and in every country, in antiquity and in modern times, in civilization and in barbarism, we find him at

---

[1] Thiers: Cons. et Emp. III. 108.   [2] Las Cases: iv. 350.

the foot of altars, either holy and venerable, or ignoble and sanguinary." He felt that as religion was necessary to man, so a national religion was essential to a state. Disinclined to invent or create a religion, he preferred to revive one that had long existed, and that a passing agitation had swept away in its tumultuous and destructive course.

France had been ten years without a national system of religion, and without established forms of worship. The churches had been at first transformed into profane Temples of Reason or of Mars. They had since been the resort of the Theophilanthropists, a sect which advocated a cold and material practice of virtue. The age was eminently skeptical; the men whose talents made them prominent, and whose acquirements gave them influence, were either carelessly indifferent or actively anti-religious. To revive Catholicism in France, therefore, to restore the spiritual authority of the pope, was a delicate and arduous task, and yet the advantages which would accrue to Bonaparte's government from a successful endeavor to reconstitute the church, were so considerable that the First Consul resolved to enter into negotiations with his Holiness. A correspondence was at once opened with Pope Pius VII.

The objects Bonaparte had in view were principally political. It is unnecessary to suppose him actuated by any of the somewhat sentimental motives that his more ardent biographers ascribe to him. It is trivial to consider him as influenced by "reminiscences of his primary education," by "memories of the pomp of Catholicism in his infancy," or "by impressions derived from his enthusiastic and melancholy temperament."[1] It is enough to believe that he understood and appreciated the force of a faith and a creed in giving a nation unity and homogeneity: that he calculated upon the dominion to be acquired by reëstablishing and controlling the hierarchy of the church; and that the pontifical organization and the discipline of the clergy which he had in

[1] St. Hilaire: Nap. au Conseil d'Etat, i. 100.

view, by making him the head of the ecclesiastical police, would give him new authority and a fresh prestige. During the progress of the negotiations with Rome, he said to Bourrienne, his secretary, "In every country, religion may be of aid to the government. It is well to use it as a means of exerting influence upon men. I was a Mahometan in Egypt, I am a Catholic in France. It is essential that as far as its police is concerned, the religion of a state be in the hands of him who governs the state."

The Pope at once sent to Paris three plenipotentiaries: Spina, the prelate, Cardinal Gonsalvi and Father Caselli. Bonaparte appointed as his representatives, the Abbé Bernier, Cretet, a Councillor of State, and his brother Joseph. These bent to the task with zeal and energy, and Napoleon, stubbornly resisting the opposition and the hesitations of his counsellors, drew up, himself, the bases of the instrument which he afterwards regarded as forming one of the most politic and astute acts of his reign.

In the face of difficulties of every kind, and opposition both open and disguised, the treaty was promulgated on Easter Sunday, the 18th of April, 1802. Its principal features were: the recognition by the French government that the Catholic, Apostolic and Roman religion was the religion of a majority of the nation, and should be freely exercised, subject only to necessary police regulations; the division of the territory of France into ten archbishoprics and fifty bishoprics; the declaration that all the episcopal and archiepiscopal dioceses existing before the Revolution were suppressed and extinguished; the assumption by the First Consul of the right to appoint the bishops and archbishops, the Pope to confer upon them the canonical installation; and the agreement by the government, that the state should secure a proper salary to the officers of the church.

The ceremony of the proclamation took place at Notre Dame, and was the first public religious act of the government since the Fête of the Federation, in 1789. A Te Deum of thanksgiving for the restoration of worship, and a mass in music, reconciling the Republic with the Church, were the prominent features of the occasion. Incense smoked upon the altars, and flowers were hung in profusion from the arches. The three Consuls were present, Bonaparte causing his servants to appear for the first time in the colors which afterwards became imperial—green and gold. The clergy sang in chorus, to an accompaniment of one hundred and one guns, the form of prayer fixed in the Concordat for the government and its officers: Domine, salvam fac rempublicam; domine, salvos fac consules. "The imposing pomp of this ceremony," says the biographer of the pope, "the joy of Christians at seeing the regeneration of the religion of Jesus Christ; the presence of the three Consuls and of all the authorities; the acclamations of the delighted public, and even the splendor of the procession and the military accessories—everything, in short, gave to this religious solemnity an interest and brilliancy which rejoiced all hearts and encouraged the most inspiring hopes."[1]

From sixty to eighty ladies were invited to accompany Madame Bonaparte to Notre Dame. "The spectacle," says Madame Junot, "was an enchanting one, seeming a magnificent conservatory filled with the choicest flowers. More than two-thirds of the ladies by whom Josephine was surrounded, were not twenty years of age: many were under sixteen, and the majority were pretty. Madame Murat's fair, fresh and spring-like face, comparable only to a May rose, was crowned by a pink satin hat and feathers. She wore a dress of fine India tambour muslin, lined with pink satin and trimmed with Brussels lace; over her shoulders was thrown a scarf of the same fabric. I have seen her more richly dressed, but never more beautiful. How many young women, hitherto unknown, on this day took their degree in the realm of beauty, beneath the brilliant beams of a mid-day sun, rendered more glowing in their passage before the stained windows of the basilic!"[2]

[1] Vie de Pie VII. 39.   [2] d'Abr. i. 561.

To augment the effect of this ceremony, Napoleon had ordered the re-publication in the Moniteur of the morning, of a review originally inserted in the Mercure, by Fontanes, of Chateaubriand's "Génie du Christianisme:" a work then exciting the utmost interest, and describing with rare eloquence the beauties of Christianity and the moral and poetic aspect of the practices of religion.

The body of the cathedral, however, did not present the spectacle of an attentive and respectful auditory. The public did not seem to be prepared for so abrupt a transition from the habits of the past twelve years. The attitudes and gestures of a large portion of the witnesses of the scene, indicated disaffection rather than assent. Murmurs, whisperings, and even audible conversations frequently interrupted and arrested the service. General Augereau had refused to attend the ceremony, till authoritatively bidden by Bonaparte to accompany him, and then talked so loud as to disturb the officiators at the altar. Rapp declined being present, and announced flatly that he should always abstain from attending mass. Delmas, in quitting the cathedral, irritated the First Consul by remarking that he thought the ceremony a "very queer sort of harlequinade." The soldiers in the barracks secretly circulated a caricature representing Bonaparte drowning in an immense font of holy water, and a crowd of bishops pushing him to the bottom with their crosiers. Moreau refused to attend the Te Deum, or the banquet given in its honor at the Tuileries. He turned the ceremony into ridicule, some time afterwards, in presence of the Minister of War. Madame de Staël shut herself up at home in order not to witness the odious procession. She had used all her influence against the revival of religion, and succeeded in uniting against it the aristocrats and the republicans. "There is not a moment to lose," she said, "to-morrow the tyrant will have 40,000 priests at his service and in his pay."[1]

"How it happened, I cannot tell," says Bourrienne, speaking

[1] Las Cases, v. 814.

of the Te Deum, "but by some fatality, many of the audience were attacked with violent hunger : people were continually observed to turn aside their heads in order to bite through cakes of chocolate : and I affirm that I saw others eating bread without the slightest embarrassment and without heeding the ceremony in the least. The consular court was in general irreligious, and indeed it could hardly be otherwise, composed as it was of those who had most contributed to the destruction of public worship in France, and of men who, having passed their lives in the camp, had been oftener to church in Italy to remove pictures than to hear mass. Those who, without being imbued with religious ideas, had received that education and were endowed with that sense which leads one to respect in others the faith he does not share, did not blame Napoleon, and behaved with decency and reverence."[1]

A shower of epigrams attended the promulgation of the Concordat. The following quatrain went from one end of France to the other :

> "Politique plus grand que Général habile,
> Bien plus ambitieux que Louis dit le Grand,
> Pour être roi d'Egypte, il croit à l'Alcoran,
> Pour être roi de France, il croit à l'Evangile."

The new order of things was from time to time disturbed by conflicts between the civil and ecclesiastical authorities. A most serious breach of good faith, on the part of the curate of a Paris church, led to the institution of rigorous measures by Bonaparte for the suppression of intolerance and fanaticism. M'lle Chameroy, a danseuse at the Opera, and openly leading a scandalous life, died, and her remains were followed to the cemetery by nearly all the actors and actresses in the city. The hearse stopped at St. Roch for the usual prayers over the dead. The curate refused to admit the corpse, and declined administering the customary rites of religion. The people clamored in the street against so gross an outrage, and were upon the point of forcing the doors, when Dazincourt, a well known comedian, prevailed upon them to remove the body to a neighboring church. Here the funeral service was performed without opposition. Bonaparte was exceedingly annoyed at this example of bigotry, for intolerance he meant should be expunged from the ecclesiastical creed. The next evening he dictated to Lagarde, the secretary to the Council of State, the following reprimand, which was at once sent to the Archbishop of Paris for his signature. It appeared in the Moniteur the next morning:

"The curate of St. Roch, in a temporary absence of reason, has refused to pray for M'lle Chameroy, and to admit her remains within his church. One of his colleagues, a sensible man, and one versed in the true morality of the Gospel, received the body into his sanctuary of the Filles St. Thomas, where the service was performed with the usual solemnities. The Archbishop has ordered the curate of St. Roch three months' suspension, to remind him that Jesus Christ instructs us to pray even for our enemies: and in order that, recalled to a sense of duty by meditation, he may learn that all the superstitious practices preserved in certain rituals, but which, begotten in times of ignorance, or created by the overheated imagination of zealots, degrade religion by their folly, were proscribed by the Concordat and by the law of the 28th of April."

Not long afterwards, one of the dramatic censors, in a report to Chaptal, Minister of the Interior, proposed to prohibit, in future, the performance at the Comédie Française, of Molière's "Tartufe," on the ground that it exposed the hypocrisies of religion, and "might therefore offend the clergy," and because the principal object of the Concordat was "to do away with every pretext for discord between the civil and spiritual authorities." This gentleman was rewarded for his suggestion by an order given by Bonaparte to Chaptal to remove him from office, and the counsel to make him inspector at the markets. "He is too stupid to hold the place he does. Give him a substitute at once, Chaptal."

Discussions between the church and the government were now of constant occurrence. The priests refused burial to persons supposed to have perished by suicide or in duels, and invoked the authority of ancient civil laws as well as of canonical rules. Legislation upon this point was declared by the government to be extinct, and the officers of religion were advised "to accord burial in every case of the kind, as dictated by the spirit of evangelical charity."

The prefects complained that parents took their children to be baptized before registering their birth upon the public records, and desired that registry before baptism might be made compulsory. Portalis, the Director of Public Worship, refused, recommending the contrary rule, on the ground that "baptism was necessary for salvation," and that it consequently could not be too promptly performed. Many priests refused to accept as godfathers and godmothers, individuals whom they pronounced out of the pale of the church, such as actors, and divorced husbands and wives. Portalis counselled them to avoid such invidious distinctions, as likely to create disturbance and to foment passion. The clergy unanimously refused to christen children by names not included in the Gregorian calendar: the First Consul declared them to be right. They refused the sacrament to such as could not show "certificates of confession," and would not bless the second marriage of parties who had been divorced. The government was thus in constant trouble, and was not always fortunate or dexterous in reconciling differences or compelling obedience.

It now appeared that the new ecclesiastical division of France reduced Rheims and Sens from archbishoprics to simple parishes. The motive was not difficult to discover. The cathedral of Rheims had been the scene of the consecration of the kings of France from the time of Hugh Capet: the vaults of Sens contained the remains of the father of the last two monarchs of the line. The

First Consul was not above the spite of seeking to degrade these spots hallowed in legitimacy, by lowering their ecclesiastical rank. The model of a monument exhibited at St. Denis soon distinctly showed the position it was meant the church should hold towards the government. It represented Religion prostrated at the feet of Bonaparte, humbly waiting his pleasure to raise her up. The police were instructed secretly to issue pamphlets against the priesthood, least they should acquire an undue influence over the people. The police engaged men to applaud the irreligious sentiments contained in the vaudeville of the "Visitandines;" and they required the frequent performance of Voltaire's "Œdipe," on account of the famous lines in derision of the clergy:[1]

> "Les prêtres ne sont pas ce qu'un vain peuple pense:
> Notre crédulité fait toute leur science."

Upon the reëstablishment of public worship, Bonaparte was strongly urged to set the example himself of religious observance, by attending mass. He refused for a long time, saying, "I have done enough: you will obtain nothing more from me; you can never make me a hypocrite." He yielded at length, however, and heard divine service, for the first time, at St. Cloud. The ceremony was performed in advance of the hour appointed and announced, that those to whom the measure was unpalatable might arrive too late to witness it.

In the newspapers published on Monday, during this period, the following item was usually to be found: "The First Consul heard mass yesterday in his private apartments." This assertion was founded on the following bit of by-play: adjoining Bonaparte's study, and communicating with it, was a bathing-room, formerly the oratory of Anne of Austria. On Sundays, a portable altar and an encircling platform restored this chamber to its primitive destination. The door was opened into the study, and mass was then performed. Bonaparte rarely suspended his writing

[1] Salgues' Memoirs, iv. 248.

or his dictation during the ceremony, which lasted usually twelve minutes.¹

Religion, in its outward observances, was an official institution : it did not hold, at the outset, nor did it obtain, during the Empire, any controlling influence upon the heart or soul of society. The attendance of the civil functionaries at the services of the church was general and punctilious : but it was in obedience to circulars from the Minister of Public Worship. The case of a prefect may be cited, whose attention to his prayer-book, during his long administration, obtained for him a wide-spread reputation for piety : he confessed, after Waterloo, that his supposed prayer-book was a volume of Lafontaine's Fables.²

Among the benefits conferred upon society by the Concordat, was the restitution to the calendar of the names of numerous saints whom the Terror had excluded from it. During that period of confusion, children had been baptized Tiger, Hemlock, Rabbit, or Wolf, instead of Chrysostom or Francis. Onion and Carrot, Robespierre and Marat, names either ridiculous or infamous, had superseded those of Vincent, Joseph and Matthew. Baron Alphée de Vatry, a gentleman of elegant accomplishments, had borne, during the first years of his infancy, the name of "trognon de chou," or Stump of Cabbage.³ The First Consul abolished this impious innovation, and when, even after the promulgation of the Concordat, Baron Pommereul published an almanac in which he had replaced each saint by a philosopher —substituting Socrates for Luke, Epicurus for Clement and Zeno for Nicholas—Bonaparte forbade its circulation and ordered its suppression.⁴

1 Bour., iv. 252.
2 Mém. d'un Bourgeois, i. 56.
3 Mém. de Madame de Genlis, 118.
4 Salgues' Memoirs, iv. 274.

CHAPTER X.

A Courtship and Marriage under Bonaparte—General Junot and M'lle de Permon—The Offer—Consultation with Bonaparte—A singular Obstacle—The Trousseau and Corbeille—The Bride's Toilet—The Ceremony—Bonaparte wagers with Josephine upon the sex of the First-Born—The Baptism of M'lle Junot.

GENERAL JUNOT, one of Bonaparte's favorite officers, was, in 1800, at the age of twenty-nine, appointed Commander of Paris, with extraordinary prerogatives. The First Consul enjoined it upon him to marry, as a home and an establishment were indispensable to him in the situation he was to occupy. "Besides," said Bonaparte, "I require it of you for your own interest." This allusion referred to Junot's African connections, an Abyssinian slave, named Araxarane, having presented him, while in Egypt, with a boy whom the army, with true military humor, baptised Othello. Junot, therefore, left Méo's inn, where he lodged, took a hotel in the Rue de Verneuil, stocked it with the best of Burgundy wines, and requested his family to seek him a wife: especially a rich one, in accordance with the recommendation of Bonaparte. To this suggestion Junot had replied, "Willingly, if she please my taste; but that is not very likely, as almost all heiresses are superlatively ugly."

The duties of the command of Paris left the General sufficient leisure, it appears, personally to prosecute his researches through the salons of the capital. As it was known that he was a marrying man, and that the instructions of the First Consul required as prompt a compliance as possible, the match-makers and gossips seconded him with praiseworthy zeal. He was advised in numerous quarters to visit Madame de Permon, a lady of the old régime, a former acquaintance of Bonaparte's, but estranged from him of late years in consequence of her rejection of him in marriage. Her daughter Laura, whom the First Consul had often familiarly called M'lle Loulou, was sixteen years old, and was violently opposed to an alliance with a "charming bachelor" of fifty, with whom Madame de Permon was anxious to unite her. Junot at first declined seeking her acquaintance, on the plea that "M'lle Loulou must be a little personage of great pretensions, a spoiled child, and thoroughly insupportable."

However, he finally overcame these unreasonable objections, and visited Madame de Permon one evening in September. A dozen guests, principally returned emigrants, were chatting and playing charades. It was a most awkward moment for a visit from a General of the Republic. The legitimist circle immediately became silent, and the stranger was received by all but the mistress of the house with coldness and distrust. She, however, exerted her tact, and soon established friendly relations between the disaffected parties. The General talked of Egypt, of his battles with the Mamelukes, and of his encounter with Ayoub-Bey. This, we must suppose, was intended for the ear of M'lle Loulou, with whom French etiquette would hardly have permitted a more direct and personal interview. Junot was in this less fortunate than Othello of Venice, who seems to have had unbounded opportunities for communicating martial information, directly, to the gentle Desdemona. It does not appear that Junot interested the daughter on this occasion, but he succeeded in inducing the mother to be present the next day at the translation of the remains of Turenne—a ceremony at which he was to preside, as Commandant of the Army of Paris. As the cortége passed the window at which Madame de Permon was sitting, he bowed to her in so marked a manner, that the crowd immediately noticed it; and one man, forgetting chronology in his anxiety to furnish an explanation, exclaimed: "She must be Turenne's widow!"

For ten days Junot regularly repeated his evening visit, confining his attentions exclusively to the mother, and never once speaking to the daughter. One day at noon, when Miss Laura was taking her drawing lesson, while Madame de Permon was still in bed, and while her son Albert was paying her his morning respects, a carriage was announced, and a servant brought General Junot's request that he might be admitted. Permission was granted, and the General, entering and closing the door, seated himself by the bed-side, and took Madame de Permon's hand. He had come, he said, to ask a favor, and an important one; "I have come to beg the hand of your daughter—will you grant it me? I give you my word for it, and it is that of a man of honor, that I will make her happy. I can offer her an establishment worthy of her and of her family. Come, Madame de Permon, answer me with the frankness with which I prefer my request, Yes or No?"

The mother and brother gave their consent with joy. "But now," said Junot, "I have another favor to ask; one upon which I set a high value, as it is most interesting to me. I desire, extraordinary as it may seem to you, to be myself allowed to present my petition to your daughter." Against such an impropriety —so violent an innovation—Madame de Permon exclaimed and protested, but upon the General's adding that it was in her presence he desired to speak to the young lady, both mother and son relented and consented. M'lle Laura was sent for: she excused herself to M. Viglians, the drawing-master, and descended to the bedroom with the utmost composure, as she supposed General Junot was gone. But she found him seated by her mother's bed-side, holding one of her hands in his. He rose and addressed her as follows:

"Mademoiselle, I am happy enough to have obtained the consent of your mother and brother to my solicitation for your hand:

but I have to assure you that this consent, otherwise so valuable to me, will become null, unless you can at this moment, here, in their presence, declare that you willingly acquiesce in it. The step I am at this moment taking, is not perhaps altogether consistent with established forms—I am aware it is not: but you will pardon me if you reflect that I am a soldier, frank even to roughness, and desirous of ascertaining that in the most important act of my life, I am not deceiving myself. Will you then condescend to tell me whether you will become my wife? and above all, whether you can do so without any repugnance?"

This stately discourse, addressed to a girl of sixteen totally unprepared for it, by a gentleman who had never once spoken to her before, produced the effect which might naturally have been expected. The young lady felt "as if it were all a dream:" she "remained for ten minutes with her eyes fixed on the ground:" "the palpitation of her heart threatened to burst her corset:" the blood mounted to her head with such violence that "she heard nothing but a sharp singing, and saw nothing but a moving rainbow." She finally escaped, ran up stairs and concealed herself in the attic. Her brother, with a knowledge of the female heart remarkable in one so young, declared to Junot that his sister would be proud to bear his name, and succeeded in partially allaying the agitation of the General. The consent of the First Consul was now to be obtained, and Junot hastened to the Tuileries. Duroc obtained for him an immediate audience, and Junot was at once introduced into the cabinet of Bonaparte. The conversation that ensued is given by Madame Junot in her Memoirs, and is guaranteed by her as exact in every particular, her established rule being—on no occasion to be departed from—never to record expressions of Napoleon upon uncertain recollection.

"General," said Junot, commencing with that abruptness which bespeaks an earnest purpose, "you have testified a desire to see me married: the affair is arranged; I am about to marry."
"Really! And have you ran away with your wife; you appear

somewhat agitated?" "No, General." "Whom are you going to marry, then?" "A person whom you have known from her childhood, whom you used to love, General, of whom all speak advantageously, and with whom I am desperately in love—M'lle de Permon."

At this moment Bonaparte, instead of walking as he conversed, as was his usual custom, was seated at his desk, which he was notching with his penknife. He started up, threw away the knife, and seized Junot by the arm, saying, imperiously, "Whom did you say you meant to marry?" "The daughter of Madame de Permon—the child whom you have so often held upon your knee when you were yourself a young man, General." "It cannot be: Loulou is not marriageable: how old is she?" "She will be sixteen next month." "This is a very bad match you are making: there is no fortune in the family: and besides, how can you reconcile yourself to becoming the son-in-law of Madame de Permon? You must take care: the lady has a temper of her own." "Permit me to observe," interrupted Junot, "that I do not propose to marry my mother-in-law." He then enlarged upon the virtues of the young lady, and referred Bonaparte for further favorable details to Josephine and his sister Caroline. The First Consul at last resumed: "She is totally without fortune, I dare say: what portion has this young person?" "I have not asked." "You were right in saying just now that you were desperately in love. What rashness! Did I not expressly recommend you to seek a rich wife? For you are not rich yourself." "I beg your pardon, General; I am very rich. Are you not my protector, my father? And when I inform you that I love a girl who is poor, but without whom I should be unhappy, I know that you will come to my assistance, and portion my betrothed."

Bonaparte smiled, urged other objections, listened, yielded and assented. "Very well; you will not marry your mother-in-law, you say; and if the young lady be really such as you describe her, I see no reason for being severe on the article of fortune. I give you one hundred thousand francs for your bride's portion, and forty thousand for her trousseau. Adieu, my friend, I wish you well!" So saying, he resumed his seat and his penknife, adding, laughingly, "But you will have a terrible mother-in-law!"

The preparations for the marriage were now urged on by Junot, who commissioned Madame Murat to superintend the preparation of the wedding gifts, and Madame Bernard, the florist of the Opera, to furnish the bride elect with a daily bouquet of the rarest flowers. The contract was signed late in October, the lady's brother endowing her with sixty thousand francs, and M. Lequien de Bois-Cressy, the intended second husband of Madame de Permon, settling upon her fifty thousand more. Bonaparte appended his signature to the instrument the next day, and was so pleased with the brother's generosity, that he made him Commissary-General of Police.

The day preceding the marriage, General Junot, accidentally discovering that the family of the bride would not consider the ceremony complete, when performed by one of the mayors of Paris, startled Madame De Permon from her propriety by asking her if her daughter expected to be married at church. "To be married at church!" she exclaimed, "why, where else would you have her married? Before your friend with the scarf?" meaning M. Duquesnoy, mayor of the Seventh Ward. "You must have lost your wits, my child. How can you suppose that we could consent to a purely republican marriage?"

Junot plead that marriage was a civil ceremony, and that the benediction of the priest was a useless formality; that the Commandant of Paris could not consistently appear in uniform, to show himself to the crowd of beggars and low people that would be sure to fill the church. M'lle Loulou was firm, urged the requirements of Christianity, declared that the union could not take place unless the church should bless it, and finally sought relief in tears. Junot stamped his foot, and it would seem that he even swore, for the biographer says that he "let slip a very unusual expression."

It appears that Junot's conduct in this juncture was partly dictated by Bonaparte. The First Consul was already accused of seeking to overturn the Republic, and one of the great conquests of the Revolution had been the secularization of legislation, and the separation of church and state in the matter of marriage. He feared lest the solemnization of the nuptials of a general officer so well known as Junot, at a church and in public, might excite surprise and distrust—for he had not yet negotiated the Concordat with the Pope. The difficulty was finally compromised by arranging a nocturnal wedding to be discreetly muffled under a midnight mass. To this the young lady consented. "So," said the mother, "this grand affair is settled. Come, fall upon your knees, sir, and beg pardon of your betrothed. Loulou, give him your hand, or rather your cheek, in recompense of this graceful act of submission."

The trousseau and corbeille were now announced as ready for inspection, in adjoining rooms: the trousseau, furnished by the family of the bride herself, and containing the more necessary articles of a wife's wardrobe, and the corbeille, the gift of the bridegroom, containing the ornamental and decorative portion. Junot was requested to withdraw during the examination of the first, permission being accorded him to return during the inspection of the latter. The bride of sixteen then proceeded to survey her accumulated treasures. The floor was strewed with packages delicately wrapped in tissue paper and tied with pink ribbons. These had been given forth from the bosom of a rose-colored sarcophagus. M'lle Loulou spent, she says, a magic hour in the midst of these nuptial magnificences; highly trimmed chemises with embroidered sleeves; handkerchiefs with embossed borders, petticoats with hems in alto relievo, dressing-gowns of India muslin, night-caps edged with Mechlin lace, and collerettes skirted with English point. Bonaparte's appropriation of forty thousand francs had been employed to good purpose. Madame de Permon was the Lady Bountiful of this happy scene, the fairy Benevola of this hour of enchantment.

The ladies now passed to what must have been, to the younger of the two, the most agreeable of the duties of the day—the examination of the bridegroom's wedding present. It was a new sensation, and to be enjoyed but once. The corbeille had been designed by Junot, improved by Caroline Bonaparte, and executed by M'lle l'Olive, the dress-maker of Josephine. It contained Cashmere shawls, India muslin by the piece, Turkish velvet by the roll, veils of English lace, and sheets of white blond; reels of Brussels point long enough to throw the log of an ocean steamer; gloves, essences, flowers, trimmings, fans; a dressing-case containing all the necessaries of the toilet in enamel; a workbox comprising all the delicate engines of feminine industry in gold set with pearls; an opera-glass of mother of pearl, effulgent with diamonds; six ears of golden corn; a diamond-set comb; a medallion portrait of Junot, by Isabey, intended to be worn upon the breast, but more fit, from its size, thought M'lle Loulou, to be suspended upon the wall of a gallery; Egyptian topazes, oriental corals and antique cameos; a bridal purse of entwined golden links, swollen with bank notes, and jingling with Venetian sequins.

Junot had proved himself an attentive and zealous lover: he had now to show himself an adroit son-in-law. Madame de Permon had for years pined for a red Cashmere shawl, an indulgence which she considered beyond her means. Forming part of the corbeille was a basket embroidered with her cipher. Within was a purse like that of her daughter, containing a pure topaz instead of sequins; two fans and several dozens of gloves: and enshrined in an envelope of white gros-de-Naples, lay a magnificent scarlet Cashmere! This delicate and graceful compliment came with peculiar effect from the soldier whose valor had made him the hero of Lonato, the pulsation of whose brain had been felt in the depths of a sabre wound upon his skull, and from whose unclosed scar, eight years after, blood flowed upon the fingers of Napoleon as he was playfully pulling his favorite's hair.

At day-break on the 30th of October, M'lle Loulou proceeded to the church of her confessor, where she received absolution and the blessing of a venerable abbé. At nine she commenced her toilet, and at eleven appeared in a costume which no one can describe better than herself. "I wore an India muslin gown, with a short waist, a train, and long sleeves that buttoned at the wrist, the whole being trimmed with magnificent point lace. My cap was of Brussels point, crowned with a wreath of orange flowers, from which descended to my feet a veil of fine English point large enough to envelop my person. My costume was a profusion of rich lace so delicate and filmy that it resembled a vapory net-work, shading my countenance and playing with the curls of my hair: the undulating folds of my robe fell around me with the inimitable grace and supple ease of the superb tissues of India; the long veil covered my form without concealing it."[1] In this guise M'lle de Permon proceeded to the mayoralty and was civilly married by its presiding officer. The market-women, then, as now, a corporation, and a somewhat intrusive and presumptuous one, insisted on paying their respects to the bride, and deputed four of their number to present her with flowers, and two to kiss her on either cheek. Junot, who could well afford to condescend on the happiest day of his life, replied to them in their own elegant dialect, the argot of the French Billingsgate. At midnight, the disguised benediction of the church was bestowed upon the impatient couple, and "at one, they entered the Hotel de Montesquieu to the sound of the most harmonious music."

Such was the courtship, such the wedding of one of Bonaparte's lieutenants with a child whom the First Consul had held upon his knee. Some time before the birth of Madame Junot's first child,

---

[1] The portrait of Madame Junot, upon the opposite page, is from a sketch in possession of the family kindly placed at the disposal of the designer.

Josephine predicted that it would be a girl. This opinion was derived from the position of certain cards in a game of patience. "Pooh, pooh," said Bonaparte, "Laurette will have a boy, I tell you." "What will you lay?" asked Josephine. "I never bet," replied the First Consul: "if you are sure of the fact, it is dishonest: if not, it is simply foolish." "Well, bet sweetmeats, then: and I will wager the worsted work for a footstool." "Agreed," said Bonaparte: "and now take care," turning to Madame Junot, "that you do not make me lose."

Some weeks after, General Junot informed Bonaparte of the birth of a daughter. The First Consul embraced him, and then said: "Give my love to your wife, and tell her that I have a two-fold quarrel with her: first, because she has not given the Republic a soldier, and secondly, because she has made me lose my wager with Josephine. But I shall not be any less her friend and yours."

M'lle Josephine Junot and Master Napoleon Lannes, were Bonaparte's first god-children. They were christened at St. Cloud, soon after the promulgation of the Concordat. The First Consul wished to hold Miss Junot in his arms, but that young lady resisted violently, and absolutely refused to quit her mother "Well, Miss Devil," said he, "stay where you are, then." While Cardinal Caprara was performing the ceremony, M'lle Josephine raised her arm, lifted his Eminence's red cap from his head, and placed it upon her own. "With your leave, my child," said Bonaparte, "give me your plaything; it is but a bauble, like so many others, and we will restore it to the Cardinal." Before the godfather could interfere, the cap had been triumphantly placed upon his own head, and upon his removing it, Miss Josephine set up a shout so tremendous that she was heard from the chapel to the court-yard. "By heavens," said Bonaparte to Junot, "your daughter has as stout a voice as the most masculine boy in France."[1]

---

[1] d'Abr. i. 11, passim.

General Junot was made Duc d'Abrantès, in 1808, for his capture of a town of that name on the Tagus, but fell speedily afterwards from grace, and died of a brain fever at the age of forty-two years. His body lies at Montbar, but his heart is at the Pantheon. Madame Junot long survived him, and has left six volumes of Memoirs of Napoleon, his Court and Family. These are very precise and circumstantial, and with some allowances for the writer's too evident partiality, form an authentic and in many respects interesting record of the period of which they treat.

CHAPTER XI.

An Evening at Madame Récamier's—The Company—The Programme—Talma as Othello—A Gavotte rehearsed—The Wild Boy of the Aveyron—A rustic Wedding—An amateur Performance by Madame de Staël—A Midnight Supper—A Sentiment by the Prussian Ambassador.

ORDER had now been completely restored, and society had recovered its tone. Nothing can give a more lively idea of the occupations and amusements of the better classes at this period—the early Consulate—than the narrative of the employment of a day and evening at the house of Madame Récamier, the most beautiful and accomplished woman of the age. Of the lady herself, we shall have occasion to speak more fully, under the Empire. The season was spring, and the scene her chateau of Clichy-la-Garenne, just beyond the walls of Paris. The invitations promised breakfast, a promenade, dinner, the reading of a new play, recitations from Shakspeare, amateur theatricals, charades, proverbs and supper.

The company began to assemble at eleven. Camille Jordan, the late republican exile, General Junot, and Bernadotte, then Commander of the Army of the West, were the first to arrive. Laharpe, the critic, who was to listen to M. de Longchamp's new play, "Le Séducteur Amoureux," and to give his opinion of it; Talma, the tragedian; the two Montmorencies, the representatives of one of the noblest houses in France, followed soon after. Five minutes before the hour fixed for breakfast, came Mr. Fox, Lord and Lady Holland, Mr. Erskine, Mr. Adair and General

Moreau, the hero of Hohenlinden. The company, thus composed of incongruous, or at least inharmonious elements, manifested at first some embarrassment. It was difficult to induce conversation between persons strangers to each other, or who had been lately separated by civil or international hostility, for conversation might often be an indiscretion and a betrayal. The hostess entered, and with a few natural words, produced among her guests sympathy, communion and accord. Addressing Mr. Fox, she said, "I am delighted to welcome to my house a gentleman who is as much esteemed in France as he is admired in England: will you allow me, and will Lord and Lady Holland as well, to present to you my friends?" She then named each guest severally, alluding to his rank and position with appropriate compliment, and the conversation at once became general and easy.

Madame Récamier was conducted to the table by Fox: Moreau sat at her left. Laharpe and Erskine, Talma and Bernadotte, Jordan and Longchamp, conversed in pairs till the circle gradually widened and embraced the whole company. The subjects were war, politics, literature, the fine arts: Fox upon Pitt, and Erskine upon the Jury. The coffee had hardly been served, when the tramp of horses in the court announced a new arrival; the tardy guest was Eugène de Beauharnais, who had come to take Fox to visit his mother at Malmaison. He sat down at the devastated board, and, with the courteous aid of the hostess, snatched a hurried and unsubstantial repast. After a short promenade in the park, the company returned to the parlor, where Talma was to give recitations from the poets. No actor ever dispensed so completely with scenic accessories as this admirable tragedian. Madame Récamier, out of compliment to her English company, requested him to make selections from Shakspeare, through the French translation of Ducis. He commenced by a scene from Othello. Madame de Staël said of him that "he had only to pass his hand through his hair, and to cloud his brow, to become the Moor of Venice in person. Terror seized you at two steps from his side, as if all the illusions of the stage surrounded him." He then recited the interview of Macbeth with the witches, and though this was a brilliant era upon the English stage, Fox and Erskine expressed an enthusiastic admiration for the poet's French interpreter. Upon Talma's leaving the chateau to attend a rehearsal at the theatre, Madame Récamier sang a ballad, accompanying herself upon the harp. Eugène de Beauharnais now renewed his invitation to Fox to visit Josephine at Malmaison, and speedily withdrew with him and Mr. Adair.

Their places were soon supplied by new-comers—the Duchess of Gordon and her daughter Georgiana, afterwards the Duchess of Bedford. M. de Longchamp now read his comedy, and Laharpe, a severe and unsparing critic, declared that he could conscientiously compliment the author. An important but unbidden personage was then announced—Vestris, the ballet-master. He had heard that Lady Georgiana was at the chateau, and as she was to dance on the morrow evening a gavotte of his composition with Madame Récamier, he thought that a rehearsal would not be inopportune. It was out of the question to think of denying him admittance, so the rehearsal was held to the music of the horn and the harp. Madame Récamier, being a married woman, and consequently supposed to possess the requisite assurance, assumed the responsibility of an Andalusian tambourine, while the blond and retiring English beauty veiled her blushes in the muslin folds of her bayadère shawl. The audience were moved to enthusiasm, and the preceptor well-nigh shed tears at the proficiency of his pupils.

The ladies next rode to the Bois de Boulogne, and, returning at five o'clock, found M. Récamier returned from his banking-house, and ready for dinner. This gentleman, whose age gave him the air rather of his wife's father than her husband, abandoned himself altogether to the calls of his business, leaving to her the entire duty of reception, entertainment and representation. Two new guests had arrived to dine, in the persons of Lalande the astronomer, and Degerando the economist. Another was expected at dessert; this was the wild boy of the Aveyron—a being who had once been human, but who, by dwelling with animals in the forest, was now, at the age of fifteen, a confirmed brute in his tastes and capacities. He was under the care of Dr. Yzard, to whom the government had entrusted him for education.

He came with his instructor at seven. Madame Récamier caused him to be placed at her side, and sought by subjecting him to the influence of eyes accustomed to win, to subdue and to enchain, to woo him back to his once natural instincts. But on this occasion, doubtless the only one, they failed of their effect, for the young savage was exclusively occupied in satisfying the calls of hunger. When he had finished, he filled his pockets with sugar-plums, and then appeared to give ear to a warm discussion upon atheism between Lalande and Laharpe. In the midst of the debate, he sprang from his seat, rushed out upon the lawn, where he divested himself of all his clothing but his shirt; this garment finally yielded to the rapidity and animation of his course, tearing in halves as he climbed a horse-chestnut and seated himself for repose in a fork of its branches. The ladies, who had followed him to the park, thought proper, upon observing this catastrophe, to remain at a distance, while Dr. Yzard, with a basket of fruit, attempted to decoy him to earth again. He yielded to the seduction: an incomplete but satisfactory garment was made for him from a petticoat of the porter's niece, and he was carried off to his home at the Garden of Plants.

At seven o'clock the guests of the evening began to assemble; Count Markoff, the Russian ambassador, and the gentlemen of his legation; the Austrian ambassador; M. de Berckeim, a friend of the Duke d'Enghien, and who afterwards lost his reason on learning the execution of that unfortunate prince. The sounds of a pipe, violin and tambourine, on the borders of the river, drew the notice of the company in that direction, and Madame Récamier, saying that the music was that of a village wedding, proposed that they should attend it. "The newly married couple," says the chronicler, "highly flattered by our visit, received us with every mark of respect, and the singular contrast produced in the tableau by our arrival, can easily be imagined. Such is the sovereign power of beauty: grave diplomatists and unbending financiers sought to vie in agility with the nimbler rustics, and the noblemen of the North ventured for the first time to stray amid the mazes of a French quadrille, in presence of the most lovely and accomplished woman in the world: a general sentiment of gaiety augmented still further the interest of a scene worthy of the pencil of Teniers or Albano."

On their return to the chateau the party found other guests awaiting their arrival: among them were Madame de Staël and the Marquis de Luchesini, the Prussian ambassador. Proverbs were at once proposed, but it was decided to begin the evening with amateur theatricals. The dramatic talent of the company was of a high order: Madame de Staël's improvisation was, by many, considered the best in Europe: Madame Viotte had been styled by Laharpe, "the Tenth Muse," and Count Cobentzel was the best amateur actor of the Hermitage Theatre, at the court of the Czarina Catherine. The first piece was "Hagar in the Desert," and as there is a lyric in Madame de Staël's works, of this name, it was doubtless the one represented on this occasion. Madame de Staël played Hagar: her son, afterwards killed at the age of twenty, in a duel at Stockholm, performed the part of Ishmael, and Madame Récamier that of the Angel. "It would be difficult," continues the eyewitness already quoted, "to depict the effect produced by Madame de Staël in this eminently dramatic part, or to give any adequate idea of the pathetic manner in which she rendered the emotions of grief and of despair, suggested by Hagar's situation in the desert. Though performed in a parlor, the dramatic illusion of the scene was perfect. With her long hair falling in the wildest disorder, Madame de Staël completely identified herself with the character. Madame Récamier, with her modest and celestial beauty, was the very personification of the messenger of heaven. One would have supposed written for her these lines of the British poet:

> 'O woman! lovely woman!
> Angels are painted fair to look like you!'"

Proverbs and charades in action followed this biblical tragedy. Count Cobentzel justified and sustained his dramatic reputation, to the great scandal of his colleagues, whose credit for gravity was somewhat endangered by the levity and versatility of his impersonations, and finally, at midnight, supper was announced. As the company sat down to table, the Prussian ambassador, though a married man, remarked that supper is always the most agreeable act of the comedy of the day. "Breakfast," he said, " is the meal of friendship : dinner that of etiquette : luncheon that of childhood ; while supper is the banquet of love, and the scene of its hushed and whispered confidence."

CHAPTER XII.

Bonaparte projects the Legion of Honor—The first conversation concerning it—The Argument and the Vote—Epigrams and counterfeit Decorations—The Artists, Scientific and Literary Men admitted—Lafayette—The Grand Eagle—Goethe—Young Lafayette—Picard, Talma and Crescentini—Madame de Genlis—Hubert Goffin—Caricatures—The Effect of the Order upon Society.

ONE evening in the month of February, 1802, Bonaparte still being First Consul, a select party dined at Malmaison. Upon the removal of the cloth, Josephine withdrew to the boudoir with the ladies of the company, while Bonaparte retired to the room somewhat ambitiously called the Council Chamber. He was followed by Monge the geometrician, Duroc, Didelot, Councillor of State, Denon, lately appointed Director of the Louvre, and Arnault, the tragic author. Bonaparte arranged them in a circle, and placed himself in the centre, as was his custom when about to enter upon an argument or to take a leading part in the conversation. "Citizen Monge," he said, "I did not see you on Sunday last at the grand reception of the ambassadors at the Tuileries. Since the palace has become the seat of government again, there has been no reception so brilliant. With what avidity the guests contemplated the diplomates and foreign ministers ornamented with the stars and ribbons of the various orders of their countries! Denon, did you not notice this eagerness?"

"Certainly, I noticed it," replied Denon, "and I shared in it myself: it must be acknowledged that these wide ribbons of striking colors, these bright constellations, these enamelled crosses, produce a marvellous effect and contribute singularly to improve the personal appearance of the individual wearing them. In fact, they 'dress' a man." "That's an artist speaking," interrupted Monge; " why, these crosses, these decorations, these cordons, are nothing but tinsel and gewgaws." " Gewgaws as much as you please," returned Bonaparte, " but people fancy them and yearn to possess them ; they are the ostensible signs of human grandeur; they strike the eye of the multitude and inspire involuntary respect. Let us attack the question fearlessly: men are fond of badges of distinction, the French more fond than other nations; they really hunger and thirst for them ; such has been their spirit in every age. See what use Louis XIV. made of the cross of St. Louis: that powerful auxiliary stimulated soldiers to perform prodigies of valor. Money was worthless in comparison with it: it was preferred to mountains of gold." " Well," said Monge, coldly, " you could not do better, Citizen Consul, than reëstablish the cross of St. Louis."

This was a direct and palpable thrust. Monge was a member of the Committee of the Convention, upon whose report that body suppressed the Order of St. Louis, in 1793, exactly one hundred years after its foundation. Bonaparte looked at Monge, remained silent for a few minutes, and then said : " Suppose we join the ladies in the parlor."

In April of the same year, Bonaparte communicated his intention of instituting an order of chivalry to the members composing a sort of informal privy council. Cambacérès favored the project, saying that these distinctive marks had not been proscribed by the republics of antiquity. Regnault de St. Jean d'Angely furnished a very acceptable argument, in the assertion that the newly-formed government of the United States had just completed its republican institutions by creating the Order of Cincinnatus. Among the people—for the plans of Bonaparte naturally became public—the opposition and disapproval was serious and prolonged. The First Consul persevered, however, and the 4th of May, 1802, was appointed for the communication of the bill to the Council of State.

The attendance on that occasion was large, and the interest manifested, unusually lively. Several of the auditors to the council were not twenty years old, and upon Bonaparte's entrance, they made such noisy haste to get into their seats, that he was obliged to call them to order. "Gentlemen," he cried, tapping his desk with an ivory knife, "you behave like veritable school boys that you are." Upon the restoration of silence, the Second Consul, Cambacérès, announced that the Bill for the Institution of the Legion of Honor was the order of the day, upon which the Councillor of State, Rœderer, proceeded to read it. Bonaparte then said: "The present system of military recompense is a system without organization. The 87th article of the Constitution secures, indeed, national rewards to soldiers; it is true also that a decree has ordered a distribution of honorary arms, which involves double pay, but the whole matter is a mass of confusion and irregularity. The spirit of the army needs to be sustained and directed. This bill gives consistency to the system of recompense, and forms a connected whole: it is a first step towards the organization of the nation."

Murmurs and whisperings followed the close of the First Consul's remarks. "Silence, I say, gentlemen!" he exclaimed, again calling into requisition his ivory paper folder. "Citizen Mathieu Dumas has the floor."

Mathieu Dumas, an upright, austere and methodic councillor, opposed the bill, inasmuch as he would prefer that the institution be exclusively confined to the army. Bonaparte's reply was remarkable, coming from a man whose sword was his fortune. After acknowledging the influence of might and force in a period of barbarism, he said: "But we must not reason from such periods to the present time. We are thirty millions of men bound together by intelligence, property and commerce. Three or four hundred thousand soldiers are as nothing compared to such a mass. When a general quits the army, he returns to civil life. The soldiers themselves are the children of citizens. The army is the nation. The soldier knows no law but force, while the citizen knows no other interest than the general good. The peculiarity of the soldier is to seek to obtain, despotically: that of the citizen to submit every question to discussion, to reason, to truth. So that I do not hesitate to think that the preëminence belongs incontestably to the citizen. If we were to divide the proposed rewards into military and civil, there would be two orders, while there is only one nation; and if we were to award honors to soldiers only, the nation would be forgotten altogether." An explosion of bravos followed this brilliant improvisation, for the majority of the council were men of civic avocations. Bonaparte, wishing to prolong the effect and rivet the impression, adroitly adjourned the meeting.

Four days afterwards the subject was revived. Berlier, a laborious and grave councillor, spoke against the bill. He began by saying: "The proposed order leads to aristocracy: crosses and ribbons are the toys of monarchy." Bonaparte, in his reply, said: "It is nevertheless with such toys as these that men are led and governed. See how the people worship the decorations of the foreign envoys: the latter are themselves surprised at it, and never fail to wear their ribbons in public. I do not think that the French love either liberty or equality: they have not been changed by ten years of revolution. They are what the Gauls were, proud and frivolous. They have but one sentiment—HONOR. It is this sentiment that we must feed: the people must have badges of distinction. Voltaire called soldiers 'Alexanders at five sous a day:' he was right: they are nothing else. Do you think you can make men fight by analysis? No: they must have glory, and the badges which show and perpetuate this glory. . . . The Revolution is over, and we are to reorganize the nation: everything is destroyed, and we are to re-create. There is a government, there are constituted authorities, but what is the rest?

Grains of sand. We are scattered, without system, without union, without contact. . . . Do you imagine we can count upon the people? They cry indifferently 'Vive le Roi!' or 'Vive la Ligue!' We must give them a direction, and for that we must have instruments. In the war of the Vendée, I saw forty men control a whole department: it is their system of which we must possess ourselves."

At the third sitting, Bonaparte skillfully turned the discussion to matters of detail, as if the substance and body of the project had already been adopted. Thibaudeau, whom the Convention had named the "Bar of Iron," from the sternness of his principles, spoke energetically against the project, denouncing it as diametrically opposed to the views professed during the Revolution; and as the legislative body was to adjourn in three days, he thought it unwise to require of it so important a vote upon so insufficient examination. Bonaparte called upon the council for its opinion: the ballot stood fifteen in favor of the bill to nine against it—the most serious opposition the First Consul had yet encountered. It was presented the next day, May 14, 1802, to the Legislature. The reporter, quoting an expression evidently furnished him by Bonaparte, said, "the idea is to create a new small change—" monnaie "—whose standard is unalterable." The opposition was violent, though the bill was finally carried by a vote of one hundred and sixty-six to one hundred and ten. The Tribunat—a body which Bonaparte declared to be composed of "taquins," or teasers—returned a ballot of fifty-six for, to thirty-eight against. So that the three chambers whose concurrence was necessary in the passage of the bill, and which consisted of three hundred and ninety-four members, gave to the Legion of Honor the very feeble majority of eighty. It thus became an institution, though it awakened a more imposing and tenacious hostility than any other of Napoleon's measures.

Thibaudeau, the Bar of Iron, said to Bonaparte soon after. "You see that we were right in the Council of State, Citizen

Consul. An opposition so earnest is always a disadvantage." "Yes," returned Napoleon, "the prejudices are still too powerful. I should have waited: the matter was not urgent. Still, France has a right to expect great results from this institution, provided my successors do not botch it."

The law was not to be put in execution for two years or more, owing to the necessity of procuring six million francs for the preliminary expenses. During this period a rain of epigrams and quolibets fell upon the new institution, from the mouths of the republicans and the partisans of the Bourbons. Napoleon, never able to tolerate ridicule, revenged himself unsparingly by exile and disgrace: at the same time, he found comfort in predicting for the order the success with which the event has crowned it. "Patience, patience," he said: "many who now make merry at the expense of the cross, will never be able to wear it: the Legion of Honor will yet become an object of ambition to all." M. de Lacépède, the naturalist, was made Grand Chancellor of the order. The Legion itself was divided into sixteen cohorts, each cohort containing seven grand officers, twenty commanders, thirty officers, and three hundred and fifty chevaliers: the whole order, therefore, would comprise six thousand six hundred and twelve members.

The students were the most active malcontents, as they have, indeed, ever been. At the moment of the first distribution of ribbons, July 15, 1804, the fields were blushing with wild carnations, a flower which in color, size and form, closely resembles the cross of the Legion. Though penal to wear the decoration without authorization, there was no clause against wearing carnations, and the streets were very soon filled with bands of young men with the deceitful flower in their button-holes. As they passed the military posts, the sentinels presented arms: the promenaders, not so easily deluded, and unwilling to believe in the existence of merit at once so abundant and so juvenile, recognized and applauded the quiz. Napoleon, in his wrath, sent for Fouché, and

ordered him to take the most rigorous measures against the
offenders. Fouché showed his tact in his reply : "Certainly, your
Majesty, these young fellows deserve chastisement : but let us
wait till autumn." The emperor was pleased with the wit of this
rejoinder, and was convinced by its spirit : the season of carnations was soon over, and with it disappeared the whole array of
counterfeit decorations.

Napoleon had the good taste and the generosity to admit into
the order, the Councillors of State and Legislators who had opposed its creation : Monge, Berlier, Thibaudeau and others : they
accepted the cross without resistance. The list of scientific and
literary men offers sufficient interest to be hastily passed in review : the names of the soldiers and government officers hardly
present the same attraction. The following were the principal
appointments in the Academy of Sciences, the First Class of the
Institute :

The four L's of Mathematics—Lagrange, Laplace, Legendre,
Lalande ;[1] Bossut, professor of hydraulics ; Delambre, astronomer ;
Prony, geometrician ; Fourcroy, chemist ; Haüy, mineralogist, cre-
ator of the science of crystallography and professor at the Garden
of Plants ; Parmentier, horticulturist, to whom was due the adoption of the American potato in France, and who had persuaded
Louis XVI. to wear in his button-hole the first potato blossom
produced on French soil ; Hallé, physician to Josephine ; Geoffroy
St. Hilaire, naturalist and professor of zoology ; Cuvier, one of
the youngest of the Academy, and at this period, 1804, just commencing the studies which have made his name immortal ; and
Conté, inventor of the hydraulic machine at Marly and founder of
the manufacture of crayons in France.

The list of men of letters—the Second Class of the Institute
— was drawn up by Lucien Bonaparte, Lacépède and Fontanes,
and was accepted by Napoleon with some modifications. The
following were the principal admissions : Collin d'Harleville, dra-

[1] Mazas, Legion of Honor, 35.

matic poet; Boufflers, a poetaster, both licentious and frivolous; Chénier, one of the first poets of the revolutionary period, and for a long time violently opposed to the First Consul: Napoleon erased his name, but restored it at the instance of Cambacérès; Andrieux, dramatist; Fontanes, a critic and essayist till proscribed by the Directory, and upon his recall by Napoleon, chosen by him to pronounce the eulogy upon Washington in 1800, and afterwards the emperor's most servile flatterer; Arnault, tragic author, whose drama of Oscar brought Ossian into high favor in France. We shall describe under the Literature of the Empire, how Lemercier, Ducis and Delille refused the proffered decoration.

Upon the list proposed by Fontanes was the name of Bernardin de St. Pierre, one of the most truly popular and widely known writers in France. Napoleon drew his pen through his name, on account of the zeal with which he had defended Madame de Staël at the time of her exile: two years later, however, he gave him the decoration. Napoleon also erased the name of Parny, author of Poésies Erotiques, and of Goddam, a philippic in verse against England: that of Domergue, the grammarian, who was thought too pedantic to be really learned: that of Naigeon, a metaphysician and freethinker, and that of Cailhava, dramatist.

Among the other distinguished academicians admitted were: Anquetil, an octogenarian, and the eldest of French historians; Larcher, the translator of Herodotus; Danse, antiquarian and professor of Greek literature, and Silvestre de Sacy, orientalist. These gentlemen belonged to the Third Class of the Institute—that of Ancient History and Literature.

The Fourth Class, the Academy of Fine Arts, furnished the following members: the section of painting, its four G's—Gros, Guérin, Girodet, Gérard—besides David, Regnault, Visconti, Vien, Redouté and Lagrenée; that of sculpture, Houdon, celebrated for his Washington and Voltaire; Pajou and Moitte; that of music, Lesueur, Gossec, Méhul, Grétry, Monsigny and Paisiello. Cherubini, an Italian by birth but a Frenchman by adoption, was excluded, for having sometime previously proved to Napoleon that though a good soldier he was a poor musician. The decoration given to Denon, the director of the Louvre, was accompanied with a flattering reminder of his apt expression at Malmaison, on the evening when the First Consul broached his project of instituting the order.

One circumstance connected with the military distribution requires mention here. Napoleon sent the cross of Grand Officer to M. de Lafayette, considering him as ex-general in chief of the National Guard. Lafayette declined it, saying that the Legion of Honor was "ridiculous." Napoleon felt that this insult was gratuitous, and afterwards spoke of it bitterly at St. Helena. The refusal was the more unexpected, as Marshal de Rochambeau, the companion in arms of Lafayette in America, and the Nestor of the old French army, had accepted the cross with expressions of gratitude.

Six months later, Napoleon added to the order a degree superior to the four already instituted: it took the name of the Grand Eagle, and the number of admissions was limited to sixty. He proposed to the crowned heads of Europe an exchange of this decoration against that of similar grade in their respective orders of chivalry. The King of Spain accepted the proposal, and sent the collar of the Golden Fleece: the King of Portugal sent the order of Christ: the King of Prussia the star of the Black Eagle. Napoleon now completed the organization of the institution, by increasing the number of legal members, and deciding that two thousand additional crosses should be distributed exclusively in the army. The opposition and the war of epigrams ceased upon the battle of Austerlitz, where the new order received its baptism of glory: those who had accepted the badge, but who had affected a disinclination to wear it, now hastened to attach it to the willing and expectant button-hole.

Some incidents connected with the Legion of Honor, showing

the esteem in which it came to be held, will not be out of place here. Napoleon, entering Weimar, in 1806, in pursuit of the fugitives from Jena, ordered the house inhabited by Goethe to be protected by a body of sentinels: he gave the poet himself the decoration of chevalier. The historians of the time compared this act to that of Alexander at Thebes, who excepted the house which had been occupied by Pindar from the destruction impending over the city. Goethe received from Louis XVIII., in 1818, a higher rank in the order and one more in accordance with his reputation.

At the battle of Eylau, Georges de Lafayette, one of Grouchy's aids-de-camp, displayed the most remarkable and the most opportune valor. Grouchy presented his name for the cross of honor. Napoleon erased it. At the battle of Friedland, young Lafayette's division decided the victory, and his name was again proposed by Grouchy. Napoleon a second time refused. He had not forgotten the expression used by his father, some years before. The opinion of the army was condemnatory of Napoleon, and, upon the advice of Grouchy, Georges de Lafayette withdrew from the service.

Four years after the institution of the Legion, every prejudice against it had disappeared, and all classes of society displayed the utmost eagerness to be admitted to its ranks. No station, no capacity, no attainment, was above the ambition, deemed innocent and legitimate, of holding a position in an order of merit so truly national and universal. Napoleon skillfully profited by this shifting of public opinion in his favor, to enter upon a system of exclusion and exaction in his awards of the decoration, which rendered it infinitely more precious, by increasing the difficulty of obtaining it.

In 1807, Picard, a dramatist and retired actor, was apprised by the Minister of the Interior that he was soon to be made a chevalier of the order. Talma, the tragedian, upon learning this decision in favor of his comrade, solicited of Napoleon, with whom he was upon terms of friendship and intimacy, a similar distinction. Napoleon replied: "Picard is to receive the cross as an author, and not as an actor, for he has quitted the stage. You, Talma, cannot quit the stage, for you are the first tragedian of the century. Society has conceived a prejudice against actors, which it is not in my power to destroy, and this motive compels me, though unwillingly, to withhold the decoration you solicit." Aware, however, that Talma would have reason to feel aggrieved if a distinction withheld from him were conferred upon Picard, Napoleon thought proper to give it to neither.

Upon this subject, Napoleon spoke as follows, at St. Helena: "My system was to confound together every species of merit, and to render one single decoration universal: I therefore wished to confer it upon Talma. Still I hesitated, in view of the caprices of our national manners, and the folly of our prejudices, and ventured to make, by giving the badge of the Iron Crown to Crescentini, the tenor, a trial of public opinion which could do no harm. The decoration was a foreign one, and Crescentini was a foreigner: the act could not compromise the government, beyond perhaps drawing upon it the wit of the jesters. But notice the power of public opinion: I distributed sceptres as I pleased, but I was unable to secure the success of a simple ribbon—for I believe that my experiment was unfortunate, was it not?" "Very," replied a listener; "it produced the utmost sensation in Paris: it received the anathema of the salons: malevolence made ample use of it; it was called the abomination of profanations."[1] Had Crescentini been merely a tenor, the public would not, perhaps, have protested: he owed the persecution of the wits to the fact that he was a soprano, and possessed a voice not conferred upon him by nature.[2]

In 1808, Madame de Genlis, lately appointed one of the librarians of the Arsenal, made an effort in behalf of the admission of ladies into the order. She composed an address in furtherance of her plan, and collected quite a convincing array of female names distinguished in literature, the arts, and even in the sciences. She cited Mesdames de Staël, Campan, Duvernoy, Cottin and herself in letters; Mesdames Lebrun, Jacotot, Lescot in painting, and M'lle Sophie Germain, geometrician and laureate in equations. The Academy of Sciences was mortified and indignant at this proceeding, which they considered at once impertinent and degrading. Madame de Genlis prevailed upon her son-in-law, General and Senator Valence, to present the memorial to Napoleon. He did so, though without any hope of a favorable result. The emperor, comprehending the whole matter at the first sentence, interrupted the unfortunate sponsor in the midst of his narrative, and energetically dismissed both petition and petitioner.

Napoleon now limited his bestowals of the cross to persons acquiring military distinction: his wars required all the stimulus of reward and encouragement that became disposable by reason of deaths in the order. Somewhat later, however, he gave the decoration to Wieland at Weimar, and to the poet Monti at Milan; to Metternich and Prince de Schwartzenberg, upon the signing of the treaty of Vienna, in 1809; to M. Oberkampf, in recognition of his successful competition with the English in certain manufactures, of which, till then, they had held the monopoly; to M. Delessert, for his efforts to obtain sugar from the beet-root; to M. Ternaux, for his French cashmeres; to David, for his Distribution of the Eagles; and to Raynouard, for his tragedy of Les Templiers.

In 1812, Napoleon made a nomination in the order which raised it still higher in the esteem of the nation. Hubert Goffin, a miner in the coal district of Liege, was surprised, at an immense distance under ground, by an irruption of water. He had one foot in the bucket at the moment of the break, and might easily have escaped by giving the signal to the men at the rope. He preferred to give his place to a blind miner, and to remain with his brigade of one hundred men, imprisoned like himself. He assumed and maintained control over the affrighted herd, now mutinous from terror, and caused the excavation of a chamber in one of the galleries, beyond the reach of the water. In the meantime, the blind man gave the alarm to the authorities of the city of Liege. After five days of arduous labor on the part of the engineers and soldiers, and of mute suffering in the darkness of the mine by those that survived the first catastrophe, a communication was effected. Seventy-two men, out of one hundred, were restored to life and liberty. All would have perished without the devotion of Goffin. Napoleon assimilated this trait of heroism to a brilliant act upon the field of battle. Goffin was made a member of the Legion of Honor, with an annual pension of six hundred francs. The French Academy offered a prize for the best commemoration, in verse, of the event; the poet Hubert Millevoye obtained it, together with a pension from Napoleon of six thousand francs. The admission of Goffin, a laboring miner, into an order of chivalry, gained the heart of the nation; and from this period, the Legion of Honor became enthusiastically popular among the people as well as in the army.

The disasters of Moscow caused numerous vacancies in the order: so numerous that Russian prisoners taken subsequently by the French, were found to have three rows of crosses sewn upon their bear-skin caps. These were torn off and returned to the chancellor's office at Paris. During the sports of the carnival of 1813, at Frankfort, a number of young men, disguised as Cossacks, drove before them through the streets a dozen persons travestied as French officers, each of them ornamented with a huge pasteboard cross. This masquerade was so acceptable to the population, that Marshal Augereau, appointed soon after governor of the city by Napoleon, condemned it to pay a fine of several millions; and to lodge and board, gratuitously, the whole French army now on its way to Saxony.

On his return from Moscow, Napoleon detached his own cross from his breast, and gave it with flattering words to Corvisart, his confidential physician. He also admitted numerous scions of illustrious families, who possessed no other qualifications than those of birth and lineage. In 1813, the number of nominations Napoleon had made since the institution of the order, was no less than forty-eight thousand, only one thousand four hundred of which were in recompense of civil service. This disparity, considerable as it is, will be largely diminished by the consideration that the forty-six thousand six hundred military members did not all exist at once. Battle, in thinning the ranks of the army, caused a constant renewal of the names composing the order. It is not likely, though no documents upon the subject have been made public, that the Legion included, at any one period, more than thirty thousand members.

We have spoken thus at length of the Legion of Honor, not only on account of the influence it exerted on society and the nation, but because it is one of the few creations of Napoleon which survived him and which still exist. Louis XVIII. decreed the maintenance of the order, substituting, upon the cross, the head of Henry IV. for that of Napoleon. He gave the badge to Ducis, the poet, who had refused to accept it from Napoleon : to Picard, whose disappointment has been described : to M. de Choiseul, the patriarch of history, to whom Napoleon did not offer it, fearing a refusal : to Arago, successor of Lalande in the Bureau of Longitudes : to Biot, his colleague : to Cherubini, who offended the emperor in 1804 : to M. Guizot : to Dupaty, dramatist ; to Villemain and Cormenin : to Firmin Didot, the typographer, and to Horace Vernet, painter. Napoleon, on his return from Elba in March, 1815, annulled all the appointments made during his exile, and restored the order to the position in which it stood at the entrance of the allies. In July of the same year, Louis XVIII. in his turn annulled these decisions, and issued a decree definitively organizing his "Royal Order of the Legion of Honor." In 1821, he admitted to the ranks Chateaubriand, Charles Nodier and Lamartine.

The institution of the Legion of Honor was one of the most daring, and it must be admitted in view of the character of the French people, and the actual condition of affairs, one of the most fruitful and beneficent acts of Napoleon's reign. In contributing to arrest confusion and consolidate society, to substitute the distinctions of merit for the divisions of caste, to conciliate faction and promote effort in the various paths to glory, it deserves to rank above the Concordat and on a level with the Civil Code. Historians whose opinions have won regard, have pronounced it altogether the first and most productive achievement of his genius.

CHAPTER XIII.

The Empire proclaimed—Attitude of the People—Jests upon the rapid Fortunes of the Bonapartes—The Clamor for Office—Bonapartists, Bourbons and Jacobins—Mock Receptions—Napoleon's Irritation—Brunet and Napoleon's Bust—The Court Journal—Extravagance.

SIMULTANEOUSLY with his labors of legislation, his revival of ancient or his creation of new institutions, and his prosecution of military designs, Bonaparte paid a constant and earnest attention to the necessary preparation of the public mind for the restoration of the throne. It is not possible here to detail the processes by which this event was realized, and monarchy revived, after an interregnum of twenty-two years. It is sufficient to say that the Empire was proclaimed on the 18th of May, 1804, and that while Paris coldly acquiesced, the provinces joyfully acceded. The epoch was unfortunate—for the Duc d'Enghien was hardly two months dead, and the deep and poignant emotion which had been excited by the catastrophe in which the young Bourbon perished, was far from having subsided. The Parisians would doubtless have welcomed the Empire with enthusiasm, had it followed either Campo Formio, Marengo, the Concordat or Lunéville. But the late execution and the impending continental wars were sinister auspices for the inauguration of a dynasty. The attitude of the people of Paris was one of indifference, not of positive hostility. Still, on occasions which seemed to call for a manifestation of enthusiasm, the public was apt to make a demonstration in a contrary sense. Thus the night before the proclamation, Carion

THE EMPIRE PROCLAIMED.   139

de Nisas produced at the Théâtre Français a tragedy entitled Peter the Great. Worthless as a literary work, it was distasteful from the excess of its flattery of Napoleon, and was hissed throughout. The police caused the pupils of the Polytechnic school—all devoted to Bonaparte—to attend the second representation, but their presence only served to increase the tumult and embitter the opposition.[1]

"The gravity with which Napoleon pursued and attained the Empire met with persistent laughter at Paris," says Capefigue; "the public could not admit these hasty fortunes, improvised as in a single day. It accepted Napoleon, because from the splendor of his glory no one could escape; but his family, his brothers, sisters and cousins—could they claim the same respect? Could the nation regard with approval these marvellous dignities tossed at them by an undiscriminating destiny? Every one knew that Cardinal Fesch had been a simple army intendant; that Madame Lætitia, poor though noble, had brought up her family with infinite difficulty; that Josephine was the hail-fellow-well-met of the commissaries of war; and Louis a young officer of no greater merit than many other graduates of the colleges. What did the public not say, in its confidential chronicles, upon the early life of this theatrically organized court? And now all these people, by a magic stroke of the pen, had become Imperial Highnesses, and the nation was to kneel in the dust before them. Parisian wit allowed itself free play with these princes so fantastically elevated, and revenged itself in puns for the forced respect it was called upon to pay to a borrowed nobility."[2]

Upon the proclamation of the Empire, and the publication of the intelligence that Napoleon's household was to be organized upon a footing becoming his new position, the clamor and intrigue for office became, on the part of persons of all shades of opinion, violent and unprincipled to a degree such as had never been witnessed in France. Not only did those who had from the beginning espoused Napoleon's cause, make a combined onset upon the various places to be created, but the most lofty families of the old nobility, the bearers of names illustrious in legitimacy for centuries, did not hesitate to lay their Bourbon allegiance at the feet of the parvenu sovereign. Stranger still, many repentant Jacobins—haunters and disciples of Robespierre—were eager and anxious to wear the new sovereign's livery.

Napoleon certainly desired to give place and preferment to members of the old nobility and representatives of the aristocracy of birth; but it does not seem, as has been persistently asserted, that he resorted to intrigue or descended to importunity to induce them to accept office. He looked upon the nobility as supple and obsequious by habit and tradition: he considered them from their education, their wealth, their connection with the aristocracies of other kingdoms, the necessary accompaniment of a throne. He noticed that their service was graceful and zealous. "A Montmorency would throw himself at the feet of the empress," he said, "to tie her shoe-strings, while the wife of Marshal Lannes would consider such an act degrading: she would fear to be taken for a waiting-maid—a hesitation which, to the Montmorency, would never be likely to occur." Still he did not forgive them for their marked avoidance of the camp and their eager preference of the court. "I showed them," he afterwards said, 'the path of glory, so honorably trod by their ancestors; all recoiled with shameful dismay. I inadvertently opened to them the door of my ante-chamber, and they at once dashed into it in throngs."

He soon saw that any attempt to listen to the innumerable demands for place, or to base his choice upon the petitions presented, or the certificates and vouchers submitted, would create ten enemies where it would satisfy one elect. He determined to apportion his household according to his own judgment, in obedience to his own preferences, and in view of the personal merit and qualifications of the candidates. The list, as he drew it up, went successfully into operation, and was never materially altered. It will be passed in review in a subsequent chapter.

The faubourg St. Germain, then, as now, the seat and centre of the old nobility, was naturally the focal point of the opposition, in spite of the numerous offices it solicited at Napoleon's hands. Unable to contend against the new order of things with any other weapon than ridicule—an efficient and deadly one, however, in France—it employed this weapon with telling and murderous effect. Epigrams upon the awkwardnesses, the improprieties and the incongruities of the new court and the new nobility, circulated through Paris with that extraordinary rapidity which characterizes the spread of jests that it would be penal to put in print. The scandalous chronicles of the imperial family, the tone, manners and spirit of those who were to develop the new institutions, afforded amusement and occupation to the idle as well as to the busy tongues of the disaffected. Ladies of the old régime held mock receptions at their houses, where the demeanor, address and costume of the ladies of the new court were caricatured and held up to ridicule, often legitimate and as often unjust.

"The faubourg St. Germain," says the author just quoted, "discontented and pouting, was proud of its disaffected fraction of royalists—an accomplished and disdainful throng who refused to accept even the benefits of the Empire. Its only vengeance, thus far, was to rail at the new régime; it composed and told endless stories upon the Tuileries, the stiffness of its manners, the awkwardness of its ceremonial and its ritual of reverences, which substituted the starched bearing of an awkward squad for the easy and respectful attitudes of persons trained to elegant life. Napoleon was weak enough to be influenced by this tattle: becoming alternately uneasy and irritated, he replied by decrees of exile to the merest jests of women; he, grand and imposing as an antique bronze, allowed himself to be afflicted by these pin-pricks and fan-strokes dealt by a provoked marchioness."[1]

The spirit of opposition broke out even upon the stage, in the form of disguised epigrams and lunges palpable only to the select few. History has preserved quite a quiverful of these envenomed shafts. One will give a fair idea of the whole. Brunet of the Variétés, the first low comedian of the time, received in the course of a farce, the bust of Napoleon, in plaster. After examining it, he said, " Je l'aimerais mieux en terre," in which the apparent meaning is that he would prefer the bust in clay—the hidden sense being that he should like to see Bonaparte under ground. Brunet was several times sent to prison for pleasantries of this sort.

Napoleon may be said to have invented the Court Journal. No sovereign before him ever admitted the public to such an intimate acquaintance with the domestic economy of the palace, or the employments and little daily recreations of its occupants. The Moniteur never failed to devote a portion of its space to a record of what their Majesties did yesterday, and what they proposed to do to-morrow. It chronicled the variations of an imperial headache with greater precision and detail than it could devote to the phases of an eclipse. A water spout was of less interest to the official organ, than a mass at the Tuileries or sherbet and syrup at Malmaison. It exhibited a similar, though very properly a subdued, delight, in chronicling the avocations of the imperial brothers and sisters ; for the Princess Pauline and the Prince Joseph had been at the same time admitted to the honors of Monitorial publicity. The movements of the favorite generals, even, were registered in this extatic column, if they offered an occasion, even the most remote, of coupling with them his Majesty's name or the most indifferent of his Majesty's acts. Thus the Moniteur of the 16th of February, 1805, gravely and conspicuously announced that General Leopold Berthier had been gratified with a seat and a ride, the day before, in one of the emperor's carriages.

Napoleon could not avoid noticing—and he did so with evident annoyance—the different use made of their money by those whose birth and former position had accustomed them to the possession of wealth, and by those whom he had himself raised from obscurity and poverty. The nobles of the old régime disbursed their salaries freely, though not prodigally, while the establishments of his own grandees testified to the existence of a spirit of parsimony and illiberality. Napoleon desired the gentlemen of his court to "spend" their money, and not to "invest" it. He did not hesitate to give currency to anecdotes upon the avarice of such of them as deserved it, and was apt to bestow upon them the unamiable title of "grigoux." He felt that they were laying by what they could spare from their necessary expenditure, for the moment when they should perchance be involved in his own fall, and he could ill excuse a forecast which implied, in the protégé, a hope of surviving the ruin of the protector.

Marmont spent more money than any other of Napoleon's generals, whence he was ironically called Marmont I. Junot was for a similar reason called Marmont II. Madame Junot's expenses for her toilet were no less than two hundred thousand francs a year. Useless extravagance such as this, Napoleon condemned, but he encouraged lavish expenditure on the part of those able to afford it.

CHAPTER XIV.

Madame Récamier—Description of her Personal Appearance—Her Character—Fouché's Proposal—Caroline Bonaparte an Accomplice—Madame Récamier's Banishment—Her Wanderings in England, Italy and Switzerland—The Prince of Prussia and the Duke of Wellington in love with her—Canova's Bust of Dante's Beatrice—The Inconsistencies in her Character—Napoleon's Rejection of the Coöperation of Women.

CONSPICUOUS for beauty, virtue and accomplishments, among the ladies of the early imperial epoch, was Madame Récamier, whose name has been already mentioned. She was a native of Lyons, her maiden name being Jeanne-Françoise-Julie-Adelaide Bernard. She was habitually called Juliet, though, as has been aptly said of her, destiny was to furnish her no Romeo. She married in 1793, at the age of sixteen, a banker by the name of Récamier. Her husband was much older than herself, and her feelings toward him seem to have been little more than filial. At the period of which we are speaking she was twenty-seven years old, and was regarded as the most beautiful woman in Europe—Pauline Bonaparte enjoying the lesser credit of being the most beautiful princess. Madame Junot thus speaks of Madame Récamier in her Memoirs:

"It was at this period that I first saw Madame Récamier. I had heard her much spoken of, and I acknowledge that my mother had prejudiced my judgment concerning her, in persuading herself, and consequently me, that Madame Récamier's reputation was wholly exaggerated, and that she must necessarily be a person of such overbearing pretensions that no moderate qualifica-

tions could expect any notice, in presence of her noisy and senseless appropriation of the homage of fashion.

"Great then was my surprise when I beheld that lovely face, so blooming, so childish, and yet so beautiful, and still greater when I observed the timid uneasiness she experienced in her triumph. No doubt it was pleasing to be proclaimed the unrivalled beauty of the fête, but it was evident that she was pained by the envious glances of the women, who could not wholly suppress the ill-will with which they witnessed her monopoly of admiration.

"Madame Récamier truly deserved this homage: she was a really pretty woman![1] Nothing is more common than those everyday faces with large eyes, a straight nose, a mouth with good teeth and rosy lips, the whole accompanied by falling shoulders and well-made limbs. But ask those eyes for a glance of fire, ask those lips to open with an intellectual smile, ask that Greek or Roman nose to derange its solemn line, to show by the smallest movement of the nostrils that this fine face can exhibit a play of the muscles; ask these things, and you will find that your statue will manifest the silence and coldness, as well as the beauty, of marble.

"These requisites Madame Récamier possessed in perfection: the expression of her eye was mild and intellectual; her smile was gracious, her language fascinating; in her whole person was the charm of native grace, goodness and intelligence. She reminded me at first sight of the Madonnas of the pious Italian painters; but the resemblance consisted wholly in expression—not in regularity of features. It was the mind which animated her eyes and blushed in her cheek: the smile which so frequently played upon her rosy lips expressed the unaffected joy of a young heart, happy in pleasing and in being beloved.

"At the time when I first met Madame Récamier, she was in the prime of her beauty and of her brilliant existence. M. Récamier was at the head of one of the first banking-houses of Paris;

---

[1] The portrait of Madame Récamier, upon the opposite page, is from the original painted by Gérard for her husband. It is now at the Abbaye-aux-Bois, at Paris, where Madame Récamier died.

his misfortunes were not then foreseen. He had, therefore, the means of giving to his charming consort all the enjoyments of wealth and luxury, as a poor return for her constant attentions and the happiness which she shed over his home and his life. M. Récamier's house was a delightful residence : nothing could be compared to the fêtes he gave to foreigners recommended to him, and whose choice of a banker was no doubt often determined by the desire of an introduction to his wife. Curiosity attracted them, and they were retained by a charm which acted equally upon old and young, male and female.

"Madame Récamier is an essential character in contemporary memoirs; it is not often that a woman is to be found to embellish the era of her life with attractions such as hers: a woman whose friendship has been courted by persons the most remarkable of the age for their talents; a woman whose beauty has thrown at her feet all the men whose eyes have once been set upon her; whose love has been the object of universal desire, yet whose virtue has remained pure; whose unsullied reputation never suffered from the attacks of jealousy or envy; a woman who could always sacrifice her own enjoyment to afford consolation—which none could do more sweetly and effectually—to any friend in affliction. To the world, Madame Récamier is a celebrated woman: to those who had the happiness to know and to appreciate her, she was a peculiar and gifted being, formed by Nature as a perfect model in one of her most beneficent moods."[1]

There is not probably another woman of modern times upon whom a similar eulogium could be pronounced. But the very fascinations and virtues of Madame Récamier were soon to bring upon her the ban of the emperor's displeasure. Napoleon exiled her from Paris, for reasons which may be briefly detailed. She was residing at her country seat at Clichy, surrounded by all that could render life happy and desirable. Fouché, Napoleon's Minister of Police, one day presented himself, and begged her to

[1] d'Abr. l. 486.

accept the post of lady of honor to the empress. "Consider the emperor's situation," said Fouché; "he wants a guide, a female friend—and where can he find one? Among the wives of his generals? Impossible, for it would excite scandal." "And why are you so obliging," asked Madame Récamier, "as to suppose that scandal would spare me?" "The case is a very different one. You are, to be sure, as young as any of them; but your marriage, and the station in which it places you, have established your reputation: it is pure and unblemished. You are privileged to be the emperor's friend, for it is a friend and not a mistress that he wants. I know the cravings of his heart; I know he is unhappy at not being understood, and that he would gladly exchange hours of victory and noisy acclamations which play round the car without reaching the heart, for a few moments of social and confidential converse. He is weary, too, of daily encountering scenes of jealousy; from this the pure and sacred connection I wish to see established between you and him would be exempt." "But," returned Madame Récamier, quite unconvinced, "how can I ascertain that it would be agreeable to the emperor that I should accept this situation; and how would it please the empress, whose whole household is already appointed? And, besides, I love my liberty."

"I ask nothing of you which will interfere with your liberty," returned Fouché. "You are not requested to undertake any burdensome duty. Your post in the household will be that of the empress's friend, but more particularly the emperor's. The friend of the emperor! The friend of Napoleon! Consider a little: reflect on my proposition, and I am certain, if you are not prejudiced, your noble and generous soul will accept it with delight."

Madame Récamier, dazzled by the seductive offer, did reflect upon the propriety of accepting it. She was yet totally ignorant of the real purpose to which it was the cover and pretext. She felt, as she said, "that in the proposed capacity she might sway with a kindly influence the destinies of millions of men."* In this state of things, she was invited by the Emperor's sister, Caroline, to breakfast at her hotel. The princess, who was either an accomplice of Fouché, or a confidante of Napoleon, conversed of friendship, and the charms of that Platonic sentiment between a man and a pure and virtuous woman. "The Emperor is worthy of such happiness," she said, "and would be fully capable of appreciating it; but he has no such friend. And how is one to be selected for him, from amongst the multitude of our court ladies?"

She then inquired of Madame Récamier if she liked the theatres, and which she preferred. "The Comédie Française," she replied. "Oh, then," said the Princess, "my box is at your service; as it is in the lower tier, it requires no ceremony of dress; promise me to make use of it." Madame Récamier readily promised, and early the next morning received the following note:

"The managers of the Comédie Française are informed that her Imperial Highness, the Princess Caroline, gives Madame Récamier admission to her box. They are likewise informed that when Madame Récamier uses the box, she is to choose her own company; and that no person is to be admitted, even though a member of the Princess's or the Grand Duke's household, without Madame Récamier's special permission."

It was impossible even for a person as guileless and unsuspecting as Madame Récamier, not to be convinced, from the tenor of this note, of the purpose of its writer. The box faced the Emperor's, and the privacy with which she was to occupy it bespoke the intention of the Princess that it was to be the scene of an appointment. Madame Récamier sent her thanks to her Imperial Highness, but never made use of the box. It does not appear that the Emperor or Fouché ever made any further overtures. The latter, however, felt inimical to her for the rejection of his proposal, and, at a subsequent date, seized the occasion of her visit to

Madame de Staël, exiled at Coppet, as a motive for banishing her from Paris. To this the Emperor consented, and her exile was soon publicly announced. General Junot, now Duc d'Abrantès, and deep in the Emperor's confidence, dared not interest himself for her recall. But he wrote thus to his wife : "Laura, my heart is oppressed and sick, when I think of the exile of Madame Récamier. I told you long ago that I had once passionately loved her; my friendship is now only that of a brother, united with a sentiment of respectful admiration. This blow renders desolate the future existence of an unfortunate woman who deserves the homage of all who pronounce her name. Laura, I conjure you, see the Empress—see Queen Hortense—see the Emperor—but no, you must not speak to him. Alas! how can he who is so just, so great, so good, how can he voluntarily oppress a feeble woman!"[1]

Madame Récamier, on being informed of her banishment, said to one of Napoleon's officers, "Ah, sir, a great man may be pardoned the weakness of loving women, but not that of fearing them."

In reference to this matter, an authority noted for its caution says: "It is believed that Napoleon, at the period of his highest glory, was taught by Madame Récamier how little calculated is the most brilliant destiny to dazzle the simple instinct of innocence, or pervert the sentiment of innate dignity."[2]

"Madame Récamier's transient visit to Coppet," says Alison, "was the pretense for including her in Madame de Staël's sentence of banishment. The graces which had won the admiration of all Europe, and which had disdained the advances of the Emperor himself, were consigned in a distant province to the privacy of rural retirement; and the ruler of the East and the West deemed himself insecure on the throne of Charlemagne, unless the finest genius then in Europe and the most beautiful woman in France, were exiled from his dominions."[3]

Pelet, the reporter of the debates of the Council of State, says upon the same subject, "Napoleon's jealousy of Madame Récamier's beauty and influence carried him to very unjustifiable lengths. Her husband, who was a great banker in Paris, became bankrupt, and he seriously proposed in the Council of State 'that she should be subjected to joint responsibility with him for the debts of the bank!' In wishing thus to render her liable, he was actuated by a special spite against that celebrated lady. The little court with which she was surrounded, on account of her incomparable beauty, excited his jealousy as much as did the talents of Madame de Staël. Elevated as he was above all others, he could not see without pain, that she shared with him the public attention. He could not even endure that M. Gall, with his well known system of craniology, should be more talked of than himself."[1]

"Madame Récamier could not love Napoleon," says Thibaudeau, apologetically, "but this was no reason why he should let fall upon her his arm of iron. Her exile has been attributed to her refusal to be lady of honor and the Emperor's mistress: Fouché is said to have managed the intrigue, and to have revenged himself for his failure. In view of the reasonable motives for her banishment, it is, to say the least, useless to suggest romantic ones."[2] He suggests no reasonable ones, however, and there appears no reason to doubt the entire accuracy of the story as we have given it.

Madame Récamier was now forced to lead an errant and a homeless life. She spent many years at Lyons, in the poor accommodations afforded by a second class inn. She amused her leisure with her piano, drawing materials and books. She was visited by many persons from Paris, sufficiently courageous to brave the displeasure of Napoleon. She went to Naples, where Murat and Caroline Bonaparte were upon the throne. Though the former had been one of her rejected lovers, and the latter was the sister

[1] Opinions de Napoléon, 261.　　[2] Thib. iv. 201.

of her persecutor, they both gave her every assurance of interest, and exerted themselves to mitigate the hardships of her exile.

At Rome, Canova executed her bust—not the bust of Madame Récamier, as he said himself, but the marble embodiment of the impression he received in contemplating her. This exquisite work does not bear the name of the model who sat for it, Canova preferring to make it an ideal; it is entitled "Dante's Beatrice," realizing, by what seems an apparition too lovely not to be celestial, the vision of the Florentine poet.

In England, Madame Récamier was received by the Prince of Wales, afterwards king, and by the Duchess of Devonshire. Her portrait was engraved by Bartolozzi; the demand for it was universal, and large orders came even from distant lands, from the Ionian Islands, and from Hindostan and China.

She made frequent and prolonged stays at Madame de Staël's residence at Coppet. This spot was the scene of the most romantic event of her life. The Prince of Prussia, being on his way to Italy, a prisoner on parole, after the battle of Eylau, stopped at Coppet, with the intention of paying his respects to Madame de Staël, and of then proceeding on his journey. But meeting Madame Récamier there, he remained all summer. The Prince and the beauty, both victims of Napoleon's ambition, soon felt for each other a mutual interest: that of the Prince ripened into passionate love. He conceived the plan of marrying her, in spite of his rank and her husband. He confided the project to Madame de Staël, who eagerly favored it, "thinking," according to Napoleon, "that it might throw a romantic interest upon her country-seat."[1] He was soon recalled to Berlin, and from thence pressed his suit by letters, with the same warmth he had used in person. Madame Récamier, who would appear not to have been indifferent to her suitor, refused, however, to share his royal honors; the manners of the age would have excused her in seeking for a divorce; but her generosity and good feeling towards

[1] Las Cases, iv. 195.

her husband. now advanced in years—to say nothing of a higher sense of duty—prevented her from attempting a release by means so unworthy. The Prince then wrote with his own blood and sent to Madame Récamier, a promise of marriage in case the death of her husband should render the alliance possible. She preserved the paper for a short time and then returned it.

Napoleon spoke of Madame Récamier at St. Helena, and said that various letters intercepted by the police and read by them, contained unequivocal proof of the extreme attachment of the Prince of Prussia. This episode in the life of Madame Récamier furnished Madame de Genlis with the subject of one of her most interesting romances : "Le Château de Coppet."

The fall of Napoleon restored Madame Récamier to Paris and to society Lord Wellington, who, it would appear, was peculiarly susceptible to the charms and attractions of women, was there in 1814. He, too, made a declaration to Madame Récamier, being, according to the Duchess d'Abrantès, keenly bitten by the epidemic ; she received his advances according to her custom, which was never to consider the proposition as insulting, and to seek to convert the lover into a friend. The Iron Duke was graciously given to understand that to indulge the hope of changing her resolution was a simple waste of time. But after the battle of Waterloo, he remembered that Madame Récamier had been exiled and persecuted by Napoleon, and thought that perhaps his victory over the tyrant would plead with her in his favor. He hastened to the house of Madame Récamier, and, throwing himself upon his knees, exclaimed : "I have conquered him!" She treated him this time with severity, and rebuked him with such sternness as she could command, for presuming to suppose that his victory over the French could be a title to favor in her eyes. She begged him to remember that the sword he had laid at her feet was stained with the blood of her own countrymen. Madame Junot does not fail to make merry over the discomfiture of the hero of Waterloo : "He was on his knees, and in a position not unlike that of the Knight of the Rueful Countenance, to whom, indeed, he bore a singular resemblance; for at this period he had all the thinness and a good deal of the figure of that cavalier: do what he would, his face and demeanor never were those of a man accustomed to conquer by the heart as by the sword."[1]

Madame Récamier received the advances of age not merely with resignation, but with satisfaction, and society was to learn from her who was deemed the most perfect woman in Europe, how gracefully the sceptre may be laid aside. "When I saw," she said, "that the little chimney-sweepers in the street no longer turned to look at me, I felt that it was all over." She died at l'Abbaye-aux-Bois, early in the year 1849.

The best appreciation of the character of Madame Récamier is that of M. de Sainte-Beuve. The following passage, though it perhaps does her injustice, by explaining her constant virtue upon the supposition that she was incapable of love, is nevertheless eloquent and descriptive:

"In regard to Madame Récamier, I ask this question: Did she ever love? I answer, confidently, no. No, she never loved; she never loved, and never felt passion. Instead of possessing that deep need of loving borne by every soul attuned to tenderness, she was actuated by an infinite desire to please, or rather to be loved, and by an active will and an ardent capacity to repay love by kindness. We who saw her in her declining years, and who caught here and there a ray of her divine goodness, we know that the source was profound and the stream abundant, and that she warmed her friendships by that fire with which she never kindled love.

"There are certain natures that are born pure, and which receive an inalienable gift of innocence. They cross, unharmed, like Arethusa, the perilous wave: they resist fire like the children of Holy Writ, whose furnace was cooled by gentle dews. Madame Récamier had need of this protecting genius around her

[1] Mémoires de la Restauration, iii. 278.

and in her, for the world in which she lived was a tumultuous and ardent one, and she never sought either to shun or to disarm temptation.

"At the moment of her first appearance, under the Consulate, already for some years married, we see her at once surrounded, feasted and passionately loved. Lucien, Napoleon's brother, was the first historical personage to love her. Lucien loved her; he was not repelled, but was never to be accepted. Such is the delicate distinction. I saw, not long since, in the palace of the late King of Holland, at the Hague, an admirable statue of Eve—Eve in that supreme crisis of innocence, in which a woman plays with the danger that threatens her, or talks of it under her voice, to herself or with another. This moment of indecision, which with Eve came to harm, was, in Madame Récamier, repeated and prolonged in a thousand shapes, during the brilliant and often injudicious years of her youth: but it was always checked and subdued in time by a stronger sentiment and her ever present virtue. Exposed to the passions which she excited and of which she was really ignorant, she was as imprudent and yet as self-reliant, as curious and yet as confident, as a child or a novice.

"She confronted the peril with a smile, and in consciousness of safety, not unlike the Christian kings of the olden time, who went forth in holy week to heal the sick. She did not doubt her own purity nor her sweet conciliatory magic. She seemed almost to seek to pierce your heart, that she might perform the miracle of restoring you. When an unfortunate complained or reproached her, she said with provoking clemency, 'Come and I will cure you.' And she succeeded with many, with the greater number even. All her friends, with few exceptions, were her lovers at the outset. She had many, and she preserved them nearly all. M. de Montlosier said to her one day that she could say with the Cid: 'Five Hundred of my friends.' She was really a sorceress in her art of converting love insensibly to friendship, at the same time that the latter was suffered to retain all the perfume of the former sentiment. She would have arrested the emotions of every heart at April. There her own had remained, at that first dawn of spring, when the orchard, yet leafless, is filled with pale, though fragrant blossoms.

"Bernadotte was one of her chevaliers. Mathieu de Montmorency loved her passionately, and was thus the rival of his own son, Adrien. He wrote to her on one occasion thus: 'My son worships you, and you know my own sentiments. It is the lot of all the Montmorencies, indeed; though we do not all die, we are at least all stricken.' Madame Récamier was the first to narrate and to smile at these incidents in her life. But serious complications sometimes followed. It was not every man thus attracted and ensnared, that would be as easily led and eluded as were this pacific dynasty of the Montmorencies. Her gentle hand could not always subdue the mutinies and the violence that her provoking loveliness produced. In playing with the passions which she only sought to charm, but which she inflamed more than she believed, she resembled the youngest of the Graces, yoking and irritating lions. Imprudent as Innocence, she loved her own peril and the peril of others. But in this cruel and dangerous practice, she troubled many hearts, and ulcerated others. Though she never knew it, women were sacrificed and wounded to the quick for her sake. This is a serious matter, and one which she finally came to comprehend; it is a lesson which the profound respect we attach to her noble memory does not forbid us to call to mind. So she did not regret her youth when it had passed, nor the storms of passion she had been wont to provoke. She could not conceive of happiness beyond the pale of duty. She placed the ideal of romance in marriage, where unfortunately she did not find it. More than once, in the midst of her triumphs, and at festivities of which she was the queen, she withdrew for an instant to weep."[1]

Such was the character of this remarkable and charming woman.

[1] Causeries du Lundi, I. 99.

as drawn by one who has made the epoch of her career his study. Her exile by Napoleon was an act not only unjust, but impolitic and injudicious in a reformer of morals and a renovator of society. But Napoleon was perversely unwilling to acknowledge the influence of women, and he probably never realized that in banishing Madame Récamier, he was positively repelling the services and the coöperation of one who, beyond all others, beyond Josephine even, was capable of gracing, ameliorating and moulding the restored society of the Empire. This influence she did exert, later, upon the society of the Restoration, at a period, too, when her beauty was less dazzling, and when there was also less need for its beneficent exercise. She might have done for Napoleon what she did for Louis XVIII. Under the latter sovereign, it was said of her that she brought the art of friendship to perfection; that she disarmed party spirit, softened the asperity of discord, reconciled hostility and arrested dispute. But Napoleon did not care to enlist this species of influence in his cause; and it was this indifference which deterred him, when Madame Récamier's exile was proposed for another motive, from opposing a sacrifice at once wrong in its principle and inopportune as to its policy.

CHAPTER XV.

The Code of Etiquette—The Grand Marshal—Governors of the Palaces—Prefects—Chamberlains—Grand Master of the Horse—The Pages—The Aids-de-Camp—Grand Master of Ceremonies—The Palace of the Tuileries—Its Divisions and Apartments—Meals—Punctilio at Table—Napoleon's Opinion on Eating in Public.

THE etiquette, the ceremonial and the ritual of observances proper for the new régime, were laboriously discussed in a sort of Council of State, assembled for the purpose, and Napoleon took an active part in the debate. He was somewhat of a formalist and martinet in these matters, and sought, by personally attending to them, to surround his throne with the traditional honors and the customary accessories of legitimacy. The division of labor and the distribution of offices grouped together in this chapter, were in a great measure the work of the Emperor himself, and form a singular proof of the versatility of the man of whom it was said that "he thought at the same moment of the invasion of England and the cut of a chamberlain's coat, and who dated from his head-quarters at the Kremlin, the famous regulations for the Comédie Française, known as the Decree of Moscow." "Whoever," said Madame de Staël, "could suggest an additional piece of etiquette from the olden time, propose an additional reverence, a new mode of knocking at the door of an ante-chamber, a more ceremonious method of presenting a petition, or folding a letter, was received as if he had been a benefactor of the human race."

The code of etiquette, a bulky collection of eight hundred and nineteen articles, was intended to anticipate every possible situation and supply directions for meeting every contingency, whether proximate or remote. Napoleon gave his reasons at St. Helena: "I was rising above the level of the crowd, and it was indispensable to create myself an exterior, to compose a dignity and a gravity, in one word, to establish a ceremonial: otherwise I should have been daily tapped upon the shoulder. In France, we are naturally inclined to ill-timed familiarity; we are instinctively courtiers and obsequious at the outset; but, if not repressed, this familiarity soon ripens into insolence."[1] On another occasion, he said that a monarch only existed in a state of civilization, and was always dressed; he could not exist naked and in a state of nature.

From this volume, we make such condensed extracts as are necessary to give the reader an adequate idea of the duties of the various ladies and gentlemen composing the imperial household; of the ceremonial customary on official as well as informal occasions, and of the salaries attached to the different situations and sinecures of the court. The names are appended of such functionaries as seem of importance, during the first period of the Empire—extending from the Coronation to the Divorce.

THE GRAND MARSHAL OF THE PALACE.

The duties of this office were the military command in the imperial palaces, the responsibility of their repair and furnishing, the control of the tables, the fire and light, the silver, the linen, the liveries and the wages. He was the head of the police, and of the detachments of the Imperial Guard, detailed for service in the palaces; he received reports of every event that happened, and of every individual who was lodged within the gates, or who obtained admittance into them. He alone was empowered to inflict punishment. No furniture could be brought in or carried

[1] Las Cases, iv. 271.

out without an order from him. When the Emperor was with the army or was travelling, the Grand Marshal provided his lodging and that of his suite. Upon the first entry of the Emperor into a palace, after an absence of any length of time, he was received at the door by the Grand Marshal, and was conducted by him to the apartment prepared for him. At ceremonious dinners, and on state occasions, the Grand Marshal announced the meals, conducted their Majesties to their seats, and served the Emperor with wine during the repast. He caused the prefects of the palace to furnish him every six months an inventory of the porcelain, glass, linen and silver belonging to their Majesties. He presented to the Emperor, at his levee, the officers who had been appointed to places in the household, and received, unless Napoleon preferred to do so himself, their oaths of fidelity and allegiance. He was responsible for the exactitude of the post-office attached to each of the palaces. The Grand Marshal was lodged, served at a table of his own, and furnished with horses and vehicles, at the expense of the crown.

GOVERNORS OF THE PALACES.

There was but one Grand Marshal for all the imperial residences, but there was a governor to each. The duty of this officer was, generally, the execution of the various details of which, in theory, the Grand Marshal was the supervisor, and for which he was in reality accountable, though he delegated all active interference. The governor made, personally, a round of inspection every night, and received constant notification of the progress of events from the sentinels, the warders, the servants and the gardeners. He received the pass-word from the Grand Marshal and gave it to those who required it.

It was natural that the governor, following the example of the Grand Marshal, should seek to throw off his burden upon the shoulders of another. In order to meet this necessity, a lieutenant governor was appointed. This gentleman, in his turn, relieved himself of a certain portion of his duties by intrusting them to a functionary called the adjutant. That this individual also succeeded in transferring a share of his business to a subaltern, the Code of Etiquette doth not affirm; all that can be said is, that it is more than probable.

THE PREFECTS OF THE PALACES.

The prefect on duty—for he was relieved every week—personally inspected once a day, the kitchen, cellars, pantries, store closets and warehouses. He counted the silver, and could call the servants by name. As the Emperor retired for the night, the prefect waited to learn the hour of breakfast for the morrow. At the family and unofficial dinners of their Majesties the prefect announced the meal, seated the persons invited, and notified the kitchen and the pantry that all was ready.

CHAMBERLAINS.

The service of the chamberlains included every thing connected with the honors and etiquette of the palace, the audiences, the prestation of oaths, the festivities, the invitations, the theatrical and operatic representations given at the Tuileries and at St. Cloud, the visits of their Majesties to the theatres of Paris, the wardrobe and library of the Emperor, the ushers and valets-de-chambre. The Grand Chamberlain controlled this whole department. At imperial banquets it was his duty to present to the Emperor, before and after eating, water to wash his hands. He presided at the designing and making of all presents to be given to crowned heads, princes and ambassadors, and which were to be paid for from the privy purse.

One of the chamberlains filled the office of Master of the Wardrobe. His duty was to order and take charge of all the objects composing his Majesty's toilet—clothing, linen, lace, shoes, costumes, cordons, scarfs, and other decorations of the Legion of Honor, as well as all the jewelry belonging personally to the Emperor—such as did not form part of the crown jewels. He took the orders of the Emperor every morning upon his apparel; and usually, in the absence of the Grand Chamberlain, assisted his Majesty in donning his coat, attached to his person the order or cordon desired, and handed him his sword, hat and gloves. On occasions of state, he placed the mantle upon the imperial shoulders.

When their Majesties desired to employ the crown diamonds, the Grand Chamberlain, or Napoleon himself, gave a written order upon the Treasurer-general to the Master of the Wardrobe for those of the Emperor, and to the Lady of Honor for those of the Empress. The Master of the Wardrobe, and the Lady of Honor, upon receiving them, signed a receipt in the treasurer's register; he, in turn, upon receiving them back again, discharged the bearers from responsibility by appending his signature to blanks held by them and prepared for the purpose.

THE GRAND MASTER OF THE HORSE AND HIS OFFICERS.

The Grand Master of the Horse held the control and surveillance of the stables, of the couriers, the pages, and the weapons of his Majesty: he was also superintendent of the stud of St. Cloud. He had the entire direction of everything relative to the journeys of the Emperor: he communicated to the persons invited on any occasion to accompany him, his Majesty's desires.

The Grand Master of the Horse always attended the Emperor when with the army. In the absence of the Constable, he carried the imperial sword. If the Emperor's horse were wounded or killed, he offered him his own. He remained, mounted, at the left of his Majesty, in order to be near the left stirrup. He lodged in the camp, within call of the Emperor. He presented to his Majesty the pages, upon the attainment of their eighteenth year, and who were therefore qualified to enter the army. He was always attended by a musket bearer, whose duty it was to keep in order, to load, and to discharge, if not used, the fire-arms of his Majesty. He was lodged at the expense of the crown, and used for his own service the horses and vehicles of the Emperor.

At official dinners, he gave the Emperor his chair, and withdrew it at the close of the meal. During its progress, he stood at his Majesty's left. When the Emperor quitted the palace to mount his horse, the Grand Master preceded him, and assisted him into the saddle, presenting him the whip, the reins and the stirrup. He was responsible for the solidity of the vehicles, the intelligence and skill of the grooms, and the soundness and breeding of the horses. He superintended the education, the meals and the lodging of the pages.

He was often replaced, in these various duties, by subordinate equerries, one or two of whom were always in attendance upon him, when personally present with the Emperor. If his Majesty let his whip or other article drop, it was picked up by the first equerry, who handed it to the Grand Equerry, who restored it to the Emperor. The first equerry, or the equerry on duty, received from the secretary of the palace, giving a receipt in exchange, the despatches to be forwarded by courier; he was responsible for the strength of the seals and envelopes. He received also the incoming despatches—if brought by a courier—and gave them himself into the hands of his Majesty, in the daytime, and, during the night, to the aid-de-camp in the ante-chamber. He scrupulously examined the courier's way-bill, to make sure that he had delivered all that had been intrusted to him; he also verified his time-table, and if he found him behindhand, sent him to the Grand Master of the Horse for reprimand or punishment.

THE PAGES.

The duty of the pages—of whom there were thirty-six at the least, and sixty at the most, and who entered the service at the age of fourteen and quitted it at eighteen, for the army—was to wait upon their Majesties, to carry messages and to bring back the answers. At Paris, two always attended the Emperor in the palace: one followed him on horseback, whether he rode or drove. At St. Cloud, only one was in attendance, but another was always in readiness, at the Hôtel des Pages, to replace him. At audiences and at mass, eight pages were usually in attendance; and when the Emperor rode in his state carriage, six sat behind the coachman, and six more in the rumble. If the Emperor had not returned to the palace at nightfall, the pages on duty waited at the gate with white wax torches, and on his arrival conducted him to the ante-chamber, where they gave up their torches to the valets-de-chambre. The pages, besides carrying the messages of their Majesties, might be sent upon errands by the princes and princesses, the aids-de-camp, the chamberlains and the equerries. They were obliged in all cases to communicate the result of their mission to the person who had charged them with it. At the chase, the first page held the Emperor's carbine. At the hunt, eight pages passed the muskets from those who loaded them to the Emperor, while a line of footmen passed them back from the Emperor to be loaded again. All game killed by his Majesty belonged of right to the first page: rank was determined by length of service.

THE AIDS-DE-CAMP.

The Emperor had twelve aids-de-camp in his service, principally generals in the army. Their rank was determined, not by military grade, but by the date of their commission as aid. One of these officers was always in attendance. He was obliged to have a horse constantly saddled, and a carriage constantly harnessed. When the Emperor slept, the aid-de-camp who watched in the room preceding the bed-chamber, became the guardian of his person. A despatch, arriving at night, was brought to the aid-de-camp's door, which was kept carefully locked. He received the missive, again locked the door, and then knocked at that of his Majesty. On parade occasions and in military movements, the aids-de-camp marched in front of the Emperor; the one on service for the day, but six paces in front, and behind his colleagues. In camp, the aids performed the entire duty which at the palace devolved upon the chamberlains.

THE GRAND MASTER OF CEREMONIES.

The duty of this officer was to draw up the plans and programmes of the rites and festivities which their Majesties attended —such as the Coronation, the Reception of the members of the Legion of Honor, the Opening of the Legislative Session, the Fête of the Champ de Mars, &c. He fixed the time and place, assigned places to individuals and corporations, according to the rules of precedence or the peculiar proprieties of the occasion. The programme became official upon the approval of his Majesty. The Grand Master received personally the Emperor's orders during the progress of any ceremony. It was also his duty, at receptions and presentations, to introduce the ambassadors into the imperial presence.

THE PALACE OF THE TUILERIES.

The residence of his Majesty was divided into three suites of rooms—the Grand or Festive Apartment, the Ordinary Apartment of the Emperor, and the Ordinary Apartment of the Empress.

The Grand Apartment consisted of a concert-room, a first and second parlor, the throne room, and the Emperor's room. The concert-room served as an ante-chamber and as a place of waiting for the pages. The two parlors were for the Grand Officers of their Majesties, the members of the Senate and the Council of State, the generals of division, archbishops and bishops. The throne-room was open to the princes and princesses of the imperial family and of the Empire, the ministers and the presidents of the Senate and Legislature. The Emperor's room was sacred to their Majesties, and no one, no matter what his rank, could enter it unless bidden to do so. A chamberlain was at hand to bear the Emperor's commands.

The Emperor's Ordinary Apartment was divided into two suites—a superior and a private suite. The latter consisted of a study, an interior study, a topographical bureau and a bed-chamber. To enter the study was simply intrusive, but to enter the interior study was sacrilegious. The door was guarded by a personage styled the Guardian of the Portfolio, who required a written order from the Emperor to allow any one to penetrate its hallowed and mysterious precincts.

MEALS.

On occasions of ceremonious dinners, the table was elevated upon a platform, and the two imperial chairs were placed under a canopy. The doors of the room were guarded by ushers. The Grand Master of Ceremonies had charge of the invitations, a list of which he received from their Majesties. He gave notice of the hour, the place of assembly, the arrangement of the tables and the rank of the guests, to the Grand Marshal of the Palace.

When the Emperor was ready, he intimated the fact to the Grand Marshal, who transmitted the intelligence to the first prefect, who at once sent word to the pantry and the kitchen, from whence everything required for the first course was immediately brought. The plate of the Emperor was placed at the right of that of the Empress; the Emperor's "nef," containing his napkin, and his "cadenas," containing his drinking-cup, were also placed at his right, those of the Empress at her left. These preparations being accomplished, the first prefect signified to the Grand Marshal to proceed to summon their Majesties. The following order was preserved in the line of march:

The pages on duty; an assistant master of ceremonies; the prefects of the week; the first prefect and a master of ceremonies; the Grand Marshal of the Palace and the Grand Master of Ceremonies; the Empress, her first equerry and her first chamberlain; the Emperor, with the Colonel-general on duty; the Grand Chamberlain and the Grand Master of the Horse; the Grand Almoner.

When their Majesties arrived at their seats, the Grand Chamberlain offered a finger-bowl to the Emperor, the first prefect offering one to the Empress; the Grand Master of the Horse presented the Emperor his chair, the first equerry performing a similar service for the Empress; the Grand Marshal unlocking the Emperor's "nef," and the first chamberlain unlocking that of the Empress, supplied therefrom their Majesties with napkins. Upon the conclusion of these preliminaries, the Grand Almoner approached the table in front of the canopy, invoked the divine blessing upon the meal, and then withdrew.

Servants in livery waited upon the guests, the grand functionaries and the pages serving their Majesties. When the Emperor desired to drink, the first prefect poured out the wine and water, handed the goblet to the Grand Marshal, who transmitted it to his Majesty, who himself conveyed it to his lips. When the Empress desired to drink, the first equerry mixed and the second prefect handed. The stewards carved, and the pages carried the plates. A prefect poured out the Emperor's coffee, a page presented it upon a golden platter to the Grand Chamberlain, who passed it on to the Emperor; the first chamberlain rendering himself similarly useful to the Empress. After the repast, finger-bowls were brought to the Emperor by the Grand Chamberlain, to the Empress by the first chamberlain; the Grand Master of the Horse drew back the Emperor's chair, the first equerry that of the Empress: the imperial napkins were received into the hands of the Grand Marshal and first prefect.

On ordinary and intimate occasions, their Majesties took their meals in their private apartments; these were as remarkable for their absence of etiquette, as the more formal festivities were for the excess of punctilio and the fantastic prescriptions of artificial decorum. Dinner was always served at six, and their Majesties dined alone, except on Sundays, when the members of the imperial family were admitted. None of them were allowed armchairs but Napoleon's mother; the royal brothers and sisters sat upon simple chairs. Dinner rarely lasted over eighteen minutes, and comprised one course and dessert: the Empress poured out the Emperor's coffee—a reminiscence of the Consulate.

The Grand Couvert, or the public state dinners of the imperial family, a prominent feature of the Code, was instituted with some hesitation, and Napoleon afterwards regretted it, as a ceremony not in harmony with the dignity of modern manners. "It is very well," he said, "to look at the sovereign at church, or at the theatre, or the promenade; but to see him eat, is ridiculous for the eater and the spectator. Royalty, when it has become a magistracy, should only show itself to the public in the garb and the exercise of office, and free from the infirmities and the needs of humanity."

CHAPTER XVI.

The Members of Napoleon's Imperial Household—The Almoners; Chamberlains; Marshals; Masters of the Horse and Hounds; Intendants; Physicians; Surgeons—The Subordinate Service—Napoleon's Fondness for Etiquette—Its Consequences.

IN the preceding chapter we described the functions and attributes of the several officers of the imperial household. In the present chapter we give the names of each of the incumbents of these various places, as they were originally appointed by the Emperor, commencing with his Majesty's Chapel.

ALMONRY.

GRAND ALMONER: His Imperial Highness Cardinal Fesch, Archbishop of Lyons, half brother of Napoleon's mother. This office was asked for by Prince Ferdinand de Rohan, the representative of a family which had held it for a century under the monarchy. Napoleon preferred to place his uncle at the head of the French clergy, and made Prince Ferdinand first almoner to the Empress. The annual salary attached to the former office was 25,000 francs.

FIRST ALMONER: M. Charrier de la Roche, Bishop of Versailles, and the largest wholesale wine-dealer in the department. Salary, 18,000 francs.

ALMONERS IN ORDINARY: The Abbés Maurice de Broglie and de Pradt. The latter was the most notorious renegade of the imperial annals. When appointed, he said that he was to be almoner to the god Mars; and upon Napoleon's fall, he called him Jupiter Scapin, or Jupiter Buffoon. Salaries, 15,000 francs.

CHAPLAINS : MM. Fournier and Lacotte. Salaries, 12,500 francs.

MASTER OF CEREMONIES OF THE CHAPEL : M. de Sambucy. Salary, 15,000 francs.

COMPOSER OF MUSIC FOR THE CHAPEL : M. Lesueur. Salary, 12,500 francs.

TENOR SINGER : Crescentini. Salary, 50,000 francs. Eleven others, with proportionate salaries.

CHAMBERLAINS.

GRAND CHAMBERLAIN : Talleyrand, Minister of Foreign Affairs. Salary, 200,000 francs.

FIRST CHAMBERLAIN : M. de Remusat, the same who held a prominent situation in Bonaparte's consular household. Salary, 30,000 francs.

CHAMBERLAINS IN ORDINARY : At first six, then fourteen, then fifty in number. Salaries, 25,000 francs.

LIBRARIANS : Denina and Rippaut. Salaries, 7,500 francs.

MINIATURE PAINTER : Isabey. This renowned artist executed the portraits of all the personages inhabiting the imperial palaces. He worked with great rapidity, throwing off three dozen miniatures in a week.

MARSHALS.

GRAND MARSHAL OF THE PALACE : Duroc. Salary, 75,000 francs.

DEPUTY MARSHALS : Colonels Reynaud and Clément, Captain Segur, and Lieutenant Tascher, cousin of the Empress. The duties of these gentlemen confined them principally to the courtyard of the palace. Salaries, 12,500 francs.

GOVERNORS OF THE PALACES : Eight in number, each with a salary of 25,000 francs.

PREFECTS OF THE PALACE : Three in number—MM. de Luçay, de Bausset and de St. Didier. Salaries, 15,000 francs.

PRIVATE SECRETARY : At one period, Clarke ; at another, Bourrienne ; at another, Meneval. Salary, 25,000 francs.

UNDER SECRETARIES : Four in number. Salaries, 12,500 francs.

MASTERS OF THE HORSE.

GRAND MASTER : M. de Caulaincourt. Salary, 50,000 francs.

EQUERRY CAVALCADOURS : Colonels Durosnel, Defrance, Lefebvre, Vatier. Salaries, 25,000 francs.

GOVERNOR OF THE PAGES : Gen. Gardanne, a stern, impassible and impartial Mentor, though the Parisians thought proper to make a pun upon his name, and to call him " Garde ânes," or Keeper of the Donkeys. Salary, 25,000 francs.

SUB-GOVERNORS OF THE PAGES : Abbé Gandon, almoner, and Colonel d'Assigny. Salaries, 12,500 francs.

INSTRUCTORS OF THE PAGES : Ten in number, with a salary of 3,000 francs each.

PAGES : Thirty-six in number at the outset, and lastly sixty. Salaries, 2,000 francs each.

MASTERS OF THE HOUNDS.

GRAND MASTER : Alexandre Berthier, Minister of War. Berthier was passionately fond of hunting, and disliked extremely to attend his Majesty to the forests, where the etiquette acted as a restraint upon huntsmen, horses and hounds. He one day told Napoleon that the weather was unpropitious, and that the dogs would be unable to keep the scent. The hunt was therefore postponed, and Berthier went on a private excursion for deer at Gros-Bois. The day was unusually fine, and the scent of the pack exquisitely keen. Napoleon laughed at the mystification, but was too fond of Berthier to reprimand him. However, he never again consulted him in regard to weather suitable for sporting. Salary, 75,000 francs.

CAPTAIN OF THE HUNT: M. d'Hannecourt, an excellent huntsman; he lived in the forests over which it was his mission to preside. Salary, 20,000 francs.

DEPUTY MASTERS OF THE HOUNDS: Twelve in number, with a salary of 15,000 francs each. The musket-bearer, M. Boterne, had but one eye. This circumstance, apparently a deficiency, was said by the wits to be an advantage, as he dispensed with the preliminary of shutting one eye, on taking aim.

CEREMONIAL.

GRAND MASTER OF CEREMONIES: M. de Ségur, a cosmopolite, linguist and courtier. He did not consider himself qualified for the office, but said that he should be glad to acquire some knowledge of etiquette. He remarked that his case was much like that of the king's new librarian, whose uncle observed to him, on his nomination, "Now, nephew, you will have a fine opportunity to learn to read!" Salary, 75,000 francs.

MASTERS OF CEREMONIES AND INTRODUCERS OF THE AMBASSADORS: MM. de Salmatoris and de Cramayel. Salaries, 25,000 francs.

ASSISTANT MASTERS: MM. d'Aignan and Dargainaratz. Salaries, 20,000 francs.

A CAPTAIN OF THE HERALDS, and four heralds.

INTENDANCE.

INTENDANT-GENERAL OF THE HOUSEHOLD: M. Claret de Fleurieu, a severe accountant, a zealous administrator and a discreet adviser. Elisa Bonaparte, in speaking of his excessive caution, remarked, "So prudent is he, that it is with visible constraint, and evident fright at his own temerity, that he ventures to ask of an intimate friend, 'My dear sir, how do you do?'" Salary, 50,000 francs.

First Painter: Louis David.

Architects: Fontaine, attached to the Louvre and the Tuileries; Raymond, to the Chateaux of St. Cloud and Meudon; Trepzat, to the palace of Versailles, the two Trianons and Rambouillet. Salaries, 25,000 francs.

MEDICAL SERVICE.

First Physician: Corvisart. Salary, 50,000 francs. Physician in ordinary, Hallé. Six physicians attached to the palace.

First Surgeon: Boyer. Salary, 25,000 francs. Surgeon in ordinary, Yvan. Six surgeons attached to the palace.

First Apothecary: Salary, 7,500 francs. Two apothecaries in ordinary; an oculist; M. Bousquet, dentist.

TREASURY OF THE CROWN.

Treasurer: M. Estève, of whose office under the Consulate, and of whose singular fate, we have already spoken. He ably seconded the Emperor in his attempts to prevent depredations and useless expenditure. Salary, 50,000 francs.

Administrator of the Crown Forests: M. Perrache-Franqueville. Salary, 25,000 francs.

Secretary of State for the Imperial Family: Regnault de St. Jean d'Angely. Salary, 75,000.

Notary: M. Raguideau.

SUBORDINATE SERVICE.

Five Valets-de-Chambre: Of whom the first was Constant —Louis Constant Wairy. His service was zealous and intelligent, and above all, disinterested, for he left Napoleon, after fifteen years' uninterrupted devotion, as poor as when he entered the palace. He abandoned him, however, upon his abdication, and wrote six volumes of imperial memoirs.

FOUR USHERS ; THREE STEWARDS ; FOUR OUTRIDERS ; TWELVE FOOTMEN.

ONE MAMELUKE : Roustan, the slave of the sheik Al-Bekey, and brought by Bonaparte from Egypt, and attached to his service. He approached the imperial person more intimately than any other domestic of the household. He, too, deserted Napoleon upon his fall.

THREE COACHMEN : One of whom, Germain, but always called Cæsar by Napoleon, on account of the bravery he displayed in Egypt, was the favorite. It was he who drove Bonaparte on the night of the explosion of the Infernal Machine of the Rue Ste. Nicaise, and to his address on that occasion was due, in some degree, the escape of the First Consul. Napoleon said at St. Helena that Cæsar was intoxicated on the evening in question, and that he took the explosion for a military salute. In this Cæsar was calumniated and Napoleon misinformed. When the latter sallied forth at night, incognito, Cæsar was always required to be upon the box, and, on these occasions, without livery.

Such is a rapid view of the household established in 1804, which was subsequently extended in number and augmented in splendor. It was Napoleon's undue love of etiquette and punctilio which rendered him accessible to many of the influences which contributed to his downfall. When Consul, he had forbidden his former equals and companions to address him with the "thee" and "thou" of intimacy; and now, as Emperor, he still further stiffened the language of friendship and the intercourse even of kindred, by a pervading leaven of formality and reserve. Well-wishers no longer dared to speak the truth, for Napoleon now preferred the tongues that dripped incense. Closing his ears and his heart to the language of disinterested advisers, he condemned himself to listen only to the poisoned flatteries of those who secretly and insidiously plotted his ruin. The Count de Narbonne, former minister of Louis XVI., was one day commissioned to give an unimportant despatch to Napoleon. He knelt upon one knee, and presented the missive upon the crown of his hat. "Upon my word, what is all this?" asked Napoleon. "This is the way we did under Louis XVI.," returned the count. "Ah! very well, very well," said the Emperor, evidently gratified by the revival of the usage. In time, this fancy for the honors and traditions of legitimacy, coupled with the desire of founding a dynasty and transmitting his name, led him to seek an alliance with a house of royal lineage. This step, involving the divorce from Josephine, was the first of a series of errors conducting at last to Elba and Waterloo.

The desire of continuing to exercise an influence, through posterity, seems to be instinctive in the human heart, and this is generally powerful in proportion to the energy and achievements of ambition. It is this sentiment which constructs a throne and encircles it with a peerage; it is this which induces, in the possessors of wealth, the founding of families and the perpetuation of estates. That Napoleon should have fallen in a measure through such temptations, may deprive him of a portion of our worship as a hero, while it brings him within the circle of common sympathies as a man.

CHAPTER XVII.

The Household of the Empress Josephine—Prince Ferdinand de Rohan—General Nansouty—The Duchess d'Aiguillon—Madame de Larochefoucauld—Madame de Lavalette—Madame Gazani—M'lle Avrillon—Georgette Ducrest—The Pages, Ushers, Valets, Footmen—Josephine's Extravagance and consequent Quarrels with Napoleon—Talleyrand and Bourrienne the Mediators between them—The Beauties of the Court—The Household of Madame Mère

THE household of the Empress Josephine, as it was organized in 1804, consisted of the following individuals, filling the various situations created by the code of etiquette:

FIRST ALMONER: Prince Ferdinand de Rohan, formerly archbishop and Prince de Cambray; the heir of one of the most illustrious houses in France. Salary, 25,000 francs.

FIRST MASTER OF THE HORSE: Count and Senator d'Harville. This was the highest officer in the household. He offered the Empress his hand in preference to any other person; he was present at all the audiences given by her, and stood behind her chair. His duty, generally, towards her Majesty was equivalent to that of the Grand Master of the Horse towards the Emperor. Salary, 25,000 francs.

FIRST CHAMBERLAIN: General Nansouty, one of the best cavalry officers of the epoch. Salary, 35,000 francs.

INTRODUCER OF THE AMBASSADORS: M. de Beaumont. Salary, 20,000 francs.

FOUR CHAMBERLAINS IN ORDINARY: Salaries, 18,000 francs.
INTENDANT OF THE HOUSEHOLD: M. Hainguerlot.
LADY OF HONOR: Countess Chastulé de Larochefoucauld. When Josephine was confined during the Terror, at the prison of the

Carmes, she shared her cell, as has been stated, with Madame Tallien and the Duchess d'Aiguillon. Reflecting on the predictions of Euphémie David, at Martinique, and of M'lle Lenormand, at Paris, she said, on the eve of the day fixed for her execution, "After all, I have no need for alarm, for I shall yet be Queen of France." "Why do you not appoint your household, then?" said Madame d'Aiguillon, smiling through her tears. "True, I had not thought of it," returned Josephine. "You, to begin, shall be lady of honor." Upon the proclamation of the Empire, Josephine attempted to redeem her promise, but, in the meantime, the duchess, having been judicially separated from the Duke d'Aiguillon, had become the Countess Louis de Girardin, and Napoleon refused to admit a divorced lady to court. He subsequently made the countess, however, lady of honor to his sister-in-law, Madame Joseph Bonaparte, Queen of Naples.

Madame de Larochefoucauld, lady of honor to the Empress, was a personage of stern and antique manners, but of irreproachable life. She accepted the office at Josephine's earnest solicitation. She proved in the sequel to be heartless and ungrateful, however, for upon the divorce of Josephine, she applied to the Emperor for his authorization to continue her service in the same capacity in the household of Marie Louise. Napoleon replied by a direct refusal, and Madame de Larochefoucauld fell into disgrace. Salary, 20,000 francs.

TIREWOMAN: Madame de Lavalette—Emilie de Beauharnais—niece of the Empress. In 1815, this lady earned a European reputation by her successful ruse to save her husband from death, sentence having been pronounced upon him for open aid given to Napoleon against the Bourbons. She gained access to him in prison, and disguising him in her own apparel, enabled him to escape. The trick was discovered in less than five minutes, and the barriers of Paris were immediately closed. Lavalette, however, made good his flight to Bavaria. His condemnation was subsequently annulled, and he was restored to his country and his wife.

LADIES OF THE PALACE: At first twelve in number, the greater part of whom have been mentioned under the Consulate; these were afterwards increased to twenty-four. The salary of each was 16,000 francs.

READER: Madame Gazani. This beautiful and celebrated person was a native of Genoa, and the daughter of a danseuse. Napoleon saw her during one of his Italian campaigns, and induced her to follow him to Paris. She was made reader to the Empress; her husband was given a situation as receiver-general. Her liaison with Napoleon was a brief one; he was afraid of becoming subject to her influence, and commanded Josephine to send her home to Italy. "No," said the Empress, "she shall stay with me. It would be wrong to drive to despair a woman whom you have led into error. We will weep together; she will understand me." Josephine already had a presentiment of the lot that was in store for her. From this moment the abandoned wife and the discarded favorite lived in close and constant intimacy. Madame Gazani never read to Josephine on account of her Italian accent.

During the period of her supremacy, Madame Gazani held a position equal to that of the ladies of the palace. This was contrary to etiquette, and annoyed Madame de Larochefoucauld; but Napoleon insisted, and it was useless to contest his will. In person, Madame Gazani was tall and slight; in complexion, a brunette, with a rare perfection and delicacy of feature; her eyes expressed what she thought, as she was speaking, and told what she heard, as she listened.

TWO FIRST LADIES IN WAITING: Madame Marco de St. Hilaire, who had the charge of Josephine's jewels and cashmeres; and Madame Roy.

FOUR CHAMBERMAIDS: Of whom M'lle Avrillon was decidedly the favorite. This young woman subsequently wrote a volume of tattle upon Josephine and her court. It was said that but three words in the manuscript, as she prepared it, were correctly spelled, Napoleon being in every instance written Napoullion.

FOUR LADIES TO ANNOUNCE : One of whom, Georgette Ducrest, niece of Madame de Genlis, and still living, has written an interesting volume of memoirs of Josephine.

SIX PAGES were constantly in attendance upon the Empress. When she left her apartment, one walked before her, and another—the elder of the two—carried her train.

TWO FIRST VALETS-DE-CHAMBRE : Freyre and Douville. The daughter of Douville married Roustan, Napoleon's Mameluke. The latter, when reproached by the public for not following his master to St. Helena, pleaded his happiness at home as a sufficient motive for remaining there. Freyre is still alive, and serves a German prince. He visits France once a year to attend the mass at Rueil, near Paris, for the repose of Josephine's soul.

FOUR VALETS-DE-CHAMBRE IN ORDINARY ; FOUR USHERS ; EIGHT FOOTMEN ; THREE COACHMEN ; of whom Dulac was the favorite and the confidant ; an ERRAND-RUNNER, by the name of Benoist.

The needs of her Majesty increasing from time to time with those of Napoleon, the number of places in her household was constantly multiplied. Her retinue was doubled between 1804 and the divorce ; and that of Marie Louise commenced more numerously than Josephine's ended.

There were certain points of difference in the characters of Napoleon and Josephine, which unfitted them in some degree to occupy the same throne. He, who restored etiquette, was fond of it ; while she found its minute prescriptions irksome and harassing. While he was strict in his accounts with tradesmen, and could not tolerate waste or fraud, she was perfectly indifferent to price and very careless about payment. This latter defect seriously embittered her relations with Napoleon. Her prodigal expenditures—a reminiscence of her life under the Directory—often drew reproach from him. Early in the Consulate, Talleyrand and Bourrienne were forced to become the mediators between them, in the very delicate matter of the liquidation of Josephine's debts. The complaints of her creditors came to be so loud that Bonaparte felt the immediate necessity of putting an end to them. Talleyrand opened the negotiation, and upon his departure, late one evening, Bonaparte said to Bourrienne : " Bourrienne, Talleyrand has been speaking to me of the debts of my wife ; ask her for the exact amount of her indebtedness. Let her confess the whole, and let her beware of such extravagance in future. Let me see the bills of every one of this pack of thieves."

Bourrienne applied to Josephine for a statement of what she owed ; she refused to confess more than the half, and implored Bourrienne to be content with this partial avowal. He replied : " Madame, I must not conceal from you the discontent of the First Consul ; he believes you owe a considerable sum, and he is disposed to pay it. You will be bitterly upbraided, and will doubtless have a violent scene with him ; but the scene will be no less violent for the sum you propose to acknowledge than for the whole amount. If you conceal a portion, the murmurs of your creditors will speedily recommence, and Bonaparte will be more angry than before. Take my word for it, and confess the whole ; the result will be the same in any case, and you will hear but once the reproaches which otherwise you must hear twice."

Josephine positively refused to follow the counsel of her adviser, and would only surrender accounts to the value of 600,000 francs, though she owed a million and a quarter. Bonaparte was indignant and hurt at the enormity even of this sum, though he placed the necessary amount at once at Bourrienne's disposal, directing him to withhold the whole from any creditor who would not abate a portion. Bourrienne examined the bills. He found that every tradesman had doubled his usual prices, in view of Josephine's carelessness, and in the fear of being compelled to wait. He found that the milliner had furnished her with thirty-eight bonnets in one month, many of them at the price of 1,800 francs, each. Nearly all of these gentry agreed to take half their first demands, and to give a receipt in full ; one, who had claimed 80,000 francs, consented to accept 35,000 francs, and boasted of his large profits, even then. Bourrienne was fortunate and adroit enough to liquidate the million and a quarter with the check for 600,000 francs. It is worth mentioning, that the funds with which this domestic quarrel was settled were derived from the Senate of Hamburg, which was compelled to pay into the private purse of Bonaparte four millions and a half francs, in apology for its conduct towards Napper Tandy and Blackwell—Irish rebels, though French officers.[1]

"Josephine was excessively extravagant," said Napoleon at St. Helena, "and possessed in an inordinate degree the recklessness in expense which is natural to Creoles. It was out of the question to settle her accounts; she was always in debt, and was continually in trouble when pay-day arrived. She often sent word to shopkeepers to keep back the half of her indebtedness. I was not secure, even in Elba, from old bills of Josephine's, which swooped down upon me from every part of Italy."[2]

On one occasion Napoleon said to Josephine, "I desire that you will be dazzling in jewelry and richly dressed; do you hear?" "Yes," she replied; "but then you will find fault with the bills, and fall into a passion, and erase my audit in the margin, 'good for payment.'" "Certainly, my love, I sometimes cancel your audits, for you are occasionally so imposed upon that I cannot take it upon my conscience to sanction the abuse; but it is not, on that account, inconsistent in me to recommend you to be magnificent on occasions of parade. One interest must be weighed against the other, and I hold the balance equitably, though strictly."[3]

No period of modern French history has been more celebrated for the beauty of its ladies than the Empire. Josephine moved and lived in the midst of rare constellations of youth and loveliness. Nature had been prodigal in the dispensation of personal attractions, and Napoleon, susceptible to everything which charmed the vision and captivated the senses, was zealous in surrounding his throne as well with fair women as with brave men.

Foremost among the belles was Madame Regnault de St. Jean d'Angely, whose style of face and feature was said to recall the Antique Niobe, and of whose life we shall have occasion to speak at a subsequent period.

Then followed Madame Maret, afterwards Duchess de Bassano, whose sweet expression of countenance and elegant manners made a powerful impression upon Napoleon. She was one of the few women who repelled his advances; " her heart must have been pre-engaged," said an eye-witness of the intrigue, "for neither reason nor virtue would otherwise have been proof against such resistless fascinations:"

Madame Savary, afterwards Duchess de Rovigo, whose want of taste in dress somewhat marred her undoubted beauty:

Madame Lannes, afterwards Duchess de Montebello, said to resemble the most exquisite of Raphael's or Correggio's Madonnas:

Madame de Canisy, whose perfect regularity of feature, indescribable charm of expression, and glossy silken hair obtained her the title of the "Muse of the Court:"

Madame de Chevreuse, "the fair one with golden locks," of whose exile for a smart speech we shall speak at the proper moment:

Madame Durosnel, "whose blue eyes were overhung by long and glossy lashes: whose fascinating smile discovered a set of the finest teeth in the world, and whose general elegance of manner indicated a cultivated mind:"

Madame Visconti, still remarkably beautiful at fifty years of age, and passionately loved by Marshal Berthier. The latter wished her to obtain a divorce from her husband, that he might marry her himself. Napoleon forbade the execution of this plan, and compelled Berthier to wed a very plain princess of Bavaria. Three weeks after the wedding, M. Visconti died. "What a pity it is too late!" wept the doubly bereaved widow. Upon her death, she left her jewels to Madame Berthier, then Princess de Wagram:

Madame, and afterwards Princess, Talleyrand, whose dazzling whiteness of skin rendered her an object of universal admiration. This lady's acknowledged liaison with Talleyrand—her name was Grandt at the time—offended Napoleon, and he resolved to put an end to so grievous a scandal in his immediate intimacy. He therefore informed his Minister for Foreign Affairs that his connection with Madame Grandt must be rendered legitimate by marriage. In the existing state of things this was impossible, as Talleyrand, in his quality of Bishop of Autun, was compelled to remain in celibacy. The church, which forbade the marriage of a priest, permitted him, it would seem, to maintain an illicit connection. Application was made to the pope to restore Talleyrand to secular life. The papal authorization was accorded, and Madame Grandt became the Princess of Talleyrand-Perigord: she was presented once, and but once, at court under this title.

The lady thus elevated and thus rehabilitated, was remarkably beautiful, but uneducated and devoid of intelligence. Talleyrand was asked how he could converse with a woman so illiterate. "She rests me," he replied, and in three words drew her character. She once spoke of the four corners of an octagonal room; this speech of a modern princess delighted the antiques of the faubourg St. Germain. Denon having published his work upon Egypt, and having been invited by Talleyrand to dinner, the prince begged his wife to read the book, that she might be able to converse upon it with the author. She promised to do so, and on the occasion in question, expressed to Denon her pleasure in reading his descriptions of an unknown but interesting country. "But why did you introduce that excellent creature, Friday, so late? He should have come earlier in the book, and I know other persons who are of the same opinion." Poor Denon was terribly disconcerted, for he saw that the hostess took him for the author of Robinson Crusoe, which she had read by mistake. The faubourg St. Germain laughed again, but no more heartily than Talleyrand himself, who told the anecdote often and with infinite zest.

Among the ladies intimate at the palace were Madame Duchâtel, who on one occasion expressed such earnest admiration of a diamond crest sent to the Emperor by the Sultan, that Napoleon, breaking it in two, begged her to accept the larger half:

Madame Basterrêche, a niece of Cambacérès, and whose maiden name was Rose de Mont-Ferrier. "No pen," we are told, "could faithfully portray her beauty. Her profile was superb, her figure sylph-like, and she possessed a complexion of which no comparison can give any idea. It breathed an animation and warmth of coloring which reminded one of the flower whose name she bore; her skin combined the delicate tints of the rose with the velvet of the peach." She married, at the age of eighteen, the most frightful and most repulsive man in France, a millionaire of Bayonne. Napoleon never forgave Cambacérès for consenting to it. "It is Beauty and the Beast realized," he said.

To these we may add Madame de Brocq, whose sentimental beauty obtained for her the title of the Statue of Melancholy.

These were all ladies either attached to the court, or admitted to it through official position or family connections. Several foreign princesses frequented the palace at this period: Mesdames Czartoriska, de Hohenzollern, de Rohan and de Courlande. The incomparable Princess Borghèse—Pauline Bonaparte—graced the scene with her lovely face and admirable diamonds. Then in financial circles was Madame Récamier—not yet exiled—and Madame Simon, lately M'lle Lange, actress of the Comédie Française, and now the wife of a banker who had begun life as a wheelwright. Madame Simon had but lately been made notorious by a vengeance of Girodet, the artist. He had painted her portrait, but her husband, not satisfied with the likeness, refused to pay for it. Girodet immediately changed the accessories of the picture, making Madame Simon a recumbent Danaë, extending her arms to catch a shower of gold. A bloated turkey and a swollen frog gazed at her in admiration. The resemblance, which had not struck M. Simon, was sufficiently marked to enable the public, at the Annual Gallery, to recognize its late favorite, and the mortified husband hastened to withdraw the caricature by paying the price of the original. When Napoleon first saw Madame Simon at the Tuileries, some years subsequent to this, he was attracted by her beauty, and said to her, smiling, " And who are you, madame?" " I am Madame Simon, sire." " Oh, yes," returned Napoleon, " I remember." And, laughing heartily, he passed on to other guests.

Such were the most conspicuous beauties admitted either to the intimacy or to the presence of Josephine. The households of Napoleon's sisters included several ladies whose appearance entitles them to notice ; they will be described in connection with the princesses themselves. The household of Napoleon's mother was formed somewhat later, upon her recall from Rome, whither she had retired upon Lucien's quarrel with Napoleon. In 1806, she was established in a position which became the Empress Dowager. She had 500,000 francs a year, one fifth of which she spent in the salaries of her household. She was, at this period, about fifty-four years of age, and still retained much of the beauty of her youth. She was a little over five feet in height ; her form was erect, and her carriage firm. Her eyes were small, black and piercing ; her smile was winning, and her expression haughty yet intelligent. Her teeth, even at this advanced age, were still perfect ; her feet were remarkably small ; her right hand presented a conspicuous defect ; the forefinger did not bend, on account of an unsuccessful surgical operation. She dressed with taste and elegance, and possessed, in a marked degree, the faculty of suiting her costume to her age, or to the requirements of occasion. She spoke, at best, but broken French, and never escaped the embarrassment which beset her from her conscious want of fluency in speech.

She possessed no influence with her imperial son, and was consequently left in isolation by the quick scented courtiers and myrmidons of the palace. The ministers paid her no attention, and generally she received only such formal marks of consideration as were absolutely indispensable. Upon her accession to the title of Imperial Highness, she took Lucien's hotel in the Rue St. Dominique, which was already luxuriously furnished. Her household consisted of a lady of honor, a reader, and four ladies companions; two chamberlains, a master of the horse, two equerries in ordinary, an almoner, and a secretary.

Madame de Fontanges was the lady of honor; she is described as a handsome, inoffensive and listless young Creole, whom Napoleon had made a baroness in order to qualify her for the place. He had mistaken her for the Marquise de Fontanges, a much more efficient and suitable person.

The reader was M'lle Delaunay, a young lady of cultivated mind and varied accomplishments. She was a finished musician and an admirable portrait painter. Madame Mère—this was the title bestowed on the Emperor's mother—gave numerous miniatures of herself as presents, and these were all executed by M'lle Delaunay.

The four ladies companions were Madame la Maréchale Soult, Madame de Fleurieu, whose husband had been Minister of Marine under Louis XVI., Madame de St Pern, and Madame Junot. Madame Soult was fat and pretentious, and one of the worst dressers at the court. Madame de Fleurieu was plain and formal, though chatty and companionable: "a spout of lukewarm water, always open and always running." She obtained her situation by convincing Napoleon that she was an authority upon etiquette. Madame de St. Pern, a Corsican by birth, and unhappy in her domestic relations, delighted the household by her amiability, and won all who saw her by her gentleness and resignation. Madame Junot's story has been already told. In case of the illness of any one of these ladies, a supplementary attendant, or as they themselves called her, their supernumerary, was ready in the person of Madame Dupuis, "an indolent and wearisome Creole."

Of the gentlemen belonging to the household of Madame Mère, there is little to say. M. Decazes, the secretary, was so fragrant and delightful, that he obtained, in time, the name of the sweet pea of the court. M. de Brissac, one of the chamberlains, had a wife who was exceedingly deaf. Before being presented to the Emperor, therefore, she prepared answers to the questions which Napoleon was in the habit of asking. The sovereign unwittingly changed the usual order of his inquiries, and said, "How many children have you?" out of its turn. "Fifty-two, sire!" was the reply, made in perfect confidence, and received in amazement by all who heard it. She had been in love with her husband in early life, and he had sworn fidelity to her, though he soon after married another woman. "Then how did you become his wife?" she was one day asked. "Oh, I waited patiently till the other died," was the triumphant and heroic answer.[1]

Some years later, Madame de St. Pern was succeeded by Madame de Bressieux, who in her youth had been M'lle du Colombier, Napoleon's first love. We shall have occasion to speak of this lady more in detail, at a subsequent period.

[1] d'Abr. II. passim.

CHAPTER XVIII.

Pauline Bonaparte—Her early Loves—Her Marriage with General Leclerc—The Expedition to St. Domingo—The Widow's Weeds—Don Camillo Borghèse—Extraordinary Scene at St. Cloud—The Statue of Venus Victorious—Pauline's Household at Neuilly—Her Receptions—Her Sedan Chair—Her Taste in Dress—M. Jules de Canouville—Pauline's Impertinence to Marie Louise—Her Banishment—Her Visit to Napoleon at Elba—Her Appeal to Lord Liverpool—Her Death at Florence.

MARIE-PAULINE-BONAPARTE, the second sister of Napoleon, and the most beautiful, wayward, fashionable and dissolute of princesses, was born at Ajaccio, in 1780. Owing to the confusion of the times, her education was superficial and incomplete. At the age of thirteen, she was compelled to fly from home with her mother; and with the family lived in exile for many months at Marseilles, upon a fund granted by the Convention to Corsican refugees. Her beauty, which was already dazzling—for Pauline was forward for her age—attracted the notice and won the heart of Louis Stanislas Fréron, the agent of the Terror at Marseilles, and the willing executor of the sanguinary decrees of the Convention. Pauline reciprocated his passion, and upon the fall of Robespierre, their union was agreed upon. The correspondence of Pauline with Fréron, which was published in Paris about the year 1830,[1] indicates a precocity of sentiment and a depth of passion astonishing in a girl of fifteen years. The marriage would have taken place, had not Napoleon been informed of the engagement—intelligence of which was communicated by Fréron's wife, whom he had deserted for Pauline.

[1] Vide "La Revue Retrospective." iii 17.

General Duphot was the next aspirant to the hand of the Corsican belle, but his sudden death in attempting to quell a riot at Rome compelled her to make a third choice. In the meantime, Junot, at this period a lieutenant, had fallen in love, and to infatuation, with Pauline. He disclosed his passion to Bonaparte, who allowed him to believe that his sister would assent with pleasure, when he should be able to offer her an establishment—or at least sufficient security against poverty. Junot could obtain nothing from his father but the assurance that his share of the family estate would one day be 20,000 francs. "You have not got them yet," said Bonaparte. "Your father wears well, my good fellow. The truth is, you have nothing but your pay; as to Paulette, she has not so much. So then, to sum up: you have nothing; she has nothing. What is the total? Nothing. You cannot, then, marry at present."

In 1796, at Milan, Pauline married Gen. Charles Emmanuel Leclerc, who had already rendered Bonaparte efficient service in the Italian campaign. Pauline neither assented to the alliance, nor did she reject it; she simply yielded to her brother's desire that it should be consummated. Professing, and doubtless feeling, the most complete indifference to her husband, she soon entered upon a career of intrigue and infidelity. Lafon, the brilliant young tragedian of the Comédie Française, was one of her first lovers. This connection became public then, and has become historical since.

Bonaparte soon formed the plan of repressing the insurrection of the blacks in St. Domingo. An immense fleet was formed, of which Villaret-Joyeuse was made Admiral, Leclerc obtaining the appointment of General-in-chief, with thirty-five thousand picked men under his command. Pauline was surprised and alarmed at receiving a requisition—not from her husband, for that she would have treated with derision—but from her brother, to accompany the general upon his expedition. Leclerc himself would gladly have dispensed with the society of his faithless and capricious, though beautiful, wife. But the First Consul dreaded the possible scandal which her conduct would occasion, if left alone, and accordingly insisted upon her following her legal guardian to the tropics. "Good heavens!" she said to Madame Junot, "how can my brother be so hardhearted and wicked as to send me into exile among savages and serpents. Besides, I am ill, and I shall die before I get there." The spoiled child here sobbed with such violence, that Madame Junot knew of but one means of consolation. She accordingly took her by the hand, and told her that she would be queen of the island, and would ride in a palanquin; that slaves would watch her looks and execute her wishes; that she would walk in groves of orange-trees, arrayed in the bright colors of a Creole costume. By this time, Pauline's hysterics had entirely ceased. "And do you really think, Laurette, that I shall look prettier than usual in a Creole turban, a short waist, and a skirt of striped muslin?" She then sent for a package of bandanna handkerchiefs, one of which Madame Junot fantastically knotted into her hair. Her delight was unbounded when she found that the country where she had expected to be devoured, might be the scene of new triumphs in the toilet, and afford her an occasion for innovations in fashion. "Oh! those lovely mountains," she exclaimed, "we will have a fête every day, and a ball every night."

While the general was organizing his fleet, Pauline was preparing her wardrobe. Madame Germon, M'lles Despaux and l'Olive, Leroy, Copp, Foncier and Biennais, contributed, each in their department, to the more harmless of the two batteries which the squadron was to convey across the seas. Had the flagship l'Océan been captured on her way, the enemy might with good reason have wondered at the prodigious store of articles of female apparel and adornment they would have found comprising her cargo—a singular equipment for a vessel bound upon so severe an errand. They might also have expressed surprise at the luxurious arrangement of the ship—at its boudoir, its conservatory, its mirrors, its pantry. Its lovely passenger meant to have no possible desire ungratified, and her reluctant husband and her indulgent brother were willing to yield to her inclinations. She sailed from Brest in December, 1801, the whole squadron consisting of twenty-two frigates and thirty-five ships of the line.

"The First Consul wished that his sister," says de Salgues, "like another Cleopatra, should embellish with her presence and her charms the admiral's vessel: in spite of her refusal, she was taken to Brest, and there put on shipboard.* This rigor of Bonaparte towards a sister whom he seemed to love tenderly, astonished the public; but justification was found in the assertion that the princess was violently in love with a young and brilliant comedian, and Bonaparte saw no surer remedy than to put 1,200 leagues between the beauty and her lover."[1]

Two poets were sent out with the squadron, MM. Esménard and Norvins. The latter has left an account of the voyage and the campaign, too poetic to be altogether reliable. He represents Pauline as reclining upon the quarter-deck, and surrounded by her court—the officers of the staff—and reminding all conversant with the classics, of the maritime Venus and the Galatea of the Greeks.

The expedition was disastrous in every sense. General Leclerc proved totally incompetent, and the splendid army under his command was well-nigh destroyed by battle and fever. The general died of a lingering disease, and Pauline caused his body to be embalmed and placed in a triple cedar coffin. In this coffin she concealed her jewels and treasures, and embarked with them on board the Swiftsure, homeward bound.

She returned to France in a costume very different from that in which she set out: she went in bandanna and returned in black. On reaching Paris, she gave way to a paroxysm of grief and despair, which seemed too ostentatious to be sincere. She even cropped her luxuriant hair, and for a time refused to be comforted.

---

* The portrait of Pauline, upon the opposite page, is from an original by David, in the Gallery of Versailles.
[1] Memoirs, iv. 495.

Society doubted the reality of her affliction, while Napoleon openly scoffed at it. "Has Pauline cut off her hair?" he asked. "Then it is because she knows it will grow again, richer and thicker than ever."

Napoleon desired that she should wear her weeds with propriety, and consequently placed her under the care of his brother Joseph and his wife. Her inclination for retirement did not last long, and she reproached Napoleon vehemently for keeping her in confinement. "Oh dear me!" she said, "I shall certainly sink under this. If my brother determines to shut me up from the world, I shall put an end to my existence at once." To this, General Junot, who was present, replied that he had often heard of the Venus de' Medici, of the Venus Anadyomene, but never of a Venus Suicide. This comparison revived the disconsolate beauty, and she requested her former suitor to come and see her frequently.

In 1803, Bonaparte's plans for making himself emperor were nearly completed. An opportunity now occurred of accustoming the French to princely honors and titles in his family. Don Camillo Borghèse, the heir to the finest villa, palace and picture-gallery in Italy, the representative of one of the most illustrious Italian families, being compelled to leave Rome for political reasons, visited Paris, and was presented to Bonaparte. The latter conceived an affection for him, made him a French citizen and major of a mounted regiment in the Consular Guard, and speedily arranged a match between him and Madame Leclerc. The prince was under the middle size; his countenance was handsome, but without expression. His education had been much neglected, and his principal accomplishments were those of a skillful swordsman and an experienced jockey. The marriage took place on the 6th of November, 1803. Pauline was thus the first of Bonaparte's family to wear a coronet. The faubourg St. Germain smiled and said, " Well, one of them is a real princess after all."

The ceremonious presentation of Pauline, after her marriage to Josephine, was an epoch in her frivolous and fantastic life. Her detestation of Josephine, which was so ill concealed as to be notorious, and which arose from jealousy, led her on this occasion to make a display of magnificence such as France had hardly witnessed since Louis XV. Josephine, in her domestic differences with Pauline, acted solely upon the defensive ; she accepted a contest forced upon her, and which she did nothing to provoke. On this occasion—one which, from the circumstances of her sister-in-law's marriage, foreshadowed the regal destinies of the family —she resolved to dispute with her at once the palm of beauty and the supremacy of taste. The presentation was to take place in the grand salon at St. Cloud, the furniture and decorations of which were blue and gold. She adapted her toilet to this condition of the accessories in the midst of which she was to appear.

She wore a dress of white India muslin, though the season was winter. The skirt was more voluminous than the prevailing fashion warranted ; this innovation was one of her own suggesting. The lower hem was trimmed with a single band of gold, of the width of the finger. The bodice was heavily draped in thick folds and fastened upon the shoulders by two golden lions' heads, set in black enamel. The girdle, embroidered with gold, was attached in front by a clasp of black enamel and gold. The sleeves were short and full, descending but little below the shoulders, and displaying the wearer's remarkably handsome arms.

Her head-dress was that represented upon antique cameos. Her hair was gathered into a knot upon the top, and enclosed in a net-work of golden chains, crossing each other at right angles, each square containing a black enamelled rosette. Her necklace, bracelets and ear-rings were of the same material. Bonaparte, on coming into the salon, was struck by this beautiful though severely simple attire, and kissing Josephine on the shoulder, said, " Why, I shall be jealous, Josephine ; have you designs on any one ?" " Oh no," she replied, " I knew you liked to see me in white, and I have dressed in white ; nothing more." " Well, if you did it to please me, you have succeeded."

Madame Borghèse was expected at eight o'clock, but as she had not made her appearance at half-past eight, Bonaparte lost patience, and retired to his cabinet. The princess, with her first chamberlain—the flattering title given by the public to her husband—arrived at a quarter past nine, and consequently did not see her brother. The splendor of her equipage was unprecedented, since the commencement of the Revolution : her carriage, built for her new dignity and decorated with the arms of the Borghèse family, was drawn by six horses : an outrider before and another behind, and three lackeys bearing torches, completed the pomp of the cavalcade. The prince and princess were announced by an usher who forgot the Republic and foresaw the Empire, for he cried, " Monseigneur le Prince et Madame la Princesse Borghèse." The company assembled in the parlor rose to their feet. Josephine stood directly in front of her chair, without advancing to meet her guests; and on the appearance of her resplendent sister upon the threshold, showed by a passing flush upon her cheek, that the lovely and gorgeous apparition had sent a pang to her heart. Pauline was that night a marvel of beauty and a miracle of effulgence.

Her robe was of pale green velvet. The front and hem of the skirt were absolutely loaded with diamonds; the bodice and sleeves were embroidered with diamond wreaths and diamond clusters. Diamonds encircled her neck and enlaced her arms. Her diadem was composed of emeralds set in diamonds; and her bouquet was formed of emeralds, diamonds and pearls. Golconda had been rifled for this incrustation of gems; and the princess who bore the burden was worth, on this memorable occasion, exactly three millions and three quarters in jewels alone!

Josephine promptly recovered from the shock of Pauline's unequalled loveliness, and the conversation became general. The following dialogue ensued between Pauline and Madame Junot, who was present at the introduction :

" Well," said the former, " how do I look to-night?"

"Deliciously! At once beautiful and magnificent."

"Oh, you love me, and so you spoil me."

"No, I mean what I say, child: but why did you come so late?"

"Oh, I arranged that on purpose: I was afraid of finding you at table. I do not mind missing Napoleon: it was Josephine that I wanted to meet and crush. Oh, Laurette, Laurette, see how disconcerted she is! Oh, I am so happy!"

"Hush, you may be heard."

"What matters that? I do not love her! She meant to annoy me, just now, by not advancing to meet me, and thus making me cross the salon, but she did me the greatest favor, on the contrary."

'How so, pray?"

"Because my train would not have had time or space to unfold, had she greeted me half way; as it was, every one could see and admire the whole of it. After all, Josephine is well dressed! White and gold make a fine contrast with the deep blue of the furniture and hangings. Oh! dear me! Ah! mon Dieu!"

"Why, Paulette, what is the matter?"

"Why did I not think of the color of the room? And why did not you, Laurette, you who are my friend and sister, why did you not put me on my guard?"

"You knew as well as I that the grand salon of St. Cloud is blue."

"Yes, but in my anxiety and hurry, I forgot it, and so I have come here in a green gown to sit down in a blue chair! I am sure I must be hideous! Green and blue! What is the name of that green and blue revolutionary ribbon? Oh, I remember: "Prejudice overcome." I must be very ugly, dear, am I not! The reflection of these two colors must ruin me. Well, it can't be helped, now. Come with me back to Paris, Laurette, to-night."

"Oh, no. Think of your husband and your honeymoon that I should interrupt."

"Honeymoon! Honeymoon with that IDIOT! You are jesting, I suppose."

"No, I was serious. But, if I shall not break in upon a tête-à-tête, I'll accept your invitation, and return with you to Paris."[1]

The prince and princess soon set off for Rome, where Pauline's son by General Leclerc, and the only child she ever had, sickened and died. It was at this time that Canova executed the statue of the princess—perhaps his chef-d'œuvre. It is a semi-nude figure, modelled from life, and represented as half reclining upon a couch; the manner and expression strongly recall the Venus of Praxiteles. The statue is known as the Venus Victorious. Pauline, whose audacity in reply was often as remarkable as the irregularity of her conduct, furnished Rome and, indeed, Europe, with a theme for scandal, by a remark made in reference to this statue, many years later, to Madame Junot. The latter expressed her surprise that the princess should have submitted to such an exposure of her person. "What, you, Madame, you were yourself the model, and in Canova's studio?" "Oh, dear me, yes; why not? There was a good fire!" The sister of Napoleon supposed that Madame Junot referred to the inconvenience of the exhibition, and not to its indelicacy. "There is in this reply," says Capefigue, "a dash of that cynic impudence of the Roman women in their decline, which the indignation of Juvenal has branded by his 'Gannit in amplexu.'"[2]

The statue was for a long time exhibited to the public, who gave it the familiar name of La Paolina, in the Borghèse palace. "Never has the chisel of the sculptor," says a critic, "given the world a more perfect gem. In the time of the Greeks, it would have been worshipped as the very incarnation of Venus. She is half reclining upon a sofa, the marble of which might be taken for down, and seems to yield beneath her weight. She holds in her hand the apple which she is supposed to have just won from

---

[1] d'Abr. Hist. des Salons de Paris, v. 66.   [2] Appula gannit sicut in amplexu.
JUV. SAT. vi. 64.

Paris, and whence comes her title of Venus Victorious. The face is charming, and the flesh possesses that morbidezza which all moderns acknowledge to have belonged only to Phidias."

Don Camillo at last awoke to the mortifying consciousness that he was exhibiting, not the nude statue of Venus Victrix, but that of the princess his wife. He removed it to Florence and subsequently to Turin, where it was concealed from observation, for some years. It may now be seen at Rome, at the Borghèse villa, the catalogue claiming the form as a Venus, and the face only as that of a Bonaparte.

The young bride soon tired of her husband, who, in a measure, seems to have deserved the humiliating title she had given him at St. Cloud. She could not be prevailed upon to remain in Rome, and, late in the year 1805, hastened back to Paris, leaving Don Camillo behind her. She graciously granted him permission to follow, or to stay away, at his choice. For a time, he chose the latter.

Napoleon had now become emperor, and was beset by a passion for royalty. He made his brothers kings, and to his sisters he gave duchies and principalities. On Elisa, the eldest, he bestowed the republic of Lucca and Piombino; Caroline he made Grand Duchess of Berg; then came the turn of the princess Pauline. She was created Duchess of Guastalla. "Even a mole-hill," we are told, "seemed too much for her to govern. Had there been kingdoms in the air, as in the time of the sylphs, she might have been enveloped in a pink and blue cloud, richly perfumed, and sent to reign in those fortunate regions, where the sceptre of government is a sprig of flowers. This, however, did not suit her: her tears and her pretty airs amused her brother for a time; but as it was not in his nature to be patient, he became angry at last. The princess Elisa discovered that Lucca and Piombino were miserable principalities. She complained; the princess Caroline complained; the princess Pauline complained: it was a chorus of grievances. 'Once for all,' exclaimed the

Emperor, 'what does all this mean? Will these ladies never be content? One would really think we were sharing the inheritance of the late king our father!'"

Napoleon now organized the household of Pauline, who preferred remaining at Paris to visiting her duchy of Guastalla. He made her the centre of a small though brilliant court, which she held at Neuilly, a mile or two without the walls. The lady of honor was Madame Champagny, Duchess de Cadore, the wife of the Minister of the Interior—a lady who was herself a model of womanly virtues, but who failed to acquire influence over her impulsive and headstrong charge. Her "ladies to accompany" were Madame de Barral, so beautiful that it was matter of astonishment that the princess admitted her to her society and friendship; Madame de Bréhan, a pretty woman with a sarcastic tongue; and subsequently Madame de Mathis, "whose grown-up face was placed upon the body of a child." Cardinal Spina, one of the negotiators of the Concordat, was the almoner; M. de Montbreton, one of the princess' successful lovers, her Master of the Horse; M. Clermont-Tonnerre and, at a later period, M. de Forbin, renowned at the time as the first gentleman of France, were her chamberlains. A pretty young lady, with a pretty name, M'lle Jenny Millot, was her reader.

As Napoleon divided the week, Pauline's evening for reception was Wednesday. She did less to promote gaiety and sociability than any member of the family. She was too indolent to make any other preparation than that of her own toilet, beforehand, or to listen during the evening to any thing beyond her own praises. She was negligent of her guests, among whom were very few handsome women—a circumstance due to a special contrivance of her own. Her list of invitations was drawn up by Duroc, Grand Marshal of the Tuileries, and when he proposed the name of any one of whose appearance Pauline was jealous, she usually induced him, by pretty airs and arch objections, to erase it. Sometimes he hesitated: "Why exclude her?" he would say; "are there ever too many handsome women?" "Oh, I shall be there, and you can admire me, Duroc, as much as you like." She would then smile, and Duroc would draw his pen through the offending name. And thus the peerless beauty was tranquillized.

Pauline was far from being a wise little body, and her listeners were often only deterred from laughing, to relieve their pent-up merriment, by the lofty rank of her imperial highness. She one day asked Madame Junot why she had never given her a fête at her country seat at Raincy. "Because, as your highness can hardly bear the motion of a carriage, I did not suppose you could hunt, which is the only amusement we have at Raincy." "And why could I not hunt?" "Because you could not ride on horseback." "But I could follow in my palanquin." "Why, no, madame, you cannot hunt in a palanquin." The idea struck Madame Junot so ludicrously—that of the princess, reclining upon a palanquin, and borne upon the shoulders of four men, careering over hill and dale, and swooping through glen and thicket, in a hopeless race with hounds and horses, that she could not restrain her laughter. "Everybody laughs," continued Pauline, "when I talk of following the hunt in my palanquin; and M. de Montbreton says that I have not common sense. Laurette, I don't think that you have ever seen my palanquin, have you?"

This conversation took place under singular circumstances. Madame Junot was in bed, and in an exceedingly interesting situation, "having," as she herself states, "confident hopes of a boy after her five girls." Pauline had clambered upon the bed, and had seated herself upon Madame Junot's feet. After having settled the question relative to hunting in a palanquin, she talked for an hour in her usual discursive and miscellaneous style, skipping from court formalities to pink satin, and from Napoleon's battles to embroidered nightcaps. Then a bright idea struck her: Laurette had not seen her newly appointed chamberlain. She leaned over the invalid, seized three bell ropes, and pulled them all together, thus summoning the valet, the waiting woman and the chambermaid at once. The new chamberlain, M. de Forbin, who was waiting below, was sent for and presented to the prostrate invalid, by the princess still seated upon her recumbent friend's feet.

With the single exception of Josephine, no lady in France displayed greater taste in dress than Pauline. In fact, she thought of little else than the prosecution of her intrigues and the occupations of her toilet. Her entrance into a ball-room rarely failed to elicit a murmur of admiration; on one occasion, says an enthusiast, she absolutely illumined the palace. She wore, on the evening in question, a dress which she said should immortalize her, and upon which she was engaged for seven consecutive days, to the exclusion of any other avocation. Her head-dress consisted of narrow bands of soft fur, of a tiger pattern; these bands were surmounted by bunches of golden grapes. Her robe was of fine India muslin, with a deep bordering of gold, the pattern being grapes and vine leaves. Her tunic was Greek in form, and displayed her figure to admirable advantage; it was attached at the shoulders by fine stone cameos. Her girdle consisted of a gold band, the clasp of which was a richly-fashioned antique stone. Her beautiful arms were adorned with bracelets formed of gold and cameos. Pauline possessed one quality, rare in so pretty a woman: she did not compromise her beauty by affectation; or, at least, her sense of her own matchless loveliness, as she manifested it in her manner, went no farther than what may be termed consciousness.

Don Camillo subsequently returned from Rome, and was made prince of the French Empire by Napoleon. He distinguished himself at several of the Prussian battle-fields, and in 1808 was made governor-general of Piedmont and Genoa, which Napoleon had just annexed to France under the title of "Departments beyond the Alps." He at once set out for Turin, his capital, taking Nice, where Pauline was spending the winter for her health, on his way, for she had consented to share his new dignity with him. Her imperial highness was a poor traveller, and bore the fatigue of posting with great impatience. The equerry, M. de Montbreton, found ample occupation in building a fortress of cushions around the illustrious invalid, while the ladies of honor relieved each other in the duty of sitting upon her feet, to keep them warm.

Pauline was not long contented at Turin, although her husband held a sumptuous vice-regal court. Her position did not please her, for she had expected to be first, and found herself only the third. The first dignitary of Piedmont was an unoccupied arm-chair, which, by a diplomatic fiction, was supposed to represent the Emperor of the French and King of Italy; behind this chair stood the highest functionaries of the government, as if attending Napoleon himself. The second dignitary was the governor-general, who subjected the imperious and haughty Duchess of Guastalla to the gross indignity of being inferior in official importance to himself. So Pauline abandoned Prince Camillo at Turin, precisely as she had done at Rome, and returned to Neuilly and Paris. Her husband did not seek to retain or to recall her; he continued to administer the government with success, and to entertain foreigners with hospitality, till the fall of Napoleon in 1814, when he restored Piedmont to Austria, and returned to his patrimonial palace at Rome.

Pauline, upon her arrival in France from Turin, divided her time between the Tuileries and her chateau at Neuilly. She had never striven to conceal her intrigues with the various gentlemen who were successively the heroes of her transitory attachments; she now even sought publicity and scandal. The most conspicuous of her liaisons, coming to the knowledge of Napoleon, ended fatally for the young man who was the object of it. M. Jules de Canouville was a young, courtly and dashing colonel of hussars, and soon became the favorite of the princess. Not satisfied with the conquest itself, he desired the reputation of it. This he soon obtained, and to his heart's content. The court dentist, M. Bousquet, one day received a professional summons from Pauline. He was conducted to her boudoir, where he found a very elegant young man, negligently clad in a dressing-gown. He was gracefully extended upon a sofa, and begged the dentist " to be careful of the teeth of his Paulette." The innocent Mr. Bousquet naturally took this considerate gentleman to be Don Camillo Borghèse. He promised to use due caution. Throughout his stay the supposed husband enjoined scrupulous attention upon the operator. As the dentist left the apartment of her imperial highness, the ladies of the household, the chamberlains, &c., gathered around him, and inquired the result of his visit. " The princess is doing very well," he replied, " and must be gratified at the tender attachment of her august husband, which he has just manifested before me in the most touching manner. His anxiety was very great, and I could with difficulty convince him of the safety of the simple measures I proposed. I shall acquaint every one with what I have seen. It is agreeable to be able to cite such examples of conjugal love in so elevated a rank. I am really quite penetrated." The ante-chamber was convulsed with laughter, but the good dentist was allowed to depart full of his generous illusion. The young man in the dressing-gown was M. Jules de Canouville. This connection came to Napoleon's knowledge in the following manner :

Alexander of Russia had given him, at Erfurth, three superb sable pelisses. One of these the Emperor sent to Pauline, and she gave it to her lover. Some days after, at a review upon the Place du Carrousel, M. de Canouville's horse became unruly, and threw the manœuvres into confusion ; the rider thus attracted Napoleon's attention. He observed that the pelisse given to his sister had been transformed into a hussar's dollman. "M. de Canouville," he exclaimed in a voice of thunder, "your horse is too young and his blood is too hot: be good enough to go and cool him in Russia." Three days afterwards, the young man quitted Paris upon his exile, leaving Pauline, for once, in a state of genuine affliction. She sent a messenger once a fortnight to see him and to speak with him, as a letter did not sufficiently tranquillize her. M. de Canouville behaved well and distinguished himself in action. He was accidentally killed by the discharge of a cannon after a battle which would have entitled him to promotion. The portrait of Pauline, surrounded with diamonds, was found upon his person: it was conveyed to Murat, who returned it to his sister-in-law.

The inconstant princess, who had already begun to forget her lover in his absence, forgot him completely upon his death. She soon resumed her fashionable career, and plunged with more ardor than ever into the elegant follies of the court. "She was one evening," says Madame Junot, "to represent Italy, in a fancy quadrille, to be danced in the theatre of the Tuileries. She was on that occasion the most perfect embodiment of beauty that can be imagined. She wore upon her head a light casque of burnished gold, surmounted by small ostrich feathers of spotless white. Her bosom was covered with an ægis of golden scales, to which was attached a tunic of India muslin embroidered in gold. The most exquisite part of her appearance was her arms and feet: the former were encircled with bracelets, in which were enchased the most beautiful cameos belonging to the house of Borghèse; her little feet were shod with slender sandals of purple silk, the bands of which were gold; at each point where the latter crossed upon the leg, was attached a magnificent cameo. The sash which held the ægis on her bosom was of solid gold, and the centre was ornamented with that most precious gem of the Borghèse collection—the dying Medusa: to all this magnificence was added a short dagger, highly embossed with gold and precious stones, which she carried in her hand. Her appearance was that of a fairy apparition, almost without substance, and as it were celestial.

"She was, indeed, an elegant nymph. Her statue, by Canova, moulded from herself, is that of an enchantress. It has been asserted that the artist corrected defects in the leg and bust.

I have seen the legs of the princess, as I believe all have who were moderately intimate with her, and I have observed no such defects: indeed the perfection of their make may be inferred from her walk: it was slow, because she was an invalid, but the grace of her movements showed that her limbs were happily formed. How finely her head was inclined, and how beautifully it turned upon her shoulders!"

She had one physical defect, however, which almost amounted to a deformity. Her ears were two thin, pale pieces of cartilage, without curl or curve. This caprice of nature was more remarkable from the contrast with her lovely features. A rival belle and haughty legitimist, Madame de Contades, who would never acknowledge either Napoleon's glory or his sister's beauty, once mortified Pauline excessively by calling attention, in a ball-room, to this unfortunate disfigurement. She noticed her reclining upon a sofa, under the blaze of a chandelier. "What a pity," she said aloud, "that such a pretty woman should be deformed. I declare if I had such a pair of ears, I would have them cut off." Poor Pauline burst into tears, and soon retired from the room. She revenged herself upon Madame de Contades by calling her a May-pole.

Pauline, who had never liked Josephine, liked Marie Louise no better. Not long after the arrival of the archduchess in France, and her marriage with Napoleon, she took occasion to insult her in a manner so public and insolent that she drew upon herself exile and disgrace. In the midst of the brilliant throng present at an official reception, and behind the back of Marie Louise, she raised her thumb and finger to her forehead, forming there a construction similar to that worn by Falstaff when disguised as Herne the Hunter, and thereby indicating the treatment her brother might expect from his Austrian bride. Marie Louise saw this extraordinary piece of pantomime in a mirror. The company laughed, while Napoleon scowled. He had but lately repudiated his wife, and he now determined to banish his sister.

The order to that effect was peremptory, and Pauline withdrew, unabashed and impertinent, to her husband's palace at Rome, where she led a brilliant and careless existence. Don Camillo remained steadfastly at Turin.

Thus far, vice and excess had been the most conspicuous features of Pauline's conduct; she now showed herself capable of heroism, sacrifice and devotion, qualities which the world has a right to expect of those who, though not born, are at least bred, upon the steps of a throne. She had spent the winter of 1813-14 at Nice, and at Hyères in the south of France. On the 20th of April, Napoleon left Fontainebleau for Elba, after what has been stigmatized as "a scene of desertion never equalled in any age of the world—tergiversations too hideous to be credible, if not recorded by eye-witnesses."[1] Pauline quitted Hyères in order to meet him near Fréjus: while waiting, she witnessed many of the fearful tumults which were excited by the passage of the "Corsican tyrant." She saw his statues overturned and his life menaced. The brother and sister met at Luc, at two o'clock in the afternoon, on the 26th of April. Napoleon entered the chamber of the princess; she extended her arms, but burst into tears on seeing that he wore an Austrian uniform as a disguise. "Why this uniform?" she asked. "Why, Pauline," returned Napoleon, reproachfully, "would you have me dead?" Pauline looked at him steadfastly, and said, "I cannot embrace you in that dress. O, Napoleon, what have you done!" Napoleon withdrew and changed his costume. He returned in the uniform of the Old Guard. Pauline pressed him to her heart again and again, astonishing those who best knew her by this unexpected burst of feeling.

But Pauline could act as well as weep. She, with Madame Mère, followed Napoleon to Elba in October of the same year. She abandoned the frivolities and gaieties to which for years she had been accustomed, and devoted herself, with untiring energy,

[1] Alison's Europe, x. 240.

to furthering the plans formed for his escape. She placed all her jewels at his disposal: Napoleon never used them; they were in his carriage at Waterloo, which was taken by the Allies, and exhibited for money at London. The diamonds had disappeared, and it was never known into whose hands they had fallen. On the 26th of February, 1815, she gave a ball to the principal personages of Elba, and that very night Napoleon stepped on board the brig l'Inconstant, and weighed anchor for France. Pauline and Napoleon never met again. She returned to Rome and he to Paris, from whence, by way of Waterloo, he passed on to St. Helena.

Don Camillo was now compelled, by the restoration of Piedmont to Austrian rule, to resume his allegiance as a Roman subject. He refused, however, to see or to receive his wife; but the pope took the matter into his own hands, and appointed a committee of cardinals to decide upon a method of reconciliation. The prince was ordered to share his palace with the princess, and to place one hundred and fifty thousand francs a-year at her disposal. He obeyed, but ungraciously, and finally retired to Florence, where he built a palace for his own private use, leaving to her the undivided control of his superb establishment at Rome.

Pauline was still marvellously beautiful, though her health was delicate, and her constitution impaired. She was surrounded with admirers, the most ardent of whom was Lord Brougham. He was admitted to the mysteries of her toilet, and she allowed him to sit upon the floor before her and hold her feet in his hands. He was also permitted, as a great favor, to hand pins to her dressing maids, when they needed them in the arrangement of her person. "How can you take pleasure," some one asked her, "in the society of men who have imprisoned your brother at St. Helena?"

"Can you not understand," she replied vehemently, "that I enjoy the sight of these men, once so arrogant, now humbling themselves to the dust of my sandals? Can you not see that the complaints of that British peer are sweet music to my soul? He stands for hours to give pins to my waiting maids, because they are to touch my person. He has the courage to confront the caprices of a woman, but he does not dare to speak before his parliament in behalf of that woman's brother, that he may be more kindly treated in his accursed dungeon at St. Helena. And this man hopes that I may love him! And the others hope I may love them! If I had neither heart nor soul, perhaps I might! Let them love on and suffer the penalty!"[1]

Pauline became convinced in 1821 that Napoleon was dying at St. Helena. She wrote a letter to Lord Liverpool, then prime-minister of England, in which she earnestly begged, in the name of all the members of the family, that her brother might be removed to a less dangerous climate. "If so reasonable a request be refused," she said, "it will be pronouncing his sentence of death—in which case I beg permission to depart for St. Helena, to join my brother and receive his last sigh. I feel that the moments of his life are numbered, and I should for ever reproach myself if I did not use all the means in my power to alleviate his sufferings and testify my devotion." The Earl of Liverpool granted the latter portion of the request, but too late. Napoleon was already dead at the date of Pauline's appeal.

She now sank into a rapid decline, though she continued to live in a constant whirl of gaiety. Foreigners visiting Rome formed her principal society; they found her receptions and entertainments hospitable, refined and sumptuous. Early in 1825, she went to Pisa for a change of air. It was evident to herself as well as to her friends, that she could not long survive. She now performed the last eccentricity of an eccentric life. Though possessed of no fortune whatever, and living upon the forced bounty of her husband, she composed and executed an imposing instrument which she called her will. In this she made large and numerous legacies, forming in the aggregate a sum of princely

[1] d'Abr. Mém. de la Restauration, iv. 164.

magnificence. Don Camillo now recalled her to Florence, where a reconciliation was effected and mutual forgiveness extended. The Princess Borghèse expired in the arms of the prince, on the 9th of June, 1825. With a generosity of which he hardly seemed capable, and which she had certainly done nothing to deserve, he recognized and paid the bequests that she had made without consulting or considering the state of his fortune.

Napoleon often mentioned Pauline at St. Helena. He considered her the handsomest woman of her time, and said that artists were accustomed to speak of her as the modern Venus de' Medici. When at Nice, she established, he said, a daily line of baggage wagons to and from Paris, to bring her supplies of the newest fashions. "Had I known it," he added, "she would have been soundly scolded. After all, she was the kindest creature in the world."[1]

The influence of Pauline Bonaparte upon public morals and the tone of society was injurious; her example, the very worst. "She placed herself," says de Salgues, "out of the pale of propriety; the interior of her house was a hotbed of corruption and scandal. This degeneracy of morals was not without its effect upon the opinion of the time, for people become vicious on seeing vice prosper."[2]

Though the sister of Napoleon, Pauline is hardly a historical character. She seems a fancy sketch, an ideal portraiture, that by some freak of nature or of the imagination, has become akin to personages in real life. By the side of her brother, she is as spun glass next to moulded bronze, biscuit of Sèvres after Parian marble. The Greeks made Mars the lover of Venus; but Corsican fact is stranger than Grecian mythology. At Ajaccio, Mars and Venus were born of the same mother—an anomaly too daring for fiction, and which history alone could have ventured to exhibit

[1] Las Cases, i. part ii. 321. [2] Memoirs, vi. 268.

CHAPTER XIX.

Literature under Napoleon—Oriani and Corneille—Bernardin de St. Pierre—Chénier—Delille—Chateaubriand—Madame de Staël—The Institute—Napoleon's favorite Authors—His Treatment of Literary Men—The Censorship—Ducis—Lemercier—Encouragement extended to Literature and the Sciences—Non-bestowal of the Awards—Liberty of the Press—An Apology for the Penury of Letters under Napoleon—Literature under Napoleon III.

WHEN in Italy, during the early part of his career, Napoleon publicly addressed a letter to Oriani, the astronomer, in which he said that all men of genius who had distinguished themselves in the republic of letters were to be accounted natives of France. "The French people," he added, "have more pride in enrolling among their citizens a skillful mathematician, a renowned painter, an eminent author, than in adding to their territories a large and wealthy city."

Afterwards, at St. Helena, regretting the penury of literature during his reign, he said, "If Corneille had lived in my time, I would have created him a prince." This was doubtless meant in all sincerity, and the fallen sovereign certainly intended to speak of literature with regard and of genius with respect. And yet had Corneille been a prince of the empire, his titles and his honors would have been extinguished at Waterloo; and the mind must be singularly warped by the contemplation of fleeting grandeurs and ephemeral distinctions, that would be gratified by the creation of a patent of parvenu nobility for the possessor of a world's admiration and a poet's immortality. It is a question whether it is extending a proper patronage to genius to class it with the fops, sycophants, renegades and bandits who have been born to titles or upon whom blazons have been conferred.

Notwithstanding the glaring poverty of letters under the Empire—which has been indeed generally confessed—a portion of Napoleon's indiscreet eulogists have created for him a creditable literary galaxy, and have presented an imposing list of the notabilities of his reign. "Though his era was prominently military," says an enthusiast, "yet at the head of the cortége, marched a grand and noble literature—Chateaubriand, Bernardin de St. Pierre, Chénier, Picard, Delille, Benjamin Constant and Madame de Staël."[1] It is not possible, however, to claim these writers for Napoleon's literary circle; the enthusiast's chronology is as faulty as his logic. The subject is worth a moment's consideration.

The literature of an age or of a reign, when attributed to, or connected with, the monarch who is the chief of the government and the head of society, must be considered as a literature bearing the impress of the national mind at the time, presenting a reflex of the manners and morals of the people, and offering, in a permanent shape, the materials for gathering an opinion of the tone of thought, of the degree of virtue and of the progress of taste, during the period referred to. No such materials have descended to us from the era of Napoleon; at least none of which he was the patron and producer. Bernardin de St. Pierre and Chénier wrote before him; Chateaubriand, the embodiment of the moral protestation of the age, and an exile for fifteen years, wrote against him: Constant and Madame de Staël wrote in spite of him. Hardly a line of pure literature can be attributed either to the spirit of Napoleon's institutions, to his influence, his example or his encouragement.

With what justice can St. Pierre be claimed for the period of Napoleon's tenure of power? Paul and Virginia was published in 1789, when Napoleon was yet unknown. Its success was immense, and its merits have given it permanence. The simple

[1] Le Siècle de Napoléon, rubric Portalis.

picture of Virginia, clad in a robe of plain white muslin and a straw hat, produced an immediate revolution in the fashion of ladies' dress, and silks and satins disappeared as if by magic, before the captivating simplicity of the island heroine's attire. Bernardin de St. Pierre was the French Goldsmith; his manner was a reminiscence and his matter a by-gone. It was illustrative of no age, and characteristic of no national feature. Least of all was it referable to the revolutionary period which actually produced it, or to the imperial episode which was twenty years subsequent to it. The enthusiast has here made an error in date.

With what propriety can Chénier, a republican poet, a revolutionary fanatic, be violently detached from the period of anarchy and confusion to which he belongs, and carried forward to the account of a succeeding period, merely because, after having hushed his muse, it was his lot to die in 1811? The enthusiast has here confounded meum and tuum.

With what propriety can Delille, who was elected to the Academy just thirty years before Napoleon was crowned, for literary distinction already acquired, who was the first poet of France before Napoleon was born, and who condescended to become Robespierre's poetaster and laureate before Napoleon had yet appeared at Toulon, but who happened to die at the age of eighty, two years before Napoleon's fall, be included in the galaxy of imperial literati? The enthusiast has here fallen into a serious anachronism.

With what propriety can Chateaubriand be included in this singular array? He was, indeed, contemporaneous with Napoleon; he was the most powerful writer of the epoch; his "Genius of Christianity" obtained for him the title of the "Last Apostle." But he wrote either in voluntary exile from the Republic and the First Consulate, at Niagara, in the East and in England, or in forced banishment from the Empire. His first offence was the following sentence, written by him in 1807, in a review of Alex. de Laborde's "Travels in Spain," and published in the Mercure:

"It is in vain that Nero prospers: Tacitus is already born in the empire: he lives in obscurity by the ashes of Germanicus. He will unmask false virtue, and will show that the deified tyrant is naught but a buffoon, an incendiary and a parricide."

Nero, in this philippic, stands for Napoleon; Tacitus for Laborde, and Germanicus for Louis XVI. Napoleon suppressed the Mercure for this single sentence, and Chateaubriand lost the twenty thousand francs which he had invested in the journal. Napoleon said, on reading the passage just quoted: "Does Chateaubriand take me for a fool? Does he think I do not understand him? If this continues, I will have him sabred on the steps of the Tuileries!"[1]

Chateaubriand, the adversary of the Emperor, and the proscribed victim of his police, devotedly and hereditarily attached to the Bourbons, minister of state and peer of the realm under Louis XVIII., belongs, not to the Empire, but to the Restoration. In preparing his list of the efficient and valid laborers of the pen, the enthusiast should not have included the octogenarian, the disaffected, the exile and the absentee.

The assumption that Madame de Staël graced and illustrated Napoleon's reign by the exercise of her transcendent talents, is perhaps more curious than any of the instances thus far adduced. In the case of Chateaubriand, the author was merely expelled the country; in that of Madame de Staël, not only was the writer exiled, but her productions were seized by the police, and their publication forbidden. They were subsequently issued in foreign lands, and even in foreign tongues, or were reserved for the Emperor's fall. The enthusiast now claims that this literature, which his Majesty considered hostile and unpatriotic, and which to him was distasteful and repulsive, was one of the luminous points of a literary age. We shall have occasion to speak more fully, in another chapter, of Madame de Staël and of her literary career.

The whole influence of Napoleon upon the letters of his reign

[1] Bour. ix. 88.

was repressive in an eminent degree. In the first place, the epoch was too troubled, and the times were too unsettled, to allow that seclusion, that application and that composure, which alone permit any sustained mental effort. And in the second place, the rigorous conditions imposed on authors by Napoleon, the jealousy of the censorship exercised over their productions, and the suspicions and exactions of the police, rendered the pursuit of literature at once dangerous and distasteful, and neither productive of wealth nor conducive to reputation. It will not be difficult to cite abundant proofs of these positions.

Early in the Consulate, Bonaparte reorganized the Institute, which at that time consisted of five academies: those of Literature, Science, Moral Philosophy, Ancient History and the Fine Arts. He suppressed the department of Moral Philosophy altogether, and inverted the order held by Literature and Science, making Science the first class and Literature the second. This was not so much in recognition of the very marked superiority of the scientific men of his time to the men of letters, as it was the consequence of his opinion that literature itself, as a pursuit and as an influence, was second to Science. "The First Consul was not sorry," says Bourrienne, "to testify the little esteem he felt for literary men. When he spoke to me of them, he called them makers of phrases. With few exceptions, I never knew a man so insensible to the beauties of either prose or poetry as Bonaparte." His love of the vague and the mysterious led him to admire Ossian, while at the same time his appreciation of what was direct and noble in conception, and fluent and manly in expression, made him a fervent partisan of Corneille. "Corneille and Ossian were his favorite authors. Beyond these writers, the finest productions of our literature were to him little more than an adroit arrangement of sonorous but unmeaning words, capable only of striking the ear."[1]

Napoleon's intercourse with, and treatment of, literary men,

[1] Bour. v. 246.

offer a multitude of incidents illustrative of the opinions which he held concerning them. Grouped together, they form a convincing and amusing commentary upon his views regarding an official and governmental literature, and the aid it should lend the administration. Early in the year 1800, Madame Bacciochi begged Bonaparte to permit Chateaubriand to return to France, which he had quitted at the time of the emigration of the nobles. Shortly afterwards, Bourrienne expressed his surprise that no office had been given to a man so eminently fitted for public duties. "Oh," said Bonaparte, "the thing has been suggested to me, but I always reply in a manner that deters the applicant from returning to the subject. Chateaubriand has ideas of liberty and independence which would prevent his adopting my system as I understand it. I like him better as a known enemy than a forced friend. Still I will bear him in mind. I may try him in an inferior position, and if he succeeds, I will help him to advance."

Upon the revival of public worship in France, Bonaparte made Cardinal Fesch, his uncle, ambassador to the court of Rome, and appointed Chateaubriand secretary to the legation. Chateaubriand wished to decline, but many influential members of the clergy insisted upon his acceptance, in the interest of religion. He was soon after made minister plenipotentiary to the Valais, and returned to Paris to prepare for his new mission. He dedicated, at this period, the second edition of the Genius of Christianity to the First Consul. He went to bid adieu to Bonaparte on the morning of the 21st of March, 1804; the Duc d'Enghien had been shot four hours before in the moats of Vincennes. On leaving the palace, he heard of the fearful catastrophe, and at once sent in his resignation as minister plenipotentiary. This public and solemn rebuke, inflicted upon the sovereign by the first mind of the epoch, made nearly as much sensation in Europe as did the crime itself. Elisa Bonaparte with difficulty succeeded in calming the wrath of her brother: the friends of Chateaubriand called every morning at his house to make sure that he had not been molested during the night. This act of courage, unhappily, did not provoke emulation; it remained without imitators, though not without approvers. "Why," said Josephine, "why is not Bonaparte surrounded with men of this character; they would arrest him in the errors which the constant flattery of his present advisers only encourages him to commit."[1]

Chateaubriand was elected to the Institute in 1811, to fill the seat left vacant by the death of Chénier. The rules require that each new member pronounce the eulogium of his predecessor, and the public evinced deep interest in that to be made by a Bourbon upon a republican—an emigrant upon a regicide. The discourse, when ready for delivery, was submitted to Napoleon for approval; after reading it, he exclaimed, "Had this oration been pronounced, I would have shut the gates of the Institute, and put M. de Chateaubriand in an under-ground cell for life."[2] The author refused to modify his language, though the manuscript was returned to him with passages marked by Napoleon in pencil for cancelling. He was immediately banished from Paris. Such were the relations between Napoleon and Chateaubriand.

Delille's experience was somewhat different. In the first year of the Consulate, he published, at the age of seventy, his "Géorgiques Françaises," of which fifteen editions passed speedily through the press. Bonaparte's police could not remain unmoved by so remarkable a literary success. It thumbed through the volume and fixed its suspicions upon the following lines:

> "Sans l'homme, dans l'univers, règne un muet effroi,
> C'est un palais désert qui demande son roi."

The evident meaning of the poet was that nature, the landscape, without man, was as a deserted palace calling for its king. The police, in the stupidity of its application, chose to regard the author as intending to hint that the deserted palace of the Tuileries was clamorous for Louis XVIII.! It compelled Delille to

[1] Bour. v. 343.   [2] Ibid. ix. 36.

substitute, in the subsequent editions, the following distich, having itself suggested the sentiment :

"Les lieux les plus rians, sans l'homme, nous touchent peu ;
C'est un temple désert qui demande son dieu."

Here the figure being altered, the prefecture became tranquil. Nature was now merely a deserted temple calling for its god.

Napoleon was said to be jealous of the glories of Delille, and to see with pain that Paris was as much interested in the author of the French Georgics as in the hero of Marengo. He commissioned Fontanes to endeavor to induce him to quit his retreat at Therapia, on the Black Sea, for a residence at Paris. The effort was unsuccessful, and Napoleon never obtained from the refractory poet one single hexameter: he remained insensible to honors, riches and decorations.

Bonaparte detested Chénier for his republicanism ; he removed him from his office of inspector-general of the schools, for his Epistle to Voltaire, a measure which compelled the poet to sell his library.[1] He disliked Ducis, who refused to accept either the title of Senator or the cross of the Legion of Honor, preferring, as he said, rags to chains. He descended so far as to bandy words with Laharpe, and charged him with dotage and second childhood in the Moniteur.[2] He said of Bernardin de St. Pierre, whose Studies of Nature he had attempted to read : "How can people write such trash! Nature, indeed! What is nature? Vague, void and insignificant. Man and the passions are the only themes worth treating of. Such writers are useless under any government. But I shall pension them, nevertheless, because, as Chief of the State, I must : they occupy and amuse the idle."[3] "What," he exclaimed, on receiving from his sister Elisa, a copy of Chateaubriand's Atala, some months after its publication, "What, another romance in A! Do you suppose I have the time to read all your nonsense?"[4] But on learning

[1] Salgues' Memoirs, vi. 406.
[2] Moniteur, 28th Feb. 1802.
[3] Bour. v. 247.
[4] Ibid. 245.

that it was by Chateaubriand, a fact which he did not know, he promised to read it. He noticed one of the ladies of his household engaged in perusing Madame de Staël's "Germany," and, seizing the volume, he threw it into the fire. He feared and disliked the poet Lemercier, for his mild but inflexible republicanism. He sought to win him to his cause, and sent him the decoration of the Legion of Honor, which Lemercier returned with a courteous but energetic refusal. "Lemercier," says Bourrienne, "was not one of the poets who were in the habit of frequenting Fouché's house, to receive occasional gratuities of fifty or a hundred louis—a sum which did not always make two and sixpence per base action."[1]

Napoleon was, in 1804, at Aix-la-Chapelle, the capital of the empire of Charlemagne, the patron of art and science, and on the 11th of September, he issued a decree, the object of which was to encourage the sciences, letters and arts. Twenty-two prizes were to be awarded every ten years to meritorious works produced during the interval, and the first award was to take place on the 9th of November, 1810. The number of prizes was subsequently increased to thirty-five—nineteen of 10,000 francs each, and sixteen of 5,000. The following was the decision rendered by the jury, composed of the presidents and perpetual secretaries of the Institute:

The prize for geometry and pure analysis was given to the Calcul des Fonctions, by Lagrange.

That for astronomy to the Mécanique Céleste, by Laplace.

That for chemistry to the Statique Chimique, by Berthollet.

That for anatomy to the Leçons d'Anatomie, by Cuvier.

That for tragedy to the Templiers, by Raynouard.

That for comedy was not awarded, though thirteen plays were presented.

That for epic poetry was not awarded, though Delille's translation of the Æneid and of Paradise Lost received an "honorable mention"

[1] Bour. v. 243.

That for didactic and descriptive poetry was given to Delille's "Imagination."

That for history was given to a History of Anarchy in Poland, while Sismondi's History of the Italian Republics obtained a mere honorable mention. This decision has been reversed by the verdict of posterity.

That for biography was given to de Beausset's Life of Fenelon.

That for opera libretto was given to M. de Jouy, for La Vestale.

That for opera composition to Spontini, for La Vestale.

That for painting to Girodet, for a Scene from the Deluge, now in the Grand Salon of the Louvre.

That for sculpture to M. Chaudet, for his statue of Napoleon.

That for architecture to Fontaine and Percier, for the Arc de Triomphe du Carrousel.

These last five decisions were condemned by public opinion at the time, and the judgment of the half century which has since elapsed has sustained it in its opposition.

The thirty-five prizes were never distributed, and the Emperor economized his 270,000 francs. Napoleon, who was dissatisfied with the awards, and who, if not desirous, was at least in this case willing, to humiliate and degrade letters and the arts, said before the Council of State "that his object had been to furnish occupation to the public mind, and to prevent it from giving attention to more important and serious matters." This singular conduct cannot certainly be taken as a proof of Napoleon's respect for science and literature. The non-bestowal of the sums awarded gave rise to a shower of epigrams upon the discomfited competitors, the incompetent jury, and the refractory sovereign.

On the 27th of September, 1807, the Moniteur published an imperial decree, destroying the liberty of the press, by assimilating books to newspapers, and enacting that the former as well as the latter must receive the sanction of the censors before publication. This, by virtually rendering the whole French press the mouthpiece, and all French authors the exponents, of imperial necessities and of governmental opinions, annihilated literature as an honorable and influential profession. No thought that did not tally with the thoughts of the Emperor, no idea that did not serve to illustrate or enforce ideas conceived at the Tuileries, no opinion that did not harmonize with opinions entertained on the throne, could by any possibility be laid before the public in print. The police of the press was active and ubiquitous, and its powers were exercised with jealous and unrelaxing vigilance. "The years of the empire," says Alison, "are an absolute blank in French literary annals, in all matters relating to government, political thought or moral sentiment. The journals were filled with nothing but the exploits of the Emperor, the treatises by which he deigned to enlighten the minds of his subjects in the affairs of state, or the adulatory addresses presented to him from all parts of his dominions; the pamphlets and periodicals of the metropolis breathed only the incense of refined flattery or the vanity of Eastern adulation. Talent in literature took no other direction than that pointed out by the imperial authorities; genius sought to distinguish itself only by new and more extravagant kinds of homage."[1]

Men of letters who were willing to prostitute their opinions, or from any reason, honorable or otherwise, to attach themselves zealously to Napoleon's cause, were sure of recompense and advancement. M. Molé, the last representative of a family illustrious in the annals of legitimacy, wrote and published an apology for Napoleon's despotism, under the title of "Essais de Morale et de Politique." He was at once made Auditor of the Council of State, and obtained speedy promotion. Napoleon never wasted his substance or his protection upon idlers or unproductive courtiers; he bestowed his favors with discernment, requiring effective service at the hands of those who had received, or were candidates for, place, emolument, or preferment.

"I have found the explanation," says Bourrienne, "of the

[1] Europe, vi. 176.

Emperor's general hostility towards literary men. It was less the effect of prejudice than a necessity of his character. Time is required merely to read, and certainly to appreciate, a literary work, and, to Napoleon, time was so precious that he would have gladly shortened even a straight line. He therefore wished men to devote themselves to things at once positive and exact; he detested economists, publicists, philanthropists—all, in short, who, directly or indirectly, occupied themselves with legislation, with public institutions, or social ameliorations. His tendency towards the positive was so imperious, that even in the sciences he only liked what concerned the earth: he never treated Lalande, the astronomer, as he did Monge and Lagrange, the geometricians. The discoveries of the star-gazers could not directly add to his greatness."[1]

"You live too much," said Napoleon to Joseph, whom he was advising upon the subject of government, "with men of letters and savans. They are so many coquettes with whom it may be very well to maintain polite relations, but whom you should never think of making either your wife or your minister."[2]

"Literature," says one of the historians of the epoch, "asks from the powers of this earth naught but liberty and tranquillity: war startles it, tyranny destroys it. While a generous protection hastens the maturity of the fruits of genius, an insolent and domineering patronage checks, if it does not arrest, their growth.

"Augustus and Louis XIV. cherished letters and arts with an elevation of mind which was repaid by the production of masterpieces in every branch of elegant acquirement.

"Domitian and Bonaparte exiled philosophers and Christians, and suborned and salaried such poets as would become sycophants and hypocrites. The protectorate that Napoleon exercised over French literature was as fatal to it as his reign was fatal to the peace of Europe.

"Let us not be unjust. He encouraged several of the arts

and exact sciences, because despotism neither fears paint nor geometry. But all noble bursts of thought, the generous intrepidity of the philosopher, the austere impartiality of the historian, which were odiously distasteful to him, were rigorously suppressed.

"It would be curious to investigate the manner and the gradations by which he succeeded in quenching the genius of his age, and in corrupting the authors who illustrated his reign. They did not all yield without resistance, while several, it is our duty to admit, fell with honor and credit."[1]

Madame de Staël thus launches her invectives at the restrictive system of the period: "When the censors of the press, not confining themselves to erasing, dictate to writers of every description the opinions they are to advance on every subject of politics, religion and morals, it may be conceived into what state a nation must fall which has no other nutriment for its thoughts than such as a despotic authority permits. It is not surprising, therefore, that French literature and criticism descended to the lowest point during the Empire. The newspapers discovered the art of being tame and lifeless at the epoch of the world's overturn; and but for the official bulletins which from time to time let us know that half the world was conquered, we might have believed that the age was one only of roses and flowers."[2]

"Bonaparte, who aspired to despotism," says Lamartine, "and who hated thought because thought is the liberty of the soul, profited by the exhaustion and the lassitude of the human mind at the close of the Revolution, to muzzle or enervate every species of literature. Of the human faculties he only honored those of which he could make docile instruments. Geometricians were men after his own heart; writers made him tremble! It was the age of the compasses. He tolerated only that trifling and futile literature which diverts the people and flatters tyranny. He would have gagged with his whole police any voice whose manly

[1] Michaud, Hist. de Napoléon Bonaparte, ii. 204.   [2] Rév. Française, ii. 377.

accent caused to vibrate the deeper chords of the human heart. He permitted the rhymes which occupy the ear, but he proscribed the poesy which exalts the soul."[1]

"He curses written or spoken thought, as a revolt of reason against fact. He imposes silence upon the tribune, the censure upon journalism, the stamp upon books, and terror or adulation upon authors. He stops the mouth of him who ventures the slightest murmur of a theory. He exiles all who will not sell their breath or their pen. He honors no science but that science which does not think: mathematics. He would suppress the alphabet, had he the power, and make men communicate by figures, because letters express the human soul, while figures express material force."[2]

The most satisfactory justification of the conduct of Napoleon towards literary men was offered by M. Thiers, in his reception discourse at the French Academy, soon after the accession of Louis Philippe. He said: "A pacific government may tolerate what a government illustrated by victory cannot tolerate. And why? Because liberty, quite possible to-day, upon the heels of a bloodless revolution, was impossible then, upon the heels of a sanguinary revolution.

"The men of that time had fearful truths to say to each other. They had shed each other's blood; they had reciprocally despoiled each other; many had borne arms against their country. These men could hardly be free to speak and write without mutually bandying bitter reproaches. Liberty would have been but an exchange of savage recriminations. Napoleon was unwilling that one man should say to another, 'You slaughtered my father or my son; you have appropriated my property; you joined the ranks of the enemy.' He gave to civil dissension the distractions of war; he condemned to the silence in which they expired the disastrous passions it was so essential to extinguish. But to-day, liberty is compatible with safety, because we, the

[1] Hist. de la Restauration, ii. 393. [2] Ibid. i. 394.

men of the present, though we may reproach ourselves with errors, need not charge ourselves with crimes."

In view of the facts we have adduced in reference to the authors claimed as shedding glory upon Napoleon's reign, and of the opinions we have cited upon his estimate and appreciation of literature, any further attempt to magnify the letters of the imperial era would seem a useless and a thankless task. The literature that illustrates and honors an epoch can hardly consist of anterior romance and verse, of subsequent and hostile essay and criticism, or of chefs-d'œuvre conceived in vagabondage, composed in exile, and either published by stealth or suppressed by force. A sovereign that thus treats authorship and thus oppresses genius, would hardly be gratified by the posthumous apologies presented by his partisans, however historical it may be that he offered citizenship to literary foreigners, and regretted that Corneille was not contemporaneous instead of classic.

It is curious to see this blockade of literature and this suspicion of the arts, renewed under the present Napoleon, the Third of his name. Without referring to the exile of Victor Hugo, the first living French writer—a measure for which sufficient political grounds may possibly be invoked—it may safely be said that every successive death in France of men great in the arts, sciences, philosophy, finds the government in dread of rebellion and disturbance at their funerals. It invariably appears that the deceased, if sufficiently distinguished to excite a national interest and to kindle general sympathy, had lived apart from the existing régime, and that the people, the students, the masses, labor and Young France, desire to extend processional honors to their remains. Under Louis Napoleon the great dead are buried by stealth, or under a cloud, or in the apprehension of revolt. Michel de Bourges, the first orator in his hold upon the popular sympathies in France, after the exile of Victor Hugo, was interred early in the morning, by orders from Paris, and in the presence of formidable preparations for defense. The road to the church was commanded by cannon; a specified number of persons only were admitted to the cemetery; no discourses were allowed over the grave. Arago, the first savant of France, and certainly the second, if not the first, of his age, was buried in the midst of an array of troops, a concourse of citizens and a gathering of police, which suggested an encampment and the state of siege. Cartridges had been distributed and passwords whispered, for the director of the Observatory had declined the oath of allegiance. Lamennais, the free-thinker, was buried by surprise: the people were to collect at nine; his body was smuggled to the Potter's Field, by a strong posse of police, at early dawn. David d'Angers, one of the two master sculptors of the early part of this century, was accompanied to his last resting-place by all the students in Paris, and as the funeral was thus a republican one, the government was on the alert. In short, the people of Paris, when they wish to count their numbers and to show their hand, select as the occasion of their assembly and the nucleus of their throng, some illustrious funeral—some hearse bearing immortal ashes. Between them and the dead there is always a bond of sympathy; while between the dead and the myrmidons of the government exist suspicion, hostility, reproach.

When Béranger dies, the drums of the garrison of Paris will beat to arms; the posts of Vincennes and Versailles will be held in readiness for sudden duty; the National Guard will be summoned to quarters; the police will be detailed as for dangerous and responsible service. The veteran chanticleer may expect tumultuous obsequies: possessing more than any other living man the affections and sympathies of the nation, his death will naturally be the object, above all others, of the fears and the distrust of the government.

CHAPTER XX.

Madame de Staël—Her Infancy and Education—Her Marriage—Her Personal Appearance—The Revolution—Her First Meeting and Conversation with Bonaparte—Interview with Josephine—Her Portrait and Character—Her Repartees—Exile—Delphine—Auguste de Staël and Napoleon—Private Theatricals—Corinne—Police Interference—Travels in Foreign Countries—Her Illness and Death—Effect of Napoleon's Persecution upon the Literary Position of Madame de Staël.

JACQUES NECKER, the father of Madame de Staël, a Genevese and a Protestant, was at the birth of his daughter Anne-Louise-Germaine Necker, in 1766, a clerk in a banking-house at Paris. He had married M'lle Curchod, a Swiss like himself, and who had, some years before, been the object of the first and last love of Gibbon the historian. Madame Necker undertook the education of Louise, plied her with books and tasks, and introduced her, even in infancy, to her own circle of brilliant and accomplished men. "At the age of eleven," writes a lady who was at the time her companion, "she spoke with a warmth and facility which were already eloquent. In society she talked but little, but so animated was her face that she appeared to converse with all. Every guest at her mother's house addressed her with some compliment or polite speech; she replied with ease and grace." She was encouraged to write, and her youthful productions were read in public, and some of them were even printed. This process of education, while it rendered the subject of it rather brilliant than profound, and encouraged vanity and a love of display, broke down her health, and the physicians ordered her to retire to the country, and to renounce all mental application.

Her mother, disappointed and discouraged, ceased to take the same interest in her talents and progress; this indifference led Louise to attach herself more closely to her father, and developed in her what became through life her ruling passion—filial affection.

In 1776, Necker, who had in the meantime become the partner of his late employer, and had attracted attention by an essay on the corn laws, was considered by the masses as the only person capable of saving the country from bankruptcy. He was, therefore, appointed to the control of the finances, being the first Protestant who had held office since the revocation of the Edict of Nantes. One of his acts, five years afterwards, having excited clamor among the royalists, an anonymous pamphlet appeared, in which his defense was warmly espoused and the propriety of his conduct successfully asserted. Necker detected his daughter's style in this production, and she acknowledged its authorship, being then fifteen years old. Necker resigned office, and retreated with his family to Coppet, on the borders of the Lake of Geneva.

Madame de Genlis saw M'lle Necker for the first time, when the latter was sixteen. She thus speaks of her in her memoirs: "This young lady was not pretty; her manner was very animated, and she talked a great deal, too much indeed, though always with wit and discernment. I remember that I read one of my juvenile plays to Madame Necker, her daughter being present. I cannot describe the enthusiasm and the demonstrations of M'lle Louise, while I was reading. She wept, she uttered exclamations at every page, and constantly kissed my hands. Her mother had done wrong in allowing her to pass three-quarters of her time with the throng of wits who continually surrounded her, and who held dissertations with her upon love and the passions."[1]

At the age of twenty, Louise married Baron de Staël-Holstein, the Swedish ambassador at the court of France. She sought neither a lover nor a friend in her husband; she treated marriage as a convenience, and became a wife in order to obtain that liberty

[1] Mem. de Madame de Genlis, 92.

and independence which was denied her as a young lady. She required that her husband should be noble and a Protestant, and as in addition to these essentials, Baron de Staël was an agreeable and an honorable man, and engaged never to compel her to follow him to Sweden, she consented to marry him. In the same year, 1786, a failure of the crops, and the consequent distress of the poorer classes, compelled the king to recall Necker to the administration of the finances.

Madame de Staël is thus described, at the age of twenty-five, by a writer who, to justify the peculiar and oriental extravagance of his style, assumed the character of a Greek poet : " Zulmé advances ; her large dark eyes sparkle with genius ; her hair, black as ebony, falls on her shoulders in waving ringlets ; her features are more striking than delicate, and express superiority to her sex. 'There she is,' all exclaim when she appears, and at once become breathless. When she sings, she extemporizes the words of her song, the ecstasy of improvisation animates her face, and holds the audience in rapt attention. When the song ceases, she talks of the great truths of nature, the immortality of the soul, the love of liberty, of the fascination and danger of the passions. Her features meanwhile wear an expression superior to beauty ; her physiognomy is full of play and variety. When she ceases, a murmur of approbation thrills through the room ; she looks down modestly ; her long lashes sink over her flashing eyes, and the sun is clouded over."

The Revolution now advanced with rapid steps. Necker, whose capabilities as a financier have been generally acknowledged, was totally deficient in the higher qualities of the statesman. He sought to assume a middle position between the court and the people, but failing of success, was in consequence dismissed on the 11th of July, 1789. Paris rose in insurrection when this event became known, and on the 14th, the Bastille was in the hands of the people. The king was forced to send an order of recall to Necker, who had left the country : this overtook him at Frankfort. "What a period of happiness," writes Madame de Staël, "was our journey back to Paris! I do not believe that a similar ovation was ever extended to a man not the sovereign of the country. Women, afar off in the fields, threw themselves on their knees, as the carriage passed: the most prominent citizens acted as postillions, and in many towns the people detached the horses and dragged the carriage themselves. Oh, nothing can equal the emotions of a woman who hears the name of a beloved parent repeated with eulogy by a whole people!" This triumph was of short duration. In a little more than a year, Necker, who had opposed some of the more radical measures of reform in the National Assembly, lost the confidence of the people, resigned, and again withdrew to Switzerland. He was now accompanied by the revilings and maledictions of the populace, and even narrowly escaped with his life.

Madame de Staël remained at Paris, and speedily became involved in the intrigues of the day. Her salon was the rendezvous of the royalists and Girondins, and the scene of ardent political discussions. In the midst of the sanguinary excesses of '92, she fearlessly used her influence to shelter and save her friends. She took them to her own house, which, being the residence of an ambassador, she presumed would be inviolable. But one night the police appeared at the gate, and required that the doors be opened for a rigid search. Madame de Staël met them at the threshold, spoke to them of the rights of ambassadors and of the vengeance of Sweden, and by dint of wit, argument and intrepidity, persuaded them to abandon their designs. She was soon compelled to flee, however, and take refuge with her father at Coppet. Here she wrote and published an appeal in behalf of Marie Antoinette, and "Reflections on the Peace of 1783." The fall of Robespierre, in July, 1794, enabled her to return to Paris, whither she hastened, upon the news of his execution.

Her residence in the capital formed an event in the annals of society at that period. The most distinguished foreigners and the best men in France flocked around her. She gave her influence to the government of the Directory, being desirous of the establishment of some guarantee for the preservation of order and of individual security.

"Madame de Staël," says de Goncourt, "was a man of genius as early as the year 1795. It was by her hands that France signed a treaty of alliance with existing institutions, and for a period accepted the Directory. Who obtained her the victory? Herself, with the aid of a friend who was the scribe of her dictation, the aid-de-camp and the notary-public of her thought, Benjamin Constant. The daughter of Necker forbade France to recall its line of kings: she retained the republic: she condemned the throne. She agitated victoriously in behalf of the maintenance of the representative system. The human right of victory was equivalent, with her, to the divine right of birth."[1]

The appearance of Bonaparte upon the stage of action produced a violent change in her life, pursuits and pleasures. She disliked and distrusted him from the first, and her drawing-room became an opposition club, or, as Napoleon himself described it, an arsenal of hostility. He, in turn, was vexed at her intellectual supremacy, and dreaded her influence. They first met at a ball given to Josephine, towards the close of the year 1797. She had long hunted him from place to place, for she was desirous of subjecting him, if possible, to the fascinations of her conversation, and he, avoiding the interview with consummate address, had always escaped her importunities. At the ball in question, he saw retreat to be impossible, and boldly seated himself in a vacant chair by her side. The following conversation, attributed to them, contains, in a concise form, the best of the authenticated sallies and repartees perpetrated by the illustrious interlocutors. After the usual preliminaries, the dialogue proceeded thus:

MADAME DE STAËL. Madame Bonaparte is a charming lady.

[1] Soc. Franç. sous le Directoire, 298.

Bonaparte. Any compliment passing through your lips, madame, acquires additional value.

St. Ah! then you appreciate my opinion and my approbation? But you have doubted my capacity, you have thought me frivolous; nevertheless, my studies in diplomacy, in the history of courts —

Bon. I implore Madame de Staël not to drag the Graces to the pillory of politics.

St. I assure you, General, that your mythological compliment is totally lost upon me: I should prefer that you judge me worthy to talk reason with you.

Bon. The right of your sex is to make us lose our reason: do not despise so excellent a privilege.

St. General, I beg of you not to play with me as with a doll: I desire to be treated as a man.

Bon. Then you would like to have me put on petticoats.

St.—TO A GENTLEMAN INTERRUPTING HER.—Sir, be good enough to understand that I desire no assistance, though certainly my adversary is sufficiently powerful to render assistance necessary.

Bon. Madame, it was to my aid that he was coming; my danger appalls him, and he was seeking to relieve me.

St. In any case, I owe him small thanks for his tardy aid, since you confess that my victory seemed certain. He is a true friend, however; he stands by those he likes, even in their absence, when, usually, friendship slumbers.

Bon. In that friendship imitates its cousin—love.

St.—NERVING HERSELF FOR AN EFFORT.—By what means, General, can an ordinary woman, without literary reputation, without superior genius, be sustained in the affection of a man she loves when separated from him by distance or a period of years? Memory, reduced to recalling her charms only, becomes gradually dim, and at last forgets, especially when the lover is a great man. But when the latter has had the good fortune to meet with a strong-minded woman, one worthy of sharing his laurels and herself enjoying a high reputation, then the distance of time and space disappears, for it is the renown of both which serves as messenger between them, and it is through the hundred mouths of fame that each receives intelligence of the other.

Bon. Madame, in what chapter of the work you are about to publish shall we read this brilliant passage?

St. It has been the constant illusion of my soul.

Bon. Ah, I understand; it is your hobby, after the manner of Sterne. So you are seeking the philosopher's stone?

St. One would think, to hear you talk, that it is impossible to find it.

Bon. There are two illusions in this world, though both flow from the same error; that of physical and that of moral alchemy. This idealistic philosophy leads to an abyss.

St. One, nevertheless, which wit and sagacity may illumine with the rays of genius to its inmost recesses. Do you never build castles in the air, General? Do you never go and dwell in them? Do you never dream, to charm away the monotony of life?

Bon. I leave dreams to sleep, and retain reason for my waking hours.

St. Then you can never be either amused or surprised? You have a scouting party stationed to watch that outpost, the imagination?

Bon. Wisdom counsels me to do so, and makes it my duty.

St.—AFTER A MOMENT'S REFLECTION.—General, who, in your opinion, is the greatest of women?

Bon. She who bears the most children.[1]

Madame de Staël turned slightly pale at this reply, and said no more. The General rose, bowed, and quitted the room. Both carried away from the interview the elements of mutual dislike and food for a life-long hostility. "Doubtless," says Lacretelle, "this last question was suggested by the vanity of the inquirer." And

Bonaparte, eager to deprive the lady of the tribute she expected in his reply, made answer as we have described. "Certainly," adds Lacretelle, "it was impossible to rebuff a courtesy with greater rudeness and less discernment, for Madame de Staël was one of the powers of the day."[1]

One evening, early in the Consulate, Josephine met Madame de Staël at the house of Madame de Montesson. Bonaparte was to come somewhat later. Josephine, knowing his aversion for her, or fearing her seductions if she were successful in obtaining his attention, received her, as she advanced, in a manner so markedly cold, if not rude, that Madame de Staël recoiled without speaking, and retreated to the extremity of the room, where she dropped into a chair.

She remained for some time apart and alone. The pretty women took a malicious pleasure in the mortification of one of their own sex, while the gentlemen indulged in impertinent and unmanly remarks. At this moment, a young girl of extreme beauty and light airy step, with blond hair and blue eyes, and dressed entirely in white, left the group that had collected in the vicinity of Josephine, crossed the salon, and sat down by Madame de Staël. The latter, whose heart was as quick as her wit was ready, said to her, "You are as good as you are beautiful, my child."

"In what, pray, madame?" asked the young lady.

"In what?" returned Madame de Staël. "You ask me why I think you as kind as you are fair? Because you crossed this immense and deserted salon to come and sit by me. Upon my word, you are more courageous than I should have been."

"And yet, madame, I am naturally so timid that I should not dare to tell you my fears and trepidation: you would laugh at me, I am sure."

"Laugh at you!" exclaimed Madame de Staël, with moistened eyes and trembling voice; "laugh at you! never! never!

[1] Lac. Rév. Française, ii. 140.

I am your sister, henceforth, my dear, dear young friend! Will you tell me your Christian name?"

"Delphine, madame."

"Delphine! What a pretty name! I am very glad of it, for it will suit my purpose exactly. You must know, love, that I am writing a novel; and I mean it to bear your name. You shall be its god-mother; and you will find something in it which will remind you of to-day and of our acquaintance."

Madame de Staël kept her promise, and the passage in the novel of Delphine, in which the heroine, abandoned, is, under similar circumstances, relieved and sustained by Madame de R., was written in commemoration of this little domestic scene.[1]

Bonaparte soon entered the room, and, ignorant of the treatment Madame de Staël had undergone from Josephine, accosted her graciously, and indeed took evident pains to restrain, during their conversation, his intuitive dislike of the petticoat politician.

Madame de Staël was now at the apogee of her talent and influence. Her conversation was not what is usually understood by the term. She did not require so much an interlocutor as a listener. Her improvisations were long and sustained pleas, if her object was to convince, or discursive though brilliant harangues, if she sought to display her wealth of thought and of words. Those that were accustomed to her ways rarely answered her, even if, in the heat of argument, she addressed them a question; well aware that it was rather to operate a diversion than to elicit a reply. She required the excitement of an audience, and her eloquence became richer and more rapid as the circle of her listeners widened. She preferred contradiction and dissent to a blind acceptance of her opinions, and the surest method of pleasing her was to adduce arguments that she might refute them, and which might suggest in her mind new trains of ideas. Controversy was her peculiar element, and she sometimes resorted to the charlatanical process of advocating two opposite opinions on

[1] Vide "Delphine," vol. ii. p. 866.

the same occasion, in order to show the flexibility of her mind and the pliancy of her logic. In the season of foliage, she invariably carried in her hand a twig of poplar, which, when talking, she would turn and twist between her fingers; the crackling of this, she said, stimulated her brain. During the season when the poplar produces no leaves, she substituted for the twig a piece of rolled paper with which she was forced to be content, till the return of verdure. In winter, her flatterers and admirers always held a supply of these papers prepared, and presented her a quantity, on her arrival at a fête or a conversazione, that she might select her sceptre for the evening.[1] The famous twig of poplar is introduced in Gérard's portrait of Madame de Staël.[*]

She was never handsome, and without the extraordinary depth and brilliancy of her eyes, would have been a plain, if not an ugly woman. Her nose and mouth were homely, and only redeemed by her ever-varying expression. Her complexion was rough, her form massive rather than graceful, and indicated indolence rather than vivacity. Her hands were beautiful, and ill-natured people asserted that the poplar twig was a mere pretext for keeping them constantly in view. She dressed at all times without taste, and this defect became more conspicuous as she advanced in years, for at the age of forty-five she wore the colors and ornaments which would befit a young lady of twenty. Her coiffure was usually a turban, though this was not the prevailing fashion. Her partisans denied that there was any exaggeration in her toilet, though they allowed that she sought to be picturesque rather than fashionable.

Biography has preserved examples almost innumerable of the readiness of her wit and the profundity of her observation. The love of truth was one of her prominent characteristics. "I saw," she said, "that Bonaparte was declining, when he no longer sought for the truth." She held long arguments on equality, and said on one occasion, "I would not refuse the opinion of the lowest of

---

[1] Ducrest, Mém. de Josephine, 23.
[*] It is from a copy of this portrait, by Gérard, in the Historical Gallery of Versailles, that the likeness of Madame de Staël on the opposite page is taken.

my domestics, if the slightest of my own impressions tended to justify his." Her respect for justice and moderation was evinced in her reply to the remark of a Bourbon after Napoleon's fall, to the effect that Bonaparte had neither talent nor courage : "It is degrading France and Europe too much, sir, to pretend that for fifteen years they have been subject to a simpleton and a poltroon!" She despised affectation, and said that she could not converse with an affected man or woman on account of the constant interruptions of a tedious third person—their unnatural and affected character. Of individuals accustomed to exaggerate, she said : "To put 100 for 10, why, there's no imagination in that." Her faith was sincere and unostentatious, and she would remark, after listening to lofty metaphysical discourses, "Well, I like the Lord's Prayer better than that." One of her best replies was made to Canning, in the Tuileries, after the exile of Napoleon : "Well, Madame de Staël, we have conquered you French, you see!" "If you have, sir, it was because you had the Russians and the whole continent on your side. Give us a tête-à-tête, and you will see!"

Madame de Staël's conduct as a wife was not irreproachable Talleyrand was one of the first, though by no means the last, of her lovers. It was after his rupture with Madame de Staël that he entered upon his liaison with Madame Grandt, and it was this circumstance that led Madame de Staël to ask him the most unfortunate question of her life, for it gave him the opportunity of making the most comprehensive reply of his : "If Madame Grandt and I were to fall into the water, Talleyrand," she inquired, "which of us would you save first ?" "Oh, madame," returned the minister, "YOU SWIM SO WELL!" She was revenged on him by drawing—though not very delicately—his character as a diplomatist : "He is so double-faced," she said, "that if you kick him behind, he will smile in front."

Bonaparte, early in the Consulate, sought, through his brother Joseph, to attach Madame de Staël to his government ; he might have done so, had he cared to conciliate her by expressing, or even feigning, deference to her talents and opinions. But he did not pursue the negotiation, and she continued her political discussions at her house, devoting her days to intrigues, and her evenings to epigrams; until Bonaparte, whose patience was exhausted, and who did not consider his power as yet fully established, directed his minister of police to banish her from Paris. She was ordered not to return within forty leagues of the city. He is said to have remarked, "I leave the whole world open to Madame de Staël, except Paris: that I reserve to myself." It was urged, too, that she had small claims to consideration; she was, though born in France, hardly a Frenchwoman, being the daughter of a Swiss and the wife of a Swede.

During a period of years, Madame de Staël remained under the ban of Bonaparte's displeasure, though, during a short interval, the intercessions of her father obtained permission for her to inhabit the capital. In 1803, she published her "Delphine," a work so immoral in its tendency that it incurred the censure of the critics and the public, and compelled the authoress to put forth a species of apology, which in its turn was considered lame and inconclusive. The character of Madame de Vernon, in "Delphine," was said to have been intended for Talleyrand, clothed in female garb.

Unable to endure the deprivation of her Parisian friends, Madame de Staël soon established herself at the distance of thirty miles from Paris. Bonaparte was told that her residence was crowded with visitors from the capital. "She affects," he said, "to speak neither of public affairs nor of me; yet it invariably happens that every one comes out of her house less attached to me than when he went in." An order for her departure was soon served upon her, and she set forth upon a pilgrimage through Germany.

In the last week of December, 1807, Napoleon, returning from Italy, stopped at the post-house of Chambéry, in Sardinia, for a fresh relay of horses. He was told that a young man of seventeen years, named Auguste de Staël, desired to speak with him. "What have I to do with these refugees of Geneva?" said Napoleon, tartly. He ordered him to be admitted, however. "Where is your mother?" said Napoleon, opening the conversation. "She is at Vienna, sire." "Ah, she must be satisfied now; she will have fine opportunities for learning German." "Sire, your Majesty cannot suppose that my mother can be satisfied anywhere, separated from her friends and driven from her country. If your Majesty would condescend to glance at these private letters, written by my mother, you would see, sire, what unhappiness her exile causes her." "Oh, pooh! that's the way with your mother. I do not say she is a bad woman; but her mind is insubordinate and rebellious. She was brought up in the chaos of a falling monarchy, and of a revolution running riot, and it has turned her head. If I were to allow her to return, six months would not pass before I should be obliged to shut her up in Bedlam, or put her under lock and key at the Temple. I should be sorry to do it, for it would make scandal, and injure me in public opinion. Tell your mother my mind is made up. As long as I live, she shall not again set foot in Paris."

"Sire, I am so sure that my mother would conduct herself with propriety that I pray you to grant her a trial, if it be only for six weeks." "It cannot be. She would make herself the standard-bearer of the faubourg St. Germain. She would receive visits, would return them, would make witticisms, and do a thousand follies. No, young man, no." "Will your Majesty allow a son to inquire the cause of this hostility to his mother? I have been told it was the last work of my grandfather; I can assure your Majesty that my mother had no hand in it." "Certainly, that book had its effect. Your grandfather was an idealist, an old maniac; at sixty years of age, to attempt to overturn my constitution and to replace it by one of his! An economist, indeed! A man who dreams financial schemes and could hardly perform the duties of a village tax-gatherer decently! Robespierre and Danton have done less harm to France than M. Necker. Your grandfather is the cause of the saturnalia which have desolated France. Upon his head be all the blood of the Revolution!" "Sire, I trust that posterity will speak more favorably of him. During his administration, he was compared with Sully and Colbert, and I trust to the justice of posterity." "Posterity will perhaps not speak of him at all," returned Napoleon.

"You are young, M. de Staël," he added, changing his tone, and taking the petitioner familiarly by the ear. "Your frankness pleases me: I like to see a son plead the cause of his mother. She confided to you a difficult mission, and you have discharged it with intelligence. I cannot give you false hopes, so I do not conceal from you that you will obtain nothing whatever. I'll have none of your mother in the city where I dwell. Women should knit stockings, and not talk politics." As Napoleon rode away from Chambéry, he said to Duroc: "Was I not rather hard with that young man? After all, I am glad of it. The thing is settled once for all. France is no place for the family of Necker."[1]

During the absence of Madame de Staël in Germany, her father died, and she hastened to return to Coppet. She collected and published his writings, and appended to them a biographical memoir. She cherished his memory with a passion bordering on monomania, which led her, whenever she saw an old man in affliction, to seek to alleviate his sorrows. She often said, upon hearing good news, "I owe this to the intercessions of my father."

She found it difficult satisfactorily to occupy her leisure. She used to say that she would prefer living on two thousand francs a year in the Rue Jean Pain Mollet at Paris, to spending one hundred thousand at Geneva. But she made no effort to obtain a recall, at least by imposing restraint upon her tongue. Knowing that she was surrounded by spies, and that her bitter allusions to Napoleon were reported at the Tuileries, she continued to exhaust her wit upon the acts of his government, and upon the tyranny of him whom she called "Robespierre on horseback."

Amateur theatricals upon a diminutive stage built for the purpose, afforded some amusement to the exile of Coppet. The audiences were principally French residents at Geneva, whose ambition to be able to boast of their admission into Madame de Staël's intimacy, induced them to travel the wearisome road which separated the two places. While waiting for the lamps to be lighted, they ate bread and chocolate in the dark—this being the traditional lunch that a Frenchman carries in his pocket. On one occasion the performance was Racine's tragedy of Andromaque. Madame de Staël played Hermione effectively, it would seem, but with a redundancy of gesture that somewhat marred the illusion. Madame Récamier acted Andromaque, the interesting widow; but the critics were so absorbed in the contemplation of her wondrous beauty that they have left little record of her histrionic ability. The characters of Oreste, Pylade and Pyrrhus were performed by M. de Labédoyère, Benjamin Constant and Sismondi, the historian. The two latter were very amusing, it appears, though the play being a tragedy, mirth could hardly have been the effect they desired to produce. Benjamin Constant, whose gestures were very broad and sweeping, once carried away a Grecian temple with the palm of his hand; Sismondi gave infinite zest to the representation by the purity of his Genevese accent. The prompter was M. Schlegel, the poet, critic and historian. His strong German pronunciation rendered him at best an inefficient assistant, for the actor whose memory was treacherous often failed to recognize the missing line, in the husky and guttural suggestions of the author of Lucinde.

The health of Madame de Staël was now declining, and in order to recruit it she undertook a journey through Italy. On her return, she published "Corinne," a poetic description of the peninsula, in the form of a novel. Though deficient in construction and dramatic power, it possesses the highest merit as a work delineating character and descriptive of scenery, and inculcates a pure morality. Incident and plot form its least attractive features; its eloquent rhapsodies upon love, religion, virtue, nature, history and poetry, have given it an enduring place in literature. She now took up her abode at the required distance from Paris, at Chaumont-sur-Loire, where she inhabited the chateau already famous as the residence of Diane de Poitiers, Catherine de Medicis, and Nostradamus the soothsayer, and at this time in the possession of one of her most attached friends. She here wrote and prepared for the press a work on the habits, character and literature of the Germans. The manuscript was laid before the censors at Paris, who expunged certain passages, and then authorized its publication. This was in 1810.

Ten thousand copies had been already printed, when the whole edition was seized at the publishers', by gendarmes sent by Savary, the minister of police. Madame de Staël was ordered to quit France in eight days. She withdrew again to Coppet, from whence she opened a correspondence with Savary upon this arbitrary, and indeed illegal, proceeding. She had been given to understand that the motive for the suppression was her omission to mention the name of Napoleon in connection with Germany, where his armies had lately made him conspicuous. She wrote to Savary that she did not see how she could have introduced the Emperor and his "soldiery" into a purely literary work. To this Savary replied that she was misinformed upon the motive which had actuated him, and that her exile was the natural consequence of her conduct for years past. "We are not so reduced in France," he added, "as to seek for models among the nations which you admire. Your book is not French, and the air of France does not suit you." This impertinent letter was prefixed to the first edition of "Germany" published in London, in 1813.

During her residence at Coppet, Madame de Staël, now a widow and forty-two years of age, became acquainted with M. de Rocca, a French officer. She felt an interest in him even before she saw him, for he was said to be young, noble and brave ; what was a still more attractive feature, he was wounded and an invalid. They first met in a public ball-room. She was dressed, it appears, in a gaudy and unbecoming style, and was followed from point to point by a train of admirers and flatterers. "Is that the famous woman?" said de Rocca. "She is very plain, and I abhor such continual aiming at effect." She spoke to him, expressed sympathy for his condition, and speedily effected a complete revolution in his opinions. From a caviller he became an admirer, and from an admirer a suitor. They were privately married, and the secret was carefully kept until the reading of her will, after her death, for she felt that the match was an ill-assorted one, and could hardly fail to excite ridicule. Besides, she was unwilling to change her name, "as it belonged to Europe," to quote her own words to de Rocca.

The tyranny to which she was subjected at the period of this marriage, by Napoleon, became annoying and perplexing. She was not only exiled from France, but warned not to go farther than six miles from Coppet. Mathieu de Montmorency was exiled for visiting her, as was also Madame Récamier, as has already been narrated. M. Schlegel, who aided her in the education of her three children, was compelled to leave her. She was seized with the gloomiest apprehensions, and resolved to escape from the sphere of Napoleon's power. The prefect of Geneva was instructed, from Paris, to suggest to Madame de Staël a means of recovering the sovereign's good graces—the publication of some loyal stanzas upon the birth of Napoleon's heir. "Tell those that sent you," she replied, "that I have no wishes in connection with the King of Rome, except the desire that his mother get him a healthy wet-nurse."

She now passed her time in studying the map of Europe, in choosing an asylum, and in devising a route by which to get to it. She at last departed for England, which she approached through Russia and Sweden. Once beyond French influence, she was treated with the highest consideration and the warmest cordiality. Among the distinguished men admitted to her intimacy, Lord Byron held the first place, and she often gave him advice both upon his conduct and his verse. It was now that she published her "Germany." She had the deep satisfaction of seeing her reputation as a critic and delineator of national manners elevated by it to the highest point.

She welcomed with delight the overthrow and abdication of Napoleon, and at once returned to Paris, where she attached herself to the party advocating a representative government under Louis XVIII. The restored sovereign caused the royal treasury to pay to her family the two million francs due M. Necker at his retirement from office—a measure of justice to which Napoleon would never consent. During the Hundred Days she retired to Switzerland, totally weaned from all interest in public life. Her health began to fail, and she still further weakened it by the use of opium. She devoted herself closely to the composition of her last work, the "French Revolution," which now ranks as one of the most philosophical, though perhaps not the most impartial, histories of that period. Her sleepless nights she spent in prayer; she became gentle, patient and devout. "I think I know," she said, in her last moments, "what the passage from life to death is. I am convinced the goodness of God makes it easy; our thoughts become indistinct, and the pain is not great." She died with perfect composure, in 1817, in the fifty-first year of her age. Her husband, who was devotedly attached to her, survived her but a few months.

Madame de Staël was the most distinguished authoress of her time. As a woman, she was always independent and sincere, and her faults—vanity and an uncontrollable thirst for applause—may easily be pardoned in view of her many talents. Napoleon could have won her to his government at any moment, had he chosen to do so. It is perhaps fortunate for literature that she was compelled to live in isolation, as neither "Corinne" nor "Germany" would have been written had she been able to reside in Paris, instead of travelling to occupy her exile. It is a singular and not unfair commentary upon Napoleon's reign, that its most remarkable literary celebrity—in point of mere chronology—owed her supremacy to his persecution; and it is a permissible inference, that had his government preferred to foster and cherish her genius, Madame de Staël would have been known to posterity as little more than a precocious child, a brilliant conversationalist, an unsexed woman, and a factious politician.

CHAPTER XXI.

Liberty of the Press—The Moniteur—Official Bulletins—Registry of Marriages—Suppression of Newspapers—The British Press—Control of Public Opinion—Mutilated Editions of the Classics—Dramatic Censorship—Edward in Scotland—Lax Criticism—Josephine and Cadet-Roussel—Violation of the Mails—The Dark Closet—Napoleon's Correspondents—Napoleon and Public Opinion.

WE have spoken, in the two preceding chapters, of the influence of Napoleon upon the literature of his time, of his relations with and conduct towards men of letters, and of his treatment and appreciation of their productions. We have now to describe the processes by which he sought, and, in a measure, contrived, to lead and control public opinion, through the daily and periodical press; to prevent the inculcation through schoolbooks and the classics, of principles which he considered antagonistic to his system; to check the liberty of the stage, by a rigid dramatic censorship; and to obtain a correct idea of the state of the popular mind, by means of a violation of the mails, and the employment of numerous persons of intelligence and good standing as correspondents and advisers—these persons not serving, it must be remembered, at all in the capacity of informers.

The preceding constitutions of France had recognized the liberty of the press. Under the Provisional Consulate, the police assumed discretionary power, and resorted to the seizure of papers and pamphlets, and to the arrest of printers. It was supposed that Bonaparte's Constitution of the Year VIII. would substitute for this arbitrary process the fixed forms of a definite legislation. But the constitution, when it appeared, was found to be silent upon this vital matter. A few weeks afterwards, January 17th, 1800, a decree appeared, suppressing all the political journals of Paris, but thirteen ; the most considerable of those allowed to remain were the Moniteur, the Débats, the Journal de Paris, the Publiciste, and L'Ami des Lois. The minister of police was directed to suffer no others to appear, except such as were devoted exclusively to commerce, science, art, literature and advertisements. The avowed and doubtless the real motive for this step was the fact that several of the suppressed sheets served the cause of the royalists and other enemies of the Republic. The latter, however, to supply their place, established numerous secret bulletins, and from time to time issued anonymous and unacknowledged pamphlets.

The Moniteur now became the "only official journal," and the First Consul made it, says Thibaudeau, "the soul and the mainspring of his government, and his vehicle of communication with the public at home and abroad."[1] The same writer says of the political and diplomatic notes inserted in it by Napoleon, that "they were either the expression of the truth or of what the government wished to have regarded as the truth. It is the duty of sound criticism to penetrate its motive, and to distinguish the true from the false : for if the ordinary reader accords full confidence to the articles of official journals, the enlightened reader is well aware that they contain, for the most part, little more than mutilated facts or designed mis-statements."[2] This admission is remarkable, proceeding from a writer so impartial and conscientious.

"It is to be desired," says Bourrienne, writing upon the same subject, "that the historian of this epoch beware of the bulletins, despatches, notes and proclamations which emanated from Bonaparte or which passed through his hands. The proverb 'False as a bulletin,' is as reliable as an axiom. Official documents were almost invariably altered ; the victories were exaggerated, while

[1] Thib. i. 403. [2] Ibid. i. 404.

loss and reverse were as constantly extenuated. A history composed solely from the official bulletins, correspondence and despatches of the period, would be a veritable romance."[1]

Napoleon began at an early age to falsify public documents. The first instance—one which may be episodically narrated here—was due to a sentiment of perhaps pardonable vanity. Josephine was six years older than himself, and this difference of age he sought, on their union, by an adroit substitution of dates, to banish from the register of marriages. He therefore gave to the proper officer his own age as twenty-eight years, whereas it was exactly twenty-six years and a half; and he gave that of Josephine as twenty-nine years, though in reality it was thirty-three. In order to justify this modification, the date of his own birth, the 15th of August, 1769, was changed to the 5th of February, 1768; and the date of Josephine's birth was removed from the 20th of June, 1763, to the 23d of June, 1767. The declaration made, however, that both were of the same age is inconsistent with these figures, which indicate that Napoleon was her junior by nearly a year. This distortion of dates is inexplicable, except on the supposition that General Bonaparte desired to equalize their two ages.

Napoleon, however, attributed this deception in Josephine's registry to that lady herself. The conversation turned, one day at St. Helena, upon the unwillingness of women to allow their age to be known. The case of a lady who preferred losing a large estate to producing her certificate of birth, which would have secured a verdict in her favor, was cited; as well as that of a lady in love, who lived unmarried rather than show the record of her age. Napoleon then mentioned the instance of "a lady of high rank, who deceived her husband, on their marriage, by five or six years at least, by substituting for her own certificate that of a younger sister, long since dead. Poor Josephine exposed herself, however, to great danger by this act, for it might have

[1] Bour. iv 349.

rendered the union null and void." The chronicler of these conversations goes on to say that Napoleon's words gave his auditory the key to certain dates, those already alluded to, which had formerly excited malicious laughter at the Tuileries, and which were then explained by the gallantry of the husband and the complaisance of the imperial almanac.[1]

The decree of the 17th of January—to return to the newspaper laws—did not define what would be considered an offence of the press, nor did it state what tribunal was to be charged with passing judgment upon refractory or erring editors. The government took the matter into its own hands, and Bonaparte's will became the law. "L'Ami des Lois" was soon suppressed, upon the recommendation of Lucien Bonaparte, then Minister of the Interior, for an article "heaping ridicule and sarcasm upon the Institute." Other suppressions were ordered for various causes. The secret and gossiping papers for a time defied the vigilance of Fouché. "L'Invisible," printed and circulated by a royalist committee, announced the intention of Bonaparte "to obtain a divorce because Madame Bonaparte could not give him an heir." "La Vedette de Rouen" dissected the character and capacity of the Council of State, mingling a good deal of offensive truth with as much scandalous fibbing. The "Bulletin à la Main" detailed the private life of Napoleon and Josephine at Malmaison. Among the subscribers to this sheet were the ambassadors of Prussia, of the Italian Republic, and of Russia, in Paris. The latter, by his influence, directed the paper in the interest of England. The editor, a person named Fouilloux, was sent to prison; but this savored so strongly of tyranny that Bonaparte was obliged to justify himself before the Council of State. "L'Antidote" was suppressed for containing "numbers of those frightful maxims which have produced so much evil in France."

These measures soon inspired a salutary terror, and during the remainder of his career Napoleon ruled the French press with a

[1] Las Cases, in. 93.

rod of iron. He had, in fact, succeeded so well, at the period of the signing of the treaty of Amiens, early in 1802, that he made an attempt to extend the sphere of his power, and to limit the liberty of the press of Great Britain. The English journals were abusive, hostile and calumnious in the extreme; a sheet called "L'Ambigu," published at London, in French, by a person named Peltier, the ex-editor of the "Acts of the Apostles," rendered itself conspicuous above them all by the violence and unscrupulousness of its attacks. Its title was as follows: "L'Ambigu, an atrocious and amusing miscellany, in the Egyptian style, published every ten days." Bonaparte, who was too susceptible to be able to treat this as it deserved, replied by articles equally ill-tempered, in the Moniteur. He instructed his minister at London, M. Otto, to protest against it; and wrote personally to the chancellor of the exchequer, to pray him to take measures for the passage of a law repressing an abuse so flagrant. The chancellor replied at length, citing the usual arguments in favor of the liberty of the press, and advising the First Consul to treat the matter with sovereign indifference. He added that any editor might be prosecuted for libel, but that his trial would involve the republication of the scandalous articles of which he—Bonaparte—complained. The First Consul abandoned for a while all attempts at retaliation, but a short time after the peace of Amiens, the French ambassador prosecuted Peltier, before the Court of the King's Bench, accusing him of advocating the assassination of Napoleon. Peltier, though defended by Sir James Mackintosh, was found guilty of libel, and was sentenced to a light fine and the costs. The requisite sum was immediately raised by voluntary subscription. This verdict was rendered on the very day of the rupture of the treaty of Amiens: the prosperity of the Ambigu, so far from being compromised, was, on the contrary, immensely benefited by the condemnation. This was the first and only instance of interference, on the part of Napoleon, with the press of Great Britain.

During the Empire, the French press remained under the

thumb-screw of the police and of the Bureau of Public Security. It would be impossible to detail all the remarkable instances of its forced silence at important junctures. Two examples will suffice. The newspapers were not allowed to chronicle the fearful naval disaster of Trafalgar: the Moniteur dismissed it in three lines. When the allies entered France in 1814, they found the greater part of the population ignorant that such a conflict had ever taken place.[1] On the day preceding the battle of Montmartre, in 1814, which decided the fate of Paris, the Moniteur omitted to allude to it, owing to a press of other matter, such as a commentary on "nosography," and a criticism upon the drama of the Chaste Susanna.

The Bureau of the "Direction of Public Opinion"—a police department—besides composing articles for the newspapers and pieces for the theatres, revised and expurgated the classics, and closely examined all elementary books intended for the instruction of youth. This they did not do in the spirit of those wise and prudent teachers who seek to remove from the perusal of their scholars passages dangerous to good morals and conducive to lax principles: their object was the suppression of sentiments which might recall and revive ideas of liberty and of the rights of humanity. They published mutilated editions of Racine, Corneille, Fenelon, Massillon, Rousseau. They announced an edition of the historian Sallust, "with the omission of exceptionable passages." Everything which proceeded from authors whose antiquity gave them authority, or whose fame gave them influence, and which tended to throw discredit upon the injustice of conquerors, upon the tyranny of princes and the calamities of war, was ruthlessly expunged.

"Frenchmen," says a modern author, "are like gunpowder: individually, they resemble the grains, smutty and contemptible; nationally, they are like the magazine, fired and exploding." We quote this opinion not for the purpose of subscribing to it, by any

[1] Alison's Europe, vi. 176.

means, but because it records an important distinction between the individual and the mass—a distinction upon which is founded the necessity of dramatic censorship in France—a subject of which we have now to speak. A man alone, and in isolation, may read with calmness what might be very exciting, were he to hear it in company with a thousand others like himself. Sentiments which are harmless in print may lead to disorder and to hostile demonstrations, if tossed from the foot-lights into an excitable and disaffected pit. Napoleon found that his subjects would severally peruse without emotion the popular and democratic language of Brutus in Voltaire's "Mort de César," but that if an actor, in the garb and with the manner of Brutus, delivered this same language in the hearing of the same individuals, collectively, they became an inflamed and menacing mob. Dramatic censorship consists, then, in the expurgation from the acting copy of matter liable to political application, which is allowed to remain in the printed edition.

The instances of this under Napoleon were innumerable. The following lines from "Britannicus" were dropped in the representation, by order of the police, in consequence of the application by the audience to Napoleon of what was said of Nero:

> "Je ne connais Néron et la cour que d'un jour;
> Mais, si je l'ose dire, hélas! dans cette cour,
> Combien tout ce que l'on dit est loin de ce que l'on pense,
> Que la bouche et le cœur sont peu d'intelligence,
> Avec combien de joie on y trahit sa foi—
> Quel séjour étranger et pour vous et pour moi!"[1]

[1] In 1851, the censors of Louis Napoleon, who was then President of the Republic and unconstitutionally a candidate for reëlection, struck out from a comedietta in verse the following passage, which, as the author is not a classic, we venture to translate:

> "I drink to harmony and that powerful accord
> Which makes a state tranquil and a people strong;
> To the day marked with white, when civic virtue
> Could alone aspire to power and public place;
> When the Chief of the State, the Guardian of Liberty,
> Deserved well of his dearly beloved country,
> In returning, his brow bound with oak-leaves,
> To prune his blooming vineyard and cultivate his field."

The objection to this tribute to Cincinnatus was, that the audience would inevitably applaud it as a disguised admonition to Louis Napoleon to retire gracefully from power, at the expiration of his term.

Agrippina's address to Nero, in the same tragedy, having caused, on one occasion, great confusion in the house, and necessitated a large number of arrests, it was also suppressed.

The opening stanzas of "Heraclius" were pointed out by certain eager courtiers as exceptionable, and the order was given that the proper expurgations or alterations be made. A "poet" was engaged to execute the necessary changes, and Heraclius was not again performed till it had undergone mutilation and adaptation. The tragedy of Cinna was represented as Corneille wrote it, and it was Bonaparte's favorite play, containing, as it does, a long and vehement tirade against popular power.

One of the censors proposed to the Minister of the Interior to withdraw the tragedy of "Tancrède" from the repertory of the Comédie Française, because its hero is an exile who returns to his country without having obtained the previous authorization of the government! This was carrying the matter too far, and the minister declined acting upon the censor's suggestion.

M. Lehoc's tragedy of "Pyrrhus," in which Talma had an admirable part, was suppressed by Napoleon, after several performances, on account of one single line. A usurper, advised to restore a throne to the rightful monarch, replies that he would rather fall than abdicate:

> "Je pourrais en tomber, je n'en veux pas descendre."

"La Mort de César," of which we have spoken, was withdrawn from the stage, in consequence of the emphatic applause bestowed upon the character of Brutus. Napoleon even caused the publication in the newspapers of an article denouncing Brutus and his opinions, and commending the sentiments expressed by the despotic Cassius.

In the opera of "Le Triomphe de Trajan," produced after the divorce, were several very flattering allusions to Josephine, whose character was favorably represented under the name of Plotine. These were suppressed by order of the police, who sought at this period to press upon the public the claims of Marie Louise. The newspapers were instructed to chronicle the suppression of the passages referred to, as a change for the better.

Though the control exercised over the stage was severe, Bonaparte had constant reason to complain of the inefficiency and indifference of the censors. Early in the Consulate, a play by Alexandre Duval, entitled "Edouard en Ecosse," had been interdicted by the Minister of the Interior, but its representation was finally authorized, upon the intercession of influential persons. The audience was largely composed of royalists and returned emigrants, and all the allusions to Edward which could be construed into references to the Bourbons and their own legitimate and exiled sovereign—le Comte de Lille, Louis XVIII.—were received with long and loud applause. Bonaparte was advised, the next morning, to suppress the play as "anti-revolutionary and anti-patriotic," and, in order to judge for himself, attended the second performance. He noticed the marked political interpretation placed upon the situation of the king in Scotland, especially by the late dukes de Choiseul and Richelieu. He left the house before the play was concluded. The piece was suppressed, the Duke de Richelieu was ordered to quit Paris in twenty-four hours, and the author was advised to absent himself for a while from France. He resided a year in Russia, and then returned without molestation to Paris.

Shortly afterwards, a ballad opera—the words by Emmanuel Dupaty—was produced, entitled "L'Antichambre." Bonaparte was told that the characters were three lackeys, dressed in a livery closely resembling the attire of the three Consuls, and that Chénard, the actor performing the principal lackey, imitated his—Bonaparte's—attitudes, gestures and utterance. The First Consul ordered the matter to be investigated, and recommended the exile of Dupaty to St. Domingo. It was found, however, that the piece had been written and costumed under the Directory and that any resemblance, therefore, was purely accidental. The opera, withdrawn for a time, was subsequently revived under the title of "Picaros and Diego," and was one of the thirteen plays offered to the jury, in 1810, in competition for the government prizes. Dupaty, who prudently retired to Brest, was subsequently invited back to Paris by Napoleon himself.

Napoleon, being at Schœnbrün in 1809, wrote, under the date of September 17th, to M. de Montalivet, then Minister of the Interior, to complain of the laxity of his control of the minor theatres of Paris. "I hear," he said, "that pieces are nightly played in which direct allusions, in the worst taste, are made to the nations I have conquered. This is indecent and ungenerous, and is unworthy of a nation like ours. You will not hereafter trust the bureau of censors; you will read all plays in manuscript yourself, that you may judge personally whether their representation will be proper and opportune."

The most remarkable instance of insufficient dramatic censure occurred soon after Napoleon's return from Wagram. It was then that he first took serious steps in view of a divorce from Josephine, though as yet no one was in his confidence, except Duroc. Josephine, however, had long entertained a presentiment of what was to happen, and the quick scent of the courtiers had set them upon the trace of the impending event. The Emperor ordered a hunt and a comedy at Gros-Bois, and made Berthier, Master of the Hounds, director of the festivities. The grand veneur summoned the company of the Variétés, and left the choice of the piece to Brunet, the favorite low comedian of the period. The latter selected Cadet-Roussel, a very popular and lively farce; Berthier, who knew that it was in its two hundreth night, ratified the selection. The performance is thus described:

"Every one had observed the profound melancholy of the Empress, upon her arrival, and the distinguished guests shared, during the dinner, her sombre humor. Napoleon, perceiving the air of constraint which pervaded the company, said, upon rising from table to proceed to the theatre, 'Gentlemen, I have bidden you here to amuse you, and I hope you will laugh a little more than you have done hitherto. I want neither etiquette nor court formality: this is not the Tuileries.' This order had the singular effect of completely paralyzing those who before were only half paralyzed. But judge of the stupefaction of the audience, when they heard, at the very commencement of the play, Cadet-Roussel complain of his childlessness in the following terms:

"'It is painful for a man like me to have no son to whom to transmit the inheritance of his glory! Upon my word, I'll be divorced from Mrs. Cadet-Roussel, that I may marry a younger woman who will make me the father of children.'

"The greater part of the other scenes turned upon this idea, and the word divorce was repeated twenty times. It is out of the question to picture the embarrassment of the company; that of Berthier was inconceivable. Josephine could hardly contain herself, and it was feared every moment that she would be taken ill. Napoleon appeared to be very much interested in the piece, and strove to laugh, but it was only with the points of the lips. No one dared to look at him, lest he might seem to be making an application. An explosion appeared imminent. This, however, was prevented by Berthier, who stood behind Napoleon's chair, and who, from time to time, indulged in noisy bursts of laughter which contrasted singularly with the consternation visible upon his countenance. Upon the fall of the curtain, the Emperor arose hastily, and taking Duroc by the arm, said to him in an under tone:

"'Duroc, I see you have kept the secret of my divorce, for had my project been known to the public, no one would have ventured upon such a piece of impertinence. How long has this piece been upon the stage?'

"'About a year, sire.'

"'Is it successful?'

"'Immensely so, I have heard.'

"'I am sorry for it. Had I known it, I should not certainly have authorized the performance—not even a year ago. Why am I never told of what is going on? One would think the censors commit follies on purpose and on every occasion they can get. I cannot understand Cambacérès either: he is constantly at Brunet's theatre, and he has never once mentioned this infamy. I must absolutely reorganize this affair of dramatic liberty; it needs a thorough reform. One would positively think,' he added, with a bitter smile, 'that I had made an arrangement with Brunet and the author of the play.'

"And he repeated several times, 'I am sorry for it, I am sorry for it.'"

It was natural that after these various measures, intended to influence and control public opinion, Napoleon should desire to know—from other sources of information than his spies and secret police—what success had crowned his efforts. The Dark Closet, where mailed letters were opened and their contents noted, furnished him a portion of the intelligence he sought.

This ominous institution originated under Louis XV.; its purpose was then less to surprise political secrets than to keep pace with the scandalous chronicles of the city. Under Napoleon, however, its character changed. "Persons who wished to injure an enemy or serve a friend, made a long and efficient use of this closet, which, though at first a simple resource of the curiosity of a king whose leisure was to be amused, became in the end an arsenal of intrigues, dangerous by the abuses of which malice rendered it capable."[1]

That Napoleon's government habitually opened and possessed itself of the contents of letters intrusted to the mails, in all cases where a sufficient motive existed, has been long known. In 1802, the public was incensed by the discovery of a violation of this sort, traced to a subaltern civil functionary. The Minister of Finance addressed a letter to Lavalette, the postmaster-general, censuring

[1] Bour. v. 176.

such acts on the part of the agents of the mails. This letter was published in the Moniteur. It was thought to signify nothing more than the assertion, by the government, of its exclusive right to tamper with the mails, and a prohibition to the postal authorities to assume any such privilege. It was felt, however, that if any man could by sagacity and discretion temper the evils of this system, that man was Lavalette."[1]

Bourrienne, the First Consul's private secretary, read every morning for three years the report made by the clerks of the dark closet. He states, however, that, with the exception of the facilities the institution offered for the denunciation of enemies, the evils of the system were far from justifying the fears or the indignation of the public. Out of thirty thousand letters mailed daily in Paris, not more than ten or twelve were copied and made use of, though many hundreds were opened. The copy or the extract was sent by Bourrienne to the minister whose bureau was interested in the discovery made or the intelligence obtained, with these words: "The First Consul has directed me to inform you that he has just received the following information." It was the business of the minister to divine from whence the information came.[2] Upon the establishment of the Empire, the violation of the mails became a matter of daily occurrence, and on the appointment of Bourrienne to the post-office, in 1814, by the Emperor Alexander, he found an immense accumulation of intercepted letters. He sent a notice to the Moniteur on the 4th of April, stating that the letters to and from England and other foreign countries, which had been lying at the post-office for more than three years, would be forwarded to their respective addresses. The revenue collected upon these detained mails amounted to no less a sum than three hundred thousand francs.[3]

One of Napoleon's ministers, conversing with the postmaster-general of a conquered kingdom, and learning that he was in the constant habit of breaking the seals of private correspondence,

[1] Thib. iii. 54.   [2] Bour. v. 177.   [3] Ibid. x. 94.

professed great surprise, and asked how so moral a government could descend to means so odious. "God," returned the postmaster, who was an Italian, "is enabled to govern the world, because he reads in the hearts of men: how could we govern the earth unless we could read in their letters?"[1] Napoleon, however, had a better and surer method of acquainting himself with the state and the mutations of public opinion. He employed correspondents residing as well in the departments and in foreign countries as in Paris, who wrote to him, at stated intervals, upon subjects of national and public interest. These were not all flatterers, and many of them told wholesome truths and administered undisguised reproofs.

The most distinguished of these correspondents was J. Fiévée, whose communications to the First Consul, during a series of years, were collected by himself, and published in three volumes, some years after Napoleon's fall. M. Desrenaudes, a friend of Talleyrand's, wrote upon subjects connected with internal administration, but was forbidden to discuss politics. Barrère, ex-member of the Convention, to whom Napoleon could not consistently give public office, was employed to enlighten him upon the state of public opinion. He wrote in this way, during four years, but as his communications consisted principally of gossip and flattery, he was recommended to devote his talents in future to journalism. M. Lemaire, professor of Latin, wrote upon literature and literary men, but was removed for personality. M. de Montlosier, ex-deputy, wrote upon administrative and religious topics. He was commissioned to compose a work upon the French monarchy, which he did; the examining committee reported against its publication as inopportune and dangerous. These gentlemen received for their services about 500 francs a month. Several gave their labor gratuitously, as in the case of an auditor at the Court of Accounts, who wrote for fourteen years under the pseudonym of Héliodore.

[1] Thib. iii. 53.

Madame de Genlis, for many years governess and instructress in the service of the Bourbons, and who had returned with the royalist emigrants to Paris, lived for some time in absolute want. The Minister of the Interior, Chaptal, gave her a temporary home in one of the public libraries—that of the Arsenal. When Napoleon became Emperor, he ordered her to receive a monthly pension of 500 francs; and, in order not to offend her delicacy, requested her to make semi-monthly communications to him upon literature, finance, or national manners. This she did, choosing for her topics, religion, philosophy and morals. She received 6000 francs a year from Napoleon till his fall in 1814.

We have thus rehearsed the facts and adduced the requisite examples in this curious matter of Napoleon's influence on letters, and his attempted control of public opinion. It is needless to pursue the subject further. It may be well, however, to remark, that as an explosion usually follows restraint, and as a reaction is the natural consequence of any violent and prolonged effort, so the scenes of desertion and treachery which surrounded Napoleon's fall, were in a measure due to the forced service he had so long imposed upon courtiers, artists, authors, and upon the countless retainers of his government. The fallen Emperor, stealing in disguise and in bodily danger across disaffected Burgundy, hostile Languedoc, and menacing Provence, was reaping the legitimate fruit of his system. Every tongue that had sworn a forced allegiance, now muttered treason; every pen that had yielded a compulsory compliance, or that had remained in sullen inactivity, was now able and rejoiced to write without dictation. All that had offered service and adherence, and had furnished their stipulated flattery or their implied adulation, now hastened to profit by their opportunity to speak either the thought they had suppressed or the truth they had disguised. France would not have presented the spectacle it did upon Napoleon's abdication—a spectacle of desertion unexampled in history—had it not been held during fifteen years in a state of mental and moral servitude.

Literature, no longer compelled to flatter, hastened to launch anathemas at the flying monarch; the arts were glad to be free from the submission in which the imperial patronage had held them; and even soldiers, weary of their service and ashamed of their prostration, assumed the white cockade and shouted welcome to the Bourbon king. This extravagance and excess of treachery was but a recoil from the state of compression in which the mind of the nation had been confined. The pen and the lips that Napoleon had condemned to servile flattery became, at his decline, hostile and impertinent. Had he allowed them a moderate liberty during his reign, he would have found them temperate, just and sympathetic at his fall.

CHAPTER XXII.

Elisa Bonaparte—Her Marriage and Residence at Paris—Her Government of Lucca—Baron Capelle—Paganini—Elisa in Tuscany—Her Exile and Death—Caroline Bonaparte—Her Marriage with Murat—Her Portrait—Intrigue with General Junot—Murat's Military Dress—The Throne of Naples—Caroline's Exile and Death.

MARIANNA-ELISA-BONAPARTE, the eldest of Napoleon's sisters, was born at Ajaccio, in the year 1777. She received a better education than either Pauline or Caroline, for during her youth Corsica was tranquil, and the influence of her family considerable. They commanded sufficient credit to obtain her admission as a free pupil to the school of St. Cyr, where she remained till revolution broke out in Corsica, in 1792, in consequence of the capture of the island by the English. Madame Lætitia and her daughters now took up their residence at Marseilles, subsisting, as has been already stated, upon a fund voted by the Convention for the support of Corsican refugees.

In May, 1797, at the age of twenty, Marianna married M. Felice Bacciochi, a Corsican like herself, of a poor but noble family, and holding the grade of captain of infantry. It is impossible, from the records now accessible, to decide whether Napoleon was favorable or averse to the alliance; one authority positively stating that he considered it unfortunate and ill advised, and another as distinctly asserting that he regarded the prescriptions of a proper ambition as fully consulted in the match. But it must be remembered that Napoleon was already married to Josephine, and had been for some months general-in-chief of the Italian army. Even at this period he might with propriety have sought husbands for his sisters in higher walks of life than those trodden by M. Bacciochi, and if in reality he did oppose the step, the thorough insignificance of which his brother-in-law gave proof during his long career, amply justified his objections.

The next year, Lucien Bonaparte was elected to the Council of Five Hundred, and Marianna and her husband followed him to Paris. Here Madame Bacciochi, whose education had fitted her for the society of men of letters, gathered around her many of the poets and critics of the time. Chateaubriand took pleasure in her acquaintance, and at a later period found her an active and willing mediatress in tempering the unfriendly relations existing between himself and Napoleon. Laharpe and Fontanes were assiduous visitors at her house : the latter soon became her acknowledged lover, the complaisant husband quietly accepting the odious position. Madame Bacciochi now affected the airs of a blue-stocking; she presided over a society of literary ladies, and invented a costume for the use of the associate members. This she wore herself on one occasion at a fancy ball, announcing her intention of recommending it to the adoption of all good Christians. In appearance Marianna Bonaparte was much less attractive than either of her sisters. A harsh and domineering expression injured the effect of features which might otherwise have been pleasing, and her manner, which was abrupt and almost contemptuous toward inferiors, rendered her address distant and suspicious. Her bones were large and prominent, and her limbs ill-shaped : her gait was not graceful, and often subjected her to the playful mockeries of her sister Pauline.

Napoleon became emperor in 1804, and in 1805 made his eldest sister Princess of Lucca and Piombino, in Italy. She now abandoned the name of Marianna, by which she had been known during her youth, using exclusively her second baptismal name, by which she is historically known—that of Elisa. She and her husband were crowned at Lucca, in July, 1805 ; this was the only act of her life as a sovereign, in which she recognized M. Bacciochi as her equal. She soon degraded him to a position which her biographers have described as that of the first of her subjects, if not that of the first of her domestics. At the parade, he was her aid-de-camp and lowered his sword as she passed; at official ceremonies of the palace, he was her chamberlain, and stood behind her or marched after her; in social life, he was the very last and least of her associates; on the coins, his profile was three-quarters absorbed and lost in hers. She seemed to make it a point to render him ridiculous in the eyes of Europe, and absurd in the sight of history.

Her government of the principality of Lucca was not an unsuccessful one. She did much to develop the resources of the country, the face of which she beautified with numerous public works. The admirable road from Lucca to the Baths, and the embankment raised for the first three miles along its borders to resist the inundations of the Serchio, remain to bear witness to her spirit of improvement. She committed, however, several ruthless acts; she caused the cathedral of Massa Ducale to be demolished, because it stood too near her summer palace; and she destroyed, from a similar motive, the church of the Madonna at Lucca. She made her government a military one, in ambitious imitation of that of France, and, for want of a war with which to gratify her martial tastes, she ordered parades, drills, musters and sham fights; of these she was the heroine, gorgeously attired and sumptuously served, her husband rendering himself useful as an orderly officer. He waited in respectful silence, and, when bidden, bore mimic despatches across the bloodless field.

The princess encouraged the arts, and protected the artists who sought her favor. She rewarded the poets who chanted her praises; and when styled, in flattering verse, "La Semiramide di Lucca," she accepted the comparison as a tribute which did her honor. She lived in open defiance of public opinion, being of a temper too imperious to pay heed to the criticisms of those who were her subjects and not her peers. One of her lovers at this period was Baron Capelle, Prefect of the Mediterranean, and in this capacity stationed at Leghorn. He often saw the princess at Lucca, and, when the proper moment for a declaration arrived, he made it in a manner at once novel and delicate. He found her suffering, on this occasion, with a violent toothache. He summoned a dentist to the palace. He said to her, "Princess, it appears the tooth is beyond saving; you must have it out." "Oh, I can never consent, I am sure," returned her highness. Capelle drew the dentist into a corner, and said, "Here, find the tooth corresponding in my mouth to the one which aches in the princess's, and draw it; make haste." The operation was accomplished quickly and noiselessly. The baron showed the extracted tooth to the princess, saying, "There, you see that it is the affair of a mere instant, and that it leaves no trace behind it." The invalid could hardly regard with indifference this chivalrous proof of interest.[1]

The Princess Elisa was instrumental in directing the efforts of Paganini to a new field of exertion. At the age of twenty he was appointed leader of the orchestra of the court: he conducted the musicians at the opera when the reigning family attended the performance. Once a fortnight he gave a concert at the palace. A lady, whom he had long loved in silence, seemed to manifest, by her constant presence at these entertainments, that she observed and perhaps returned his passion. Their position, however, enjoined upon them discretion and mystery. On the day preceding one of his concerts, Paganini caused a message to be conveyed to the lady, to the effect that he was arranging a musical surprise for her. The programme for the evening announced a "Novelty," called a "Scena Amorosa." The court curiosity, thus enlisted, was stimulated to a high pitch by the appearance of Paganini with a violin of two strings, the sol and the chanterelle. The piece, executed entirely by him on this instrument, represented a

[1] Mém. d'un Bourgeois, i. 45.

passionate dialogue between a lady of soprano register and tender sentiments, and a jealous lover of tenor compass and pleading accents. To the reproaches of the tortured gallant succeeded the consolations of his yielding inamorata; a reconciliation soon followed, the whole concluding with a merry rigadoon danced by the happy couple, which the audience interpreted as an elopement and a lesson to obdurate parents.

The Princess Elisa complimented the musician upon his extraordinary performance, saying, "You have accomplished an impossibility with two strings; could you not execute a similar feat upon one?" Paganini hesitated, but promised to make the attempt. Three weeks afterwards he played before the court, and upon the fourth string alone, a sonata entitled "Napoleone." His success was immense, and from this concert dated his predilection for performances upon a single string. This is Paganini's own account—given some years subsequently—of the manner in which he was led to attempt a task apparently so impossible. The popular explanation had previously been, that having committed a terrible murder, he was confined for many months in a dismal cell, where a violin formed his only resource and furnished him his only occupation. The jailer, fearing that he might hang himself with the strings, prudently removed all but one! From this solitary chord the patient artiste speedily learned to draw the various sounds which, until then, had only been extorted from four!

Napoleon recognized the administrative capacities of his sister, in 1808, by making her Grand Duchess of Tuscany, thus largely extending her dominions. She now resided alternately at Florence, Pisa, and Poggio. She felt that she might presume, in her diplomatic relations with France, upon the indulgence of her brother, and the correspondence of her government with the French Minister of Foreign Affairs, which she dictated herself, shows how jealous she was of French encroachment or interference, and how adroitly she made her influence with Napoleon tell in favor of Tuscany and its interests. She stimulated agriculture by offering prizes for successful cultivation of the land, or amelioration of the breed of domestic animals. She made forays against the bandits that infested the forests. She built fortifications and erected school-houses and asylums for orphans. Her reviews and parades were now upon a grander scale; she disciplined raw recruits, instituted a system of military encouragement, promoted favorites and cashiered the objects of her dislike. Her husband had not participated in her late advancement; while she rose from the rank of a princess to that of a grand duchess, he still remained the citizen husband of a regal wife. She never allowed him any other position than that of a submissive official and an obedient subaltern.

Upon the fall of Napoleon, she commenced, like all her family, a life of exile and vagabondage. The Austrians would not permit her to reside at Bologna, and Murat, the husband of her sister, would not receive her at Naples. She remained for a time at Trieste, and upon the death of Murat, in 1815, she retired with Caroline to the vicinity of Vienna, and afterwards to the chateau of Brunn, in Moravia. She was finally permitted to reside at Trieste, under the name of the Countess of Campignano, where she died in 1820. She was the first of the eight sons and daughters of Lætitia Bonaparte to descend to the tomb.

During the period of her wanderings, Napoleon said of her at St. Helena: "Elisa has a masculine brain and a lofty soul; she doubtless displays great philosophy in adversity." Upon hearing of her death, he desired to be left alone. Being interrupted in his meditations, he said, "I used to think that death had forgotten our family; but now he has begun to strike. He has taken Elisa, and I shall soon follow her." His own death took place in less than six months from this date.

Caroline-Maria-Annonciada Bonaparte, the youngest sister of Napoleon, was born at Ajaccio in 1782. She was, therefore, eleven years old when her mother and family were compelled to leave Corsica for Marseilles, and to accept the bounty of the

Convention. On going to Paris the next year, she was placed at Madame Campan's boarding school, where she acquired some accomplishments and many affectations. In 1798, her brother Joseph was appointed ambassador of the Republic near the Papal government, and Caroline spent some time with him at Rome. Though only sixteen, her rather precocious beauty attracted many admirers, among whom were Joachim Murat, aid-de-camp of Bonaparte, and the young Prince de Santa Croce. Murat was evidently the favorite, but he was unable to prosecute his suit, as he fell at this period into disgrace with the General-in-chief, on account of an unskillful manœuvre before the walls of Mantua. He lingered for many months under Bonaparte's displeasure, but redeemed himself in Egypt, at Aboukir, and in the struggle with Mourad Bey. On his return to France, Josephine strongly urged him to apply at once to Napoleon for the hand of his sister Caroline, hoping by thus espousing his interests, to secure to herself a partisan in the very bosom of her husband's family.

Murat preferred his request to Bonaparte at the Luxembourg. It was received coldly, and Murat obtained no immediate satisfaction. In the meantime occurred the revolution of the Ninth of November; Murat's dashing charge of grenadiers in the Hall of the Five Hundred, greatly facilitated Bonaparte's usurpation of power. The aid-de-camp received the command of the Consular Guard, and the First Consul yielded to the pressing solicitations of Josephine, Hortense, and Eugène, in behalf of his marriage with Caroline. "Murat is the son of an innkeeper," said Bonaparte, hesitating; "but, after all, the alliance is a proper one, and no one can say that I am proud, and that I seek grand matches." Joachim Murat and Caroline Bonaparte were married at the Luxembourg on the 29th of December, 1799, and in the second month of the Consulate. Bonaparte could only give his sister a portion of 30,000 francs; the wedding present which he made her was a diamond necklace, abstracted from

Josephine's jewel-box, in the vain hope that that luxurious lady would not notice its absence. He was soon able, however, to purchase her a country seat called Villiers, at Neuilly.

Caroline Bonaparte, at the age of seventeen, and at the period of her marriage, is said to have possessed the most beautiful complexion in France. Her skin was thought to resemble white satin seen through pink glass. Otherwise, she was not to be compared to her elder sister, Pauline. Her head was large, and her shoulders were round; her arms, hands, and feet were perfect, like those of all the Bonapartes; her hair, which in infancy, had been almost white, was now neither light nor dark; her teeth were white, though not so regularly beautiful as those of Napoleon; she kept them constantly visible by a permanent sneer. Jewelry, which so well became Pauline, was detrimental to the pure, pale colors of Caroline's complexion.[1] Heavy stuffs, brocades, and satins were equally prejudicial, and she seldom wore them in consequence.

Napoleon soon left Paris for the second Italian campaign, and taking Murat with him to St. Bernard and Marengo, left the youthful bride to play her part in the reviving gaieties of the metropolis. On the proclamation of the Empire, Napoleon made Murat Grand Duke of Berg and Cleves, his dominions including the possessions of the house of Nassau and the principality of Munster. Caroline was not content with this allotment, and left her husband to assume and to administer his government as he thought fit. She saw very little of her capital city of Dusseldorf, preferring to remain at Paris and to reside in the Elysée Impérial. During the winter of 1806–7, she led the festivities of the court, of which she was the undisputed belle. Her sister Elisa was at Lucca, Pauline was an invalid, Hortense was in Holland, Josephine had abandoned dancing, and Napoleon and Murat were absent at the wars. It was at this period that she

---

[1] The portrait of Caroline Bonaparte, on the opposite page, is from the original by Gérard, at the Historical Gallery of Versailles.

enticed General Junot, now Governor of Paris, into a gallant intrigue, which drew upon him the wrath of Napoleon, and which consequently reduced his wife, the Duchess d'Abrantès, to the necessity of writing her memoirs for a subsistence.

Napoleon returned to Paris in July, 1807, having but lately received full and written details of Junot's intimacy with his sister. Their first meeting was a stormy one. Napoleon accused Junot directly of having compromised, by his assiduities, the good name of the Grand Duchess. "Sire," exclaimed Junot, "I loved the Princess Pauline at Marseilles, and you were on the point of giving her to me. I loved her to distraction, yet what was my conduct? Was it not that of a man of honor? I am not changed since that period. I am still equally devoted to you and yours. Sire, your distrust of me is unkind." Napoleon listened with a menacing brow. At last he said, "I am willing to believe what you say, but you are none the less guilty of imprudence; and imprudence in your situation towards my sister amounts to a fault, if not to worse. Why does the Grand Duchess occupy your boxes at the theatres? Why does she go thither in your carriage? Hey, M. Junot! You are surprised that I am so well acquainted with your affairs, and those of that little fool, Madame Murat. Yes, I know all this, and many other facts which I am willing to consider as imprudences only, but which are nevertheless serious offences on your part. Once more, why this carriage with your livery? Your servants should not be seen at two o'clock in the morning in the court-yard of the Grand Duchess of Berg! You, Junot! You, compromise my sister!"

"I do not hesitate to ascribe all my husband's misfortunes," writes Madame Junot, "and even his death, to his unhappy entanglement with Caroline Murat. I do not charge this connection with real criminality: I even believe that there was only the appearance of it: but the suspicious appearances which really did exist, led to the most fatal consequences: they kindled the lion's wrath. A family bereft of its head, children made orphans, an illustrious name assailed, are sufficient grounds for conferring on my history all the solemnity it merits, and preserving it from the insignificance of an amorous intrigue. I shall entertain my readers neither with jealous passions nor with romantic sorrows: it is facts alone that I shall record." General Junot was soon after sent to take the chief command of the army of observation, now assembling at Bordeaux and Bayonne. "So then you exile me?" he said to Napoleon. "What more could you have done, had I committed a crime?" "You have not committed a crime, but you have erred. It is indispensable to remove you from Paris, to silence the current reports respecting my sister and you. Come, my old friend—the marshal's baton is yonder."

Murat spent the winter of 1807-8 at Paris, and for a time plunged into the follies of what he supposed a life of fashion and elegant debauch. As a gallant, his connections were of the lowest sort, and had it not been for his splendid military reputation, his affected manners and harlequin dress would have driven him from society. Even in the field and as a soldier, he had made himself notorious by his fantastic costume. He gathered together scraps of military uniforms from the armies of every nation in Europe, and huddled them upon his magnificent person with an utter disregard of epoch, fitness or color. He invented a series of military head-dresses that rendered the leader of the cavalry of France a pompous and flaunting caricature. His feathers cost him 7000 francs a month. He was called "l'homme aux panaches." The most severe language that Napoleon ever listened to from any one of his generals, was provoked by Murat's mountebank attire. "That brother-in-law of yours is a pretentious knave," said Lannes, "with his pantomime dress and his plumes like a dancing dog." Murat's eccentricities could not diminish his merits as the most brilliant cavalry officer of the age; but his curls, furs, plumes, feathers, and his wardrobe generally—that of a strolling player—with corresponding manners, rendered it vain for him to aspire to the position of a gentleman and a courtier. Napoleon once called him a "Franconi King."

In July, 1808, Joseph Bonaparte, King of Naples, was transferred to the throne of Spain by Napoleon. Murat was appointed to the vacant crown of the two Sicilies. Queen Caroline entered the capital of her realms on the 25th of September, 1808; her subjects extended to her a genial and flattering welcome. "This same Caroline Bonaparte," says de Salgues, "who might have been seen some years before at Marseilles, dressed in humble garments, bringing home from market, in early morning, the frugal meals of the family for the day, was now to replace upon the throne of Naples the daughter of the Cæsars."[1] While Murat remained in Naples, he administered the government in an enlightened and merciful spirit; during his various periods of absence, to attend Napoleon in his wars, Caroline acted as regent, and displayed shrewdness, activity and liberal views in her conduct of affairs. At other times, Murat remained in Naples, while she spent a season of gaiety and relaxation from the cares of state, at Paris. The husband and wife, when together, led a discordant and quarrelsome life; the palace often presented the spectacle of conjugal dissensions. Murat felt that he was unduly subject to the influence of his wife, and once, in a spasm of resistance, declared that he would not be a "second Bacciochi!" He was disgusted with the reverses and horrors of the retreat from Moscow in 1812, and in 1813, after the disastrous battle of Leipsic, he finally abandoned Napoleon. He associated himself by treaties with Austria and England, and for a time preserved his throne. On Napoleon's return from Elba, he attempted to form a league of the Italian States, and to induce them to arm for their national independence. This brought him into hostility with Austria, and left him no support in any reliable quarter. He fled to the island of Ischia, and from thence sailed for France, leaving Queen Caroline regent of the kingdom. The Austrian army had entered the

[1] Memoirs, vii. 333.

territory, and Naples was agitated with apprehension. Queen Caroline mounted a war-horse, reviewed the troops, and addressed them in words of encouragement and in a spirit of resistance. She remained on horseback for six hours during this, the last day of her reign. Open resistance was, however, hopeless, and she finally surrendered herself to the English Admiral commanding the harbor, after obtaining a promise from him to give her an unmolested passage to France. From this vessel she was compelled to witness the return of the Bourbons into Naples. The royal Prince Don Leopold entered the city on horseback, in the midst of the rejoicings and acclamations of the people, who had already forgotten their late popular sovereign, Murat, the King of Feathers.

Caroline soon afterwards claimed the protection of the Austrians, the English commander failing to execute his engagement to place her on the soil of France. She assumed the title of Countess of Lipano, and Murat, now in Corsica, was invited by the Austrian government to take that of the Count of Lipano, to reside in Bohemia or Moravia with his wife, and to give a bond not to quit the Austrian states without permission. He preferred to stake his fortunes upon a rash and hopeless expedition. He landed at Pizzo, in Calabria, with twenty-eight followers, was taken, condemned, and shot. Caroline resided successively at Brunn, at Rome, and at Florence, devoting herself zealously to the education of her five children. She died at Florence, in 1839.

"Caroline," said Napoleon at St. Helena, "was adroit and capable; she possessed great character and an insatiable ambition; her capacity rose with her trials." Of Murat he said, "he was one of several that I made too great; I elevated him beyond his level. It is difficult to conceive of greater turpitude than that displayed in his late proclamation. He says it is time to choose between two banners, that of virtue and that of crime. He means mine by the banner of crime. And it is Murat, my work, who would have been nothing without me, the husband of my sister, who writes these words. It would be difficult to abandon a sinking cause with greater brutality, or to embrace new fortunes with more shameless treachery."[1]

As we shall not have occasion again to speak of the imperial family, we may properly insert here the estimate placed upon their achievements by Napoleon himself. "It is very certain," he said at St. Helena, "that I was poorly seconded by my family, and that my brothers and sisters have done great harm to me and my cause. Much has been said of the strength of my character, but I was reprehensibly weak for my family, and they were well aware of it. After the first storm of resistance was over, their perseverance and stubbornness always carried the day, and they did with me what they liked. I made great mistakes in this. If each one of them had given a common impulse to the different masses I had intrusted to them to rule, we could have marched together to the poles; everything would have fallen before us; we should have changed the face of the globe. I did not have the good fortune of Genghis Khan, with his four sons, who knew no other rivalry than that of serving him faithfully. Did I make a brother of mine a king, he at once thought himself king 'by the grace of God;' so contagious has this phrase become. He was no longer a lieutenant in whom I could repose confidence; he was an enemy more for me to beware of. His efforts did not tend to second mine, but to make himself independent. Every one of them had a mania to believe himself adored and preferred to me. They actually came to regard me as an obstacle, and as a source of peril. Legitimate sovereigns would have acted exactly as they did, and would not have believed themselves a whit better established. Poor things! When I succumbed, their dethronement was not exacted or even mentioned by the enemy; and not one of them is capable now of exciting a popular movement. Sheltered by my labors, they enjoyed the sweets of royalty; I only bore the burden."[2]

[1] Las Cases xi. 371.   [2] Ibid. III. 196.

CHAPTER XXIII.

Science under Napoleon—The Institute—Speculation and Theory—Progress of Physical Science—Mathematics—Chemistry applied to the Arts—Chaptal, Cuvier, Jussieu, Geoffroy St. Hilaire, Volta, Fulton—The Gregorian Calendar restored—The Republican Year—The Decimal System—Dr. Gall—Maelzel's Automaton—The Comet of 1811—Napoleon's Influence upon Science.

THE Institute, one of the creations of the Convention, was, at the period of the election of Bonaparte to the Consulate, the embodiment of the science and erudition of France; at the same time that, owing to its origin and the antecedents of many of its members, it was still tinctured with republicanism and inclined to independence. It was the most vigorous existing souvenir of 1789; given to free-thinking, Jacobinism and metaphysics. In its present organization it showed no tendency toward monarchy, and the reaction which was visible in the nation had not yet reached those, the most able by their attainments and influence, to precipitate and accelerate it. Bonaparte sought for the reason of this, and found it in the Academy of Moral Philosophy and Political Economy.

This academy was one of the five composing the Institute; the other four being, as we have already had occasion to state, Science, Literature, Ancient History, and the Fine Arts. Bonaparte drew his pen through that portion of the constitution which created the fifth academy; thus suppressing all that class of investigation into mind and the unseen world that he regarded as useless, if not injurious: he considered such labor as misapplied exertion and bad philanthropy. He would have no speculation, no theory, no metaphysics; his government required the aid of statistics, of axioms, of mathematics; the dominion at which he aimed needed the concurrence of historians, poets-laureate, artists, inventors, discoverers, not rhapsodists nor visionaries. The epoch was to be one of action, not of dreaming. The empire called for earnest work upon matter and masses; inquiry into the nature of the soul and the origin of life could be spared for a fitter and less agitated period.

The progress of physical science during the previous twenty years had been immense. The theory of crystallization, the analysis of light and air, the resolution of the four so-called primitive elements into their constituent parts, the explanation of the laws of evaporation and vaporization, of galvanism, of combustion, the discovery of new acids, of the method of producing all mineral waters artificially, were long strides in the path of progress, due to Berthollet, Monge, Haüy, Humboldt, Aldini and Buffon. Meteors had been decomposed; the bowels of the earth had been summoned to reveal their secrets, and races extinct and worlds forgotten were called back from beneath the new formations which had buried them. Cuvier had just commenced his theory of fossils and petrifactions, which he lived magnificently to complete; Hallé had published his researches upon digestion. Botany, anatomy, geology, were all the subjects of profound inquiry, and the sources of untold benefits to mankind.

The advance of the sciences of which mathematics form the bases, had been equally striking. Algebra, the mechanic arts, astronomy, navigation, geography, all seemed to put on the seven-league boots of progress, and had added largely to the stock of human knowledge, and to the comforts and blessings of existence. Vaccination, the signal telegraph, the hydraulic ram, stereotyping were either discovered or applied at this period, or were materially improved and modified. The metrical system of weights and measures—an institution of the republic—had also done its share in facilitating research, by simplifying calculations and all operations of figures.

That Bonaparte should desire to perpetuate in France, at the institution established in that view, such splendid traditions of useful labor and beneficent inquiry, to the exclusion of metaphysics and philosophy—which yielded, as he maintained, results either nugatory or pernicious, and which at any rate could not contribute to his advancement or his glory—was but natural. That the Institute should cherish the achievements of his ambition and illustrate his career, was his motive in changing its organization. Even his most uncompromising eulogists admit that his action in this matter was due to selfish considerations. "The exact and physical sciences," says Capefigue, could embellish and dignify his reign; the Academy could chant his praises; historians could perpetuate his name, coin medals and compose inscriptions; the fine arts could reproduce his image, whether amid the eternal snows of St. Bernard, or at the coronation in Notre Dame; sculptors could hand down to future ages his antique and accentuated features, and could cast bronze columns to his memory; musicians could sing hymns and celebrate his triumphs. The Institute became, for him, not only a means of warping contemporaneous judgment, but of preparing history and of influencing posterity."[1]

It would seem that the scientific conquests of the republic had left but little field of exertion to the science of the empire; but Napoleon's era is, in this respect, one of the richest in French annals. Chemistry applied to the arts was the most striking feature of the investigations of the period. It replaced the cochineal of Oaxaca and the indigo of Hindostan—products that were with difficulty obtained in time of war—by distillations from indigenous plants. It extracted brandy from potatoes. It sought a substitute for West India sugar in grapes and figs, and at last found it in the beet-root. In many ways, it contributed to render life more agreeable, subsistence less costly and labor more remunerative. Jean Antoine Chaptal, the first

[1] L'Europe sous Napoléon, iii. 289.

producer of sulphuric acid, was at the head of these beneficent and fruitful investigations.

In other fields of inquiry, equal success was obtained. The capacity of heat was determined by the calorimeter; the solar spectrum, the chemical action of light, the effect of surface upon radiation, were the objects of eager study. The gases of the air and water were separated, and the first experiments upon illuminating gas were made. Steel was brought to perfection, the atmosphere was weighed, a theory upon fulminating powders was produced, the diamond was analyzed, fossils and petrifactions were restored.

Cuvier now completed his sublime interpretation of the geology of the book of Genesis. Jussieu perfected and extended the botanic classification of Linnæus; he advised the introduction into France of the Malaga sweet potato, and the Swedish rutabaga. Geoffroy St. Hilaire measured the muscular power of the electric eel and the torpedo, and studied the habits of the kangaroo. The Academy busied itself with the architecture of bees, with the sensitive wings of the bat, with the reproductive capacity of the salamander, with the torpor of the marmot and dormouse during their lethargic winter slumbers, and with the inky discharges of the cuttle-fish. All these studies were encouraged by Napoleon, while successful application was munificently rewarded. The Voltaic pile was to the Emperor an object of intense interest and curiosity; and he for a time believed, that this singular instrument would reveal the origin of life, and snatch from the grave its secret and its mystery.

In his relations with scientific men, Napoleon made an immense and fatal error. He regarded the application of steam to locomotion as puerile and visionary. As early as 1802, a rough experiment had been made with a barge fitted with a clumsy engine, upon the canal de l'Ourcq, near Paris; its success was sufficient to demonstrate the feasibility of the project. In 1803, Fulton, who had resided at Paris for seven years, made a trial of a steamboat of his construction upon the Seine. He offered the invention to Napoleon, whose Committee on the Navy rejected it, as inapplicable and useless. The French have since regretted this indifference of Napoleon for the most powerful motor of modern times. "His disdain for this invention," says Capefigue, "is an unfortunate circumstance in his history. Steam would have bridged the English channel, and have landed an army without obstacle upon the shores of Great Britian. This gigantic bridge Napoleon had often dreamed of, as of Dante's in the Inferno. When seas of a thousand leagues shall be crossed in a week, it will be sad and fatal that the name of Napoleon can have no place in the annals of the new civilization."[1]

One of the scientific glories of the Empire was the return to the Gregorian calendar, in the computation and measure of time. Laplace, the astronomer, recommended the change, in a memorial addressed, by order of Napoleon, to the Senate. The republican calendar was instituted by the Convention on the 5th of October, 1793, and declared to have gone into operation on the 22d of September of the preceding year, the day of the installation of the Convention. The republican year was divided into twelve months of thirty days each. Each month consisted of three decades of ten days ; Sunday, instead of returning every seventh day, and being called Dimanche, returned every tenth day, and was called Decadi. As this division of the year accounted for three hundred and sixty days only, the other five were called supplementary days, or "sans-culottides." The three hundred and sixty-sixth day of leap year received the name of "franciade." The names of the days in the decade were as follows : primidi, duodi, tridi, quartidi, quintidi, sextidi, septidi, octidi, nonidi decadi.

The confusion resulting from this innovation was indescribable. The necessity of double dates isolated France commercially from the rest of Europe. Its trade was large with Russia, and

[1] L'Europe sous Napoléon, vii. 7.

as the Greek calendar of that power was, as it still is, twelve days behind the Gregorian, three dates were required in all correspondence with the dominions of the Czar. The inconveniences of the decade were harassing, and indeed odious. A lady who gave receptions on quintidis, expected her guests Wednesday in one week, Saturday in the next, and, omitting the third week, on Tuesday of the fourth. Decadi came on Friday and on Monday, and alternately on every day of the seven.

The newspapers of the period were full of amusing chronicles of the struggles for supremacy between Monsieur Dimanche and Madame la Decade. The government manufactory of Sèvres, following the republican calendar, rang its bell to summon the hands to labor on the Gregorian Sunday; while they, faithful to tradition and the almanac of their youth, chose to employ it as a day of rest. Upon the republican Decadi, on the contrary, they gathered to their allotted tasks, unsummoned by the bell. M. Genissieux, Minister of Justice, publicly reprimanded a provincial functionary for holding audience on decadis, and reposing on the Sabbath.

On the other hand, the advantages of the new calendar were manifest. The months were of uniform length, and the seasons commenced with the months, instead of on the 22d day of the months of the Gregorian calendar. The name of each month suggested its characteristic in the meridian of Paris—as the month of wind, the month of rain, the month of blossom and the month of harvest, instead of a system of nomenclature derived obscurely from mythology and classic history. The French reformers of fifty years ago did not consider themselves bound by the views which had governed Numa Pompilius, who gave February 28 days. that the month of Expiation might be a brief one ; nor by those which had actuated Julius Cæsar in his distribution of seven odd days between January, July, August and December ; nor yet by the considerations held by Pope Gregory XIII. Again, the year of the new calendar commenced at the autumn equinox, the 22d of September, when the days and the nights were twelve hours each, while the Roman calendar placed the first of January nine days after the winter solstice.

The decade fell into disrepute as early as 1797, in which year a Gregorian Sunday, falling upon New Year's day, was feasted and fêted like a prodigal son recovered. Under the Empire, the provinces, which had never become accustomed to the change, were clamorous for the cities and the capital to return to the Old Style of computation. On the 1st of January, 1806, France resumed the reckoning of time by the Gregorian calendar, after thirteen years' trial of the calendar of the Republic. The imperial decree to that effect was received with gratitude throughout the country. L'An XIII. and last of the republican era, consisted of fourteen months, to compensate for the short measure of 1793, l'An I., in which there had been but ten.

The abolition of the calendar did not draw with it, as was feared, the suppression of that other republican conquest—the decimal system of weights and measures. The government pronounced strongly for the maintenance of this system, and promised to generalize its use by all means in its power. Biot and François Arago were sent to continue to the Balearic Isles, the measurement of the arc of the meridian, already carried to Barcelona by Delambre and Méchain. The system has triumphed over opposition and tradition; the metre has successfully replaced the aune, and the kilogramme has triumphantly superseded the pound.

We have already had occasion to speak of Napoleon's high appreciation of men of science. One instance of his treatment of theorists will suffice. He placed no confidence in the phrenological system of Dr. Gall, and on all occasions sought to throw ridicule upon him and his labors. He said one day to a lady who was inclined to patronize the doctor, "Well, I suppose we must have some consideration for men of science, even though they be fools. And what has the doctor told you?" Upon being acquainted with certain predictions he had made regarding one of her children, based upon an examination of his infant skull, he replied, "Ah, he said that, did he! A man like Dr. Gall is good for something, after all. I think I shall establish him in a professorship, so that he may teach his system to all the surgeons and midwives in Paris. As soon as a child comes into the world, they will at once ascertain what it is destined to be: if it is strongly marked with the organs of murder or theft, they shall drown it at once, just as the Greeks used to stifle the bandy-legged and the hunchbacked."

In consequence of this imperial estimate of Dr. Gall and his labors, burlesque of his system and theory was one of the principal features of the carnival of the winter spent by the doctor at Paris. A troop of harlequins, pierrots, clowns, and fishwomen passed through the grand thoroughfares, feeling of their heads and seeking for the tell-tale protuberances. One of them bore a quantity of pasteboard heads, divided into bumps and localities, each marked with some ridiculous appellation, such as "Skull of a Thief," "Skull of a Bankrupt," "Skull of a Gentleman of the Nineteenth Century." Seated upon a donkey, and his head towards the animal's tail, was a figure representing Dr. Gall himself. Mother Goose rode behind him, and offered him trophies of scalps crowned with dandelion. The procession was closed by a colossal head upon diminutive shoulders, offering in its enormous and absurd phrenological developments, an amusing caricature of the learned doctor's hobby.

At Schœnbrün, near Vienna, Napoleon, on one occasion, saw Maelzel, the mechanician and inventor of the metronome and the Automaton Chess-player. He admired several of the artist's artificial limbs, and commissioned him to construct a new and commodious van for carrying the wounded from a field of battle. He expressed a desire to see the automaton, which was accordingly set up in one of the rooms of the palace. The Emperor sat down at the table opposite the Mask, saying. "Now, sir, for us two." The automaton bowed, and signified by a motion of the hand that Napoleon was to play first. The latter executed two or three moves, therefore, and then made a false play with a knight. The automaton bowed, took up the piece, and restored it to its place. Napoleon played unfairly again, and the automaton confiscated the piece. "That's just," said the Emperor, and cheated still again. The automaton shook his head, passed his hand across the board, overturned the men, and broke up the game. Napoleon complimented Maelzel highly, saying that he admired the very natural conduct of his mechanism in unexpected situations more than he should have done any exhibition of regular and methodical skill.

Upon the apparition of a comet of unusual size and remarkable brilliancy in 1811, the question was asked and debated in council, whether it was safe and advisable to allow the newspapers of Paris to discuss its mission, and the Academy of Sciences to chronicle and publish its behavior. It was decided that the community was sufficiently enlightened and free from superstition, to hear the truth in regard to the errand and the conduct of the celestial stranger. The public bore the visitation with equanimity, though the lurid effulgence of its tail was well calculated to kindle dismay. The police employed writers to ridicule and caricature the comet, in order to laugh the people out of any lingering belief in its dread and mysterious influence. This was the more necessary, as the constantly occurring conflagrations and even earthquakes might reasonably seem to be connected with the coming of the errant planet. Never did the vineyards of France yield a more luxurious return than under the gaze of this appalling, yet innocent, meteor. The "wine of the comet" obtained currency as the finest crop since the Revolution; large quantities of it were carefully hoarded in cellars, that it might receive the benediction of time—the sacrament and flavor of dust. From that period to this, it has graced state occasions, and high nuptial and family festivities. The supply is now exceedingly scarce, if, indeed, it be not more prudent to believe that it was long since exhausted. The guest before whom it is placed may reasonably believe that it is some other vintage in the masquerade of an assumed name.

Thus it has been shown that Napoleon's reign was illustrated by numerous and useful discoveries and by uniform progress in science, and that men devoted to scientific pursuits were admitted to his intimacy and rewarded by his munificence. Still, the immense strides that had been made before his accession to power show, that in this branch of labor, France had little need of stimulus. It is more correct, therefore, to say that Napoleon recompensed science, than that he encouraged it; he was its patron rather than its promoter. He was the Mæcenas of savans, not their Charlemagne.

CHAPTER XXIV.

Hortense de Beauharnais—Her Education—Talent for Amateur Theatricals—Calumny—A Maniac Lover—Duroc—Louis Bonaparte—Official Poetry—The Throne of Holland—Death of Napoleon-Charles—Birth of Louis Napoleon and de Morny—Hortense at Aix; at Malmaison; at the Court of Louis XVIII.—The Return of Napoleon—The Necklace—Chateau of Arenenberg—Death and Will of Queen Hortense—Education and Life of de Morny—Modern French Biography.

HORTENSE-EUGÉNIE, daughter of Josephine by her first husband, Vicomte Alexandre de Beauharnais, was born at Paris, on the 10th of April, 1783. Three years afterwards she accompanied her mother to the island of Martinique, the home of Josephine's now aged and infirm relatives. They returned to France at the commencement of the revolution. Their poverty was such—for Josephine was alienated from her husband, and had no resources of her own—that Hortense was glad to accept, from the boatswain's mate of the vessel in which they had taken passage, a pair of shoes that his daughter had already worn. On their arrival at Paris, influential friends sought to bring Beauharnais and his wife together again. Hortense was the means of effecting a reconciliation. She was presented to her father in the costume of a Creole boy. The vicomte, who had till that moment doubted her relationship to himself, and had for this reason separated from Josephine, exclaimed, " 'Tis I, I myself at the age of seven years! I recognize my own features!" Turning to his father, who was present, and who had been much afflicted by the estrangement, he said in Latin, " Verum putas haud ægre, quod valde expetis :" " It is not difficult to believe true what we ardently wish may be so."

At the commencement of the revolution, Hortense and her brother Eugène were intrusted to the care of the Princess de Hohenzollern-Sigmaringen. Their father was arrested upon the charge of giving his influence to the monarchists, and soon perished upon the scaffold. Their mother was thrown into prison, from whence the fall of Robespierre delivered her, as has been already narrated. At the age of thirteen, Hortense became the daughter-in-law of Napoleon Bonaparte, and was placed under the care of Madame Campan, at St. Germain. She received at the hands of this celebrated lady the showy and somewhat unsubstantial education given at that time to the daughters of people of fashion and of elegant associations: that education which regards accomplishments as superior to acquirements; a finish of the person, of the manners, of the exterior, rather than a cultivation of the mind. Hortense was an apt scholar, and her charming disposition rendered her the favorite of the school and the cherished pupil of the instructress. During the absence of Bonaparte in Egypt, Josephine recalled her home, and from this moment to her marriage the mother and daughter were inseparable companions.

Bonaparte became consul in December, 1799, Hortense attaining about the same period her eighteenth year. She was at this time a very pretty and pleasing young lady. Her light silken hair played round a face of pure pink and white, though her color was slight, and her complexion therefore rather pale than florid. Her eyes were of a soft and penetrating blue. Her figure was slender, and her carriage graceful. Her hands were white, her feet small and well made. Her manner was engaging, combining the stimulating vivacity of a Frenchwoman with the languid suavity of a Creole.* She was witty but not caustic. She cultivated flowers, and successfully transferred their color and forms to paper. She composed and sang ballads, and was an excellent amateur actress.

---

* The portrait of Hortense, upon the opposite page, is taken from a copy of David's original, in the Historical Gallery at Versailles. The original is in the possession of the present Emperor of the French.

To the chateau of Malmaison was attached a private theatre, and in 1800 it was resolved to make it subservient to the amusement of its inmates. Hortense had been successful at Madame Campan's in the character of Esther—a tragedy written expressly by Racine for amateur performers—and her mother thought her dramatic talents might be usefully employed in diverting the First Consul. Napoleon assumed the duties of director: that is, he selected the plays and distributed the characters. "The Barber of Seville," by Beaumarchais, the comedy upon which Rossini's opera of the same name is founded, was the first selection. The cast was as follows:

ROSINA,	Hortense de Beauharnais,
ALMAVIVA,	General Lauriston,
FIGARO,	M. Didelot,
BASILE,	Eugène de Beauharnais,
BARTHOLO,	Bourrienne,
L'EVEILLÉ,	Savary.

Napoleon startled his actors by informing them, during the last rehearsal, that he had invited forty persons to dinner, and one hundred and fifty besides to witness the performance, including the cabinet, the senate, and the diplomatic corps! He himself sat in a stage box, and succeeded in disconcerting his troupe by a quizzical smile and an incessant scrutiny. The stars of the company were Bourrienne, Eugène and Hortense. The latter charmed the auditory by the graceful and yet spirited manner in which she rendered the character of the fair Andalusian. Her costume—the traditional pink and black assigned to Rosina—became her complexion in its color, and her form in its fashion. General Savary's character, though not arduous, was certainly fatiguing, for it compelled him to sneeze at intervals during three mortal hours.

The affection of Bonaparte for his amiable daughter-in-law, which was very marked, and the simple fact that she never looked nim in the eye and always quailed before his glance, gave rise to an odious, persistent and wide-spread calumny. It incensed Bonaparte, harassed Josephine, afflicted Hortense and afterwards embittered her relations with her husband, and was in a great measure the cause of their discord and consequent separation.

One of the earliest victims of the beauty and graces of M'lle Hortense was a poor lunatic, whose weak brain was quite overpowered by so many attractions. He followed her with frantic declarations of love, and lamentable prayers for compassion; he tossed odes in at her carriage window, sent her locks of hair through the mail, and besieged her door and lattice at night. This amused her for a time, but the unhappy maniac soon required the restraint of a strait-jacket, and Bonaparte sent him to a retreat for the insane, many leagues removed from the cruel object of his affections.

M'lle Beauharnais was herself destined to be crossed in love. She cherished a secret and a hopeless passion. Bonaparte, in the meantime, was desirous of bestowing her hand upon Duroc: he was ready to give the bride half a million francs in dower, and to make Duroc commandant of the eighth military division. Josephine opposed the plan with all the force of her arguments, her caresses and her tears. Her own desire was to unite her daughter with Napoleon's moody brother, Louis Bonaparte. He was the only one of her brothers-in-law to whom she could look for friendship and protection against the hostilities and persecutions of her husband's family; and she devoted herself with untiring perseverance to effect her object and consummate the alliance. The First Consul, in the full expectation that Hortense would marry Duroc—for she had expressed her willingness—had given to the latter the very flattering mission of complimenting Alexander upon his accession to the throne of Russia. During his absence, his correspondence with Hortense passed through the hands of Bourrienne, who was in the habit of playing chess in the evening with her, and who used to whisper across the board

"J'ai une lettre." Duroc, on his return, did not press his suit, either because his own feelings were not deeply enlisted, or because he was acquainted with the young lady's prior attachment. Josephine's influence would, in any case, have been too powerful for resistance. On the 7th of January, 1802, the marriage was solemnized between Hortense de Beauharnais and Louis Bonaparte. The bride wept during the ceremony, and after it was performed, withdrew in tears to the embrasure of a window, while her taciturn husband, with discontented and lowering brow, stood aloof from the assembled guests. "Never," says Louis himself in his memoirs, "was there a more gloomy ceremony; never had husband and wife a stronger presentiment of all the horrors of a forced and ill-assorted marriage." It was, indeed, one of the most uncongenial matches ever formed from considerations of personal advantage or the exigencies of state policy.

The alliance took the public by surprise, and the calumnious report of which we have spoken now spread from one extremity of Europe to the other. The marriage was put forth in pamphlets and libels circulated with zeal by the royalists, as a cover and a diversion; Louis was mocked and derided as the scape-goat of his brother's immoralities. Seven months afterwards, the English papers stated that Hortense had given birth to a son. Bonaparte was shocked at this premature announcement, knowing as he did that it was intended to give color to the story of his relations with his daughter-in-law before she became the wife of his brother. The means he adopted to refute the calumny evince a remarkable turn for petty machination. He ordered a ball to be given at Malmaison, and insisted that Hortense should dance a quadrille, in spite of her situation. She resisted, but was compelled to yield. The next morning a piece of poetry appeared in one of the papers, complimenting Hortense upon the grace she had displayed under trying and unusual circumstances. The subject of the verses was mortified, and complained to Bonaparte, saying that however ready and facile might be the poets of the time, she hardly believed that the stanzas in question had been composed and printed between twelve at night and six in the morning. Bonaparte replied vaguely, and changed the subject. Hortense subsequently learned from Bourrienne that the poetry was written before the ball took place : that the ball was given to furnish an occasion for the poetry, and that she had been made to dance in order to justify its theme. The motive for this little intrigue was the necessity of showing the statements of the English papers to be unfounded ; and the refutation was the more efficacious from the fact that it was thus indirect and apparently accidental.

Some time afterwards, Bonaparte said to Bourrienne : " That story of my connection with Hortense is still circulating." " I confess," said Bourrienne, " that I did not suppose it would live so long." " I expect of you," returned Bonaparte, " if you ever write your memoirs, that you will wash my hands of this infamous accusation : I do not wish such a reproach to escort me to posterity." [1]

Josephine was naturally afflicted by the rumor thus revived, and Napoleon in reassuring her unwittingly augmented her distress. He sought to persuade her that the extraordinary publicity which had been given throughout France to the report, was due to the desire of the country that he should have an heir, and that, despairing of one from a legitimate source, it seized with avidity upon a story which attributed to him even a bastard offspring. This singular method of administering consolation very naturally added to Josephine's apprehensions of a divorce, of which, thus early, she had an anxious presentiment.

" Louis and Hortense lived happily but a few months," said Napoleon at St. Helena ; " great exactions on his part, and great inconstancy on hers—these were their mutual wrongs. She was capricious, and affected independence. Louis placed no reliance on the rumor which made me the father of her first son, but his

[1] Bour. v. 276.

self-love and peculiar temper were shocked by it, and he afterwards made it the pretext for misconduct of his own. The match was due to the intrigues of Josephine, who was prompted to it in furtherance of her own private interests."

The first son of Hortense was born towards the close of 1802, ten months after her marriage. The infant was held at the baptismal font by Napoleon, who would have adopted him and made him his heir to the throne, had not Louis withheld his consent, to the great chagrin of Josephine, who already despaired of again becoming a mother. Napoleon, however, considered him as his heir, though he could not make him his son. A second son was born to Hortense and Louis in the year 1804.

With the proclamation of the Empire, came the distribution of thrones among Napoleon's brothers and sisters. Hortense would have preferred that of Naples, but political necessities conferred the Sicilian crown upon Joseph. "I would have re-kindled," says Hortense in her memoirs, "the flame of the fine arts in Italy. I would have revived the reign of the Medici, and of the house of Este. But alas! I was destined to reside in Holland, a kingdom heavy with fog, without sun, and without poetry, a country of thick and phlegmatic burgomasters." She spent a part of the years 1806–7 at her capital city of the Hague. The portion of the palace occupied by her was plainly and unexpensively furnished, in order not to shock the simple tastes of her thrifty subjects. Her life here was unhappy for many reasons: she had no affection for her husband; she was separated for the first time from her mother; the landscape of marshes and dikes which surrounded her, and the wearisome Dutch society with which she was brought in contact, were saddening features of a disheartening exile. A calamity now occurred, which changed the fortunes of the whole Bonaparte family; her eldest son died of a sudden attack of croup. The shock of this loss, and the consequent grief and despair in which it plunged her, exerted a lasting and injurious effect upon her constitution. The blow was a fatal one to Josephine; for she felt that her divorce was involved in the death of Napoleon's heir adoptive. The Emperor had been very fond of his nephew, and had encouraged his early fancy for drums and mimic fire-arms. He, too, was deeply affected by the loss, and from this moment his intercourse with Josephine became reserved and unsympathetic. The remains of young Napoleon Charles were removed to Paris, and temporarily deposited in the cathedral of Notre Dame.

Queen Hortense was ordered by her physician to travel in order to recruit her health, undermined by the grief consequent upon her loss. She at once left Holland, and never resumed her position as the wife of Louis Bonaparte. She spent some time in the Pyrenees, winning the affections of the peasants among whom she dwelt, by her benevolence and the placid graces of her manner. In the autumn, she visited Paris, and her house became the resort of the artists and musicians of the time: David, Isabey, Gérard. It was at this period that she composed the ballad of "Partant pour la Syrie," which has since become the present Emperor's March. Much to the regret of Napoleon, she lent her great artistic influence to the introduction of the Gothic style of furniture. This style, now known as that of the Empire, fell into disrepute with the restoration of the Bourbons.

Madame Mère was dissatisfied with the conduct of her daughter-in-law, whom she considered as playing truant from her husband at the Hague. She, therefore, wrote a paragraph to the effect that Queen Hortense, having somewhat recovered from her late indisposition, intended to return at once to Holland. This she caused to be inserted in the Journal des Débats of October 17th, 1807. Hortense was naturally indignant at this piece of dictation, but as it was impossible to contradict the Empress Dowager in a newspaper, she could only publish the certificate of her physicians, to the effect that in spite of her ardent desire to rejoin her husband, the state of her health necessitated a prolonged stay in France.

On the 20th of April, 1808, she gave birth, in the palace of the Tuileries, to her third son, CHARLES LOUIS NAPOLÉON, now Emperor of the French. This prince was the first of the Napoleon dynasty to receive military honors at his birth, which was welcomed throughout France by the official rejoicings of government cannon. Shortly afterwards, Louis Bonaparte begged Napoleon to grant him a divorce from Hortense. Napoleon refused, though he promised, at a more fitting period, to arrange a separation.

At the divorce of Josephine, Hortense supported her mother to her chair. The former was dressed in white muslin, the latter in black velvet. Napoleon afterwards reproached her for what he pronounced an unseemly affectation of woe, in her choice of a costume and a color.

Louis Bonaparte was soon compelled, by political complications, to abdicate his throne. He retired to Gratz, in Styria. He was declared to be separated from Hortense by Napoleon, who endowed the late queen with two million francs a year, and intrusted to her the care and education of both her sons. She continued to reside in Paris, visiting her divorced mother at Malmaison on every alternate day, giving the other days of the week to formal attendance at the palace of Marie Louise, whose train she had been compelled to bear, on her marriage with Napoleon at Notre Dame.

On the 22d of October, 1811, Hortense gave birth to a fourth son, on whom was bestowed the name of de Morny. No secret was ever made of the paternity of this child, it being attributed to, and tacitly acknowledged by, M. de Flahaut, general of division and aid-de-camp of the Emperor. Of the son we shall have occasion to speak presently ; of the father, Napoleon himself has left a description. This is doubtless in some degree unjust, owing to the antipathy the Emperor felt for elegant accomplishments and the ordinary qualifications of a man of fashion. Josephine one day said of M. de Flahaut that he possessed a variety of talents. "What are they?" said Napoleon. "Sense? Bah! who has not as much as he? He sings well, you say; a fine thing for a soldier, who should be hoarse by profession. He is a beau, you mean; that is what pleases you women. I see nothing so extraordinary in him; he is just like a spider, with his eternal legs; his legs are quite unnatural; to be well-shaped"—looking at his own and acting, though not uttering, the concluding phrase—"to be well-shaped, his legs should be like these."

During the summer of 1813, Queen Hortense lost by a terrible accident her earliest and most constant friend—Adèle Auguié at school, the Countess de Brocq by marriage. During an excursion in the neighborhood of Aix, this unfortunate lady fell from a precipice into a mountain torrent. Her body was recovered mutilated and lifeless. By order of Hortense a marble monument was erected to her memory upon the scene of the catastrophe.

During the calamities of 1814, Hortense and her ladies busied themselves in preparing lint for the military hospitals. Upon the fall of Napoleon, she joined her mother at Malmaison, where they received Alexander and the other monarchs of the alliance. The attentions of Alexander to Hortense were very marked; she reciprocated his kindness by saving his life. He was visiting with her the machine at Marly, by which the water-works and cascades of Versailles are fed from the Seine. An incautious movement placed the Czar within reach of the ponderous wheel, from which nothing but the energetic and well-timed effort of the queen could have extricated him in time. The interests of Hortense were consulted by the allies. Talleyrand, who had joined them, said of her: "She is the only lady of the family that I esteem." Louis XVIII. erected her country seat of St. Leu into a duchy, transmissible to her children.

When Hortense laid aside the mourning which she had assumed upon the death of her mother, she paid her respects to Louis XVIII. at the Tuileries. The sovereign seemed to take great pleasure in her conversation, and she repeated her visit One of his intimate courtiers said to him, "Why does not your

Majesty arrange her divorce and marry her? But your Majesty might do better than receive with this marked favor one whose relations with the enemy are so well known." Louis XVIII. never saw Queen Hortense again. She had endeavored to play a double part, and succeeded in offending both Bourbons and Bonapartes. Napoleon, on his return from Elba, received her coldly, and told her she should either have followed him to Elba, or her husband to Rome; and that she was wrong in accepting St. Leu from the Bourbons. But as she was the only lady of his family present in Paris, he restored her to favor, and she did the honors of the Hundred Days. After the battle of Waterloo she attended upon Napoleon at Malmaison, and as he departed upon his exile, gave him a diamond necklace for which, in happier days, she had paid eight hundred thousand francs. It was under Napoleon's pillow when he died at Longwood, and, by his order, was subsequently restored by General Montholon to Hortense.

Upon the second restoration of the Bourbons, she was naturally regarded with suspicion, and consequently lost her duchy of St. Leu. A verdict rendered in a suit brought against her by her husband, compelled her to give up to him her eldest son. Falling into want, she sold for a trifling sum a picture given her by Talleyrand, the cost of which had been sixteen thousand francs. An order was served upon her to leave Paris within two hours. She departed, refusing however the proffered escort, and taking no one with her but an Austrian aid-de-camp of nineteen years. In her wanderings, she was repulsed from Savoy and from Baden. She finally bought the chateau of Arenenberg, on the banks of Lake Constance, in the Swiss canton of Thurgovia, where she spent her summers, retiring to Rome in the winter, and sharing the Borghèse palace and la Paolina villa with the princess Pauline.

In 1830, her eldest surviving son married the second daughter of Joseph Bonaparte, and died the year after of inflammation of the lungs complicated with measles. Her third son, Louis Napoleon, entered the school of engineers at Thün, in Berne. She was compelled to dispose of the necklace that had been restored to her by General Montholon. The King of Bavaria entered into an arrangement by which he agreed to take the jewels, and in return pay Hortense an annuity of twenty-three thousand francs. He was called upon to fulfill this stipulation for two years, only. The sagacious Bavarian obtained for the sum of forty-six thousand francs, diamonds valued at eight hundred thousand! In 1836, Louis Napoleon made his adventurous attempt at Strasburg, in consequence of which he was compelled to expatriate himself to America. The dying summons of his mother called him back to Arenenberg, early in the following year; he arrived there in time to close her eyes and receive her blessing. She died on the 3d of October, 1837. The government of Louis Philippe permitted her remains to be placed side by side with those of Josephine, in the village church of Rueil.

The following is an extract from the will of Queen Hortense:

"May my husband bestow one souvenir upon my memory, and may he believe that my greatest regret in dying is that I was unable to render him happy.

"I pardon all the sovereigns with whom I have had relations of friendship, for the hasty judgment they passed upon me.

"I pardon all ambassadors and chargés d'affaires for the constant inaccuracy of their reports concerning me.

"I pardon the few Frenchmen to whom I have been useful, for the calumnies with which they have loaded me, in acquittal of their obligations. I pardon those who believed them without examination, and I hope to live for a time in the remembrance of my countrymen.

"I HAVE NO POLITICAL ADVICE TO GIVE MY SON CHARLES LOUIS NAPOLEON. I KNOW THAT HE UNDERSTANDS HIS POSITION, AND APPRECIATES THE DUTIES IMPOSED UPON HIM BY HIS NAME."

The young man to whom this closing paragraph referred is now Emperor of the French.

We now return to the fourth son of Queen Hortense, the

Count de Morny, who was born, as we have said, in 1811, at Paris. As it was impossible that he should remain at the residence and under the charge of his mother, he was placed in the hands of his grandmother, once the Countess de Flahaut, but now, by a second marriage with a Portuguese noble, the Countess de Souza-Bothello. This lady, the authoress of "Adèle de Senange," and "Eugène de Rothelin," two novels illustrative of the manners of society before the revolution, devoted herself zealously to the education of her grandson. He became a favorite with Talleyrand, and it is said that the latter predicted of him, when but twelve years old, that he would one day become a cabinet minister. He was graduated at the College Bourbon, a proficient in Greek and English, and as he grew in years, offered in his person and manners a lively souvenir of the grace and distinction which characterized the aristocracy of the old regime. He wrote verses, for which he also composed the music—a talent which he inherited from his mother; he would even sing these ballads to intimate friends, in an agreeable, though somewhat feminine, tenor voice.

He now entered one of the military schools, which he left at the age of twenty-one, entering the army as sub-lieutenant of lancers. Being quartered at Fontainebleau, he obtained from M. de Montalivet, Minister of the Interior, free access to the library attached to the palace. He studied, principally, works upon metaphysics and theology, giving as a reason for his inquiries into religion, that "he wished to settle that question at once." He joined the African army, and was present at the siege of Constantine as orderly officer of General Trézel, whose life he saved. For this act, and for having received four Arab bullets, none of which injured him, Louis Philippe made him Chevalier of the Legion of Honor. At Mascara, de Morny was lying one evening, wrapped up in his cloak, on the banks of a river. He was suffering from an attack of fever and ague. An officer whom he did not know, approached him, and said, "M. de Morny, you are unwell; will you permit me to offer you an orange?"

"Many thanks," returned de Morny. "To whom do I owe this kindness?" "To Captain Changarnier." On the 2d of December, 1851, Captain, now General Changarnier, was exiled from France, by order of the Minister of the Interior, de Morny.

M. de Morny resigned his commission in the army in 1838, having been refused a furlough which he considered essential to the restoration of his enfeebled health. He bought large landed estates in the department of le Puy-de-Dôme, and introduced there the manufacture of native sugar. He was so successful in this that the congress of sugar-raisers which assembled soon after at Paris, and which consisted of four hundred members, made him, the youngest delegate, their president. The shire town of his department, Clermont, sent him to the Chamber of Deputies, in 1842. His promises to the electors, he used to say, were limited to the prediction of an eclipse of the sun for the 10th of the month. He obtained credit as an orator and as a publicist, and M. Guizot, the President of the Council of Ministers, was disposed on one occasion to make him cabinet minister.[1] He espoused the interests of his half-brother, Louis Napoleon, in 1848, and was one of his most active coadjutors in the coup d'état of December, 1851. He became Minister of the Interior on the consummation of that event, and remained so till the 23d of January of the following year. Occupying a position which afforded him both opportunity and capital, he entered the field of industrial and real estate speculation; the result showed him to be possessed of high financial and commercial capabilities. He became one of the railroad kings of France, and in a comparatively short period realized a princely fortune. He was made Grand Cross of the Legion of Honor, in 1852, on the anniversary of the coup d'état; President of the Legislative Assembly, in 1854; and upon the restoration of peace with Russia, early in 1856, French ambassador to the court of St. Petersburg.

The rigid system of censure to which the press is at present

[1] Mém. d'un Bourgeois, vi. 113–120.

subjected in France, has produced a new style of biography, which may be called with propriety the inferential style. On one subject —parentage—it leaves the reader either in profound ignorance, or compels him to undertake a tedious process of deduction. Thus Dr. Veron, in his sketch of the life of de Morny—which the subject of it has publicly declared "to be of the most scrupulous exactitude," and which is the only biography of that gentleman yet issued in France—avoids all mention of his mother; not even by an indirect allusion giving the inquirer the least enlightenment in the matter of his maternity. He resorts to an ingenious circumlocution to acquaint the reader with the facts of his origin on the father's side. Young de Morny was educated, he says, by his grandmother, Madame de Souza. He then details the history of Madame de Souza, and states that she had previously borne the title of Countess de Flahaut, and had a son by her first husband. As it does not appear that she ever had any other son, it is clear to the mind that is awake to processes of ratiocination, that it could only be he that had made her a grandmother. She had one son, and one grandson; the former is, therefore, by inference, the father of the latter. The Parisian reader is to presume, therefore, that M. de Flahaut was the father of M. de Morny. It is nowhere said, however, that M. de Morny had a father, or that M. de Flahaut had a son, but Madame de Souza had a grandson. M. de Flahaut and de Morny are never represented as in each other's company but once, and then on Talleyrand's staircase, the former holding the latter by the hand.

This school of biography is in direct opposition to that whose practice it is to trace the ancestry of its subject back to the Crusades or the Norman Conquest, or to the Mayflower and the Pilgrim Fathers.

On the eve of the coup d'état, de Morny was told by a lady that he must expect to be swept away in the revolution the people were preparing. "Madame," he replied, "if there is to be any brooming in Paris, I shall try to be on the side of the handle."

CHAPTER XXV.

The Art of Painting under Louis XIV.—Watteau—Painting under Louis XV.—Boucher—Napoleon and David—The Picture of the Coronation—Cardinal Caprara and his Wig—The Portrait of Napoleon and the Marquis of Douglas—David's Coat of Arms—Gérard—Girodet—Guérin—Isabey—Gros—The Plague of Jaffa—Napoleon and Desgenettes—Géricault—The Spoliation of Italy—Foreign Works of Art at the Louvre—Their Restoration by the Allies—Sculpture under Napoleon—Canova at Paris—His Interview with Napoleon—Houdon—Chaudet—Music during the Empire—Méhul—Lesueur—Boieldieu—Spontini—Cherubini—Napoleon's Influence upon Art.

THE art of painting, in France, during the century preceding the Revolution, had been singularly neglected. Its scope had been narrowed, its aim and purpose degraded. The age of Louis XIV. was, nevertheless, one, it would seem, to stimulate to the production of epics and chefs-d'œuvre, as well in the arts as in literature. And yet Watteau, the fan-painter and illuminator of screens and panels, was the grand monarch's artist-laureate; he was too, the favorite during the Regency. His subjects were fawns, satyrs, fêtes champêtres and masquerades; nymphs, hoydens and soldiers. Dolce far niente was their occupation; basking in the sunshine, seeking shade and shelter in bowers or beneath fringy parasols, their pastime; and, from time to time, piping upon a bunch of tuneful reeds, the application of their feeble energies. In painting, at least, the age was bucolic, pastoral; the woods were peopled with the grotesque creations of mythology, and the lawns dotted with beings quite as fanciful—ladies of rank habited as shepherdesses, and fashionable courtiers in the guise of rustic swains; and all engaged with crooks and wands in guarding troops of sentimental and coquettish sheep. Watteau's figures, says an authority, are imaginary, and illustrate the impossible;

yet, to the eye, they present that familiar grace which we call gentility. His soldiers are careless and slouching, and aspire to be agreeable as well as victorious.

Under Louis XV., Boucher was the court painter, and his amative pastorals and rural elegies soon obtained for him the name of the Anacreon of his art. Like Watteau, he illustrated the court festivities, and represented the age as tawdry, frivolous and lackadaisical. They both of them employed to good purpose the colors of the prism, while they neglected or disregarded the pure lines and correct drawing of that useful little trihedron. Their works are acknowledged to have done great and lasting injury to French art, and to be poor and paltry representatives of a school and a century. They are, nevertheless, pleasing to look upon, and repose the eye agreeably after a battle-piece, a storm at sea, or a martyrdom from Scripture.

A reaction took place, just before the Revolution, under the auspices of Jacques Louis David. Drawing had previously been sacrificed to color, and now color was, in its turn, sacrificed to drawing. David's style is a labored imitation of the Greek sculptures: his figures are like statues colored and endued with motion; his subjects were usually groups, either partially or totally naked; the composition was classical, the color hard and glaring, and the effect artificial and theatrical. It has been aptly said that his pictures recall the uplifting of a stage-curtain when the whole company are assembled in one tableau. He executed his Belisarius, the Death of Socrates, the Loves of Paris and Helen, and the famous Oath of the Horatii, before the advent of Napoleon.

"The Emperor," said David, some years subsequently, "without, perhaps, being a passionate lover of the Fine Arts, knew their importance in a state. He was anxious that they should engross a large share of public attention. I went to pay my respects to him immediately after the 18th Brumaire. As soon as he saw me, he saluted me by the title of the French Apelles, and asked me upon what subject I was engaged. I replied, 'Leonidas at Thermopylæ.' He shrugged his shoulders, and said:

"'Ah, David, you are always painting the Greeks and Romans, and, what is worse, the conquered! Yes, citizen David, the conquered! Is it conformable to the principles of reason that three hundred men should face three millions? If they do so, they are not heroes, but madmen, and should be sent to Bedlam. All resistance should be rational, and should be founded upon a probability of success; otherwise, whatever name may be given to it, it is pure extravagance, and ought not to be recorded in pictures, on account of the bad example which would thus be conveyed. A small number of men may cause the failure of a great movement by an imprudent and obstinate defence. I advise you to make choice of some incident in our own history. Modern times offer plenty of good subjects.'

"I was somewhat astonished by these remarks, which were by no means in accordance with my predilection for the antique. I approached the First Consul, and said, in a voice to be heard by him alone: 'Perhaps a coronation might meet with approval.' 'Not just yet,' he replied, laughing. 'There is a wide difference, republican, between that and Thermopylæ. However, do what you please; your pencil will confer celebrity on any subject you may select. For every great historical picture you may choose to paint, you shall receive one hundred thousand francs.'"

Upon the proclamation of the Empire, Napoleon made David his painter in ordinary, and instructed the Minister of the Interior to order of him six large pictures for the Louvre. The Coronation was one of this series, the execution of which cost the artist many years of labor and involved him in constant annoyance and conflict. He could not resign himself to the painting of modern costumes, and he was compelled to submit to the exactions and encounter the susceptibilities of the numerous political personages who were to appear in the picture, and it was not till the spring of 1808 that Napoleon was admitted to see it. He expressed great admiration, and recognized the various portraits; he said of Murat that his head was a Vesuvius, of Talleyrand that he was perhaps a little flattered, and of Fouché that his likeness was so correct as to be startling. As he was leaving the studio, he lifted his hat from his head, and, turning to the artist, said: "David, I salute you!" "Sire," replied David, "I receive your salutation in the name of the artists of France, and am happy to be the one to whom it is addressed."

Cardinal Caprara, one of the aids of the Pope at the coronation, wore a perruque. In his portrait of the ceremony, David represented him bald. The cardinal begged the artist to restore the wig, a favor which was steadfastly refused. He then flew to Talleyrand, Minister of Foreign Affairs, and laid the case before him. "David represents me without my wig, when it is notorious that I wear one. Now, as no pope ever covers his head with a perruque, it will naturally be supposed that I am an aspirant for the pontifical chair, in case of a vacancy!" This argument was communicated to David, who replied, "Caprara knows my taste for the nude; he ought to be thankful that I have taken off nothing but his wig, and represented bald nothing but his head!"

About this time, David painted for the English Marquis of Douglas a standing portrait of Napoleon of the size of life. He was accustomed to paint the imperial features without requiring Napoleon's personal attendance. The Emperor, therefore, knew nothing of this portrait, till it was brought one day to the Tuileries, for his inspection. It represented his Majesty in his cabinet, as he had risen from his desk after a night spent in writing—a circumstance indicated by candles burning in their sockets. Those who had seen it, considered it, as far as the head and features were concerned, the most perfect resemblance that had yet been obtained.

Napoleon was delighted with it, and eagerly complimented David. "Still," said he, "I think that you have made my eyes rather too weary; this is wrong, for working at night does not fatigue me; on the contrary, it rests me. I am never so fresh in the morning as when I have dispensed with sleep. Who is the portrait for? Who ordered it? It was not I, was it?" "No, sire, it is intended for the Marquis of Douglas." "What, David," returned the Emperor, scowling, "is it to be given to an Englishman?" "Sire, he is one of your Majesty's greatest admirers, and is, perhaps, the most sincere living appreciator of French artists." "Next to me," replied Napoleon, tartly. After a moment, he added, "David, I will buy the portrait myself." "Sire, it is already sold." "David, I desire the portrait, I say; I will give thirty thousand francs for it." "Your Majesty, I cannot change its destination," said David, indicating, by a descriptive gesture, that he had already been paid. "David," exclaimed Napoleon, "this portrait shall not be sent to England, do you hear? I will return your marquis his money." "Surely your Majesty would not dishonor me?" stammered the artist, at the same time noticing that the Emperor, having exhausted persuasion, was preparing for active interference. "No, certainly; but what I will not do either, is to allow the enemies of France to possess me in their country, even on canvas." So saying, he directed a sturdy kick at the painting, and the imperial foot passed vigorously through it. Without a word, he quitted the apartment, leaving a wonder-stricken audience behind him. David had the picture carried back to his studio, and subsequently mended and restored it, and forwarded it to its owner. It is likely that the merit of the portrait, as a work of art and as a likeness, is now somewhat lost in the superior attractions of the patched rent, and that its value is considerably greater as a memento of his Majesty's wrath, than as a specimen of the skill of his artist-in-ordinary.

Two days after the scene just described, David was summoned to the Tuileries, where Napoleon, taking and pressing his hand, begged him to bear no malice. "You see David, I am jealous of the glory of French artists, and should be better pleased if all your chefs-d'œuvre could be collected in the Louvre. Adieu, my friend; both of us must forget what has happened." The next morning, David was promoted in the hierarchy of the Legion of Honor, and received the title of Baron of the Empire. Napoleon himself designed his coat of arms—a palette upon a golden ground, with the uplifted arm of Horatius holding the three swords intended for his sons. This was taken from David's composition of the Oath of the Horatii. Upon the fall of Napoleon, David was exiled by the Bourbons, with those who had voted for the death of Louis XVI. He retired to Brussels, where he established a school, and painted his celebrated Cupid and Psyche, now in the Louvre. He died in 1825.

Gérard, born in 1770, was a pupil of David, and for a time, in connection with Gros and Girodet, continued and confirmed the peculiarities of his style. His Battle of Austerlitz, and Entrance of Henry IV. into Paris, gave him a high reputation at an early age. He felt, however, that he was better fitted for the execution of poetic subjects than for the illustration of history. He became, under the Empire, the first portrait painter of the day; his gallery of Historical Portraits contains eighty-four likenesses, full length and of the size of life, besides two hundred of half length. Napoleon made Gérard also a Baron of the Empire.

Girodet was, towards the middle of his career, the successful rival of his master, David, his "Deluge" obtaining a higher rank from the examining jury, than David's "Rape of the Sabines,' its competitor. This decision, however, has been reversed by posterity. Girodet's "Burial of Atala" has been rendered familiar to Europe and America, by means of innumerable copies.

Guérin illustrated mythology and classic history. His "Phèdre et Hippolyte," "Andromaque et Pyrrhus," and other similar works, now at the Louvre, are pleasing and poetic examples of the school of which David was the founder.

The court portraitist was Jean Baptiste Isabey. He had studied for some time with David, but want of success in the speciality of that artist determined him to adopt portrait painting. Before the Revolution, he had obtained sufficient patronage to enable him to take the miniatures of Marie Antoinette and the Duke de Berry. After the revolution, he painted the portraits of Josephine, Hortense, and General Bonaparte. He soon became the fashionable artist, and was attached to Madame Campan's seminary in the capacity of drawing master. When Napoleon became Emperor, he was appointed portraitist to the Ministry of Foreign Affairs, and in this capacity was afterwards sent to Vienna, to perpetuate upon ivory and other substances, the lineaments of the members of the House of Hapsburg. He made designs for Sèvres porcelain, painted scenery for the Grand Opera, managed the court theatricals, and at last gave lessons in water colors to Marie Louise. The style that he founded, the great merit of which was the giving to miniatures all the depth and vigor of oil paintings, has survived him, though it has been since professed by artists immeasurably his inferiors.

Gros, one of the pupils of David, and, perhaps, after him, the first painter of the epoch, furnished the world in his splendid composition of the Plague of Jaffa, with the most audacious instance on record of falsification of history. The painting represents Bonaparte in the hospital at Jaffa, touching the pustules of the sick and dying, and thus reassuring his soldiers. The truth is, this act of heroism was not performed by Bonaparte, but by Dr. Desgenettes, of the medical staff.[1]

A modern biography, written and published under Louis Philippe, not only excuses, but applauds, this proceeding on the part of Gros. The following passage occurs in the French Plutarch, and is from the pen of a member of the Academy of the Fine Arts, the Vicomte de Senonnes : " Certainly if there is a fact contested

---

1 Salgues' Memoirs, vi. 117.

in history, it is that which suggested this magnificent work. The conscientious historian will assuredly not consult it as a reliable authority. A painter may dispense with that dry precision which forms the merit of the chronicler; his mission is to furnish emotion and not documents, and when he hears of an incident, distorted but poetic, atoning for its lack of truth by its grandeur, he is not called upon to make further researches; it is not his task to discuss probabilities, to dissipate doubts, to measure testimony, to determine conviction. He must move, seduce, startle. Whole generations will believe, through this painting, that the general-in-chief of the army of Egypt did not fear to show himself in the terrible hospital where death was accumulating its heaps of victims, and to appear as a father and a friend; that he touched with his own hand the fearful marks of the scourge, and by this sublime act of virtue restored hope to the sick and confidence to the living. This is probably all that the people will know of the awful episode of the plague of Jaffa, and it is to the pencil of Gros that the memory of Bonaparte is indebted for this service. Such an act more than acquits the great painter of his obligations towards the great conqueror."[1]

How many admissions in this short extract—one emanating from the French Academy of Art! A painter may falsify fact, if he have court to make or protection to repay; a painter of history may pervert history and be approved in it, if he succeed in embellishing reality by the seductions of fiction, and in replacing, in behalf of a monarch, an awkward truth by a fawning and soothing falsehood. It is a merit in an artist to mislead posterity and abuse the world, when Mæcenas calls for flattery and Cæsar clamors for incense. A painter may pay his debts by falsehood on canvas; he may acquit his obligations by treacherous perversions in oil. How degrading to art is such service, and how disgraceful in a Royal Academy is the holding and the propagation of such opinion!

[1] Plutarque Français, viii. Art. Gros.

It is certain that the heroism of the surgeon Desgenettes has been forgotten by the world, and is scantily mentioned in history. And yet it as fully deserves a place in the kindly memory of mankind as the fidelity of Casabianca, the fortitude of Guatimozin, or the devotion of Pocahontas. Why has it disappeared from the well-thumbed and familiar chronicles of deeds of courage and self-sacrifice? Ask the gallery of the Louvre, where a picture, whose artistic merit makes it immortal and whose reputation gives it currency, has dressed the surgeon in the apparel of the general-in-chief, and has given him the stature and the lineaments of Napoleon. Such is history, as illustrated by an officious art and a subservient artist; such is one phase of the patronage of art, during the Consulate and the Empire.

The popular story of Bonaparte's having touched the tumors of the plague-stricken was first denied by Bourrienne in his Memoirs. "I walked," he says, "by the general's side, and I assert that I never saw him touch any of the infected. He proceeded quickly through the rooms, tapping the yellow top of his boot with a whip he held in his hand." This was in turn denied by the intendant-in-chief d'Aure, in a letter to the Journal des Débats, which that paper refused to insert. It was subsequently incorporated in a volume entitled "Les Erreurs de Bourrienne," published at Brussels. The official report of what occurred at Jaffa was drawn up by Berthier, under Bonaparte's eye. It does not contain the slightest mention of his touching the plague-spots; and the "Scientific and Military History of the Egyptian Expedition" is equally silent, though it chronicles, and of course establishes, the devotion of Desgenettes. The article we have quoted plainly shows, by the apologies it offers for Gros, that he must be considered as having illustrated an event which had no existence except in complaisant and obsequious legend.

It is worth mentioning that the Plague of Jaffa was executed upon a portion of the canvas, forty feet square, which had served for the rough draught of an intended painting of the Battle of

Nazareth, of which Junot was the hero. As the character of Napoleon developed itself, Gros became convinced that the First Consul and Emperor would prefer himself to furnish the themes for pictorial illustration, and that the artist who should devote his labor to embellishing the career of his lieutenants, would be more likely to compromise than to establish his reputation.

Later artists emancipated themselves from the influence of the school of David and his pupils. Géricault commenced this important reform. It occurred at the period of the immense popularity of the works of Lord Byron and of Schiller—whose themes are the dominant passions of humanity, and stirring passages in modern and contemporaneous history. He felt that this field was open to artists of the brush as well as to artists of the pen. He chose for a subject the most harrowing incident of the century in French maritime annals: the Wreck of the Medusa. No picture has been more criticised and more extolled than this. Whatever may be its merits or demerits, it was the first of a school and contributed to the overthrow of what had been called "le beau idéal"—the illustration of the classics and of mythology. Gods, demigods, Horatii, Sabines, Dido, Phèdre, Coriolanus, Andromaque, were abandoned for the study of nature, the delineation of the passions and the illustration of history. David's pictures still occupy the walls of the Louvre, but he has ceased to serve as a model or a teacher. The patronage bestowed by Napoleon upon French art may be said, as far as painting was concerned, to have given undue encouragement to a false and artificial school, and to have maintained by favor a system destined to fall, of its own weight, when that favor should be withdrawn.

A work published expressly to present, in a concise form, a view of the achievements of France in every branch of acquirement, thus speaks upon this subject: "Painting under the Empire is now appreciated at its proper standard. It is confessed that the compositions of the imperial era were forced and affected, too dramatic to be natural, and artificial in color. Still, the works of David, Girodet, Gros, Gérard and Guérin will always be remarked for qualities which it would be idle to contest. A few years later, Prudhon and Géricault restored, by solid and powerful compositions, the legitimate influence of color."[1]

Though this is the opinion held by the French critics and connaisseurs themselves, yet authors writing, as it would seem, for the express purpose of eulogizing the Emperor with indiscriminate zeal, have frequently indulged in such panegyric as the following: "Napoleon and David! Two men who owed to their genius only, their elevation, their popularity and their misfortunes! Two men moved by the same principles, swayed by the same ambition of immortality! Two men, in short, who, after having attained a degree of glory to which none others would have dared to aspire, fell by the same blow, and perished at nearly the same period, in a land of exile!"[2]

The most remarkable exemplification of Napoleon's taste for the Fine Arts, was his spoliation of Italy, after his memorable campaign in that country. The Louvre had already been made a National Museum by the Convention, and the country possessed valuable artistic cabinets in the collections of Francis the First and Louis XIV. To these Napoleon, ordering a razzia among the galleries, churches and palaces of Italy, Spain and Holland, added the accumulated treasures of centuries and the idols of Christian and of Pagan Art. The Venus de' Medici was torn from the tribune at Florence and sent to adorn the Grand Salon at Paris; the Florentines begged Canova to execute a Venus for her deserted pedestal, that they might name it "La Consolatrice." The Apollo Belvidere—to mingle the classic with the commercial—was shipped from the Vatican to Marseilles; the Laocoön was invoiced in the same consignment; Correggio contributed his St Jerome at Parma, though the Duke offered one million francs for its ransom; Raphael contributed his Transfiguration, at Rome; Domenichino his Communion; Paul Veronese his Marriage of

[1] Patria, ii. 2240.   [2] Le Siècle de Napoléon, Art. David.

Cana, at Venice ; Rubens his Descent from the Cross, at Antwerp ; Murillo his Assumption of the Virgin, at Madrid. The Bronze Horses, whose migrations from Corinth to Rome and thence to Constantinople, and thence again to Venice, had been for many years suspended, were re-jostled into motion, and sent to grace the triumphal arch of the Tuileries at Paris.

"What is this cloud of dust," says de Goncourt, "hanging over the post roads that centre at the Louvre? It is the priceless booty of art trundled to Paris from conquered kingdoms. The national highways are worn into gulleys under the weight of pictures which were before the envy of the world, and the dower of nations. Paintings, woven of purple and sunlight, arrive by cartloads ; and Berthollet's Assumption serves to stop a rent in a baggage van. Paris is to be the Pantheon of the human demigods, and Italy is summoned to contribute Raphael and Michael Angelo, Titian and Veronese. The legacy of antique art to the Italian peninsula—immortal bronze and marble—shall come and inhabit France. Victory is abroad, and at every halt in the world's museum, she indites, on a drum-head, the way-bill of some chef-d'œuvre. Milan shall lose the Cartoon of Raphael's School of Athens, its Giorgionis, its Leonardos : Parma its Correggios : Plaisance its Caraccis : Mantua its Guercinos. Like widows despoiled, the cities of the peninsula shall weep over the lost pride of their galleries. Rome will no longer be at Rome ; ten chariots will not hold the fastidious choice made from her artistic wealth. The Louvre will be too small to contain Belgium, Holland, Italy and Greece. To think of the accidents, the losses, and the breakages, in this crash and pell-mell of art! The Dutch and Flemish school huddled into a damp store-house on the ground floor! Belgian masterpieces tossed under the staircase ! Canvas jammed against canvas by careless truckmen, and Madonnas pierced by unwary ladders!"

The arrival of the spoils of Italy at Paris, which took place on the 10th Thermidor of the year VI., was the most wonderful fine art spectacle that the world has ever seen. Twenty-nine huge chariots laden with marble and pictorial trophies marched in procession over the Boulevards. There were the Venetian Horses, the Dying Gladiator, the Venus of the Capitol, the Disk Thrower, the Apollo Belvidere, the Venus de' Medici, the Laocoön, the Marriage of Cana, the Transfiguration; Mercury, Terpsichore, Erato, Urania, Polyhymnia, Euterpe, Cupid, Psyche, Antinoüs, Meleager, Ceres, Brutus, Cato, Clio, Adonis, Calliope, Melpomene, Trajan, Hercules and Thalia. In the train followed wagon loads of exotic plants, of petrifactions, of medals, manuscripts, Swiss bears and African dromedaries. The cortége was headed by the students of the Polytechnic School, the directors of the Museum, the professors of the School of Fine Arts, and the commissaries of the army of Italy. The chariots were arranged, at the close of the promenade, around the statue of Liberty, on the Champ de Mars; and then Citizen Thoin, the orator of the day, thanked the goddess for thus avenging the humiliated arts, and breaking the chains which bound the renown of so many illustrious dead.

The French have justified this rapacious pillage on very singular grounds. Madame Junot, who was requested by the French Consul to do the honors of the Louvre to distinguished strangers, states that "these chefs-d'œuvre had been conquered from barbarism and indifference, and in many instances from approaching ruin." The catalogue of the Louvre, published by the Minister of the Interior, says: "We are sorry that our space will not permit us to enlarge on the efforts and success of those honorable administrators, who, by their skill and care, saved from certain ruin the paintings whose preservation Italy had so much neglected."

The French were very anxious, upon the fall of Napoleon, that an arrangement be made by which the works of art collected at the Louvre and in the capital might be suffered to remain. Wellington wrote to Lord Castlereagh a letter upon the subject, in which occurs the following passage: "The allies being now in legal possession of the pictures and statues of the museum, they can not fail to restore them to those from whom they had been violently taken, contrary to the usages of regular warfare, and during the fearful period of the French Revolution and the tyranny of Bonaparte. . . . . . The desire of the French to retain these works of art is nothing more than a sentiment of national pride. They wish to retain them, not because Paris is the most proper spot for their assemblage, but because they were acquired by conquest, of which they form the trophies. The same sentiment naturally guides the nations despoiled, now that victory is upon their side, in their desire that these works be restored to them, the legitimate proprietors. The allied sovereigns are bound to give favorable attention to this desire. My opinion, then, is, that it would be unjust in the sovereigns to yield to the requests of the Parisians. The sacrifice they would make would be impolitic, for they would lose the occasion of administering to the French a grand moral lesson."

Napoleon's gallery of plundered art was therefore broken up in 1815, and its treasures were restored to their respective states. The Place du Carrousel, which covers the space in front of the museum, was occupied by English and Prussian soldiers during the boxing and removal of the precious absentees. Very few were allowed to remain. Austria, which at the Congress of Vienna was confirmed in the possession of Lombardo-Venetia, acknowledged that, in view of the dangers and difficulties of its transport back to Venice, the Marriage of Cana, by Paul Veronese, was safer where it was, and consented to leave it; but exacted, in exchange for it, a picture by Lebrun, representing Jesus, Judas and Mary Magdalen at the house of Simon the Pharisee. Canova, who had been sent to Paris by the Roman government to attend to its interests in the surrender of the works of art, consented to the retention of the colossal statue of the Tiber, and the magnificent Pallas of Velletri, as voluntary gifts from Rome. The Florentine commissaries agreed to a compromise, by which several works by Ghirlandaio were suffered to continue in Paris. The robberies committed by Soult, in Spain, were principally on his own account, and upon his death, in 1852, his Spanish gallery was sold at auction for the benefit of his estate. Murillo's Assumption was bought by the government for the Louvre, for the sum of about 600,000 francs.

The dispersion of Napoleon's collection was a sore mortification to the Parisians. "A melancholy humiliation," says Alison, "now awaited the nation. The justice of the demand could not be contested; it was only wresting the prey from the robber. . . . . . Nothing wounded the people so much as this breaking up of the trophies of the war. It told them, in language not to be mistaken, that conquest had now reached their doors; the iron entered into the soul of the nation. They had come to regard these matchless productions, not as the patrimony of the human race, but their own peculiar and inalienable property, and had thus prepared themselves for the mortification which now ensued, upon the restoration of these precious remains to their rightful owners."

"With whatever enthusiasm," says Lacretelle, "this new species of tribute may have been received in France, it is impossible not to discern in it a triple outrage upon the rights of nations, upon a true taste for the arts, and upon a wise and moderate policy. Was it right to revive, in the processes of war, a violence of which the ancient Romans alone had set the example? The evils of war are transitory, and often a few years of peace are sufficient to obliterate its traces. But the pride of a nation is permanently wounded, when its titles to glory are despoiled by force. A desolate pedestal, a vacant niche, a mutilated fresco, are pointed out by the aggrieved nation with sighs to the traveller, with indignation to the subject of the despoiling monarch. From hence comes that continuance of national dislikes which even during peace may lead to a renewal of hostilities. Besides, it is to renounce all noble rivalry in the arts, thus to establish their supremacy by theft. And the constantly returning idea of the ravages of war diverts the attention and disturbs the enjoyment of the amateur in his contemplations of a gallery of art......

"The possession of masterpieces obtained by violence is uncertain, as we have seen. Transported as they were from one country to another, what danger did they not run from military precipitation and neglect! And again, if this sort of rapine were to be established as a consequence of war and conquest, might it not one day happen that a nation should destroy, rather than submit to the humiliation of restoring, the chefs-d'œuvre it had obtained?"[1]

The visitor at the Louvre to-day will thus find the works of art which Napoleon purchased and the school which he fostered, without followers, without traditions, and without influence; and he will discover few remains of those which he obtained by plunder. Its walls are certainly adorned with many specimens of the Italian, Spanish, and Flemish schools; but these were obtained by other sovereigns and at other periods, and generally by gentler processes and means more commendable than pillage and confiscation.

The French sculptors of the imperial era were by no means equal to their comrades of the palette and brush. Napoleon felt their inferiority, and in 1802 summoned Canova from Italy, that he might model his statue of colossal size. He caused his travelling expenses to be paid, and a carriage to be given to him. The offer made the artist for the statue was 120,000 francs. After having moulded the model in clay, Canova returned to Rome to execute the statue in marble. One of the arms being outstretched, a large block of stone remained to be cut away from beneath it. "From under the arm of Mars," said Canova, "I will get the material for my Venus." The Venus ordered by the Florentines to replace the Venus de' Medici, and now to be seen at the Pitti Palace at Florence, was in fact thus chiselled in the fragment of marble taken from under Napoleon's arm.

This statue of the Emperor is not by any means the best of

[1] Lac. i. 174.

Canova's works. It did not satisfy the Emperor, and was in consequence concealed in a closed room of the Louvre. It passed into the hands of the Duke of Wellington in 1815, who paid 80,000 francs for it. This sum was devoted by Louis XVIII. to the repairs of the Louvre. The year after, David d'Angers, a French sculptor, walking in the streets of London, noticed a crowd of persons standing before a palace door. He looked in and saw, in the entry and at the foot of a staircase, Canova's colossal Napoleon. One of the Duke's lackeys had flung his livery over its shoulders. David wrote to Paris that the statue had become a "hat-tree."

Canova was summoned to Paris a second time, in 1810, for the purpose of executing the statue of Marie Louise. The sculptor has himself detailed the circumstances of his presentation to the Emperor, at Fontainebleau:

"You have grown somewhat thinner, M. Canova," said Napoleon. Canova replied that it was the consequence of incessant application; and then thanked his Majesty for having called him to France for the purpose of employing him professionally. He did not conceal, however, that it was impossible for him to fix his residence permanently out of Rome.

"Paris," returned Napoleon, "is the capital of the world; you must remain here; we shall make much of you." "Sire, you may command me, but if it please your majesty that my life be devoted to your service, permit me to return to Rome, after having completed the object of my visit here." "But you will be in your element, here in Paris; we have all the masterpieces of art, the Farnese Hercules alone excepted; and we shall soon have that too." "May it please your Majesty, pray leave Italy, at least, something. These monuments of antiquity are inseparably connected with many others, which it would be impossible to remove either from Rome or Naples." "Italy can indemnify herself by excavations; I shall order some to be made at Rome. Pray, has the Pope been at much expense for excavations?"

Napoleon subsequently expressed regret that his statue had

not been in modern dress. "Omnipotence itself," said the sculptor, "would have failed, had it attempted to represent your Majesty as I now see you, with small clothes and boots. In statuary, as in all other arts, we have our sublime style : the sculptor's sublimity is nudity, and a kind of drapery peculiar to the art." "Then why is my equestrian statue, upon which you are engaged at Rome, to be draped?" "Because in this case, the figure must be in the heroic costume ; it would not be correct to represent a sovereign on horseback, at the head of his army, in the nude state."[1]

Canova worked for Napoleon with evident distaste. The Emperor was an impatient sitter, and was always nervously anxious to bring the hour of posturing to a close. Canova often complained of the little interest he seemed to take in the details and niceties of the art. He considered him, too, the despoiler and oppressor of his country. He was still engaged upon the bronze equestrian statue, in 1814. He had foreseen the impending disaster, and had taken the precaution to mould the horse separately. Upon the saddle intended for Napoleon now rests, at Naples, the form of Charles III. of Naples, the father of Ferdinand, at that time the reigning sovereign.

The French sculptors of the period may be dismissed in very few words. Houdon, whose Washington has furnished the type for innumerable copies, had nearly finished his career upon Bonaparte's accession to power. He executed the busts, however, of Napoleon and Josephine. He was bald and venerable in 1800, and Gérard introduced his portrait into his " Entrance of Henry IV.," as the face of one of the patriarchs commissioned to present the monarch with the keys of the city. Chaudet, whose statue of Napoleon obtained the prize for sculpture, in 1810, might have reached the highest rank in his profession, had it not been for an incurable disease and an early death. Pajou and Moitte were anterior to Napoleon, being respectively sixty and seventy years

[1] Entretiens de Canova avec Napoléon.

old at his coronation, while David d'Angers and Pradier did not acquire distinction till after his fall.

The musicians and composers of the Empire were men of high attainments; their names are still familiar. The majority of them, however, were Italians: Cherubini, Spontini, Paër, Paisiello. The first French composer was Etienne Méhul, a native of Givet, on the northern coast. He was peculiarly Napoleon's contemporary, for he was born but five years before him, and died two years after his exile.

During the period of Méhul's studies, the musical world was divided into two camps—the admirers of Piccini, and the partisans of Gluck, called respectively Piccinistes and Gluckistes. Méhul strove to combine the merits and avoid the defects of both masters. During the Revolution and the Consulate, he produced Euphrosine, Stratonice, l'Irato, and Joseph en Egypte. These works placed him at once in the highest rank, and caused the formation of a third party of dilettanti—the Méhulistes. The duo of Euphrosine was pronounced quite equal to any piece of concerted music in existence.

Paisiello, the idol of Italy, was, during the Consulate, composer of sacred music to Bonaparte. The position, however, became soon vacant, upon his return to his native country. It was generally believed that Méhul would be appointed to the place, and an article in the Journal de Paris set forth this choice as the only one that Napoleon could consistently make. The Emperor, who would listen to no dictation, immediately sent word to Lesueur that he made him his maître de chapelle. As a compensation for this marked and intentional slight, Méhul received an annual pension of 2,000 francs, and was admitted to the hospitalities of Malmaison. Sometime after, he was summoned to the imperial box at the Opéra Comique, where Napoleon told him that he had lately visited the fortifications of the north of France, and at Givet had been accosted by an old man, who desired to know how his son, Etienne Méhul, was progressing at the capital

Napoleon replied that Méhul was a great musician and an honest man, and that on his return to Paris he would tell him of his interview with his aged father, which he now did in presence of many gentlemen of the court.

Méhul was the first to introduce wind instruments into the orchestra; they had only been used previously in detached choruses. His strict probity, liberality and disinterestedness reduced him on several occasions to the verge of starvation; and a letter written by him is still in existence in which he implores Elleviou, the tenor, to hasten the production of one of his operas, "if he does not wish to see the author of Stratonice and of Ariodant perish of hunger." He died in 1817, of a pulmonary complaint, and was buried at Père la Chaise. One hundred and forty musicians executed a requiem over his grave.

Lesueur, the composer of La Caverne, Télémaque, Les Bardes, and of numerous oratorios, masses and other church music, was the favorite and protégé of Napoleon. He gave him a jeweled snuff-box bearing the inscription, "L'Empereur des Français à l'auteur des Bardes," and he held his first child upon the baptismal font—a special and exceptional favor. Méhul and Lesueur were the types of the musical taste of the Empire: the characteristics of their style were energy rather than grace, concentration rather than vivacity, and a scientific combination of harmonies rather than an agreeable flow of melody. This school of composition was superseded towards the close of the Empire by that introduced by Boieldieu, who succeeded completely in winning over the popular taste to a mode of composition which has since been perpetuated under the auspices of Auber, forming a school eminently and exclusively French—that of the opéra-comique, or ballad opera. Boieldieu produced "Le Calife de Bagdad," in 1799; "Jean de Paris," "Ma Tante Aurore," and "Les Voitures Versées," during the Consulate and Empire. His most esteemed and celebrated work, "La Dame Blanche," was not written till after the fall of Napoleon. His manner was light, facile, elegant, coquettish even, without practised or studied effects. He is not considered, historically, as belonging to Napoleon's time. He was the opponent of a school which, chronologically and from its characteristic features, is regarded as that of the Empire, the school of Méhul and Lesueur—and if we include the foreign composers resident in France, that of Cherubini, Paër, and Spontini.

Many hundreds of operas were composed and produced in France during Napoleon's reign. So complete has been the change in musical taste, that hardly ten of these works have retained possession of the French lyric stage. "La Vestale" of Spontini has been once revived, in obedience to the commands of an imperious prima donna; "Le Maître de Chapelle" of Paër maintains an uncertain place in the current repertory of the Opéra Comique; "Joseph" and "Le Jeune Henri" of Méhul are from time to time restored to the admiration of the lingering veterans of the Empire. Of Lesueur nothing remains but his motets, oratorios, and cantatas. Cherubini survives in memory and tradition only; the once famous and admired Lodoïska is silent and forgotten.

No sovereign has ever bestowed a more liberal patronage upon the fine arts than Napoleon. And yet the fact is notorious that the painters, sculptors, and musicians of the Empire, though they have left great names and famous works, are rarely cited as authority, and are seldom consulted as models. The walls of the Louvre occupied by the masterpieces of imperial art, though always viewed with interest and often with admiration, are as completely useless for all purposes of instruction to youthful artists as are the frescoes of Pompeii; and the portfolios of the Conservatory and of the Academy of Music, laden with the treasures of imperial composers, are rarely if ever opened either to guide the student or to gratify the dilettante. Napoleon was in fact destitute of taste and real appreciation of the arts, and hence his encouragement was merely that of money, without the inspiring influence of enlightened and sympathetic genius.

CHAPTER XXVI.

Astrology during the Empire—M'lle Lenormand—Her first Prophecy—Her Education and Choice of Studies—Predictions made to Mirabeau, M'lle Montansier, Bernadotte, Murat, Robespierre, St. Just—The Horoscope of Josephine—Napoleon—M'lle Lenormand's Cabinet of Consultation—Her Prediction to Madame de Staël—Her Arrest, Interrogatory and Release—Predictions to Horace Vernet, Potier, Alexander and Von Malchus—Her Adventures in Brussels—Her Works—Her Death and Character—Her Faith in her own Powers—The Processes to which she had Recourse—Hermann the Soothsayer—An Intrigue at the Tuileries.

THE arts of astrology and divination occupied a large share of public attention during the Consulate and the Empire. M'lle Marie-Anne Lenormand, the most distinguished sibyl of modern times, the counsellor of Robespierre, Napoleon, and the Czar Alexander, the confidante and biographer of Josephine, and who possessed the ability to subject the most brilliant and enlightened court of Europe to the authority of her shuffles of cards and perusals of palms, merits more than a passing notice. The epoch in which she lived was a period of incredulity upon religious subjects, and consequently one likely to invest a skillful professor of the black art with marked consideration. "Evocations and necromancy," says Chateaubriand, "are nothing more than the instinct of religion, and form one of the most striking proofs of the necessity of worship. A nation produces somnambulists when its prophets depart, and resorts to witchcraft when it abandons the rites of religion; the dens of the sorcerers are opened when the temples of the Lord are closed."

M'lle Lenormand, who was born at Alençon, in 1772, of a respectable family, was, as she herself declares, a "waking somnambulist" at the age of seven years. She was placed in the

Royal Abbey of Benedictines, and speedily became the oracle of the convent. The superior having been dismissed, and the king hesitating for many months in the appointment of a successor, she predicted that a lady by the name of Livardrie would finally be selected by his majesty. This was soon realized, and at the installation the young priestess was made to fill an important post, and was even presented as "one supernaturally inspired," to the notice of Bishop Grimaldi.

She read little else than books treating of the forbidden art, and even at this early age spent much time in the compilation of a sort of history of divination from the earliest period to her own day. She versed herself thoroughly in the annals of Greek and Roman oracles; in those of the Gallic Druids, of the prophets of Baal, of the Hebrew philosophers, and of the miracle-workers of antiquity. She studied the interpretation of dreams and the doctrines of second sight, and at the age of twelve was a complete adept in the practice of judicial astrology, in the drawing of horoscopes, and in the combination of cabalistic figures. She examined the mysteries of the white of eggs and the grounds of coffee, but only to reject them. She inquired what degree of confidence was to be placed in the assertions of Plato, Aristotle and Plutarch, that Socrates foretold the principal events of his own life, and in that of Tacitus, that Tiberius and Marcus Aurelius expounded dreams. She investigated the cures effected in the middle ages by amulets and the relics of saints, and the power of healing the king's evil, said to have been possessed by the kings of France since the time of Clovis.

But her principal study was that of chiromancy, or the art of reading the lines and signs of the human hand. She declared that both Job and Moses had used language which implies belief in the revelations of the hand; and claimed Solomon as an entire believer, upon the strength of the passage, "Length of days is in her right hand, and in her left riches and honor."[1]

She asserted that Ptolemy, Plato, Galen, and in modern times, Lavater, regarded chiromancy as an exact science, and even treated of it in their writings at length. She resolved to adopt divination and hermetic science as a profession. She adopted, as its regular and avowed bases, somnambulism, magnetism, astrology, chiromancy, and physiognomy. The white of eggs, though, according to Suetonius, of Roman origin; coffee grounds, though not, as she said, without scientific and chemical authority; the divining rod, though a time-honored tradition, dating from Circe and Medea; and numerous other practices which she considered degrading and superstitious, were severally rejected. She also rejected cartomancy, or the art of reading cards. It is true that she used cards, but this was merely cabalistically, for the sake of the figures upon them, and to aid her in numerical processes. She made her first important prediction at the age of seventeen, at the moment when Louis XVI. convoked the States-General. She foretold the downfall of that monarchy which numbered eight centuries of existence, the dispersion of the clergy, and the suppression of the convents.

Upon the realization of this prediction, she established herself in Paris, where her reputation had already preceded her.* Her cabinet of consultation was overrun with applicants of all ages and ranks, anxious to obtain a glance at the future which was to succeed this terrible period of anarchy. She foretold her fate to the unfortunate Princess de Lamballe, and received a letter from Mirabeau, written in the dungeon of Vincennes, and imploring her to tell him when his captivity would cease. To General Hoche she predicted a short but glorious military career, and to Lefebvre, a marshal's baton: both these predictions were realized. To M'lle Montansier, who expected to be guillotined the next day, she wrote, "You will live to a good old age." This prediction threw the prisoner into such a state of delirious

---

* The portrait of M'lle Lenormand, upon the opposite page, is taken from an engraving at the Bibliothèque Impériale, in Paris, believed to be the only authentic likeness of her in existence.

joy, that her execution was postponed; the fall of Robespierre saved her, and she lived to number her one hundredth year. To Bernadotte she announced that he would become King of Sweden. He promised to settle upon her ten thousand francs a year, if her prediction were fulfilled. He forgot, or at least never executed, his engagement, when, in the course of events, he became Charles XIV. She was especially consulted by the most advanced partisans of the Revolution, and on one occasion gave audience to Marat, Robespierre, and St. Just. To the first, she announced a speedy death, and magnificent honors at his funeral: to the two last, an ignominious fate at the hands of an indignant people. It is impossible not to admire the fearlessness with which she announced to her ferocious auditors that "they would be devoured by their own work, and become victims of the bloody drama which they were themselves enacting."

M'lle Lenormand espoused the cause of the Royalists, and made several attempts to save Marie Antoinette, to whom she gained admittance in her dungeon. The administrator of the Temple was dismissed for complicity in this act, and M'lle Lenormand was arrested and confined at the Petite Force. She here predicted that Robespierre would speedily perish by the guillotine; and this was realized while she was still in durance.

A more extraordinary prediction than this was made by her during the same captivity. It is true that we have little other guarantee for its authenticity than her own assertion, but the intimacy between her and Josephine, which is historical, can be explained in no other manner than by assuming its accuracy. Josephine, then Madame de Beauharnais, was at this period confined at the prison of the Carmes; she learned from the newcomers who were successively brought to share her captivity, of the singular predictions of the prisoner of the Force. She and several other ladies determined upon sending to the sibyl the data necessary for drawing their horoscopes, and to request her to enlighten them upon the epoch of their restoration to liberty.

Each of them collected the details forming what is called a "thême de naissance"—a document giving the applicant's age; the month and the day of the month of her birth; the time, whether day or night; the initials of her baptismal names; her favorite color, flower and domestic animal. All these papers were secretly conveyed from the Carmes to the Force, and placed in M'lle Lenormand's hands. The latter replied to each, being of course ignorant of the names and positions of the applicants. She announced to Josephine that she would soon suffer the greatest of calamities, but that she would survive her affliction, and marry a man destined to attain the loftiest dignities and to astonish the world. The horoscope concluded by hinting at the possibility of a divorce. Josephine was naturally surprised at this prediction, and the more so as it coincided with that of the famous negress of Martinique, Euphémie David, who had, many years previously, promised her the empire of the Gauls. Soon after her release from prison, Josephine inquired the address of M'lle Lenormand, who was also restored to liberty. She found her in the Rue de Tournon, No. 1153, since No. 5, and instituted further inquiries into the fate that awaited her. It does not appear that she learned anything beyond the general features of the prediction already made.

Soon after, Napoleon Bonaparte, then an officer of artillery, was taken to the cabinet of M'lle Lenormand, by an old general of the name of Lasalle. He submitted his hand to the sibyl, and asked for the interpretation of its lines. She declared that the applicant would gain battles, marry a widow, conquer kingdoms, distribute thrones, and astonish the world; he would finally die in exile. She gives, in one of her works, a full description of Napoleon's hand, its signs, raxetes and restraintes, and declares it to have been a chef-d'œuvre of chiromancy. Napoleon and Josephine were married in 1796, and thus were three points of the horoscope of the latter fulfilled: she had suffered calamity in the death of her husband, she had survived her grief, and had united her fate with a soldier—and one who, in the belief of all who knew him, was capable of rising to the promised elevation. M'lle Lenormand became, therefore, the protégée, and was, in a certain sense, the object of the affectionate consideration, of Josephine. Her cabinet was now crowded with the elite of Parisian society—priests, nobles, magistrates and soldiers. The visitor to the dwelling of the pythoness was shown into a room in which books, prints, paintings, stuffed animals, musical and other instruments, bottles with lizards and snakes in spirits, wax fruits, artificial flowers, and a medley of nameless articles, covered the walls, the table and the floor, leaving the eye scarcely an unoccupied spot to rest upon.

The furniture of the cabinet of consultation was in maple; the walls were adorned with portraits of the Bourbons, with a painting by Greuze of great value, and with her own portrait by Isabey. Her cards, which were of large size and covered with colored hieroglyphics, were painted by Carle Vernet.

Madame de Staël also visited her about this period, though with considerable reluctance. The sibyl made her the following speech: "You are anxious about some event which will probably take place to-morrow, but from which you will derive very little satisfaction." Public rumor completed the story as follows: Madame de Staël met Bonaparte, the next day, at an evening party. Bonaparte said to her, "Have you seen the Thieving Magpie yet, madame—the play which is now so much the rage?" As she hesitated to answer a question so unexpected, he added, "They say we are soon to have the Seditious Magpie, too." Poor Madame de Staël, the story went on to say, withdrew in deep confusion, and remembered the prediction of M'lle Lenormand.

On the 2d of May, 1801, the sorceress was summoned to Maimaison. She supposed, on obeying the invitation, that it came from one of the ladies attached to the person of Madame Bonaparte. She was introduced into the presence of Josephine herself, however, who asked her at once whether she was destined to reside much longer at Malmaison, and what was to be her future life. M'lle Lenormand took her left hand—of which, in her memoirs, she gives a diagram—and, according to her own version of the interview, replied as follows: "You cherish projects, madame, for the advancement of your husband. Take care! If he should ever grasp the sceptre of the world, he would abandon you, for he is ambitious. Nevertheless, you are destined to enact the first part in France, and the day is not far off."

Josephine then asked if her own fate was to be indissolubly connected with that of the First Consul, and if the new government was to experience the inconstancy of fortune. M'lle Lenormand replied: "You will sit upon the throne of the kings; the force of your genius promises you a grand and inconceivable destiny, but the day may come when your lord will forget his solemn promises, for, unhappily, his sincerity will not always equal his greatness."

Some years later, when Josephine had become Empress of the French, she consulted her friend the pythoness upon Napoleon's designs against Rome. "He means to become master of it," was the reply: "but let him beware of any interference in the spiritual government of the Church, for his efforts would be frustrated." Josephine communicated this to Napoleon on his return from the Congress of Erfurth. "Oh, ho!" said he, "you seek to penetrate my designs, do you; and for this purpose you consult oracles! Learn, ladies, that I do not like to be divined, so, to-morrow I will have your demoiselle Lenormand arrested; and never speak to me of her again." Josephine sent one of her attendants, M'lle Aubert, at once to Paris, to warn M'lle Lenormand of her impending arrest, and to advise her to conceal herself till the fit was over. "Tell your mistress," replied the sibyl, "that I thank her for her kindness, but that I have nothing to fear from the Emperor." The next morning Josephine repeated this rather presumptuous rejoinder to Napoleon, who laughed and said, " Well, I believe she is right ; where the deuce does she get all she says? I don't mind her meddling with your affairs ; but tell her to let mine alone, for the slightest interference would cost her her liberty."

On one occasion M'lle Lenormand was summoned by Fouché to his cabinet. He reproached her for the aid and comfort she had given to the Bourbons by her late predictions. She paid no attention to his complaints, being engaged in shuffling a pack of cards, and muttering from time to time, " The knave of clubs !" He then said that he intended to send her to prison, where she would probably remain a long time. " How do you know that?" she returned. "See, here is the knave of clubs again, and he will set me free." " Oh, ho ! the knave of clubs will set you free, will he ? And who is the knave of clubs ?" " The Duke de Rovigo, your successor in office."

About this period, Talleyrand consulted her personally and by letter. One of these epistles, still in existence, commences thus : " Illustrious sibyl, will you never predict me aught but misfortunes ?"

During the period preceding the divorce of Josephine, M'lle Lenormand made numerous political predictions, which again drew upon her the anger of Napoleon, and again called for the intervention of the Empress. At last, however, she placed herself beyond the reach of Josephine's protection, by announcing to her on the 28th of November, 1809, during the interpretation of a dream of serpents, that on the 16th of December following, "an infamous deed would be accomplished." For this she was arrested, and the furniture of her cabinet seized. The police astonished and amused the city by putting the seals upon four volumes of Lavater and nine tables of logarithms. She was conveyed to the Prefecture, where, in a solitary cell, she occupied her leisure by the evocation of spirits. In the interrogatory which followed, she was skillful enough to invert the order of characters, and to lead the judge to a discussion upon hermetic science, in the course of which he acknowledged "his intimate conviction of the existence of supernatural and invisible beings." Her interrogatory was brought to a close by a prediction regarded by the French as the most remarkable of modern times. Being urged to explain a vague observation she had made, she replied, "That is a problem which will be resolved on the 31st of March, 1814"—the date of the occupation of Paris by the allies. There is an apparent flaw in the proof of the authenticity of this prediction. It was not made public till after the abdication of Napoleon, and therefore seems made to suit the occurrence; but as M'lle Lenormand states the prediction to have been uttered to M. Dubois, prefect of police, and to the examining judge, neither of whom denied it, and as no refutation of the assertion was ever drawn from the archives of the Prefecture, where the report of her interrogatory was deposited, it is fair to regard the prediction as a genuine one. She was set at liberty after twelve days of solitary confinement, and seven days after the accomplishment of Josephine's divorce. She wrote a letter of adieu to M. Dubois, concluding with these lines:

> "De vous aimer de loin, je m'impose la loi,
> Mais, de grâce, Monsieur, ne pensez plus à moi."

This interference of the police produced a very natural result. She became the object of increased interest and curiosity, and her den was a more fashionable resort than ever. A learned abbé, in a work entitled "Error and Prejudice," bore witness to the intelligence of the class that now thronged her ante-chamber.

She predicted to Horace Vernet, a child at the time, that in about thirty years from that period he would stand in such high consideration as an artist, that the king then upon the throne would send him to Africa to paint the storming of a fortress there by the French army. Louis Philippe fulfilled this prophecy in 1839.

In 1810, the famous comic actor Potier met M'lle Lenormand,

though with no intention of employing her services. The conversation turned on lotteries. She told Potier that two and even three prizes were assigned by destiny to every man; and that if she could collect about her the individuals to whom fortune was favorably disposed, all the lotteries in Europe would not be able to pay the immense winnings she could enable them to claim. Potier asked what were his fortunate numbers. M'lle Lenormand examined his left hand, and said: "Mark the numbers 9, 11, 37, and 85; stake on these in sixteen years from now, at Lyons, and you will win a quatern." In 1826, Potier chose these four numbers, with a fifth, 27, the number of his birth-day. He won 250,000 francs, and so well did he invest it, that he died worth a million and a half.

The influence of M'lle Lenormand augmented so rapidly, that an edict for her exile was signed, though afterwards revoked. In 1811, the plan was formed of attaching her to the secret police, in the capacity of a detective; and on the 1st of May she was summoned to the Prefecture, when the proposition was made to her. She rejected the overtures of M. Pasquier with dignity and firmness, on the ground of their immorality.

On the invasion and occupation of France by the allies, the sibyl's abode was crowded by foreigners of all nations and conditions; among them was the Czar of Russia, Alexander. President Von Malchus, a Westphalian statesman of ability and credit, who had been Minister of Finance, of War, and of the Interior, under Jerome Bonaparte, was induced, in March, 1814, to visit her. He wrote and published an account of the interview. "Of my past history," he says, "she told me, to my infinite astonishment, much that I had myself forgotten, and which was certainly known to no one in Paris. She placed before me the various sections of my past life in so definite and distinct a manner, that I began to feel a kind of horror creeping over me, as if I had been in the presence of a spirit." She told the President that in eight days he would receive a letter from his wife; he would hear four times from Germany in the coming week; predictions that the event justified. She said that before the 23d of November of the same year an unacceptable decision would be made concerning him. On the 21st of that month the Hanoverian minister made known to him that his claim to the estate of Marienrode was rejected. Upon the conclusion of the interview, Malchus requested her to commit to writing what she had orally communicated to him, for which additional labor he would pay an additional sum. She required three weeks in which to perform the work; in a month she handed him the papers, written out in full. There was no perceptible variation from the previous spoken predictions. This Malchus considered good and sufficient proof that she drew her deductions from positive and fixed data. As it was impossible she could remember, in the multiplicity of her avocations, any one individual statement for the space of a month, it seemed clear that she had reconstructed the horoscope, and that, proceeding from the same premises, she had naturally arrived at the same result.

M'lle Lenormand now became an authoress, and published numerous works treating of divination, the most interesting of which is "Les Souvenirs Prophétiques d'une Sibylle." She was arrested in Brussels in 1821, and tried by the tribunal of Louvain, for having boasted of enjoying the society of the genius Ariel, of possessing a magic eye-glass and a precious talisman, and for having exercised her art in the dominions of his Hollando-Belgic majesty. She was condemned to a year's imprisonment. This sentence was quashed by the high court of Brussels, and the pythoness was carried in triumph through the streets by a delighted and infatuated mob.

In 1820, she published two volumes of memoirs of the Empress Josephine. This work was dedicated to the Czar Alexander, and the authoress received from that sovereign a diamond ring, in acknowledgment. It contains a large quantity of interesting, though unauthenticated, anecdotes of Napoleon and Josephine.

It gives an engraved fac simile of the letter by which the Empress in November, 1809, summoned M'lle Lenormand to her presence, and in reply to which the latter predicted the impending divorce During the reign of Charles X., she declared that the Duke of Orleans would come to the throne, and saw the prediction realized, in 1830, by the accession of Louis Philippe. She now retired from business, and soon after returned to Alençon, where she built a small house which she called the Cottage of Socrates. She refused to exercise her vocation there, saying that she drew horoscopes only at Paris. She owned a large mansion at Paris, and a chateau at Poissy. She had collected a gallery of good pictures, and possessed autographs and confidential letters from the principal personages in Europe. Her property was estimated at half a million of francs.

M'lle Lenormand died in 1843, at the age of seventy-one years, though several of her works contain the enunciation of her belief that she should attain the age of one hundred and twenty-four years. She was buried at Père la Chaise. She had never been married, and was never known to desire marriage or to think of it. She never had an attachment, and her life furnished no ground for scandal.

M'lle Lenormand can hardly be considered a vulgar charlatan. She is saved from this accusation by the extent of her erudition, which, in her branch of study, has probably never been surpassed; by her courage and sincerity; by her preservation of an illustrious friendship; by the character of the society which frequented her cabinet; and by her merits as a writer and her constancy as a partisan. Her history and achievements are as remarkable in the nineteenth century as those of Nostradamus in the time of Charles IX., or those of the Cumæan sibyl during the supremacy of Rome.

It would appear that M'lle Lenormand had faith in her own powers, for she was known to consult her sources of information, whatever they were, in reference to the affairs of herself and her family. On one occasion, she felt anxious concerning the fate of her brother, who was absent with the French army. After passing the night in various cabalistic processes, she gave way to a paroxysm of tears, and ordered a suit of mourning garments. Letters soon announced the young man's death. She possessed unbounded confidence in her means of discovering character. On the approach of the allies, she desired to place her money and valuables in the hands of some trustworthy person. None such being at hand, she chose the first that offered; previously subjecting him, however, to a test. "For what animal have you the most repugnance?" she asked. "For rats." "What animal do you prefer?" "The dog." She gave him her treasures without hesitation; aversion to rats indicating a sound conscience, and partiality to dogs proving fidelity and sincerity.

The processes to which M'lle Lenormand had recourse are not distinctly known. A late work, entitled "Modern Mysteries," thus speaks of her: "All who visited her, from whatever part of the kingdom or of the world they came, were astonished and not unfrequently confounded by the minute and specific revelations of their past history which they would receive through the pythoness. In her case, there would be equally strange revelations in regard to the future, and other facts unknown to her visitors; she, no doubt, while in a magnetic state, being a very powerful clairvoyant. The visitor has in his mind visions and plans in regard to the future. Social and especially domestic connections may be formed, desired or intended, with specific individuals or with imaginary personages figured forth in his mind, in conformity with the heart's beau ideal. In the presence of the fortune-teller, and in anticipation of such revelations, these plans and persons, real or imaginary, are of course suggested to the inquirer. Through his or her mind they are reproduced in that of the pythoness, and by her given forth as revelations communicated by higher powers to her mind. It is thus, no doubt, that the image of the person with whom conjugal relations are afterwards consummated, is sometimes presented as a prophetic enunciation to the inquirer, and by him ever after regarded as proof of real prophetic foresight in the fortune-teller."

However this may be, as one of the biographers of M'lle Lenormand has remarked, witch or no witch, a certain share of admiration will always be due to her, for having contrived to be believed in an age which neither believed in God and his angels, nor in the devil and his imps.

Madame Junot, speaking of Josephine and of her connection with M'lle Lenormand, says: "The fancy, or rather the mad passion of Josephine for fortune tellers and everything relating to necromancy, is well known. Though she at one time promised Napoleon never to see M'lle Lenormand again, she continued secretly to admit her to her intimacy, and overwhelmed her with presents; she also summoned to the Tuileries every man and woman that professed to be skilled in the forbidden mysteries."[1] One incident of serious moment in the life of Josephine—for it convinced Napoleon's mother of the necessity of a divorce—sprang from her inclination for the black art and its adepts. This incident was as follows:

Early in November, 1809, the Emperor, learning that a woman who was a dealer in second-hand jewelry and wearing apparel, had been seen in the palace, gave orders that no person exercising such a calling should thenceforward be admitted. He also forbade Josephine to receive, as she desired to do, a German sorcerer named Hermann—a man of imposing manners and of remarkable personal attractions—on the ground that his character was doubtful and his purpose in Paris suspicious. On the night of the 5th of the month, Napoleon returned unexpectedly from an intended hunt at Fontainebleau, and proceeding noiselessly to Josephine's apartment, opened the door and entered. He found her closeted with two persons: the forbidden dealer in jewelry and the prohibited necromancer.

He strode forward to the Empress, and raising his hand over

her as if to strike her, said in tones of concentrated wrath: "How dare you thus violate my commands? How can you be willing to give audience to such people as these?"

"It was Madame Lætitia that sent her to me," stammered Josephine.

"And this man, how came he here?" pursued Napoleon.

"He came with the woman," returned Josephine.

Hermann here stepped forward, and drawing himself up to his full height, said in a firm voice to his Majesty: "In coming to the imperial palace of France, I did not suppose I was risking either my life or my liberty. I obeyed the call made upon me; I have endeavored to unfold the future to her who has faith in my science, and I have not to reproach myself with having withheld my assistance. As to you, sire, you would do better to consult the stars than to brave them."

Napoleon looked at this singular and fearless being with curiosity not unmixed with admiration. "Who are you," he asked, "and what are you doing at Paris?"

"You know already what I do, sire"—showing the cards upon the table. "What I am, would be more difficult to tell; I hardly know myself; who does know himself?"

Napoleon stepped to the door and summoned Duroc. "Put this woman at once out of the palace," he said, "and let M. Hermann go with her." This was done, and the handsome fortune-teller disappeared speedily from the palace and as speedily from Paris.

The next morning, early, Madame Mère was awakened by a message from Josephine. The Empress implored her, in case she was questioned by Napoleon, to say that she had sent her the day before a woman with shawls and a German with cards; and Madame Lætitia, believing the matter to be no more serious than Josephine's usual indiscretions, and desirous of preventing a quarrel, consented to assume this responsibility. She did so, upon being interrogated by the Emperor; but upon learning from him that Hermann was believed to be an adroit spy in the pay of England, and that he had obtained access to Josephine by playing upon her superstitions; upon hearing further that Napoleon had positively forbidden the admission of dealers in secondhand wares to the palace, and that Josephine's disobedience was willful, she acknowledged that she knew nothing of the affair, and that her alleged complicity was a stratagem contrived by Josephine. Madame Mère said to Madame Junot, after narrating this incident, "I hope that this time the Emperor will have the courage to resolve upon a step that not only France, but Europe, awaits with anxiety: the divorce is an act of necessity."

In detailing the incidents of M'lle Lenormand's life, we have sufficiently described the state of the art of fortune-telling in France and the consideration with which it was regarded, during the period of her professorship. Her success does not seem to have been derived from any previous credit accorded to the art of necromancy, but was the result rather of her remarkable skill and the tendency of an atheistic age to fill the void it had itself created, with superstitious dreams. She established a faith in astrology and chiromancy, for a time; they fell, however, into disrepute at her death, being afterwards exercised only by acknowledged charlatans, and obtaining support only from the ignorant and the credulous.

CHAPTER XXVII.

Napoleon's Early Loves—M'lle du Colombier—M'lle Eugénie Clary—Madame de Permon—Josephine—Her Education and First Marriage—Separation from her Husband—Josephine and Barras—Josephine's Marriage with Napoleon—The Honeymoon at Milan—M. Charles—Bonaparte's return from Egypt—His quarrel and reconciliation with Josephine—The conduct of the latter during the Consulate—Her Jealousies—Her proposal to resort to a Political Fraud—The Divorce—Josephine at Malmaison and Navarre—Her Death—Misapprehensions in regard to her Character—Reasons for this Misapprehension—French views of Private Character—Marie Louise—Her Youth and Education—The Overtures of Napoleon—A Marriage by proxy—Journey to Paris—Proceedings upon the Bavarian Frontier—The first interview of Napoleon and Marie Louise—The Marriage—Organization of the Household—Adventures of M. Biennais, M. Paër, and M. Leroy—Birth of the King of Rome—The Russian Campaign—The Treaty of Fontainebleau—Marie Louise at Blois—Her life at Parma—The Count de Neipperg—Death of Marie Louise—Napoleon's Ignorance of her Conduct.

NAPOLEON BONAPARTE did not marry his first love, nor his second, nor even his third. Before speaking of his two Empresses, Josephine de Beauharnais and Marie Louise, it may be well to mention briefly the three ladies to whom in early life he had been attached—by one of whom he was accepted, and by two of whom he was refused—M'lle du Colombier, M'lle Eugénie-Désirée Clary, and the widow de Permon.

The account of his love-passage with M'lle du Colombier we give in words attributed to Napoleon himself, who speaks in the first person. The period in which he thus narrates the adventure is the year 1799; he has just been appointed First Consul, and is alone at the Luxembourg with Cambacérès, the Second Consul, and Maret, Secretary of State; Josephine, Hortense, Pauline and Caroline Bonaparte are at the opera, to witness the new ballet of Psyche. Napoleon appears absorbed in reflections excited by a letter which he has read and re-read, and which he still holds open in his hand. The conversation turns upon early loves, and at the request of Cambacérès, Napoleon gives the following account of his first passion—one which, at the age of sixteen, he fully believed would be his last. This account, though in language put into the mouth of Napoleon for the author's own purposes, contains none but incidents which have been well authenticated, and which have passed into the domain of veritable history—with the exception of those of the pet dog and the pocket mirror. We retain these episodes of the narrative, though clearly apocryphal, for the purpose of showing, by a single example, to what an extent the practice was carried, after Napoleon's fall, of gratifying the public curiosity concerning him by the publication of amusing details of his private life, though without any pretence to historical accuracy. The First Consul speaks substantially as follows:

"I had just left the military school, proud as a peacock, and ignorant as a priest. I was transferred to the Grenoble regiment of artillery, and my detachment was quartered at Valence. I had the good fortune to be admitted to the acquaintance of Madame du Colombier—one of those ladies who are the honor of their sex, and whose qualities, virtues and merit replace their beauty at its decline. I felt myself attracted towards this respectable matron, and she felt a similar sympathy for me, for on my third visit she said, 'I am depressed in spirits to-night; enliven me by narrating your history.' 'That of a lieutenant of artillery is short,' I replied. 'No matter,' she returned, 'it is always well to know those towards whom our inclinations impel us.' So I rehearsed our genealogical tree, and traced my pedigree back to Pepin the Short. Madame du Colombier was amused, and presented me, with marked emphasis, to the Abbé de St. Ruffe, and interested in my welfare the commander of my detachment.

"Soon after, I felt myself yielding to the influence of a most tyrannical sentiment; in short, I was in love with her daughter, or, at least, I thought so. This young lady, sixteen like myself, more winning than beautiful, mild, good, modest and sincere, appeared to me like a nymph, the first time I saw her. One of the manias of young men is to suppose themselves stricken for life, the moment their poor hearts are taken captive. So, after holding counsel with myself, I imagined that I had found in M'lle du Colombier the partner of my whole existence.

"My passion was a violent one; I lost my appetite; I passed sleepless nights; I abandoned my studies, or prosecuted them with distaste. Do not suppose that I had confessed my love to the object of it; I did not feel that I possessed the necessary courage. But though I spoke not by word of mouth, I pursued my lovely charmer with significant glances; my steps waylaid hers; I followed her close, I drank from her tumbler, I ate from her plate. She had a dog named Médor, a fat, surly, tailless and earless animal, who was the object of her tenderest regard. No courtier ever showered such incense on a king as I did on this hideous beast. I patted, petted, carried and kissed him; I felt that every act of degradation committed before this wretched creature, was so much ground gained in the heart of his mistress.

'It is rare for a girl of sixteen not to divine a passion that she has inspired. M'lle du Colombier was not long in making the discovery. I saw it by her altered manners, by her embarrassment when I spoke to her, by her following my movements with her eyes, by a singular mixture of coquetry, innocence, pride and satisfaction, by her morning welcomes, which were now gracious and now cold; and by a way she had of seeming to avoid me, but as it were on condition that I should pursue her. Later in life, I should have perfectly understood this system of proceeding; but it rendered me then cruelly unhappy, and I accused her of indifference and taxed her with trifling, and often left the parlor to retire alone to the garden and weep.

"One morning I read, intending to profit by it, Ovid's Art of Love. One item of advice struck me: that which consists, according to the Latin poet, in giving a refractory lady to understand that others than herself may kindle the tender passion. So

I bought a small case covered with morocco, containing a pocket-looking-glass set in silver-gilt. Its oval form naturally suggested the presence of a portrait, and several times that day I drew it stealthily forth, and contemplated it in silent extasy, taking good care to place myself in full view of my ungrateful mistress.

"Her first glance enlightened her. She cautiously approached me; I brought matters to a climax by imprinting a passionate kiss upon the reflection of my own lips. She abruptly fled from the parlor. I hurried into the garden, sat down upon a rustic staircase and waited. A shadow fell upon me, and the silhouette of a young lady darkened the gravel walk. I feigned surprise, hurriedly thrust the morocco case into my pocket, and prepared to withdraw. But she retained me in a voice at once imperious and sweet, and said, not without emotion:

"'Come, Monsieur Napoléon, give me that portrait; it must be the lady that you love, and I want very much to know her.'

"'Very well, you shall be satisfied; but if you are offended, do not accuse me, for I only yield to your express commands Within this case you will find the portrait of the girl I love.'

"I then stepped aside, proud of my ruse, and believing myself the author of an invention which many lovers had employed before me, and usually with a success which justified the means. The poor child worked at the spring of the case, with an impatience truly feminine; at last, the clasp fell apart under the pressure of her tiny fingers. She fixed her eye upon the glass, from whence her own image was reflected, and a suppressed cry of joy, terror, wounded pride, offended modesty and gratified hope, escaped from her lips. She stood motionless, and seemed to be seeking for the means of administering a reproof, for appearance sake, which, in her heart, she did not believe either necessary or opportune.

"At this juncture, the idea occurred to me that if timidity became the tender sex, resolution and audacity became mine. I threw myself at the feet of my enchantress, begged her to pardon me and to believe in the sincerity of an affection which I was ready to sanctify by the holy bonds of wedlock. This last word has an all-powerful charm for young women. I saw that I was loved, by her blushes, her pallor, her laughter and her tears. I seized her hand and covered it with kisses, supposing that I was thus obtaining the supremest favors she could grant. We both of us dreamed of a rose-colored future. No culpable thoughts soiled our imaginations. My whole happiness consisted in the frequency of my visits, in the divine smile with which I was received, in a hurried phrase half uttered and half heard, and in a chance pressure of her hand. One morning, at six o'clock, we both stole to the orchard which adjoined her mother's house. We were absolutely alone ; you will hardly believe me, but the two sweetest hours of my life were passed in playing at battledore, and in eating a huge basketful of cherries." *

Here the First Consul suspended his narrative, and remained for a while pensive. At last Maret asked, " But what became of M'lle du Colombier, General? What was the sequel of this chaste adventure ?"

" It never had any, citizen : or at least none other than the usual sequel to the dreams and romances of lieutenants of artillery. The Revolution broke out, and I was sent to another garrison. We swore eternal fidelity, but the impossibility of corresponding hopelessly separated us. Carried on by the course of events, I married Madame de Beauharnais in 1796. And I now hold in my hand," showing the open letter, "a petition from M'lle du Colombier, in which I learn that she is the wife of M. de Bressieux. Citizen Maret, you will read the petition, and you will grant the request which it contains."[1]

It does not appear, however, that the favor asked was accorded at this period. Napoleon saw Madame de Bressieux at Lyons, in 1805, when he expressed astonishment at the ravages

---

* The portrait of M'lle du Colombier, upon the opposite page, is taken from a picture by an unknown artist, placed by its possessor at the disposal of the designer.

[1] Napoléon et ses Contemporains, i. 51.

of time and the desolation wrought by twenty years. He gave her husband a lucrative office, and made his first love a lady companion in the household of his mother.

Madame Junot thus speaks of her at the age of thirty-five; "I had heard from Napoleon himself that there had existed in early youth a project of marrying him to M'lle du Colombier; and I had in consequence a strong desire to see her. I found her witty, agreeable, mild and amiable. Without being handsome, she was very pleasing, her form was graceful, and her address remarkably engaging. I easily understood that Napoleon might have gathered cherries with her without any improper thought, and confining himself entirely to harmless chat. One peculiarity which struck me the first time I saw her, was the interest with which she watched Napoleon's slightest movement, her eye following him with an attention which seemed to emanate from her very soul." Madame de Bressieux was the successor of Madame de St. Pern in the establishment of Madame Mère; she did not yet form part of it at the period to which our enumeration of the ladies composing it, in a previous chapter, refers.

In 1795, Joseph Bonaparte married M'lle Julie Clary, daughter of a rich Marseilles merchant, and Napoleon being thus thrown into the society of her younger sister, Eugénie-Désirée, became much attached to her, and would gladly have married her, had her family been willing. But the father was of opinion that to give two daughters to two Bonapartes would be an imprudence if not a sacrifice, and opposed the match. M'lle Eugénie, we are thus authorized to believe, might have become Empress of the French in 1804; but by marrying Bernadotte, she became Queen of Sweden in 1818.

Napoleon at Paris wrote as follows to Joseph at Genoa, in 1795: "You never speak to me of Eugénie; no more do you of the children you are to have with Julie. Give us a little nephew, won't you? Good heavens, man, you must make a beginning!

"Give my compliments to Julie, and my regards to her silent sister."[1]

Writing to Joseph some thirty days later, he said: "Think of my little matter, for I have the folly to want a home; my relations with Eugénie must either be arranged or broken off. I await your reply with impatience."[2]

Again, he wrote as follows: "Désirée has asked me for my portrait, and I mean to have it taken. You will give it to her if she still desires it, if not, you may keep it for yourself. . . . . I have heard nothing from you since your departure for Genoa: to get there, I should suppose you had crossed the river Lethe, for Désirée writes me not a word."[3]

Joseph, in his memoirs, thus refers to the marriage of Napoleon and Josephine: "This event dissipated the hope entertained by my wife and myself, that our project, formed several years previously, of an alliance between her sister and my brother, might yet be realized. Time and absence disposed of them otherwise."[4] This was Napoleon's second love.

On the 8th of October, 1795, Madame de Permon, a lady of Corsican birth and of Greek descent, became a widow. She was exactly the age of Napoleon's mother, and that lady and herself—Lætitia Ramolini, and Panoria Comnenus—had been in their youth the beauties of Ajaccio. Their attractions, however, were of so opposite a nature, that jealousy never occurred to them, and their friendship endured through life. M'lle Panoria married M. de Permon, and M'lle Lætitia married Carlo Bonaparte. Madame de Permon, herself the mother of a family, often carried her playmate's second son, Napoleon, in her arms, and even danced him on her knees. When, therefore, she became a widow, at the age of forty-four, Napoleon being but a few months over twenty-six, she was certainly justified in expressing astonishment at, and in treating with levity, a proposition which the young officer one day made to her.

1 2 3 Mém. du Roi Joseph, i. 131-139.   4 Ibid. i. 60.

She was in deep mourning, and lived in absolute retirement. Her physician having advised her, however, to allow herself some recreation, she consented to an incognito attendance at the opera, for a short season. Napoleon, who was a constant visitor at her house, profited by the opportunities thus presented, and passed every evening in the society of the widow. A few days afterwards he proposed to her an alliance, which should forever unite the two families. "It is," added he, "between my sister Pauline and your son Albert. Albert has some fortune ; my sister has nothing ; but I am in a condition to obtain much for those who are related to me, and I can get a good office for her husband. The alliance would make me happy. You know what a pretty girl my sister is. My mother is your friend. Come, say yes, and the matter shall be settled."

Madame de Permon replied that she could not answer for her son, and that she should not influence his decision. Napoleon then proposed another match between his brother Jerome and Madame de Permon's daughter, M'lle Laura. "Why, Jerome is younger than Laurette," said the widow, laughing. "Indeed, Napoleon, you are playing the high priest to-day, and marrying everybody, even children." Napoleon then confessed that that morning a marriage-breeze had blown over him, and that he had a third union to propose—an alliance between her and himself, as soon as etiquette and a regard to propriety would permit it.

Madame de Permon was at first amazed, and then amused. She burst into a hearty laugh, at which the petitioner was sorely vexed. "My dear Napoleon, let us talk seriously. You fancy you are acquainted with my age. The truth is, you know nothing about it. I shall not tell it to you, for it is one of my little weaknesses. I shall merely say that I am old enough to be your mother and Joseph's too. Spare me this kind of joke ; it distresses me, coming from you." Napoleon assured her that he was serious ; that the age of the woman whom he should marry was indifferent to him, provided, like herself, she did not appear to be past thirty; that he had maturely considered the proposal he had made; that he wished to marry, and that the idea he had suggested suited him in every respect. At any rate, he asked her to think of it. She gave him her hand, and said that her pretensions did not aspire to conquer the heart of a young man of twenty-six, and that she hoped their friendship would not be interrupted by this incident.

Madame de Permon spoke to her son that evening upon the subject of a marriage with Napoleon's sister. The young man declined promptly and decisively. The proposed alliance between Jerome and Laurette was never taken into serious consideration. That between the widow and Napoleon was defeated—if, indeed, it was ever entertained by the lady—by a quarrel which ended in mutual hostility. She had previously applied to him for a commission for a Corsican cousin, and Napoleon, having promised it twice for the following day, twice forgot it. The widow was incensed, and as Napoleon once offered to kiss her hand, she drew it from him with violence and struck him, unintentionally but severely, in the eye. This was in presence of several of his aids-de-camp, and seriously mortified him. He never forgave her. He considered himself to have been treated like a child, or a school-boy fresh from Brienne. The rupture was complete, and in the sequel produced ill-will and acrimony on both sides.

Napoleon's motive in proposing this alliance was an ambitious one. At this period, he looked upon marriage as a means of advancement, and the union of the name of Comnenus with that of Caloméros—the ancestor of the Bonapartes—seemed to offer every guarantee of speedy promotion. Soon after, Madame de Permon lost her eldest daughter, Cécile; Napoleon called to pay her a visit of condolence, and to assure her of his unaltered friendship. He was already married to Josephine de Beauharnais.[1]

"Never," says Alison, speaking of the period in which these events took place, "never did such destinies depend upon the

---

[1] d'Abr. i. passim.

decision or caprice of the moment. Madame de Permon, a lady of rank and singular attractions from Corsica, in whose family Napoleon had from infancy been intimate, and whose daughter afterwards became Duchess d'Abrantès, refused in one morning the hand of Napoleon for herself, that of his brother Joseph for her daughter, and that of his sister Pauline for her son. She little thought that she was declining for herself the throne of Charlemagne ; for her daughter that of Charles V. ; and for her son, the most beautiful princess in Europe."[1] The historian has, however, committed an error in substituting Joseph for Jerome. Joseph was already married to M'lle Clary.

A word or two will now be necessary to prepare the American reader for an estimate of the character of Josephine—the next in chronological order of Bonaparte's attachments—which will probably be a surprise and a disappointment. By the graces of her mind and disposition, by the simple grandeur with which she bore her elevation and the dignity with which she sustained affliction, Josephine has, as it were, tampered with her biographers. She has suborned history by her amenity, and corrupted the judgment of the world by the temper with which she supported misfortune. No historical personage has been so misrepresented as Josephine—no character has been so distorted as hers. Extenuation, concealment, apology, have been exhausted in behalf of the winning Creole and the repudiated Empress. The chroniclers who have written for English and American eyes have sought to forget or to ignore the vices and the debaucheries of her early life. They have succeeded in producing a universal and persistent misapprehension respecting her. They have presented as a model of womanly virtue, one who, during thirty years of her life, offered a dangerous and pernicious example. We shall inquire into the causes of this remarkable perversion, when we have briefly and impartially rehearsed the principal incidents of her career.

[1] Europe, iii. 179.

Marie-Joseph-Rose Tascher de la Pagerie, known in history by the feminine diminutive of Josephine, was born in Martinique, on the 24th of June, 1763. Her parents were French, and had settled in the colonies in the hope of bettering their fortunes. They gave their daughter the best education the island could afford, and as Martinique was at this period the asylum of many French families of wealth and refinement, who had fled from disturbance in the mother country, this was nearly as perfect as she could have obtained in France. The cultivation thus furnished was bestowed upon a propitious and grateful soil, and Josephine, at the age of fifteen, was already a young lady of remarkable beauty and of many accomplishments. It would appear that she was thus early attached to a Creole youth of her own age, upon whom she lavished all the ardor of her precocious tropical passions.[1] Though thus devoted to another, she married, at the age of sixteen, through considerations altogether foreign to her inclinations, the Vicomte Alexandre de Beauharnais, a resident in, but not a native of, Martinique, and like herself, attached in another quarter. They at once embarked for France. The union was an unhappy one, being disturbed by mutual suspicions of infidelity. Beauharnais soon became aware of the presence in France, of Josephine's island lover, whom he had supposed abandoned in Martinique; and Josephine was made acquainted with the birth of a natural son of her husband. Upon her presentation at the palace of Marie Antoinette, the grace of her manners and the charm of her conversation drew around her a throng of admirers of rank and official position. She soon became a participator in the scandals and the excesses of a corrupt court. Her conduct was such as amply to justify her husband in the steps which he took to procure a divorce. He sailed for Martinique to obtain details respecting her behavior previous to her marriage, and upon his return, applied to the Parliament of Paris for a separation. Josephine controlled powerful protection, and the verdict

---

[1] Michaud, Biog. Univ., Supplément, lxviii. 225.

was altogether in her favor. It was enjoined upon Beauharnais to receive his wife to his bed and board, if she desired to return, otherwise, to secure her an annuity of 10,000 francs. No reconciliation took place till three years from this time, when, as has been already stated, Hortense convinced her father, by her resemblance to himself in a boy's costume, of the injustice of his suspicions of his wife—for he had never before considered Hortense as his daughter.

The Revolution now speedily ensued. Beauharnais lost his life upon the scaffold, and Josephine was herself a prisoner. When released by the sudden fall of Robespierre, she found herself wellnigh friendless and alone. Her late associates were royalists, and consequently had been dispersed by the Reign of Terror. Madame Tallien, whose acquaintance she had made in the dungeon of the Carmes, was almost her only resource: her friendship procured her amusement, occupation, and finally protection. She presented her to Barras, the most influential of the Five Directors. His relations with Madame Tallien were at this time of the most intimate nature, but so sincere was the attachment of the latter for Josephine, that she consented to her admission, upon an equal footing with herself, into the advantages and pleasures of the partnership. Josephine became the acknowledged favorite of the great voluptuary.[1] It was during this connection that she acquired those habits of extravagance which afterwards so embittered and embroiled her relations with Bonaparte, and which conduced so largely to his estrangement. The purse of Barras was for a time open to all her necessities and exactions; the sums which she thus lightly obtained and recklessly spent, were sufficiently large to induce in her that contempt for money and that indifference to pecuniary responsibility, which is an invariable characteristic of women who draw their means from corrupt and illegitimate sources. It was the careless license of the salon of Barras which gave to Josephine that readiness for making

[1] Alison's Europe, iii. 11.

acquaintances, that tendency to the formation of hasty and improper intimacies, which afterwards so harassed Napoleon.[1]

Josephine had been twice encouraged to look forward to a brilliant and regal destiny; the throne of France had been twice promised her by persons whom she believed or affected to believe. Her life at this period was nevertheless not that of one preparing to sustain the position of the first lady in Europe. The epoch was venal and dissolute, and Josephine was in no respect above the manners and morals of the age. She who was to occupy the throne with a grace and dignity which should charm the world, and to fall from it with a resignation which should move all hearts; she who was to fill history with the records of her amiable supremacy and of her beneficent reign, led at this disgraceful period, the life of a fashionable, though exclusive, courtesan.[2] Barras was her protector: General Hoche was her lover.

Bonaparte could hardly have been ignorant of the gallant adventures of Josephine, at the time of his first acquaintance with her. It was during her liaison with Barras that the latter proposed an alliance between herself and Bonaparte—an important condition of which was to be the appointment of the young general to the command of the Italian army. Such a knowledge would have arrested a more scrupulous admirer, but it seems, on the contrary, to have decided the aspiring officer. Barras was exceedingly anxious that the marriage should take place, for Josephine had become a heavy encumbrance upon his resources, and Bonaparte felt that in espousing her, he should relieve his influential patron of a wearisome burden, and save him the fatigues and the annoyances of an exhausted passion.[3] Nevertheless, ambition was not his only motive, for he was at the time deeply impressed by Josephine's many attractions, and he gave her, during the early years of their union, proofs of a real and disinterested attachment.

On her part, Josephine was not by any means prepossessed

[1] Capefigue, ii. 233. [2] Michaud, lxviii. 229. [3] Capefigue, ix. 286.

in favor of Bonaparte, nor was she at all desirous of contracting a second marriage. Her first union had been unhappy, and she had found, besides, greater satisfaction in the independence of a widow than in the responsibilities of a wife. A letter written by her at this period gives a picture of the irresolution by which she was beset:

"I am advised to marry, my dear friend; all my acquaintances desire it, my aunt insists upon it, and my children urge me to accede. If you were but here to give me your counsel at this important juncture, and to persuade me that I should be right in putting an end, by this union, to the embarrassment of my present position! You have seen General Bonaparte at my house: it is he who offers to supply the place of their father to the orphans of Alexandre de Beauharnais.

"'Do you love him?' you will ask me. Well—no. 'You feel aversion towards him, then?' No. But I am in a state of indifference which annoys me—a condition which the devout consider a most dangerous one in religion—for love is a species of worship. This is why I have need of your advice, to stay the perpetual irresolutions of my feeble character. To have a will of my own always seemed an effort to my Creole listlessness, which is infinitely more ready to follow the will of another..... Barras assures me that if I marry the general, he will obtain for him the Italian command.....

"Were it not for this project which harasses me, I should be happy enough As long as it is a project, I shall be uneasy: once concluded, come what may, I shall be resigned.

"We have agreed to suppress the usual conclusions of letters: so, adieu, dear friend."[1]

Napoleon Bonaparte and Marie-Joseph de Beauharnais were civilly married at Paris on the 9th of March, 1796; the religious ceremony took place, five years afterwards, in the chapel of the Tuileries, but Napoleon forbade that any announcement of the fact should be made in the Moniteur. Twelve days after the civil marriage, Bonaparte departed for the Italian campaign.

His letters, during the early portion of the war, breathed the most ardent love, mingled with reproaches for Josephine's coldness and distrust of her constancy. In one of them he accused her of loving her favorite cat, Papin, better than him. He begged her to follow him to Lombardy, and after a long delay, and many hesitations, she complied. It was under the escort of Junot that she travelled to Milan, where her husband awaited her. Junot paid assiduous court, on the road, to Josephine's chambermaid, M'lle Louise, for which indecorous act, by the way, the future Empress never forgave him.

Napoleon's honeymoon was passed at the Serbelloni palace, in the capital of Lombardy, where Josephine was established in sovereign state. It was marred by an unpardonable piece of levity, if not worse, on the part of the bride. A young man of twenty-eight years, by the name of Charles, of slight form and dark complexion, with black hair, and wearing a superb hussar's uniform, obtained an introduction to her in his capacity of aid-de-camp to General Leclerc, the husband of Pauline Bonaparte. Napoleon was frequently absent, and when Josephine did not breakfast with her husband, she breakfasted with M. Charles. She thus furnished the army and the town of Milan with a theme of scandal and a ground for accusation. She was closely watched by Pauline, who felt that her brother's honor was in jeopardy. Bonaparte was at last informed of what was passing in the palace. Charles was arrested, and a rumor spread through the camp that he was to be shot. His punishment was, however, dismissal from the army. He returned to Paris and entered mercantile life. We shall find him, three years subsequently, during Bonaparte's absence in Egypt, passing the summer with Josephine at her country-seat of Malmaison.

Pauline said of this intrigue, some time afterwards: "In short, Laurette, Josephine nearly died of vexation, and we certainly do not die of vexation in merely parting with our friends. There must be more than friendship concerned in this matter. For one, I comforted my poor brother, who was very unhappy."[1] Bonaparte was severely tried by this and other improprieties on Josephine's part, and once, in a fit of jealousy, he killed, with a single blow of his foot, a lap-dog that had been given her by General Hoche. Regretting his violence, he afterwards caused a small monument to be erected to the pet in the gardens of Mondeze, in the vicinity of Milan.[2] Josephine returned to Paris before Napoleon; her conduct gave him constant cause for apprehension, so much so that he descended to the indignity of placing his coachman, Antoine, as a spy upon her movements. When he left for Egypt, in 1798, it was with a despondent feeling of the danger he was incurring.

Josephine had not yet resolved to break loose from the connections she had formed and the habits she had contracted. She was constantly in the society of Madame Tallien, despite Bonaparte's prohibition. He had left her 40,000 francs for the first year of his absence, but was twice obliged, during that period, to forward her an equal amount. He had authorized her to purchase a country-seat; she chose Malmaison, agreeing to pay a sum more than treble that to which she had been limited. This unacquitted debt hung over her for years.[3] She borrowed money of numerous persons—of Ouvrard, the army contractor, especially—few of whom were ever paid. It was now that she invited M. Charles to visit her at her chateau. She paid no attention to the representations of friends that his residence under her roof compromised her in the eyes of the world. "Divorce from Bonaparte and marry Charles," said Gohier, a member of the government and one of her advisers. "You tell me that it is only friendship that exists between you and M. Charles; but if that friendship is so powerful that it impels you to violate the observances of society, I say to you, as if it were love, obtain a divorce;

[1] d'Abr. i. 409.   [2] Michaud, lxviii. 234.   [3] Ibid. 236.

a friendship so exclusive will stand in place of all other sentiments."[1]

When Bonaparte, still in Egypt, was informed of the renewal of the intrigue with Charles, he said to his future secretary: "Bourrienne, I must exterminate this race of sparks and coxcombs."[2] The brothers and sisters of Bonaparte, who had from the commencement disliked Josephine, never pardoned her for her present conduct, which compromised the honor of their brother—their common patrimony. How could a woman, they said, be so wanting in self-respect as to forget, in her Creole sensuality, the hero of Marengo and Egypt?[3] In their letters to Bonaparte, they strongly urged the propriety, the necessity even, of a divorce. When Bonaparte's sudden and unexpected return and arrival at Fréjus was announced, Josephine's manner plainly showed to what deep uneasiness she was a prey. She resolved upon instantly setting out to meet him, and after borrowing one thousand francs of Barras,[4] she started for Lyons with her brother-in-law, Louis. She missed him, however, through a change of route on his part, and on his arrival at Paris, where he was at once waited upon by mother, brothers and sisters, he found his home silent and deserted; he never forgot the impression made upon him by his desolate and abandoned fireside. He declared the journey to Lyons to be a mere pretext to avoid him, and believed that Josephine had fled from consciousness of guilt.

"All is finished," he said to M. Collot, the financier, "between her and me!" "Now is not, at any rate," returned Collot, "the proper time for such a step. Think of France; her eyes are fixed upon you. She expects your every instant to be devoted to her salvation; if she sees that you allow yourself to be tormented by domestic grievances, your greatness disappears, and you become, in her esteem, but as a husband in Molière. Forget for a time the misconduct of your wife. If you are dissatisfied

[1] d'Abr. i. 411.
[2] Michaud, lxviii. 237.
[3] Capefigue, ii. 233.
[4] Michaud, lxviii. 238.

with her, remove her when you have nothing better to do, but
begin by restoring the state." "No," interrupted Bonaparte,
vehemently, "my mind is made up; she shall never again set
foot in my house! What care I for what the world says? Paris
will gossip for a day or two over it, and forget it the third. In
the midst of this daily throng of events, what is a rupture between man and wife? Mine will pass unnoticed. She shall go
to Malmaison, I will stay where I am. The public knows already
enough of the affair not to be deceived upon the cause of the
separation."[1]

Bourrienne seconded Collot in his attempts to effect a reconciliation. He represented to Bonaparte how injudicious and dangerous it would be, at this turning point of his fortunes, to occupy France and Europe with the scandalous details of a suit at
law—a public accusation of adultery. When Josephine returned
from Lyons, Bonaparte for three days refused to see her. Every
member of his family, with the exception of Louis, encouraged
him to persevere. One evening Josephine and her two children
approached in tears and in distress the forlorn house in the Rue
Chantereine. Eugène was now nineteen years old and Hortense
sixteen. Leaving their mother below, they ascended to the room
occupied by Bonaparte. The interview was a long and painful
one. The two petitioners, who were really ignorant of the nature
of the accusation under which their mother labored, and to whom
—on account of their youth—Bonaparte could not communicate
it, besought him not to abandon his wife, nor to deprive two orphans of the support Providence had sent them in place of their
natural protector. To such an intercession Bonaparte could
make no reply; his just resentment melted away before these
unhappy children, pleading for a mother of whose offence they
were unconscious. Seeing that he was moved, they descended
to where Josephine was lying prostrate, sobbing and heartbroken,
at the foot of a stone stair-case. They took her up, conveyed

[1] Bour. iv. 116.

her to Bonaparte's study and placed her in his arms. This was a decisive and resistless argument. The offended husband relented, and folded his repentant wife to his bosom. The reconciliation was complete. Josephine took the lesson to heart and thoroughly reformed her conduct. She became an altered woman from that day forward. It is pleasing to have arrived at the conclusion of this chronicle of error and dissipation.

It was during the period which now followed—the first three years of the Consulate—that Josephine displayed those qualities of mind and heart which have endeared her to the world, and which have caused so many to forget, or to reject as calumnious accusations, the transgressions of her youth. She devoted herself with sincere purpose to rendering Napoleon's home happy and his palace imposing. She read to him in those fascinating tones which led him afterwards to say—"The first applause of the French people sounded to my ear sweet as the voice of Josephine." With her diligent needle, she worked tapestry for his feet and scenic embroidery for the panels of his cabinet. She employed her retentive memory in his service, and he familiarly called her his "agenda," or memorandum. She resumed her neglected harp; she cultivated and acclimated exotic flowers. She bent her efforts to surrounding the Consular throne with an atmosphere of elegance, dignity and refinement. She had indeed lost the power of fixing his wayward and capricious heart, as his constant infidelities and his intrigues within the very gates of the Tulleries amply prove. But his estrangements were of short duration, and he always returned gladly to Josephine, sometimes to confess and sue for pardon, always to feel that his affection for her would outlive his fugitive attachments. She even interested herself in political affairs; she hastened the return of many emigrant nobles; she mitigated the harshness of the tribunals, and obtained the reversal of decrees of confiscation. She begged for the life of the Duke d'Enghien. She advised Napoleon to be content with the Consulate, and to abandon all thought of an Empire and a crown.

Though her conduct was in these respects irreproachable, she still committed numerous and serious errors. We have shown elsewhere how she sacrificed the happiness of her only daughter in the furtherance of her domestic schemes. We have shown how Bonaparte was compelled to employ the services of Talleyrand and Bourrienne in settling her tradesmen's bills. We have shown how she continued to receive Madame Tallien, in spite of Bonaparte's prohibition. We have shown what intimate relations she maintained with M'lle Lenormand, notwithstanding his opposition. She was often disobedient and refractory. She preferred prevarication, in case of discovery, to a frank confession. "A marked feature in her character," said Napoleon at St. Helena, "was her constant system of denial. No matter at what moment, no matter what the question, her first impulse was a negative—and this was not exactly a falsehood, but rather a preparation of precaution and defense."[1]

As time advanced, the temper of Josephine was soured and her life embittered by her childless condition. Her jealousy and her exactions augmented, and long before the coronation, Bonaparte escaped from what he called "the subjection of a citizen husband," by occupying apartments distinct from those of his wife. The poor Empress, whenever for a night Napoleon resumed his allegiance, allowed her satisfaction to be seen by all the officers and domestics of the palace. "I rose late this morning," she would say, rubbing her hands with delight, "but then, you see, Bonaparte was with me!"[2]

The death, in 1807, of the eldest son of Hortense—Napoleon's heir adoptive—thoroughly alarmed Josephine ; her anxieties now became impending and threatening realities. "A son by Josephine was essential," said Napoleon ; "it would have rendered me happy, not only as a political advantage, but as a domestic comfort. It would have tranquillized Josephine and put an end to her jealousy, which left me no repose ; for her jealousy was much more

[1] Las Cases, ii. 806.   [2] Michaud, lxviii. 255.

political than sentimental. Josephine foresaw the future, and was alarmed at her sterility. She felt that a union is only complete when blessed by children; and at the time of her marriage with me she was incapable of again becoming a mother. As her fortunes rose, her fears augmented; she employed every resource of medicine, and often pretended to have derived benefit from it. When compelled to abandon all hope, she hinted at the feasibility of resorting to a political fraud—a substitution—and finally, openly proposed it." [1]

So spoke Napoleon at St. Helena. Bourrienne, in his memoirs, throws doubt upon the statement. His ground of doubt, however, is nothing more than the belief that his close intimacy with Josephine would have led her to communicate this project to him, as she had done many others. Whatever the truth may have been, a report was prevalent in Paris, in 1809, that Josephine was to assume as her own offspring, the child—if a boy—to which Madame Walewski, who had followed Napoleon to France from Warsaw, and for whom a sumptuous residence had been purchased in the Chaussée d'Antin, was soon to give birth. A son was born of this lady to the Emperor, but he was not adopted by Josephine. He was created a count, by Napoleon, on the day of his birth; he received the name of Alexandre, though he has since been known under that of Colonna Walewski, as Louis Napoleon's Ambassador to the Court of St. James, and upon the retirement of M. Drouyn de Lhuys, in 1855, his Minister of Foreign Affairs.

Madame Junot, in rehearsing the preliminaries of the divorce, uses the following language in reference to this subject: "The Emperor had loved Josephine, but he loved her no longer. But what heart that has loved fails to retain a profound sentiment of friendship for the object of its passion! Napoleon was deeply influenced by the sentiment which had firmly attached him to his wife, and who can tell what would have been the result of an explanation in which Josephine had proposed to adopt one of his

[1] Las Cases, ii. 804.

natural children—both boys—Count Walewski or Count Léon,[1] and his own flesh and blood?"

In October of the year 1809, Napoleon returned suddenly from Wagram, and the court was established at Fontainebleau. By the Emperor's orders, the private access from Josephine's rooms to his own was closed. They seldom met, and when they did, they avoided each other's eyes. Their demeanor was constrained, though they both endeavored to be composed and natural. It was known to the whole palace that the divorce had been decided upon, and the manners of the officials bore witness to this knowledge. "Ah!" said Josephine, "what looks are those which courtiers suffer to fall upon a repudiated wife!" "Josephine!" said Napoleon, when the time for speaking the words now so memorable had arrived, "my excellent Josephine! Thou knowest if I have loved thee! To thee, to thee alone, do I owe the only moments of happiness which I have enjoyed in the world. Josephine, my destiny overmasters my will. My dearest affections must be silent before the interests of France." "Say no more," returned Josephine, "I was prepared for this, but the blow is none the less mortal." She became unconscious, and, on recovering her senses, found that she had been conveyed to her chamber. The act of separation was read on the 16th of December, in the grand salon of the Tuileries, in the presence of the Emperor, Josephine, her two children, all the members of the imperial family present at Paris, and the grand dignitaries of the empire. Josephine, who was simply dressed in white, was pale, but resigned. The tears coursed down her cheeks, as with tremulous voice she pronounced the oath of acceptance, and signed

[1] Of the birth of the former of these children we have spoken. Count Léon was the son of a young lady by the name of Eléonore, employed in the household of Madame Murat, as reader. He was born in 1804 or '5. The name of Léon was given to him, from the fact that it occurred both in the name of his father and in that of his mother. He was made a count upon his birth, and a pension of 30,000 francs a year was settled upon M'lle Eléonore. He has lived an unsettled life, and owing to a previous quarrel with the present Emperor, derived no benefit from the restoration of the Bonapartes in 1848. His resemblance to his father is very striking. As nearly as it is possible to ascertain, he is now interested in an ink manufactory at St. Denis, near Paris. Count Léon, born in 1805; Count Walewski, born in 1809; and the King of Rome, born in 1811, were Napoleon's only children. He never had a daughter, and never expressed a desire to have one.

with unsteady hand the deed of divorce. She performed her part in this scene without precedent—one which in all probability will never have its parallel in the annals of the world—with a grace and a dignity which, as we have said, has disarmed history and seduced the judgment of posterity.

Josephine survived this catastrophe but five years. Napoleon gave her the means of continuing, at her chateaux of Malmaison and Navarre, the regal state to which she had been accustomed. Though a large part of her resources were squandered in heedless extravagance—for in her small palace no less than twenty-two dinner-tables were set every day, and twenty-one cords of wood burned[1]—she devoted considerable sums to the improvement of her lands, to the amelioration of the soil, to the education of orphans and to the relief of distress. She was the benefactress of the poor and the sympathetic friend of the afflicted, as well now in her fallen, as before in her prosperous, estate. Six weeks after the entrance of the allies into Paris and the departure of Napoleon for Elba, she was taken seriously ill. The Czar Alexander was unremitting in his attentions to her, and to him, on the 28th of June, her last words were addressed: "I shall die regretted; I have always desired the happiness of France; I did all in my power to contribute to it. I can say with truth that the first wife of Napoleon never caused a tear to flow." She lingered, though lost to consciousness, till the next morning, when her breath passed gently and painlessly away.

Such, without extenuation, and certainly without malice, were the life and character of the Empress of the French, as we have sought briefly and impartially to sketch them. It is worth while to inquire the causes which have conspired to render the popular idea of her—at least in America—so erroneous and incomplete. One reason, doubtless, is this: English books, English newspapers and periodicals—which, up to the period of the divorce, had represented the Empress in her true colors, though they had

[1] Ducrest, 59

certainly done so in a hostile spirit—sought to gratify their hatred of Napoleon, upon the accomplishment of this event, by extravagant eulogies of the worth and merits of the lady he had repudiated. By exalting her character, they rendered the act of separation more odious and revolting. By representing him as a man repelling a woman possessed of all the domestic virtues, they enlisted against him every wife, every fireside in the kingdom. From that time to this, the embellishment and fanciful retouching of the character of Josephine, have been a part of the machinery employed in the denunciation and degradation of Napoleon. The American mind has, in this way, through the British press, been abused and misled.

And this misapprehension has been perpetuated among us from another and a very different cause. Josephine is in the United States a popular idol. The Americans are hero-worshipers, and in a much stronger sense are they the worshipers of the beautiful, the oppressed and the virtuous of the gentler sex. Being without heroines in our own history, we have unreservedly bestowed our sympathies upon the amiable and unfortunate Empress of the French. It is not too much to say that she holds altogether the first place, among the women of modern history, in the imagination of the American people. Now it is always an easier task to follow than to stem the current, and it is a more gracious duty to praise a woman than to condemn her. So the pens employed upon this subject have fallen in with the prevailing tenor of the English sources of information which they consult, though such a system compels the writer either to the propagation of manifest untruth or to the exhibition of revolting ignorance. The biographies of Josephine to which the American public have access, are characterized by studied omissions or bold fabrications. It requires nerve to attack a settled prejudice or a cherished opinion, and it is ungallant to seek to divest, even in behalf of the truth, an amiable and an unfortunate woman of the romantic halo which has been thrown around her history.

Therefore it is that the public has been served with sentimental fictions in the place of harsh and disenchanting realities. One would, nevertheless, suppose the American reader to be able to hear the truth, and to be above and beyond the subjection of listening to a prepared literature and a distorted biography. He has certainly a right to insist that a subject belonging to the domain of Gibbon be not handled in the manner of Æsop. He is of age and a citizen of the world; he ought to be secure from the imposition of ingenious fables, disguised in the masquerade and the caricature of history.

In France, the name of Josephine is remembered with respect, and pronounced with benedictions. This is in spite of the immoralities of her early life, of which none of her countrymen are ignorant. The French have a way of thinking in these matters peculiar to themselves; a woman's public character—her character as a sovereign, as a historical personage—is but little concerned or interested in the opinion held upon her private and domestic character. Talent, wit, beauty, sense, benevolence—the elements which win a people and create a name—are all independent of private virtue—a matter in France beyond the scope of the biographer's vision. But in America it is otherwise, and a woman's virtue is her first and highest renown. Josephine must be judged, in this country, by the standard that society has established among us. Up to the Revolution which made her husband Consul, her life was a series of gross departures from rectitude; her conduct was, in these respects, irreproachable, from the moment she discovered that in him were vested the power and the glory of France. She cannot have forgotten, when divorced from considerations of state policy in 1809, that she had stood within the same peril, in 1799, from misconduct of her own.

We have chronicled Napoleon's divorce: we have arrived, therefore, at the period of his second marriage. Marie Louise, Archduchess of Austria, the eldest daughter of the Emperor Francis I., and grand-niece of Marie Antoinette, was born in the year

1791, at the imperial palace of Vienna. She was educated with great care, and was one of the most accomplished princesses in Europe at the time when Napoleon, released from Josephine, was seeking to ally himself with a lady of royal birth. In 1809, when he was besieging the Austrian capital, he was told that Marie Louise—whom he was then far from supposing would ever be his wife—was ill with the small-pox, and was unable to leave the city. His majesty forthwith ordered the palace to be spared. In 1810, Marie Louise, now nineteen years old, possessed a majestic form, an imposing walk, and an elegant deportment; her hair was blond; her complexion fresh and florid; her eyes were blue and deep; her hands and feet were small and beautifully formed. Her smile was expressive, her conversation gracious and amiable, when she was in the society of those she loved, or with whom she was intimate; but when surrounded with strange faces, and irked by the restraints of etiquette, she became reserved and distant. Her temper was mild, her mind cultivated; her tastes were simple and her talents useful as well as agreeable. She spoke French with facility, though with a decided German accent.

Napoleon's divorce rendered him a suitor at the palace doors of Europe, late in 1809. His first application was addressed to the sister of Alexander of Russia. The Czar would gladly have consented, but the Empress Dowager objected, and by the delays which she interposed, succeeded in exhausting Napoleon's patience. His Majesty next caused advances to be made to the Austrian ambassador at Paris on the subject of an alliance with the Archduchess Marie Louise. The negotiations were zealously pushed, and the contract of marriage was signed at Paris on the 7th of February, 1810, and at Vienna on the 16th. Marie Louise, who had never seen Napoleon except through the aid of a miniature, spoke of herself as a "victim sacrificed to the Minotaur:" but she soon yielded a dutiful obedience to the desires of her family. The marriage took place at Vienna on the 11th of March, her uncle, the Archduke Charles, standing proxy for Napoleon.

She set out the next day with her own household for Paris. The cavalcade consisted of eighty-three carriages and baggage-wagons, drawn by four hundred and fifty-five horses. At Braünau, on the Bavarian frontier, she exchanged her Austrian dress for one in the fashion of the French Empire ; all the members of her houschold bade her adieu, with the exception of Madame de Lajanski, her governess. Her French household, appointed by Napoleon, entered upon its duties at this point: Madame Lannes, now Duchess de Montebello, being the lady of honor, and the Countess de Luçay the tire-woman. The jealousies of these ladies and their suite soon necessitated the dismissal of Madame de Lajanski, who took leave of her mistress at Munich.

The young Empress travelled by short stages; at each village where she rested for a night, a rural fête was ordered to amuse her. At Munich, she received her first letter from Napoleon, and every morning afterwards, during her fifteen days' journey, a page, arriving from Paris, brought her a fresh epistle. She entered the French territory at Strasburg, where she received, with the Emperor's letter, the choicest green-house flowers and several brace of pheasants of Napoleon's shooting. The cortége advanced through Nancy, Bar-le-Duc, Châlons, Rheims, towards Soissons, where the first interview was to take place. But Napoleon was impatient, and mounting a horse, he set forward to meet the Archduchess. Rain was falling heavily, and before he joined the cavalcade he was wet to the skin. He descended from the saddle, opened the carriage door, and with one bound placed himself at the side of Marie Louise. Caroline Murat reassured her by introducing the intruder as "her brother, the Emperor." The postillions were ordered to post on at once to Compiègne, where they arrived late in the evening. There Napoleon imposed on Marie Louise a tête-à-tête which lasted through the night—a proceeding which the young bride resented at the time, and which, indeed, she never forgot.[1]

[1] Capefigue, x. 52.

On the first of April the civil marriage took place at the Tuileries, and the next day the benediction of the Romish church was pronounced over the imperial pair by Cardinal Fesch. The train of the bride was borne by Queen Hortense, Queen Julie of Madrid, and Queen Catherine of Westphalia. Napoleon now escorted his Empress upon a visit to some of the great public works of the Empire, and points of interest in the northern departments. He showed her the naval docks of Cherbourg, and in her presence the first waters of the English channel were admitted within the gates. He conducted her to Brussels, where, amid the festivities of welcome, his sister Pauline put upon her the extraordinary insult we have elsewhere recorded. On their return to Paris, Napoleon devoted himself to the organization of her household, the principal members of which had already been chosen, and, as far as possible, from the faubourg St. Germain: for the old nobility, who had refused to serve the Creole Empress, would gladly accept place at the hands of an archduchess, who was the daughter as well as the wife of an Emperor. The etiquette to which she was subjected was far more rigid than that which had been imposed upon Josephine. A body guard of four, and afterwards of six ladies, bearing at various periods the titles of "ladies to announce," "first maids of honor," and "readers," followed all her movements and haunted her footsteps. They were more constant than her shadow, for that attendant deserted her when the sun set or when his light was veiled. They were never absent during the day, and one of them slept at night in a room adjoining hers, and with which her chamber communicated by an open door. The Emperor could not visit the Empress except through this anteroom. With the exception of the secretary and treasurer of Marie Louise, no man could set foot across the threshold of her suite of apartments, without an order from the Emperor. One of her ladies invariably attended her when she took her lessons in music or drawing. They wrote all her letters, either from her dictation or in accordance with a general outline furnished by her.

It was the Emperor's intention that no man whatever should be able to say that he had been, for a single instant, in tête-à-tête with her Majesty. On one occasion, one of the ladies of honor was severely reprimanded by Napoleon for remaining at the extremity of the room, while the court jeweller, M. Biennais, was showing to the Empress the secret springs of a writing-desk, and on another occasion, the same lady nearly lost her situation, for a similar reason, during M. Paër's lesson upon the piano. The gossips of the time went so far as to say that M. Leroy, the man-mantuamaker, was excluded from the palace for having dared to say to the Empress, in the confidence and intimacy of a measurement, that she had magnificent shoulders. It is quite impossible that M. Leroy was ever admitted to such privy and delicate relations with the imperial person. Measures were taken, garments were tried, and changes ordered, by the ladies of the household. M. Leroy had a lay-figure at his establishment, which presented an exact fac-simile of her Majesty's proportions, and the attire which fitted this manikin, usually adjusted itself with equal precision to the living contour of the Empress of the French.

On the 20th of March, 1811, Marie Louise gave birth, after a laborious and perilous travail, to a son, to whom was given the name of Napoléon-François-Joseph, and upon whom was conferred the title of King of Rome. A salvo of one hundred and one guns announced to the people of Paris that the child was of the male sex. Napoleon's subjects seemed to testify, by their expressions of satisfaction, their sympathy with the sovereign at this realization of his ardent and long cherished hopes. In less than a week, over two thousand odes and epistles in rhyme had been addressed to the happy father by the poets and poetasters of France. One of the sub-intendants of the Tuileries, M. de Quevauvilliers, was instructed to distribute the sum of 100,000 francs among the obsequious authors of this loyal verse.

On the 14th of April, 1813, Napoleon left Paris for the Russian campaign, making Marie Louise Regent of the Empire during his absence, and his brother Joseph, President of the Council of Regency. He received numerous letters from the Empress, in which she strongly urged the necessity of making peace, and spoke of the murmurs and clamor of the provinces against the continual drains of men and money. On the 23d of January, 1814, she was again made Regent, as Napoleon departed to oppose the entrance of the allies into France. The Russians soon appeared in the forest of Vincennes, and Marie Louise, having received additional instructions to that effect from Napoleon, abandoned Paris on the 29th of March, with the King of Rome and the court, for Rambouillet. On the 1st of April she received orders from Napoleon to establish herself at Blois. The allies had already entered Paris. Of this event Marie Louise was kept in ignorance till the 7th; a portion of her advisers were then of the opinion that by returning at once to Paris, before the arrival of a prince of the house of Bourbon, she might yet secure the regency for herself and the crown for her son. But Marie Louise preferred to espouse the interests of her father, the Emperor of Austria, and the treaty of Fontainebleau, signed by Napoleon on the 11th, renounced for himself, for her and their son, the thrones of France and Italy. Marie Louise was to continue to bear the title of Empress, and upon her were conferred the duchies of Parma, Piacenza, and Guastalla. She returned to Austria through Switzerland and the Tyrol, which she visited with all the satisfaction of a midsummer tourist.

When Madame Walewski, mother of the Count Alexandre, learned that Marie Louise had not followed Napoleon to Elba, she hastened there with her son, intending to remain in the quality of a friend whose society might be agreeable to the prisoner. Napoleon, however, would not consent, being unwilling that the place which should have been filled by his wife, should be occupied in history by another. Madame Walewski stayed but three days, and then returned to Naples. The resemblance of her son to the Emperor caused, for a time, the circulation of a report that

Napoleon had been visited in Elba by the King of Rome and Marie Louise.

On Napoleon's return from Elba, the next year, Marie Louise openly expressed her hope that the allies would be successful in the impending struggle. She allowed Madame de Montesquiou, the governess of the prince her son, to be dismissed, and a German woman to be appointed in her place. She willingly signed a paper renouncing all claim to the title of majesty, and to the throne of France. She was henceforth to be known as Archduchess of Austria and Duchess of Parma; her son was to be called Hereditary Prince of Parma. The mother and son were soon definitively separated; the former to retire to her Italian capital, the latter to remain at Vienna, and to be educated as a German prince, under the title of the Duke de Reichstadt.

Marie Louise administered the government of her duchy with success and in a mild and liberal spirit. New codes were compiled, and a wise system of civil and criminal justice was introduced. Many benevolent institutions were founded; among them were a hospital for incurable patients, a poor-house, an asylum for the insane, and a school for midwives. The private life of the duchess was such as to obtain for her the scorn of her subjects and the reprobation of history; no sovereign in Europe led a more infamous existence than the late Empress of the French. For years she maintained an adulterous connection with the Count de Neipperg, her chamberlain and prime minister. She gave birth to three children while Napoleon was yet alive, and, translating the Wirtemberg name of Neipperg into Italian, gave them that of Montenuovo. Neipperg was secretly married to Marie Louise, on his death-bed, in 1829. His eldest daughter, by Marie Louise, married the Viscount de San Vitale; his oldest son became an officer in an Austrian regiment; the third child, a daughter, died early.

The Duke de Reichstadt died of consumption, at Vienna, on the 22d of July, 1832. As he left no will, his mother inherited his large property—nearly a million of florins a year. After a reign of thirty years, Marie Louise died at Parma, in 1847, leaving an infamous memory and a fatal example. Her heart was placed in a chapel of the Church of the Madonna della Steccata; her body was conveyed to Vienna.

Napoleon lived at St. Helena in happy ignorance of the criminal debaucheries of his wife and empress. He often spoke of her, and it was evident that he pictured her as placidly subsisting on the memories of the past, and as supporting with dignity and resignation her fall from her high estate. On one occasion he said, "Be persuaded that if the Empress makes no effort to alleviate my sufferings, it is because she is surrounded by spies who prevent her knowing how I am treated—for Marie Louise is the soul of virtue!" Napoleon certainly suffered enough upon his rocky fastness, to be spared the humiliating and afflicting knowledge that his wife was the paramour of a mutilated and disfigured officer of her household. His lot was less deplorable than it has been represented; for if he was harassed by captivity and unworthy treatment, he was happy in the unconsciousness of his wife's disgrace, and of the existence of the nameless children to which she had given birth.

The French have effaced the name of Marie Louise from their annals, as far as it is possible for a people to forget history and to renounce the past. Josephine was the first Empress of the French; Eugénie is the second.

CHAPTER XXVIII.

Napoleon's Manners towards Women—Grace Ingersoll, the Belle of New Haven—Her Marriage and Transfer to the Court of the Tuileries—Her Presentation to Napoleon—His Amiable Speech—Death of Grace Ingersoll—Her Two Daughters—Madame de Chevreuse—Her Epigrams and Smart Speeches—Her Persecution by Napoleon—Her Exile and Death—The Journey to Cythera—Napoleon appointed Doorkeeper—Madame Charpentier—A Scene in the Gallery of Diana—Madame Fourès—Her Connection with Napoleon—Her Divorce and Second Marriage—Napoleon's Estimate of Women—His Opinions upon Love—"How many Children have you?"—Perpetual Vows—Madame Regnault de St. Jean d'Angely—Napoleon's Speech to her—Her Reply—Napoleon expresses Regret at St. Helena.

WE have been compelled somewhat to anticipate the promised details upon the estimate placed by Napoleon upon women, and the harsh treatment to which he often subjected them. Chronological propriety and other considerations have forced us to narrate at intervals the exile of Mesdames Récamier and de Staël, the repulse from the palace of Madame Tallien, and the repudiation of Josephine. These, however, were ladies whose persecution was due to public and political motives. It is our purpose now to speak of the private relations of Napoleon with the ladies of his court; to describe his manners towards them, and his conversation with them; to state his opinion upon the social mission and the domestic duties of women, and to illustrate these various points by authentic and historical examples. This will call upon us to introduce into the dazzling circle of the Tuileries during the most brilliant period of the Empire, one of our own fair countrywomen, suddenly transplanted there from her home in Connecticut. The episode of her translation to Napoleon's imperial court we quote from one who knew her, copying from the proof-sheets

of a forthcoming work.[1] The author thus narrates the prominent incidents of her life:

"Jonathan Ingersoll, of New Haven, had a large family— sons and daughters: the names of the former are honorably recorded in the official annals of their native State—nay, of the United States. The daughters were distinguished for personal attractions and refined accomplishments. One of them claims a special notice—Grace Ingersoll:[*] how beautiful the name, how suggestive of what she was in mind, in person, in character! I saw her once—but once, and I was then a child—yet her image is as distinct as if I had seen her yesterday.

"In my boyhood, these New Haven Ingersolls came to Ridgefield occasionally, especially in summer, to visit their relations there. They all seemed to me like superior beings, especially Mrs. Ingersoll, who was fair and forty about those days. On a certain occasion, Grace, who was a school companion of my elder sister, came to our house. I imagine she did not see or notice me. Certainly she did not discover in the shy boy in the corner her future biographer. She was tall and slender, yet fully rounded, with rich, dark hair, and large Spanish eyes—now seeming blue, and now black, and changing with the objects on which she looked, or the play of emotions within her breast. In complexion she was a brunette, yet with a melting glow in her cheek, as if she had stolen from the sun the generous hues which are reserved for the finest of fruit and flowers. Her beauty was in fact so striking—at once so superb and so conciliating—that I was both awed and fascinated by her. Wherever she went I followed, though keeping at a distance, and never losing sight of her. She spent the afternoon at our house, and then departed, and I saw her no more.

"It was not long after this that a Frenchman by the name of Grellet, who had come to the United States on some important

---

[1] Recollections of a Lifetime, by S. G. Goodrich.

[*] The portrait of Grace Ingersoll, upon the opposite page, is from an original sketch by Sully, now in the possession of Hon. Ralph I. Ingersoll, of New Haven.

commercial affairs, chanced to be at New Haven, and saw Grace Ingersoll, whom he had already met at New York. Such beauty as that of the New Haven belle is rare in any country; it is never indigenous in France. Even if such could be born there, the imperious force of conventional manners would have stamped itself upon her, and made her a fashionable lady, at the expense of that Eve-like beauty and simplicity which characterized her. It is not astonishing, then, that the stranger—accustomed as he was to all the beauty of French fashionable life—should still have been smitten with this new and startling type of female loveliness.

"From the first view of Miss Ingersoll, M. Grellet was a doomed man. Familiar with the brilliant court of the Parisian capital, he might have passed by unharmed, even by one as fair as our heroine, had it not been for that simplicity, that Puritanism of look and manner, which belonged to the social climate in which she was brought up—so strongly in contrast to the prescribed pattern graces of a French lady. He came, he saw, he was conquered. Being made captive, he had no other way than to capitulate. He was a man of good family, a fine scholar and a finished gentleman. He made due and honorable proposals, and was accepted—though on the part of the parents with many misgivings. Marriage ensued, and the happy pair departed for France.

"This took place in 1806. M. Grellet held a high social position, and on his arrival at Paris, it was a matter of propriety that his bride should be presented at court. Napoleon was then in the full flush of his imperial glory. It must have been with some palpitations of heart that the New Haven girl—scarcely turned of eighteen years, and new to the great world—prepared to be introduced to the glittering circle of the Tuileries, and under the eye of the Emperor himself. As she was presented to him in the midst of a dazzling throng blazing with orders and diamonds, she was a little agitated, and her foot was entangled for a moment in her long train—then an indispensable part of the court costume. Napoleon, who, with all his greatness, never rose to the dignity of a gentleman, said in her hearing, "Voilà de la gaucherie américaine!" American awkwardness! Perhaps a certain tinge of political bitterness mingled in the speech, for Jerome had been seduced into marriage by the beauty of an American lady, greatly to the chagrin of his aspiring and unprincipled brother. At all events, though he saw the blush his rudeness had created, a malicious smile played upon his lips, indicative of that contempt of the feelings of women, which was one of his characteristics.

"Madame Grellet, however, survived the shock of this discourtesy which signalized her entry into fashionable life. She soon became a celebrity in the court circles, and always maintained preëminence, alike for beauty of person, grace of manners and delicacy and dignity of character. More than once she had her revenge upon the Emperor, when, in the centre of an admiring circle, he, with others, paid homage to her fascinations. Yet this transplantation of the fair Puritan, even to the Paradise of fashion, was not healthful.

"M. Grellet became one of Bonaparte's receivers-general, and took up his residence in the department of the Dordogne—though spending the winters in Paris. Upon the fall of Napoleon, he lost his office, but was reappointed during the Hundred Days, only to lose it again upon the final restoration of Louis XVIII. The shadows now gathered thick and dark around him. His wife, having taken a violent cold, was attacked with pleurisy, which resulted in a gradual decline. Gently, but surely, her life faded away. Death ever loves a shining mark, and at the early age of five and twenty she descended to the tomb. With two charming daughters—the remembrances of his love and his affliction—M. Grellet returned to the south of France, and in the course of years, he too was numbered with the dead."

Such is, in part, the story of our fair countrywoman. The

two daughters of Madame Grellet are still living in the south of France. One is married and has children around her; the other is in a convent, and has taken perpetual vows. "How strange, how affecting," continues the author we have quoted, "are the vicissitudes of life, as we read them in the intimate personal chronicles of homes and hearts! The direct grandchildren of the Puritan minister of Ridgefield—the one a mother, blending her name, her lineage and her language in the annals of a foreign land; the other a devotee, seeking in the seclusion of her cell, and perhaps not altogether in vain, that peace which the world cannot give! What romance is more deeply and touchingly tinted than this simple page of family history!"

From the remark made by the Emperor on the occasion of Madame Grellet's presentation, the reader will see that sympathy with women, or at least the habit of expressing sympathy at a trying moment, was not one of his characteristics. It would be easy to adduce many similar instances. The narrative which follows will show him to be incapable of even forgetting or forgiving an epigram which had fallen from the lips of a sarcastic beauty.

M'lle Ermesinde de Narbonne became Madame de Chevreuse, in 1798, upon her marriage with the son of the Duke de Luynes and de Chevreuse. Her father-in-law was the representative of a family of immense wealth and of high ancestral pride. In 1804, she was remarkable as having obtained the reputation of being the most thoroughly elegant and accomplished woman in Paris, without possessing any of the elements of beauty. Her hair was reddish, if not red; her features were irregular, and in form she was thin and angular. But her manners were so charming, and yet so dignified, her movements were so graceful, and her assertion of her proud birth-right was so amiable, that during her short and brilliant career at the court, she was one of its most lofty and dazzling ornaments.

During the formation of the imperial household by Napoleon,

a parchment signed by the Emperor was placed in her hands : it was her appointment as lady of honor to the Empress Josephine. "I refuse," she said, after she had read it. "But think of what may be the result," interposed her husband and her father-in-law "It is useless," she returned, "to repeat what I have already said a thousand times : I hate and despise the imperial court! After that, you can hardly desire me to form part of it." But Napoleon had given this haughty family to understand that a refusal on the part of Madame de Chevreuse might provoke reprisals which would endanger their fortune ; to save the estate, therefore, she assumed the distasteful service. Her conduct at court was that of a frondeuse, a malcontent ; her epigrams upon the new régime circulated through Paris and the departments. She would not deign to appropriate to her own purposes her salary as lady of honor. She made a point of giving the whole sum, twelve thousand francs a year, conspicuously and contemptuously, to the poor.

Napoleon was wounded by the smart sallies and the disaffection of Madame de Chevreuse ; and one night, in the midst of a brilliant throng at the Tuileries, he said aloud to her : "Dear me ! How red your hair is !" "Perhaps it is, sire," she retorted, "but this is the first time a man ever told me so !" The Count de Survilliers, one of the authors of "Les Erreurs de Bourrienne," says upon this subject : "This was an indirect compliment to Madame de Chevreuse, but she did not so understand it. She should have thought that the Emperor had eyes as well as other people, and that her beautiful blond hair was no redder to him than to any one else. With more wit, she would have modestly blushed, and this blush would have told her appreciation of the indirect compliment, and her gratification at the intention, in which a woman is rarely deceived ; but Madame de Chevreuse was prejudiced and hostile."[1]

It is certainly worth remembering that the apologists of

[1] Erreurs de Bourrienne, i. 236.

Napoleon reproach a lady of the court for not blushing with delight at hearing an Emperor call her blond locks red. The intimation, too, that a person may blush to order, is, to say the least, singular. It was said, at the time, in reference to this incident, that it would be quite as easy to sneeze at the word of command, to dream dreams at will, to sleep voluntarily, to wake appropriately and to expire opportunely.

By thus persecuting the sprightly lady of honor, Napoleon only succeeded in rendering her interesting, and in drawing upon himself the blame of the palace. He next sought his revenge by attempting to fasten a stain upon a pure and guileless life. He sent her superb anonymous presents, flowers, rare plants; but she soon put an end to this gallant persecution by ordering her servants to repulse the imperial offerings from her door. The Emperor now abandoned his system of mysterious devotion for one of open and undisguised attention. One day at the close of a hunt, he ordered one of the whippers-in to present, in his name, the stag's severed foot to Madame de Chevreuse. The courtiers exchanged significant glances; the lady of honor saw the impending danger. She crossed the circular space enclosed by the huntsmen, and presenting the foot to Josephine, said, "The man has made a mistake, madame: he probably does not know you. I thus repair his error." Her pale cheeks were flushed with indignation as she repelled the insult of his Majesty.

Napoleon soon came to fear Madame de Chevreuse, and necessarily to dislike her. She speedily drew upon herself the rigors of his wrath by two speeches, one of which was a mere extravagant bravado, the other a noble and dignified reproof. She came one night to the Tuileries, literally blazing with diamonds. Some one asked her if they were all genuine, or, as is sometimes the case, if they were mingled with paste. "Dear me! I hardly know," she replied, "but even if they were all false, they would be quite good enough to come here with." Any other sovereign but Napoleon would have laughed at the malice of this sally, but his incensed

Majesty indited a decree of exile. This he withheld for a time, but signed it soon afterwards under the following circumstances: In 1808, his Spanish campaign deprived Charles IV. and his queen of their crowns, and the dethroned sovereigns were compelled to accept the palace of Compiègne in France as their residence in exile. Napoleon drew up the list of ladies who were to wait upon the queen. Upon this list he placed the name of Madame de Chevreuse first. "Tell his Majesty I decline," she said; "there are no jailers in my family!" The heavy hand of Napoleon fell upon Madame de Chevreuse as it had fallen upon Madame Récamier. She was banished from Paris, and warned not to return within the distance of fifty leagues. This was a cruel and indeed fatal blow for the young duchess, who was already suffering from the first attacks of consumption. Her exile and her martyrdom hastened and aggravated her disease. She led an errant life, wandering from Tours to Rouen, and from Rouen to Caen. Josephine frequently interceded with Napoleon in her behalf; his invariable reply was, "No, I say, no! I'll have no impertinent spoiled children here!" Madame de Chevreuse died at Lyons early in the year 1813. Napoleon's querulous and unmanly persecution had killed her in the maturity of her beauty and the prime of her years.

Napoleon was not destitute of gallantry, however, and when in the humor, could converse amiably, and even condescend to agreeable trifling, with ladies whose attractions rendered it worth his while. An incident may be mentioned in this connection, which took place at Boulogne, in 1803, during the visit of the First Consul to the fleet. A lady from Dunkirk, noted for her elegance, wit and beauty, was turning the heads of the grand personages assembled there. General Soult and Joseph Bonaparte were her acknowledged favorites, and of the two, the latter was in reality and in secret, the successful suitor. The lady gave numerous evening parties, and one of them Bonaparte determined to attend, with a view to penetrate, if possible, his brother's mystery. He assumed citizen's costume, and wore a wig and spectacles. General Bertrand, similarly disguised, accompanied him, and the two caused themselves to be announced as commissaries of war. They entered unrecognized, the company being absorbed over the bouillotte table. Bonaparte was soon satisfied that intelligence existed between Joseph and his hostess, and was preparing to depart, when she retained him in order to play at forfeits. He was obliged to give a pledge, and being unfortunately without either handkerchief or other small article, was obliged to pawn a piece of paper upon which he had prepared a list of colonels. He stipulated that it should remain unopened. Upon the delivery of the sentences, it was decreed that Bonaparte should enact the part of door-keeper, while Joseph and the lady from Dunkirk "made the journey to Cythera."

This game, which is still in vogue in certain circles of French society, consists of the following features: Any two persons, a lady and gentleman, whose relations are supposed to be confidential, or whose pairing is not believed to be distasteful to either, may be sent upon this journey in an adjoining room, while the door-keeper guards the entrance. The imprisoned parties, whose time is short, are expected to make such hurried use of it as their intimacy may authorize, or their inclinations may suggest. The door-keeper is responsible for the entire seclusion of the interview.

Bonaparte performed this duty with as good a grace as could be expected, for the character he sustained is usually given to jealous husbands and to persons whom the company wishes to quiz or to tease. He soon after left, and entering the room of a carpenter who inhabited the ground floor, wrote a note which he at once sent to the fair occupant of the story above. This note ran as follows:

"I thank you, madame, for the amiable welcome you have extended to me this evening. Should you ever visit me in my tent, I will again enact the door-keeper, if such be your pleasure;

but I will not leave to others the duty of accompanying you in your journey to Cythera.—BONAPARTE."

This adventure was soon noised abroad, and the public made merry over the ludicrous sentinel duty which had been imposed upon the head of the state.[1]

At the ball given at the Tuileries in 1806, in honor of the marriage of the Princess Stephanie de Bade, Napoleon accosted a lady whom he did not recognize, thus: "Who are you, madame?" "Sire, I am Madame Charpentier." "The wife of General Charpentier?" "Yes, sire." "Dear me, how ill you look in that dress! You are very much changed!" With these words, the courteous monarch passed on. In the Gallery of Diana, a lady with trembling hand presented him a petition. This person was one who had received Napoleon into her house when he was a lieutenant of artillery, and found it difficult to live upon his meagre salary; she persuaded him that to occupy one of her vacant rooms would be to oblige her by airing the furniture, and that to eat at her table would oblige her still more, by occupying her solitude. She rendered him long and important services at a moment when he most needed assistance. Being subsequently totally ruined, she bethought herself of applying to the lieutenant whom she had befriended. She handed her petition to Napoleon as he advanced along the Gallery of Diana. The Emperor looked at her, changed color and said in a loud and menacing tone, "By what chance come you here?" The unfortunate woman fell fainting upon the floor, and was borne away from the palace. The next day the Emperor settled upon her an annual pension of twelve hundred francs, in atonement for his harshness and in acquittal of his obligation.[2]

Bonaparte's treatment of Madame Fourès, whom he had once called by the affectionate sobriquet of Bellilotte, and whom the public styled the Eastern Queen, may be briefly referred to here. This lady followed her husband, who was attached to Bonaparte's

[1] Constant, ii. 197.   [2] Ducrest, 54.

Egyptian army, to Cairo. Here an intrigue was set on foot, and Fourès was sent to France with a package of worthless duplicate dispatches. He embarked at Alexandria, was captured by the English squadron under Commodore Hood, and landed again on the Egyptian coast. He hastened back to Cairo, where he found his home abandoned and his name dishonored. His wife was occupying the quarters of the General-in-chief—the palace of Elfy-Bey. His grief and consternation were poignant; and his wife, to escape his persecutions and importunities, obtained a species of military divorce from the commissary-general of the army.

Bonaparte's attachment to Madame Fourès seems to have been profound and sincere. He wore constantly upon his person a lock of her hair, in exchange for which he had given her his portrait. During his absence in Syria, he wrote her the most affectionate letters, and in one of them is said to have promised to obtain a divorce from Josephine and marry her, if she made him a father.[1] This tenderness endured till his dreams of ambition compelled him to sacrifice her.

Bellilotte arrived at Paris from Egypt several weeks after Bonaparte; she found him reconciled to Josephine, and deeply involved in cares of state, for he had become in the meantime First Consul. He did not see her; Duroc, however, has declared of his personal knowledge, that the separation cost Napoleon a severe internal struggle. Josephine, who was aware of the whole intrigue, seasoned her jealous quarrels with constant references to her history, and made frequent and bitter use of her name. Napoleon instructed Duroc to obtain a lodging for her at Belleville, just without the walls. She sometimes attended the performances of Talma at the Comédie Française, where she excited the utmost interest and curiosity. She was then about twenty-three years of age, but with the fresh, florid complexion of a girl of sixteen. Her hair, which was flaxen, fell in natural ringlets about her neck; she sat wrapped in a white

[1] Hist. Scientifique et Militaire de l'Ex. en Egypte, iv. 76.

Cashmere shawl, with an embroidered border. It was at this period that the public gave her the title of the Eastern Queen.

Her husband soon returned from Egypt, and upon the expiration of the period in which the military divorce must be confirmed or become void, reclaimed her. She resisted, and Napoleon was informed of the angry disputes which followed. He ordered her, though legally the wife of Fourès, to marry again, and promised a distant consulate as an inducement to the future husband. One M. Ramchouppe presented himself, and with disgust and shame, the unhappy woman resigned herself to her fate.[1] She left France, and was absent many years. She did not return from Brazil—the scene of her husband's duties—until after Napoleon's death, when the public had naturally lost all interest in her.

"Bonaparte's opinion of women," says Alison, "was very low; he never could be persuaded to converse with them seriously on any subject, or regard them as anything but playthings or objects of pleasure; he felt, with Bacon, their value to young men as mistresses, to old as nurses; but utterly denied their utility even to middle life as companions. It was his favorite opinion that the Orientals understood much better how to dispose of the female sex than the Europeans; that the harem was the true scene both of their respectability and their usefulness; and that if it were not for the object of having a family, no man of sense would ever marry. His infidelities were, nevertheless, frequent; but none of his fancies ever influenced his conduct or affected his judgment, and they were generally of very short duration. There was a brusquerie and precipitation in his manner towards women, both in public and private, which his greatest admirers admit to have been repugnant to every feeling of female delicacy. He had hardly any conversation to address to them in the salons of St. Cloud. He never got the better, as hardly any one ever does, of the want of the society of elegant women early

[1] d'Abr. i. 848.

in life ; and on the occasion of his marriage with Marie Louise, in 1810, he accosted her rather as a grisette who had been won by a three weeks' fidelity, than the daughter of the Cæsars who had been the prize of a hundred victories."[1]

"Love," said Napoleon at St. Helena, "is the occupation of an idle man, the amusement of a busy one, and the shipwreck of a sovereign."[2]

The Duke de Vicence, referring to the same subject, says: "The Emperor, who knew men so well, was ignorant of women. He had not lived with them and did not understand them ; he disdained so futile a study. His sensations, entirely physical in regard to them, admitted no influence from liveliness, intelligence, or talents ; he had an aversion to their being learned or celebrated, or emerging from their ordinary domestic sphere. He placed them in the social order at the lowest scale, and never could admit that they should have any influence over the will. A woman was in his eyes an agreeable piece of creation, a pretty plaything, an amusing pastime, but nothing more. 'Love,' said he, 'is a foolish preoccupation, be assured of that.'"[3]

"His heart," says Channing, "among all its wild beatings, never had one throb of disinterested love. . . . . Not even woman's loveliness and the dignity of a queen could give shelter from his contumely."[4]

Napoleon often startled women by the abrupt inquiry, "How many children have you?" This was not a chance question, but one demanding a mathematical, statistical reply. He regarded women as the cause of a grand result—the principle of population. He interrogated the maternal heart to learn how many conscripts it could yield.[5] Mothers furnished him his "chair à canon ;" they were responsible for the supplies of food for powder. Therefore he organized the lyceums and colleges for the instruction of boys upon a military footing ;[6] they mustered for

---

[1] Europe, ix. 151.   [3] Caulaincourt, i. 158.   [5] Capefigue, ii. 241.
[2] Las Cases, ii. 15.   [4] Napoleon, 34–48.   [6] Mém. d'un Bourgeois, i. 55.

recitation or dispersed for recess to the beat of the drum; they underwent, from the tenderest infancy, the discipline of the uniform. He materialized education and converted schools into barracks.[1] His famous reply to Madame de Staël—which we have already recorded—to the effect that the greatest woman was she who had the greatest number of children, was not a mere casual, flippant repartee, but the felicitous expression of his deliberate opinion.[2]

He expressed the same idea in another form, when speaking to Madame Campan of perpetual vows. When he established the Sisters of Charity, he was importuned to allow the veil for life; this he refused. "Tastes may change," he said, "and there is no good reason for depriving society of women who may afterwards be useful. Convents attack the principle of population at its very root. The loss, to a state, can hardly be calculated, resulting from ten thousand women confined in the cloister. War is less injurious, because the number of males is at least one twenty-fifth greater than that of females. I would permit women of fifty to take perpetual vows, for then their task is done."[3]

The instances and opinions we have cited, amply suffice to show the esteem in which Napoleon held women, and the limits he imposed upon their mission and their duties. We have to mention one more example, however, as the scene was one of the most remarkable ever witnessed in a palace, and as the lady addressed by the Emperor made a reply at once so spirited and so graceful, that the audience of imperial courtiers involuntarily murmured their approbation. The scene of the incident was the chateau of Neuilly, the residence of Caroline Murat, then the Grand Duchess of Berg. "Every one knows," says Madame Junot, "the manner in which Napoleon's court circle was formed; a triple row of ladies, behind whom were ranged a triple row of gentlemen, all listening with as much curiosity as the females to hear the speeches, polite or impolite, which the Emperor should

[1] Lam. Rest. i. 402.   [2] Las Cases, v. 242.   [3] Journal de Mme. Campan, 18.

address to them. It is now quite easy to speak as we please upon this subject, and to affect courage when the battle is over, but I will affirm that when, on a court-day, the Emperor appeared at the door which is in the angle of the throne room, with a cloudy brow, every one was awed; first the ladies, then the gentlemen, and last, but not least, that group assembled in the deep window to the left—that group generally complete, with the single exception of England, covered with jewels and orders of chivalry, and trembling before the little man who entered with a quick step, dressed simply in the uniform of a colonel of chasseurs. I have known women—and I have a right to place myself among the number—who preserved in his presence a dignity of manner which pleased him far better than silly fear, or base flattery. When he made an unpleasant speech to a lady, and it was received with respect and spirit, he never returned to the charge. For myself, in cases where I have offended him, he has often passed me at two or three successive court circles without speaking, but he never said a word which could wound my feelings or my proper susceptibilities. I have heard him do so by others, however, and once in particular by Madame Regnault de St. Jean d'Angely."

Madame Regnault was the wife of the Secretary of State for the Imperial family—a man distinguished for his devotion and fidelity to Napoleon throughout the Consulate and Empire, as well as during his misfortunes. She was one of the most beautiful women of the court, and we have already spoken of her as recalling the antique Niobe by her style of face and expression. Her head was a perfect Greek model in its proportions and in the exquisite outline of the profile. Her hair was deep black, and curled in natural ringlets. Her teeth were white and regular. Her figure was so symmetrical that she never had recourse to the aid of corsets, even when she wore a court dress. She was intelligent, witty, and modest. Her portrait was painted by Gérard, and may be found in his engraved gallery of Historical

Portraits. It has also been engraved separately and is usually sold, in this form, under the title of Sappho.*

Madame Regnault was one of the many women who had incurred Napoleon's dislike. He never treated her with even ordinary politeness, without, however, alleging any motive for his conduct, and probably conscious of no reasonable ground of aversion. On the evening in question, he was out of humor, and made his customary round of the company with evident distaste. He stopped opposite Madame Regnault to examine her toilet. This consisted of a simple dress of white crape, trimmed with alternate tufts of pink and white roses. The glossy black ot her hair was relieved by white roses deeply imbedded in its tresses. Her toilet was considered faultless—for the events of the night caused it to be critically examined and canvassed. As his Majesty prepared to address her, she presented as perfect an embodiment of youth, beauty and taste, as was to be found in the court. Napoleon was all the more incensed at her irreproachable appearance. Justice was the last feature which characterized his criticisms upon ladies, and the remark which he now made was certainly the last which a regard to truth and the most ordinary courtesy would have suggested to him. With a bitter smile, he said in a deep, sonorous voice:

"Do you know, Madame Regnault, that you are looking much older to-night?"

These words were uttered in the hearing of several hundred persons, half of whom were women, doubtless gratified at the beauty's humiliation. She hesitated for a moment, as if framing her reply. At last she said with a smile, and in a voice sufficiently firm for all who heard the attack to hear the rejoinder:

"What your Majesty has done me the honor to observe, might have been painful to hear, had I reached an age when youth is regretted."

---

* The original picture is now in possession of the present Regnault de St. Jean d'Angely, the commander of the Imperial Guard. A copy has been placed at the Historical Gallery of Versailles; and it is from this that the portrait of Madame Regnault upon the opposite page is taken.

The Niobe of the court was hardly twenty-eight years old. A murmur of approbation ran through the room, which not even the presence of Napoleon could repress. The Emperor afterwards regretted his treatment of Madame Regnault. He was told at St. Helena, in 1816, that she had manifested constant attachment to him during his confinement at, and upon his return from, Elba. "Is it possible?" he exclaimed, with marked satisfaction. "Poor lady! How badly I treated her! Well, this compensates for the ingratitude of the renegades for whom I did so much! How true it is, that we can neither judge of the heart nor the sentiments, until they have been exposed to trial!"[1]

[1] Las Cases, iv. Part vii. 111.

CHAPTER XXIX.

The Drama under Napoleon—Imperial Patronage of Actors—The Decree of Moscow—Epigrams upon this Decree—Talma—His Education and Early Tastes—His First Appearance—Charles IX.—Talma a Girondin—Talma and Napoleon—Character of Talma's Genius—Criticisms of the Emperor—Talma at Erfurth—His Letter to John Kemble—His two Marriages—His Death—Lafon—Fleury—St. Prix—M'lle Mars—Character of her Talent—The Mysterious Ring—Political Constancy of M'lle Mars—M'lle Duchesnois—M'lle Georges—Circumstances attending her Birth—Her infant Performances—Her First Appearance—Stage Riots—M'lle Georges and Lucien Bonaparte—M'lle Georges and Napoleon—She Visits St. Petersburg, Stockholm and Dresden—The Romantic School of Modern Dramatic Literature.

THE dramatic literature of the Empire suffered from the repressive system to which the mind of the nation was subjected, as well as general literature, whose condition during this period has already been described. Though the production of works intended for the stage was thus limited in number and inferior in quality, the scenic interpretation of the classic repertory was, under Napoleon, the most brilliant and complete in French histrionic annals. The performers gathered at the Comédie Française, and coöperating in the representation of the tragedies of Racine, Corneille, Voltaire, and of the comedies of Molière, Beaumarchais, Marivaux, formed a constellation of talent whose equal is not presented by any previous or by any subsequent epoch. Napoleon, finding the stage thus efficient at his accession, bestowed upon it a bountiful and enlightened patronage. He paid 20,000 francs a year for his box at the Comédie. He gave Talma 10,000 francs for a few performances at the Congress of Erfurth; he gave 10,000 to M'lle Mars at the armistice of Dresden. He admitted Talma to his intimacy and friendship. He caused theatres to be attached to all the imperial residences; and during the Empire alone, forty-five tragedies and seventy-nine comedies were enacted in the palaces of the Tuileries, St. Cloud, Fontainebleau, Malmaison, Compiègne, Trianon and the Elysée.

For many years Napoleon cherished the project of giving a constitution to the Comédie Française, and of thus conferring upon the company a permanent organization. For various reasons, he never took the plan seriously into consideration, till after the disaster of Moscow, in 1812, when he found himself, for the second time, at his head-quarters in the Kremlin. His chief anxiety now was to sustain the courage and hopes of France, and for this purpose he aimed at appearing, amid the ruins of the capital of the Czars, to have both the time and the spirit to attend to matters of little or no national importance. He thus signed, at the Kremlin, a decree regulating the duty on Illyrian lead, and one establishing a warehousing tax in favor of the docks of Trieste; he ordered the construction of a theatre for the soldiers, upon the still smoking ruins of Moscow. But the most remarkable of these ordinances was that by which, in the midst of wreck, blood and desolation, he fixed the duties, privileges and responsibilities of the actors and actresses of the Comédie Française. This document, containing one hundred articles, was discussed at length by Napoleon and Maret during the autumn spent in Moscow. It was published in the Moniteur, on Napoleon's return from Russia, in December of the same year. It still governs the action of the theatre and its company, and has contributed to make them what they are—beyond possible competition the first dramatic establishment in Europe. The "sociétaires," members for life, and the "pensionnaires," members upon a salary and candidates for life-membership, take infinite pride in the Decree of Moscow, and would hardly exchange the consideration and position it has given them, for a patent of nobility or a liberal investment in the national funds. In 1813, the members, in order to acquit their obligations, voted the purchase of three horses of pure blood for the service of Napoleon's armies.

As Napoleon left Paris for the Russian campaign, an epigrammatist gave utterance to a prediction which was in accordance with the despondency and discouragement of the people. He said: "Napoleon will lose the Grand Army for the satisfaction of signing a decree at Moscow."[1] When, therefore, the intelligence was received of his Majesty's theatrical signature in the midst of the horrors of conflagration and ruin, the indignation of Europe found vent in a rain of sarcasms and maledictions. "A decree from Moscow," exclaimed Le Corréspondant de Hamburg, "upon the French comedians! We admire, sire, that force of genius, that heroic insensibility which permits you to busy yourself with the concerns of a dozen actors, in the midst of the most fearful disaster ever inflicted upon a nation by the wrath of offended heaven!"

The principal performers who shed lustre upon the stage during Napoleon's time were Talma, Lafon, Fleury, St. Prix; M'lles Mars, Duchesnois and Georges. A few words upon the nature of their talents and the achievements of their lives are due to artistes of such just celebrity.

François-Joseph Talma was born at Paris, in 1763, on the anniversary of the birth of Molière. His father and uncle were dentists; he was intended to succeed them in their profession, and received, in that view, a thorough education at one of the first seminaries of Paris. He was studious and appeared ambitious, though he manifested no particular bent towards any special pursuit. At one of the public exhibitions at his school, he performed a part in a tragedy entitled Tamerlane, written by the principal of the institution; his emotion was such that his voice failed him, and he was carried off the stage in a paroxysm of grief. On quitting college, he applied himself to the study of medicine; but scandalized his uncle, at whose house he lodged, by a habit of mounting upon the dinner table, and reciting Molière to the water-carrier and the cook. So young

[1] Michaud, Hist. de Napoléon, iii. 440.

Talma was sent off to his father, now exercising his profession at London. He here joined a company of French amateurs, and, acquiring the English language with facility, he frequented the theatres where Shakspeare was represented. He attended assiduously the performances of John Kemble and of Mrs. Siddons. Through his father, he made the acquaintance of a distinguished anatomist, with whom he practised dissection; he also studied the relations of the passions with the muscles, and inquired into the laws which connect emotion with the features.

At the age of twenty-one, he returned to Paris, and on the 21st of November, 1787, he made his first appearance upon the stage, in the tragedy of Mahomet, the bill of the Comédie Française simply stating, without giving any name: "A new actor will make his début in the character of Séide." The young stranger interested the audience by his penetrating voice, his sombre physiognomy, and his courageous deviation from the classic traditions, in passages where it is safer to trust to inspiration than to memory. Still the critical authorities hesitated before pronouncing an opinion, and Talma was obliged to fight his way, slowly, and without assistance from others. He was engaged at the Comédie upon a salary of twelve hundred francs a year; he played any and all characters, filling, at slight notice, parts left vacant by indisposition. But he could not hope for distinction, unless he could "create" a character, and it was unlikely that any author would intrust him with the responsibility of an important original delineation. But he was unexpectedly served in this matter by St. Phal, the leading tragedian, who declined studying the character of Charles IX., in Chénier's tragedy of that name. Chénier at once gave the part to Talma; and the result justified the choice. Talma procured a portrait of Charles IX., and employed the several weeks that the rehearsals lasted in contemplation of the royal physiognomy, penetrating himself with its expression, its features, its manner. "At the performance," writes one of his biographers, "the tragedy was not on the boards of a theatre, but in the halls of the Louvre. How could one avoid yielding to the illusion, when, after hearing the murderous alarm-bell of St. Germain l'Auxerrois, Charles IX., pursued by the bloody phantom of Coligny, uttered cries so lamentable, cast about him glances so full of agony and horror, and fell trembling and desperate under the anticipated maledictions of posterity, that it was not only the form and features of the king of the St. Bartholomew that the spectator saw before his eyes, but his voice, his soul, his crime and his remorse!"

The dramatists now applied themselves to the production of works worthy the interpretation of the magnificent innovator. Legouvé gave him "Néron," Arnault "Blanche et Montcassin," Lemercier "Plaute." Ducis translated for him Macbeth and Othello, and remodeled his version of Hamlet. Every author that wrote for him remained his constant friend through life; Talma retained their affection by his efforts in their behalf and his interest in their success. On the first night of Soumet's "Clytemnestre," he said, "I tremble for two."

The Revolution divided the Comédie Française into two camps. Those who had acquired distinction, and had become accustomed to privilege and the favor of the court, remained royalists; those who had everything to gain and nothing to lose, espoused the cause of the republic. Talma was the leading Girondin of the revolutionary party; he avoided the Terrorists, though by so doing he compromised his safety. Marat visited his house one night uninvited; upon his departure, Dugazon, a fellow-actor, caused perfumes to be burned upon a shovel to clear the air. Talma nearly suffered death for this untimely jest, for "L'Ami du Peuple" denounced him the next day. Like his comrades, his poverty was at this period extreme, and when the performance announced for the evening required but little effort and would permit an insufficient meal, he dined abstemiously upon bread and grapes. At other times he frequented a humble restaurant in the Rue de la Michodière, where he made the acquaintance, through a professor of mathematics who knew them both, of a young man of pale face and slender proportions, some years his junior. They often dined together, and conversed upon their respective aspirations: the one aiming at scenic renown, the other at military glory. These two young men were the first of actors and the first of modern conquerors—Talma and Napoleon.

With the restoration of social order, Talma, delivered from the denunciations of the Terror and the misgovernment of the Directory, applied himself ardently to the serious and sustained studies which made him the Roscius of his age. His talents were constantly improving, and his hold upon his audience increased with his years; his last characters in Charles VI. and L'Ecole des Vieillards—the latter a comedy in verse—were his best. No art could surpass these marvellous impersonations, and the actor, having attained the zenith of tragic renown, sickened and died at the age of sixty-three. He expired without a struggle, though after a distressing illness, muttering disjointed phrases, among which could only be distinguished the words, "Voltaire! like Voltaire!" His funeral was attended by a throng of persons distinguished for their talents and virtues; the concourse of mourners evinced the esteem in which he was held by the court and the city. The actors wore mourning for him for forty days.

It was said of Talma, that his head and profile presented the Greek type in all the purity of an Athenian medallion struck in the time of Pericles. His physiognomy, completely under his control, was naturally melancholy, but became, at will, terrible or placid, winning or repellant. His voice was penetrating and magnetic, and he possessed the art of speaking audibly in an extinct whisper. His gestures were the perfection of grace; his pantomime, whether illustrative of the text, or itself supplying the place of language, was singularly expressive. He was the first to bestow attention upon the art of costume, consulting medals, statues, manuscripts, black letter folios, for authority upon the accessories of dress, armor and drapery. He never had a rival upon the French stage. His immediate predecessor, Lekain, who enjoyed an immense reputation, was unequal and incomplete. Perfect in the delineation of the more violent passions, he failed in representing them when in repose, in rendering passages of transition from agitation to tranquillity, and in descriptive recitation. In all this Talma was as effective as in the more startling features of his art. The French classic stage is indebted to him for the present system of dramatic declamation. It was the custom previously to make both the sense and the punctuation subordinate to a distinct coupling of the rhymes. Each alexandrine fell in cadence, and the duty of the actor was especially to impress upon the ear of the listener the rhyming syllables at the end of it. Talma reversed this habit, and made it the object of his delivery to preserve the sense even if he somewhat slurred the rhyme. He breathed at the pauses; his predecessors had always taken breath at the ends of the lines. This avoidance of the jingle of rhyme was a happy innovation; and in thus improving an art intimately connected with oratory and elocution, Talma is likely to exert a more durable influence upon literature and rhetoric than usually falls to the lot of an actor, however great he may be.

Throughout the Consulate, Talma remained on terms of intimacy with Bonaparte, being habitually present at his levees, upon a footing with Monge and Lagrange. When Napoleon became Emperor, he thought it prudent to cease his attendance at the palace. He was summoned, however, to the Tuileries, on the morning of the day when the authorities were to compliment the Emperor upon his elevation to the throne. His Majesty compelled several deputations of government functionaries to wait without, while he took the tragedian to task for alleged exaggerations in the performance of Nero. On another occasion, speaking to Talma of his tendency to overact, he said: "You visit me often, Talma; you see around me princes who have lost their dominions, princesses who have lost their lovers, kings who have lost their thrones ; you see generals who aspire to crowns ; you see disappointed ambitions, eager rivalries, terrible catastrophes ; you see afflictions exposed to the public view, and you may guess at many sorrows nursed and hidden in the heart. Here is tragedy, certainly ; my palace is full of it ; and I myself am assuredly the first tragedian of my time. Do you ever see us lift our arms in the air, study and prepare our gestures, take attitudes and affect airs of grandeur? Do you hear us utter cries and shouts ? Certainly not ; we speak naturally, as every one speaks when urged by interest or inspired by passion. So have done before me the various persons who have occupied the attention of the world, and like me have played tragedies upon the throne. Here are examples to meditate upon !"

Again, one morning after the performance of "La Mort de Pompée," Napoleon said : "I am not entirely satisfied ; you use your arms too much ; monarchs are less prodigal of gestures ; they know that a motion is an order, and that a look is death ; so they are sparing of both motions and looks. For instance, how often has it happened to me to awaken to activity three hundred guns, by a sign of my little finger!" Talma profited by the advice thus given ; and if the second part of his career showed a marked improvement upon the first, the criticisms of Napoleon may be supposed not to have been without influence in inducing reflection and reformation. During the Revolution and under the Directory, he had been clamorous, turbulent, demonstrative ; under the Consulate and Empire, he became simple, impressive, majestic. He produced his effects by more natural and legitimate means. "No one but Talma," wrote Madame de Staël, "ever attained that degree of perfection in which art is combined with inspiration, reflection with spontaneity, reason with genius."

At the Congress of Erfurth, where the company of the Comédie played to an audience of kings, Talma carried the bill for the evening, every morning to the Emperor. He was never detained without, being always admitted to the table or the dressing-room of his Majesty. On one occasion, as he was entering unchallenged, the King of Saxony, who had penetrated no further than the antechamber, said to him, "Do tell the Emperor that I am waiting!"

Talma was a good English scholar, and when writing to persons who understood the two languages, would employ them both indiscriminately. The following passage is from a letter written by him to Mr. Kemble, and dated in 1814, just after the return of the Bourbons:

. . . . "Le roi a d'excellentes intentions, des lumières et un caractère ferme, mais que nous sommes poor and miserable! Adieu, mon cher Kemble, mon plus grand désir est de vous voir, et de shake hands with you. Adieu, à vous de cœur.

"TALMA.

"My best repects to Mrs. Siddons."

Talma was twice married: once to a courtesan, "capable by her talents of being a second Madame Roland, had she led an honorable life,"[1] and by whom he had two sons, baptized Charles IX. and Henry VIII.; and again in 1802, after being divorced from his first wife, and after her death by grief in consequence, to Madame Petit-Vanhove, the widow of a ballet-master, and herself a member of the Comédie Française. Napoleon held Madame Talma in profound aversion; he would never see her play when he could avoid it. She survived her husband, and at the age of sixty, became, by a third marriage, Madame la Comtesse de Chalot.

Lafon, the son of a physician of Bordeaux, and distinguished early in life for his success in rhetorical exercises and his passion for poetry, the author of a tragedy at the age of sixteen, a truant from home, a soldier, a strolling actor, and a protégé of Barras, appeared for the first time at the Comédie Française in the year 1800, when twenty-five years old. He

[1] Soc. Française sous le Directoire, 345.

captivated and subjugated the town by the magnificent warmth of his manner, the tumultuous pomp of his diction, and the heroic fervor of his passion. His southern ardor atoned for his Mediterranean accent, and he became the idol of the ladies, through his convincing and irresistible style of paying court and professing admiration. Talma prudently withdrew for a while, till the brilliant Gascon should have run his brief career. Lafon remained a favorite, however, for a quarter of a century, and his presence was really beneficial to Talma, by furnishing him a direct and obvious contrast. Talma was epic, erudite, classic, solemn; Lafon was audacious, enthusiastic, impulsive. Talma was all concentration, Lafon all expansion. Women of the world and the court found Talma wanting in sensibility; while women of a sentimental or serious turn thought Lafon superficial and wanting in earnestness. Lafon, when speaking of Talma, never called him by name; he expressed his meaning by saying "l'autre;" "the other one."

Fleury was a remarkable instance of the triumph of patient and determined application over natural and apparently insurmountable defects. Without attractions of either form or face, embarrassed by a short breath and a halting gait, he became, after the retirement of Molé, the first light comedian and the most finished and courtly stage roué among the imperial company. He has never been replaced, as a representative of the manners, deportment and tone of the elegant society of the old régime.

During the Reign of Terror he had been thrown into prison, together with all the prominent actors of the day, and was there in imminent danger of death. The Count de Perigord, likewise in durance, often met Fleury in the gloomy galleries of their dungeon, and never failed to make him a low bow, at the same time saying, "How does your Majesty do?"—referring to his famous performance of the character of Frederic the Great. "Instantly," said the count, who often afterwards related the incident, "the King of Prussia stood before me such as we have seen him in the "Two Pages," and such as he was at Potsdam two years before his death; his back bent, but with imposing carriage nevertheless, with the same air, the same play of countenance. And this total change was effected in a few seconds, in a damp prison, by the light of a grated casement, and where a turnkey might at any moment interrupt our dramatic entertainment by marching us off to death. The mental firmness of the man, which permitted him to exercise these faculties in the midst of the most imminent danger, seemed to me still more worthy of admiration than the powers of the actor." Prince Henry of Prussia shed tears at what seemed the resuscitation of his brother, and on one occasion presented Fleury with a jeweled snuff-box bearing the portrait of Frederic the Great.

St. Prix—originally a sculptor—was an actor of towering stature, of noble mien, and strongly characterized features. His voice was a deep and guttural bass, eminently suited to the walk to which his physical development condemned him. No actor could better depict the jealousy and remorse of Cain, in La Mort d'Abel; none was more suited to the Cimbrian soldier, in Marius. The austere virtue of the Grand Master in Les Templiers, the imposing sanctity of the high priest in Athalie, the majesty of Agamemnon, the stoic dignity of Seneca, have never found since his death so capable an interpreter. With more depth of soul and more control over the tenderer chords of the human heart, St. Prix would have been justified in disputing the tragic sceptre with Talma himself.

M'lle Hippolyte Boutet Mars, the natural daughter of the "pathetic comedian" Monvel and Madame Mars, a provincial actress—whose southern accent condemned her to play to none but Gascon or Languedocian ears—was born at Versailles, in 1778. Her father divined her dramatic capabilities at an early age, and placed her upon the stage of the Montansier theatre when fifteen years old. M'lle Contat, the first actress of the epoch, took her into her affection, aided her by her counsels, and upon the re-organization of the Comédie Française obtained her admission as a member for life. Like Talma, M'lle Mars undertook and effected a reformation in the traditions of her art. She found that it was the habit of the stage to idealize comedy as well as tragedy. While she recognized the propriety of clothing poetic thoughts, expressed in poetic language and illustrating the master passions, in a garb befitting a theme so lofty, she considered that nature, society and every-day life should furnish comic artists with their models and their standards. M'lle Contat had somewhat sacrificed nature to dignity ; she was serious in her gaiety, and consulted a sort of distant, unbending propriety even in her moments of passion. M'lle Mars lowered the tone of comedy to a point where the stage held the mirror up to nature ; and in achieving this reform, she conferred a lasting benefit upon her art.

Possessing a voice of inimitable sweetness, a delivery rendered pleasing by a peculiar saccade acquired in her efforts to avoid contracting her mother's accent, a scrupulous purity of pronunciation, features of extreme mobility, an attractive person, graceful and winning manners, an infallible memory, and great fondness for study, M'lle Mars was endowed with all the accessory qualities necessary to sustain her unrivalled native talent. She was the first comédienne of her time, and her retirement left a void, difficult, if not impossible, to fill.

M'lle Mars, though not strictly beautiful, inspired many ardent passions. At the outset of her career, an incident occurred which filled the rest of her life with that species of interest which springs from an unexplained mystery. She was playing, night after night, a comedietta entitled Brueïs and Palaprat—one which required her to wear upon her finger a diamond ring. At this period of her life she possessed no jewels, and consequently wore the glass diamond set in brass which the stage-manager presented to her, as the performance commenced. One night, in place of the spurious brilliant, he brought her a blue velvet case containing a note and a diamond ring. The note was thus conceived:

"The ring which M'lle de Beauval wears upon her finger is worthy neither of her nor of you. Accept this one, madame, without hesitation for the present, without apprehension for the future. It conceals no profane intent, no culpable desire. It is offered to the artiste alone, not to the woman. He who sends it will remain through life the most obscure and unknown of her admirers—a promise to which he engages himself upon his word, as a true and loyal gentleman."

In spite of this assurance, M'lle Mars would have refused the gift, but the curtain had risen, and an imperious call compelled her to put it upon her finger. The court jeweller, who saw it after the performance, estimated its value at 30,000 francs. Some years after, it was stolen, together with the accumulated treasures of the actress; the police recovered nearly the whole, but the mysterious ring was not among them.

Some years later, a baroness of the faubourg St. Germain gave a masked and fancy ball, to which M'lle Mars was invited. As she was on the point of leaving the festive scene, at three in the morning, a hand was placed upon her arm, and she found herself alone with a masked seigneur of the time of Charles VII.; his gait, his dress and his manner betokened youth, elegance and nobility. "Calm yourself, my child," he said, "and do not open those inquisitive eyes so wide." Then changing his tone, and with a trembling voice, he asked, "Have you forgotten the third representation of Brueïs and Palaprat?" "No; how could I forget it?" returned M'lle Mars. "Thanks, a thousand thanks," exclaimed the stranger; "I hardly had a right to hope that you would remember it. But the other, the visible souvenir of that night, have you regretted its loss?" "Certainly, I have regretted it, not on account of its value, but because there was a mystery about it well calculated to impress the imagination of a woman and an artiste." "And if you were to recover it, madame, would its recovery afford you gratification?" "Very great gratification I assure you." "Above all, I suppose, if it were returned with its halo of romance and mystery."

The stranger took the actress's hand in his and pressed it to his lips. She was on the point of beseeching him to throw off the disguise which had been for years so unsatisfactory to her and so oppressive to him, when he said in resolute accents: "A man of honor must sacrifice the most imperious desires of his heart to his word. I have made you a promise, madame, and whatever it may cost me, I shall remain what I have been, the most unknown of your admirers. Adieu. We shall meet no more!" M'lle Mars, too violently agitated to pursue the retreating phantom, sank into a chair; on collecting her thoughts, she found upon the finger where she was wont to wear it, the ring of Brueïs and Palaprat. The donor remained forever a mystery; she never saw his face nor learned his name. It is probable that he admitted no one to his confidence, for the secret has not since transpired.

On the occasion of a review in the court of the Tuileries, one Sunday morning, Napoleon perceived M'lle Mars in the crowd, looking on. He spurred his horse through the piquet of soldiery, and said to her, "So you have come to return the visits we have so much pleasure in paying you at the theatre?" She remained faithful to the Emperor in adversity, and suffered persecution in consequence. The first time that she performed after the return of Napoleon from Elba, she expressed her delight by wearing a profusion of violets in her hair, at her waist, in her bosom. On her first appearance after the restoration of Louis XVIII., the public, unwilling that an actress should exhibit stronger political constancy than themselves, called upon her during the third act of Tartufe, to renounce the Emperor and acknowledge the King. "Cry Vive le Roi!" shouted the veterans of the orchestra stalls. whose memory and whose antecedents told them how easy was apostasy. "Make her cry Vive le Roi," shouted the renegades of the pit. M'lle Mars remained calm during the passage of the tempest. She then employed a stratagem to escape further annoyance: "Why, gentlemen," she said, "I have cried Vive le Roi!" This was untrue, but it allayed the disturbance, and no subsequent disorder marked her career. She died at the age of seventy-one, the last of the grand school of comédiennes.

M'lle Catherine Rafin, better known under her assumed name of Duchesnois, was born near Valenciennes, in 1777. In the midst of poverty and ignorance, she evinced a marked literary tendency; her language indicated a superior taste. At the age of twenty, she played, as an amateur, the character of Palmyre in Mahomet. The performance was for the benefit of the poor; the receipts purchased five hundred suits of winter clothing. She soon came to Paris, and endeavored to obtain the means of appearing before a metropolitan audience. Chaptal, the Minister of the Interior, positively refused her the necessary authorization to play at the Comédie Française, on account of her repulsive ugliness. Madame Lebrun, the first woman admitted to the Academy of Fine Arts, and Madame Montesson, interested themselves actively in her behalf. The latter invited two hundred persons to an entertainment at her house, at which M'lle Duchesnois was to read the character of Phèdre; she obtained the promise of Chaptal and Madame Bonaparte that they would attend the performance. Madame Lebrun arranged the hair and the toilet of the plain, angular, bony little woman, who dared, in the face of such physical disadvantages, to aspire to the tragic sceptre. She placed the lamps in positions which should embellish. if possible, her who so much needed scenic illusion. M'lle Duchesnois read Racine's verse in a manner which dissipated every prejudice conceived against her, and Chaptal, upon the formal demand of Josephine, signed an order for her début at the Comédie Française. Josephine gave her a wardrobe consisting for the most part of India goods richly embroidered, and a superb set of topazes which had been presented to her by the Portuguese ambassador. M'lle Duchesnois was sent to perform a few nights at the theatre of Versailles, in order to accustom her to the stage. Finally, in August, 1802, she made her first appearance in Paris, as the heroine of the tragedy of Phèdre.

The performance recalled the best days of Clairon and Dumesnil, whom the habitués of the orchestra never hoped to see replaced. The monarch of the feuilleton, Geoffroy, wrote thus of the débutante, in the Journal des Débats : " Familiarized by experience with tragic effects, fortified by habit against the illusions of the stage, and more prompt to seize the ridiculous than to appreciate the pathetic, I was wont to defy all scenic emotion ; I thought myself superior to common weakness. I owe it to M'lle Duchesnois that I know it was not my fault, if I was never moved ; she has given me a better opinion of myself ; I feel that my heart was not hard, but that my taste was difficult. I surprised myself with pleasure giving way to sensations altogether new ; involuntary tears have reëstablished my claim to sensibility, and I am truly proud of my defeat. My opinion, then, upon M'lle Duchesnois, is that of Louis XV. upon Lekain : She made me weep—I who weep but seldom."

The critic did not remain faithful to his first impressions, however, and shortly after penning the passage we have quoted, perhaps the most eulogistic he ever wrote, he threw up his allegiance and deserted to M'lle Georges. During the weeks of disorder and tumult which followed the début of this, her dazzling rival, Duchesnois had for partisans the Polytechnic School, and the students of the Law and Medical Colleges ; Madame de Montesson, who, though a Bourbon, possessed the confidence and the esteem of the First Consul, continued to afford her encouragement. In defiance of the evident partiality of Napoleon for M'lle Georges, and in spite of the malevolence of the now hostile Geoffroy, she continued the struggle with desperate earnestness. It was the interest of the government to direct the activity and the spirit of the youth of Paris into a field where it could spend itself harmlessly, and the cabals and the riots which at this period disgraced the stage, the pit, and the press, received no hindrance from the authorities or the police.

Catherine Rafin now assumed the name of Joséphine Duchesnois, acknowledging, by her choice of a Christian name, the aid she had received at her début from Madame Bonaparte. Both she and M'lle Georges were admitted by the Comédie as members for life, in March, 1804. M'lle Duchesnois achieved the greatest triumph that an actress can obtain—her plainness of feature disappeared in the glow of inspiration with which her countenance became illumined. In spite of her physical disadvantages, she won many victories over M'lle Georges, whose beauty was positively without a rival. Duchesnois remained the tragic queen of the French classic stage, while Georges played truant in Russia, and on her return, devoted her talents to the interpretation of the modern romantic drama.

M'lle Georges was born towards the close of the last century, and before the end of Louis XVI.'s reign. Her father was leader of the orchestra at the theatre of Bayeux, a village of Normandy. One evening, during the performance of La Belle Fermière, he was observed to receive a message, and straightway to lose all control over his instrument, and to plunge his band and the actors upon the stage into the direst confusion. He finally threw down his violin, disappeared beneath the footlights, and wildly ran home. The audience obtained a clue to the explanation of his conduct from the following words spoken by the trombone to the oboe: "Both mother and child are doing well." This, however, was premature; and when the orchestra, upon the fall of the curtain, repaired to the house of their leader to serenade the young mother—the soubrette of the company—they found the event they had supposed concluded, still in process of accomplishment. M'lle Marguerite Georges Weimer, the most beautiful, and the second, if not the first, tragic actress of the Empire, was born in the midst of this grotesque and untimely harmony

The fairies which preside at the births of the illustrious, we are told, invoked upon Marguerite, now sleeping the first human sleep, all the gifts that mortals can desire—beauty, goodness, majesty, generosity, health, prosperity, longevity! She was baptised, the next morning, at the church of St. Exupère.

Her father soon became manager of the theatre of Amiens, and Marguerite, at the age of five years, was the pet of that portion of the public that affects precocity and infant phenomena. She was the dairy-maid in "Les Deux Chasseurs et la Laitière;" her childish stature compelled her to replace, upon her baby head, the traditional milk-pail by a sugar-bowl. The public would have spoiled her with flowers, sweetmeats and indulgence, had nature intended gifts so magnificent to be exhausted during immaturity. She became, when fifteen years old, the pupil of M'lle Raucourt, then without a rival at the Comédie Française. This person lived in the cottage lately occupied by Madame Tallien, in the Allée des Veuves, and here she gave a daily lesson to Marguerite Weimer. The latter, after fourteen months' study, obtained from the Minister of the Interior the necessary authorization for her début at the theatre; and the evening of the 27th of November, 1802, was fixed for the occasion, Clytemnestra being the character to be sustained. The supremacy of the tragic scene was now held by M'lle Duchesnois, whose first appearance had taken place some months previously. Her admirers thronged to her support on this eventful evening, and partisan feeling ran high between the two camps. The scene has been thus described:

"The audience was attentive and agitated. For many days, the literary and dramatic public had talked of little else than M'lle Raucourt's pupil. 'A marvel!' said one party. 'We'll see that!' said the other. The latter were Duchesnois' admirers, and they brought no bravos in their clenched hands. In the orchestra stalls were those rows of bald heads that so terrify débutants; heads that have forgotten their by-gone enthusiasm, and would rather abjure their own youth than smile at youthful talent appearing before their aged sight; exacting old men who forfeit the respect that might be paid to their experience by the manner in which they treat inexperience. Obstinate veterans, discouraging invalids, are they—claiming our regard, nevertheless, as the chevaliers of the past. In his curule chair sat the prefect of public opinion, the Aristarch of the Journal des Débats, the monarch of the feuilleton, the inflexible censor who caused Talma so many sleepless nights, the decisive, the redoubtable and renowned critic, Abbé Julien-Louis Geoffroy. He was an erudite, honest and indefatigable judge. He felt what he said, and he said what he meant. One of his errors was to recognize no talent without beauty; he would have shut the door of the theatre to every actress not possessed of charms equal to her capacity. This preoccupation rendered him unjust towards M'lle Duchesnois, the fire of whose soul burned with sufficient intensity often to transform her ugliness into beauty.

'M'lle Georges appeared. Before she spoke she had gained her cause. She might now lose it upon opening her lips, but her voice confirmed the effect of her personal splendors. The partisans of M'lle Duchesnois adjourned the commencement of hostilities. The bald heads postponed the delivery of their opinion. They listened in a great measure with their eyes, and their shrivelled lips simultaneously quoted Virgil:

'Et vera incessu patuit dea'"

M'lle Raucourt encouraged her brilliant though docile scholar by loudly whispering from a stage-box, before each critical passage, "Ferme, Georgine!" At the close of the tragedy, the public called for both pupil and professor, and Georgine led forth to the foot-lights the patient benefactress who was the first to discern her genius, and had been alone in developing it.

The feuilletonists were clearly dazzled by the débutante's luxurious display of beauty. Geoffroy had discovered that happy combination of mental and physical charms of which he had so long dreamed. He wrote as follows in the columns intrusted to his charge—the feuilleton of the Débats: "Preceded upon the stage by an extraordinary reputation for beauty, M'lle Georges appeared in every way to deserve it ; her countenance joins French grace to the regularity and nobility of the Greek outline. Her form is that of the sister of Apollo, when surrounded by her nymphs, and overtopping them in stature, she walks upon the banks of the Eurotas Her whole form is a model for the pencil of Guérin.* Within this splendid body is a soul impatient to expand ; she is not a statue of Parian marble, but the Galatea of Pygmalion, full of warmth and life, and as it were oppressed by the throng of emotions now tumultuously awaking in her bosom."

Such was her first début ; Paris custom requires three. Her second took place in the arduous character of Aménaïde. Now commenced the struggle so famous in the annals of the French stage. Duchesnois and Georges collected their partisans. The battle was long and desperate ; it was opened with hisses, continued with blows, and ended with small-swords and pistols. When the rival divinities played in the same tragedy, the two armies tore up the benches of the pit and hurled them at each other's heads. The honors of these demonstrations, said Geoffroy, belonged to the débutante ; the dust to Duchesnois. At the close of the fourth act of Phèdre, during which Duchesnois' cabal had been unusually fierce, Georges fainted and was dragged off the stage. The minister of the interior soon authorized her to assume all the characters of the tragic repertory, upon a footing with Duchesnois ; she was admitted to the company as a member for life, and received an annual salary of 4,000 francs. This sum, then deemed adequate, would now be insignificant. The hostility of the two cabals gradually died away.

* The portrait of M'lle Georges, upon the opposite page, is taken from a miniature in the possession of the actress, which was kindly placed by her at the disposal of the designer.

The first protector of M'lle Georges—we use the word in its primitive and paternal, and not its derived and scandalous, sense— was the Polish prince Sappia. He possessed a yearly income of two million francs, and begged the young tragédienne to assist him in spending it. He furnished her a suite of rooms with oriental magnificence, stocking the drawers with cashmeres and the jewel-boxes with diamonds. She accepted the key to this marvellous establishment upon the prince's solemn declaration that no second key existed.

Her first conquest was Lucien Bonaparte; the orator was assiduous, impassioned, unsuccessful. He had a formidable rival in the person of his First Consular brother, who, one night after the performance of Andromaque, summoned Hermione to St. Cloud. Hermione went at midnight, and returned at dawn ; victorious, say the chroniclers, fallen, thought the public. The audience present two nights afterwards, at a representation attended by Napoleon, showed how perfect was its knowledge of events transpiring in high places, by the crash of applause it bestowed upon the following line, spoken by Georges :

"Si j'ai séduit Cinna, j'en séduirai bien d'autres."

At this period some trivial circumstance rekindled the warfare of the opposing factions. The adherents of M'lle Georges were called "Georgiens;" the adverse party received the name of "Carcassiens," from the extreme thinness of M'lle Duchesnois, their leader. French gallantry and Parisian chivalry will hardly refer to this period for illustration of the national and traditional courtesy towards women.

In 1808, M'lle Georges yielded to the solicitations and offers of the Russian ambassador, and accepted an engagement at the Imperial theatre of St. Petersburg. She remained four years in Russia, the idol of the Czar, kindly treated by the Empress-mother, and playing loto every evening with the Grand Duke Constantine. Upon the approach of Napoleon, she fled from St.

Petersburg to Stockholm. A year after, she left Stockholm for Brunswick, and was accompanied upon her perilous journey—for the country was in arms—by an escort furnished by Bernadotte. Jerome Bonaparte received her, and hurried her off to Dresden, to take part in the theatricals of the armistice. Upon the fall of Napoleon, the Duke de Duras, then the intendant of the theatres, threatened her with exile, if she did not submit to the restoration. "Never," she replied; "Vive l'Empereur!"

She absented herself again for five years, striding over Europe from conquest to conquest; at last, the Bourbon ministry consented to reinstate her at the Comédie Française, but the influence of Duchesnois being still in the ascendant, she was fain to reign at the Odéon instead. This circumstance was a fortunate one; for it was the first step in a chain of events which led her to exchange tragedy for the drama, and to become the priestess of a contemporaneous literature. She left the classic for the romantic school, and made herself the interpreter of the vigorous and palpitating prose of Victor Hugo, Alexander Dumas, Alfred de Vigny, Soumet, Mallefille, Liadières, Fontan. No actress ever "created" so many masterpieces: Cléopâtre, Jeanne d'Arc, Christine, Jeanne la Folle, Marguerite de Bourgogne, Lucrèce Borgia, Marie Tudor, La Nonne Sanglante. Victor Hugo was so delighted with her rendering of his Lucretia Borgia, that he said of her: "Sublime as Hecuba, touching as Desdemona!"

M'lle Georges is still living, though she has disregarded the counsel of her friends and the admonitions of her own conscience, in persisting in maintaining a precarious hold of the sceptre she once wielded so proudly. At the age of seventy-two, she still performs from time to time the characters that she played in her teens. She gathers the élite of Parisian society, and still inspires the critics with glowing and impassioned periods. She is a valiant, though a solitary example of that splendid race of dramatic artistes who rose with the Revolution, and disappeared with the Empire.

CHAPTER XXX.

Features of Society under Napoleon—Mystification: the Princess Dolgoroucky and the Institute—Cafés under the Empire—Gastronomy—Conversation—Effect of Official Eulogy upon the French Language—Affectation and Exaggeration—The Soldier in Society—Epigrams. Jests and Libels—Moreau and the Legion of Honor—Napoleon's Mother and the Pope nicknamed—Napoleon and the Beet-root—Puns at the expense of Marie Louise—Desertion of Napoleon—The Race of Apostasy—Adhesion and Renunciation—The allied Sovereigns at the Theatre—Defection in the Army—Napoleon's Fall hailed as a Deliverance—Conclusion.

WE have barely space in this concluding chapter, to refer to a few of the more marked features which characterized Parisian society during the reign of Napoleon. One of the most noticeable of these was the taste for hoaxing, which pervaded the upper and even court circles. This amusement was called "mystification," and often trod upon the dangerous limits of practical jokes. A person by the name of Musson obtained a national reputation for his ingenuity in inventing, and his skill in executing, tricks and impositions of this sort. One example will suffice to give an idea of this intellectual recreation.

The Russian Princess Dolgoroucky inhabited a house so small that she never could invite more than eight persons to dinner. One evening, as she was on the point of sitting down to table, M. de Lacépède, the naturalist, was announced. She was not acquainted with the gentleman, but her interest in science enabled her to sustain an agreeable conversation. Soon after, Lalande, the astronomer, was introduced, and then Monge, the geometrician. In half an hour, a large delegation from the Institute had gathered in the confined parlors of the princess. The unfortunate lady found her situation a most distressing one.

especially as the conversation had now centered on the subject of fossil ivory, upon which she knew little and cared less. At last, she was relieved by the arrival of one of her intimate friends, who, however, reproached her for having concealed from him the interesting fact which was the occasion of the present assemblage. She then learned to her dismay, that the most distinguished members of the Institute had been invited, in her name, to visit a cabinet of natural history which she had just received from her estates in Siberia, and which she intended to present to the Academy of Sciences. M. de Lacépède had come in the full hope of seeing the skin of a serpent one hundred and eighty feet long, and Lalande was confident that he should gaze at last upon the moon-stone. The discomfited philosophers stole gradually out of the house, and endeavored to prevent the story from obtaining currency. Napoleon was seriously offended when he heard of it; and the more so, from the fact that he had set his face against the practice of mystification. He never failed to reprimand any of his courtiers who were guilty of it, and in time the custom fell into disrepute.

Cafés, estaminets, and restaurants were largely multiplied during the Terror and the Empire. Places of public resort had become necessary during the storms of the revolution. Persons interested in the progress of events met there to read the newspapers in print, and the libels in manuscript. Anarchy had rendered the Parisians gregarious, and they talked, read, thought, ate and drank in groups. The Café des Trois Frères Provençaux, the Café Foy, the Café Tortoni, were founded during the ten years previous to Napoleon; the Café Véry, the Café Lemblin, the Café du Caveau, the Café des Mille Colonnes, the Café de la Rotonde, were established during the Empire. Their kitchens and cellars were under the control of the stewards and butlers of noble families ruined and dispersed by the revolution. Beauvilliers, who had once cooked for the Prince de Condé, now cooked for a promiscuous paying company. The military element prevailed largely at these establishments, and the manners of the cafés were visibly corrupted by an invasion of the manners of the camp. An officer of rank would not hesitate to take a newspaper from the hands of a citizen, without offering apology or expecting resistance.

The First Consul was the most abstemious man of his time; Cambacérès, the Second Consul, was the most gluttonous. The example of the latter was more followed than that of the former, and to exhibit prowess in digestion was as creditable as to display valor in arms. Gastronomic wagers were constantly proposed and won; the most famous was that of one hundred dozens of oysters at a breakfast.[1] One of the features of the public festivities was the tossing of sausages and roast turkeys, from tribunes erected for the purpose, into the hungry and clamorous crowd. The public thirst was quenched on these occasions from tuns and pipes of wine, flowing from morn to night at the municipal expense.

The French language is so adapted to the requirements of easy and graceful conversation, that it possesses a term for the art, which no other language can adequately render—"la causerie." The Terror introduced into the vocabulary in daily use a spirit of exaggeration and affectation; this, the wars and excitements of Napoleon's reign fastened for a time upon society. The extravagant eulogies of the Emperor and the government, with which the journals were filled, and which were the burden of all official language, naturally rendered the language of compliment, and even that of ordinary intercourse fulsome and bombastic. For years, the government organ, and in fact the newspapers generally, contained almost daily installments of such ecstasy as the following, the effect of which, by constant repetition, may easily be imagined:

"Happy the prince who may be worthily and yet truthfully lauded!—As the Christian's God is alone worthy of worship

[1] Mém. d'un Bourgeois, i. 37.

so are you, sire, alone worthy of governing France.—You are beyond human history and above admiration.—Let the whole earth be hushed; let it listen in silence to the voice of Napoleon.—Like the god of Day, who animates all nature, Napoleon spreads everywhere his beneficent influence.—God in his mercy chose Napoleon to represent him on the earth.—Who ever healed so many wounds, dried so many tears, ended so many calamities, and made so many people happy?—With his nod he makes the globe quake.—Some god must have made the Code!—The heart of Napoleon is sparing of the blood of his subjects.—Yes, sire, the late conscriptions have contributed to an increase in the population!—When God had made Napoleon, he rested himself!"

A natural consequence of the introduction of such habits of thought and expression was, that the speaker—one engaged in the most ordinary conversation—no longer sought to express in precise terms his meaning; he sought, by asserting much more than he felt, to produce an impression upon the mind of the listener, even after the latter had eliminated a large portion of his emphasis, as due to the prevailing spirit of exaggeration. Ladies were horror-stricken and dismayed at events which, twenty years before, would hardly have been startling; they were enthusiastic and delirious over incidents which might possibly please but could hardly enrapture. Beauty was "celestial," and was told so to its face; plainness was "frightful," the simplest error was "inconceivable," the most trivial incident "monstrous." A gentleman who denied himself to an unwelcome visitor, was "harrowed" at having been unfortunately out; the visitor was, in his turn, "afflicted" at his ill fortune. A person could hardly make a series of calls, without exposing himself to the remorse of plunging a large number of his friends into profound and poignant despair.

The military element prevailed so largely under Napoleon, that the manners of the parlor suffered by the contagion of the barracks. The bearing of the soldier in society was marked rather by intrepidity than ease; he aimed at forcing admiration rather than at winning it. His entrance into a room was noisy and boisterous ; his address to the lady of the house, long, verbose and martial. Instead of withdrawing at a moment when his departure would be unperceived, he again addressed the hostess noisily and conspicuously, thus drawing upon his exit the attention of the assembled company. Anecdote, accompanied with vigorous pantomime, supplied the place of conversation ; the conclusion of a story elicited applause and laughter as hearty as though the narrator had been upon the stage. Unconsciously civilians assumed or caught this military energy and turbulence of style, of language and of bearing ; and a certain emphasis of manner succeeded the subdued elegance of the old régime. This subsisted through the Empire, but disappeared under Louis XVIII.

We have often spoken in the course of this work, of the epigrams and jests of the Parisians at the expense of Napoleon and his court. It is proper to give a few examples of these, as the Emperor was known to be exceedingly susceptible on this point, and as he bore witness, at St. Helena, to the terrible effects of ridicule. "The salons of Paris are really to be dreaded for their sarcasms," he said ; "and this because the greater part of them are replete with wit and well seasoned with salt. They are sure to make a breach in the object of their attack, and it is rare that you do not succumb beneath them."[1]

At the time of the creation of the Legion of Honor, General Moreau, a stern republican, held himself aloof from the Tuileries and enjoyed his own glory in isolation. He made merry, on one occasion, over Bonaparte's bestowal of rewards of merit. "My cook," he said, "has really excelled himself to-day ; I must encourage the rogue with an honorary stew-pan." Bonaparte never forgave this stinging criticism. When M. de Lacépède, the naturalist, was made Grand Chancellor of the Order, the public observed that a better man could not have been found to preside over a "menagerie ;" and the faubourg St. Germain expressed a hope that the distinguished savant would add a new chapter to his late "Treatise on Reptiles."

At the time of the execution of the Duke d'Enghien, it was said that Madame Mère had implored her son to spare the unhappy prince; and that, on being violently repulsed, she said, "Can you treat your mother thus?" He retorted in these words, added the story: "I have no mother; I made myself." It is not probable that Napoleon ever uttered this bit of profanity: it was doubtless invented by the wits to suit his character. The people gave to Napoleon's mother the offensive sobriquet of "la mère la Joie:" old mother Joy. Some one of them had borrowed and consulted a Latin Lexicon, and had translated the proper name, Lætitia, as if it had been a common noun.

When it was announced that Pope Pius VII. had consented to visit Paris for the purpose of crowning Napoleon, the students expressed their opinion in the form of a play upon words: "Le pape Pie se tache." This, which in its apparent sense, charges his Holiness with disgracing his name and mission, gives him, in the sliding pronunciation necessary to the double meaning, the irreverent appellation of Pape Pistache—Pope Peanut. Napoleon, in his weak dread of punsters, caused one of his poets, at this period, to compose a satire upon them, in which they were compared to harpies, defiling all they touch. The epigrammatists only railed the harder for this mythological invective, and the city laughed good-naturedly at the sensitive and thin-skinned demigod.

At the time of the scarcity and dearness of sugar—its price being nearly six francs a pound—and when Napoleon was encouraging the cultivation of the beet-root, a caricature was published representing the Emperor breakfasting with his Majesty of England. King George was sweetening his coffee from an enormous and well supplied sugar-bowl; while Napoleon, in an attitude denoting a violent effort of pressure, was endeavoring to squeeze into his cup the juice of an arid and refractory beet.

Upon the marriage of Napoleon with Marie Louise, the

University offered a gold medal to the author of the best Latin oration upon the alliance. M. Martainville, a popular rhymster, composed a song in French, which was intended, said the title, to compete for the prize. The lines were set to music, and were sung in one half of the private houses in Paris. The following couplet was invariably encored:

> "Oh! she'll be the idol of the nation,
> —For I read so in a proclamation."

The following paraphrase of a couplet referring to the diamonds given by the city to the Empress, conveys very nearly the sense of the original:

> "The lady, I very much suspect,
> Likes the present better than the prospect."

It must always be a matter of wonder that Napoleon should have been so harassed by these witty gibes. But that he was keenly sensitive to the jests which involved a criticism or a reproach, we have seen from his decrees exiling epigrammatists, and from his language at St. Helena, declaring that "ridicule kills."

The last phase of society under the empire was that presented by France, and especially by Paris, during the presence of the allied sovereigns, and upon the abdication of Napoleon. The allies entered the capital on the 31st of March, 1814. The mass of the people took but little part in the saturnalia of welcome extended to them by the partisans of the Bourbons, who rent the air with their acclamations, and whose wives waved their handkerchiefs before the conquerors, and even kissed their feet. The attitude of the people was that of hesitation, for the moment was one of uncertainty and transition. But no sooner was it evident that the coalition of sovereigns possessed the power to impose their will upon the country, and that Napoleon was no longer able to assert authority, to command obedience, or to reward servility, than the nation suddenly presented to the world the revolting spectacle to which we have already alluded—a spectacle of abandonment of a fallen sovereign and prostration before a new régime, altogether unprecedented in history. Talleyrand received Alexander at his hotel, and pronounced in favor of the restoration of the Bourbons. At four o'clock in the afternoon, the proclamation of the allies that they would neither treat with Napoleon nor with any member of his family, and announcing their desire that the Senate appoint a provisional government, was posted by order of the prefect of police. Caulaincourt was the only man of Napoleon's multitudinous retinue, who ventured to visit Paris and speak in his behalf; his appeal was of no avail, and he returned hopeless to Fontainebleau.

The race of apostasy now commenced in earnest. The municipality of Paris issued an edict, declaring the Bourbons "the legitimate masters of France;" the Senate, convoked by Talleyrand, met to the number of thirty members out of one hundred and forty, and appointed a provisional government of five officers —four of whom had been functionaries under Napoleon. This was on the 1st of April; on the 2d, the Senate pronounced Napoleon's fall, and liberated the army from the oath of fidelity. The next day, the Senate, with largely increased numbers, placed upon record, by a unanimous vote, their reasons for this step, which were none other than Napoleon's tyranny and ambition!

The Legislature followed the Senate, ratified its decisions, and promised adherence and concurrence. The University handed in its acceptance of the new régime; its Grand Master, Fontanes, who, in a series of discourses, had declared Napoleon to be greater than Charlemagne, now pronounced the future Louis XVIII. superior to them both. The clergy, led by Cardinal Maury, the Institute—Napoleon's especial pride—the municipality, the judiciary, every functionary in the realm who had a place to keep or an ambition to serve, either signed addresses by the gross, or paid homage in procession. While many contented themselves with expressing good will towards the dynasty

now to be restored, others sought to forget or deny the past;
they cast reproach upon their by-gone fidelities, and to the spontaneous graces of adhesion added the impressive act of recantation. The Tribunal of Senlis expressed sentiments of attachment,
which, it declared, it had been forced, for twenty years, to repress
within its own bosom; and the Supreme Court, upon its own
testimony, had never once ceased to offer secret prayers for the
downfall of the tyrant! The provisional government issued an
address to the army, in which it was said that "Napoleon was
not a Frenchman, even;" and in a proclamation to the people,
characterized his administration as that of a barbarian king.

The theatres sang cantatas to the glory of the coalition. At
the Comédie Française, a performance was given to the Czar of
Russia and to the King of Prussia. It was with difficulty that
the guards stationed at the door of Alexander's box could restrain ladies from forcing themselves into his presence; children,
eluding the vigilance of the sentries, begged imperial kisses from
his Majesty. A man sprang upon the stage, and attached to the
curtain the Bourbon arms. A white veil was thrown over the
Napoleonic eagle, which the pit now called a "turkey," and which
they insulted accordingly. At every allusion which could be
applied to the Czar, the audience rose and made the house ring
with their plaudits. Alexander acknowledged the compliment
by bowing with emphasis. A paper, containing a string of
rhyming invectives against Napoleon, was thrown upon the stage,
and Talma was compelled to read them, notwithstanding his
well-known devotion to Napoleon.

Russian and Prussian officers were the privileged guests at
the festivities of the aristocracy. The insignia and emblems of
the Bonapartes were effaced from the public buildings. An
officer of the Legion of Honor tied his decoration of that order—
given him by Napoleon—to his horse's tail, and dragged it
through the streets. The busts of Napoleon were mutilated and
defiled. The bronze statue of the Emperor upon the Column of

Austerlitz was taken down, and removed by order of the allies, after a vain attempt made by several ex-chamberlains to drag it from its pedestal with a team of twenty-four horses, and another to saw it through at the ankles. The press teemed with pamphlets, libels, and aspersions. Chateaubriand published his "Bonaparte and the Bourbons," just before the entry of the allies; this eloquent and powerful, though occasionally vehement, work was circulated with zeal by the wives of the royalists.

While, at Paris, the functionaries in the civil departments were thus deserting and renouncing the Emperor, the defection in the army at Fontainebleau was no less remarkable. The most eager to transfer their allegiance were those whose debts of honor towards Napoleon could only have been discharged by devotion to the last. Desertion became an epidemic, and spread with the celerity of a contagion. Marshals of France, Princes, Dukes, hurried away to acknowledge the Restoration. Marmont was already a zealous Bourbon; Berthier collected signatures for the act of dethronement; Ney, Prince de la Moskowa and Duc d'Elchingen, bore to Talleyrand at Paris the act of abdication which he had aided to draw from his fallen benefactor. Jourdan adopted the white cockade, and commended his example to the troops under his command. The National Guard assumed the white cockade, and lastly, the army, by order of the provisional government; the navy was instructed to substitute the white flag for the tricolor. Napoleon, appalled by blows so stunning, and hopeless of retrieving fortunes so desperate, swallowed poison on the night of the 11th of April; its efficacy had been impaired by time, however, and its effects were therefore but transitory. The next morning, Berthier, commander of the army of Fontainebleau, asked Napoleon's permission to visit Paris upon business of a private nature, engaging to be absent but a day. He went, but did not return. His adhesion to the Bourbons, as well for himself as for his army, appeared soon after in the Moniteur. Napoleon, now preparing for exile at Elba, was literally friendless and

alone; with few unimportant exceptions, all had disappeared—
from Talleyrand, the prime minister, to Constant, the valet-de-
chambre.

A work treating of society under the Empire would have
been incomplete without this picture of its fall and dispersion.
We have elsewhere said that the explosion of recantation and
apostasy which attended Napoleon's decline, is in some degree
to be considered as an extravagant, almost a grotesque, reaction
after an unduly prolonged confinement. The country, finding
itself at liberty to renounce him whom it had lately seemed
to worship, made an unseemly and violent use of this, its first
moment of independence. If there is any moral to be drawn
from the fact that France hailed the fall of Napoleon with joy,
and accompanied his flight to Elba with menace to his person and
maledictions on his name, it is that the French people will not
long submit to a jealous and unrelaxing tyranny. They had welcomed the dictatorship of Napoleon, fifteen years before, as a relief from social anarchy, and as the least of two evils. As time
progressed, all symptoms of disorder disappeared; absolutism,
rigidly applied and enforced, had worked a speedy and radical
cure. But Napoleon continued to subject the nation thus recovered of its disorder, to the same system he had employed to
combat the evil; the physician persisted in administering to the
convalescent patient the same remedies he had used in the crisis
of the disease. Here was Napoleon's error—an error fatal and
irreparable. His system was not progressive; it was sullen, sta-
tionary, inflexible. He exiled a woman early in the Consulate—
and as if the world had not lived ten years in the meantime, he
exiled another late in the Empire. There was no graduation, no
adaptation, no relaxation; iron he began and iron he ended. His
despotic temper did not permit him to perceive that there are
milder systems and gentler influences that may be often substituted for the ruder processes of force and compression. He
chose to effect by might what another would have effected by

persuasion. He seized the nation in his relentless gripe, and maintained his hold till a power stronger than his own compelled him to abandon it. He had doubtless imagined that time and habit had moulded the people into a form that they would mechanically retain even when the compulsory force was withdrawn. He had sought to reduce the nation as the ship-builder bends the ash, which pliantly assumes a shape and still faithfully preserves it. But Napoleon had labored upon a very different material. France is like a Damascus blade—elastic and readily yielding to pressure, and yet ever returning to its original form. Whoever disregards its temper is sure to feel its edge. Napoleon's mistake was radical; he was always and everywhere a despot. He mastered the continent of Europe, but was himself destroyed by the recoil; he mastered France, but his overthrow was hailed by the people as a deliverance. Such is the lesson taught by the incidents attending the fall of Napoleon: that a nation—and especially the French nation—may yield transiently to tyranny and bow with apparent satisfaction to despotic control, and yet upon the day of reckoning, compensate for the servility of its submission, by the fervor of its apostasy and the vehemence of its renunciation. The descendants of Napoleon may make useful commentaries on this painful chapter in the history of the first of their race.

THE END.